Ancient Ways

The Roots of Religion

Diane Mulberger Olsen

Ancient Ways

Copyright © 2016 by Diane Mulberger Olsen

All rights reserved. No part of this book may be reproduced, scanned, or distributed in any printed or electronic form without permission, except for brief quotations for personal, non-commercial uses or embodied in critical articles or reviews.

Published by:
Applegate Valley Publishing
Grants Pass, OR 97527

ISBN: 978-0-9967565-5-6

Front Cover Concept: Andrew Olsen

Front Cover Illustration: Tara Thelen "Spiritual Ascent"

Back Cover Illustration: Carrie Voorhees, "Sidrah Tree"

Book Cover and Interior Design: Illumination Graphics

Ancient Ways: A Holistic Treasury

A traditional approach to the dawn of religion is that it happened in baby steps. Fear of the unexplained, animism, ancestor worship, shamanism, etc.; and monotheism finally arrived, with Moses, Christ, or fill in the blank.

> *"But how was religion born? It has been said that it arose out of the fear of primitive man, face to face with nature. But fear has nothing in common with reverence and love. It does not unite fact and idea, visible and invisible, man and God. As long as man did nothing but tremble before nature, he was not yet man. He became man when he seized the link which connected him with the past and the future, with something superior and beneficent, and when he worshipped that mysterious unknown. But how did he worship for the first time?"*
> —Edouard Schure, *The Great Initiates*, 1889

One premise of this study is that monotheism always existed, and revelations were given to all human forms. We should not assume primitive peoples weren't smart enough to grasp the concept of a Single Creator, because they always were! Remnants of guidance exist from a variety of human branches – not just modern mankind. Examples surface in scriptures, apothegms and archaeology.

The second is that religion is holistic. What if it is Monotheism and Polytheism have been the undulating, ultimate definition of Yin and Yang? A constant interaction of two complementary, as well as conflicting forces, and energies. The world, as a result of this ongoing process, exhibits both **organic unity and dynamism**.

> *"Blessed art thou, O night! For through thee was born the Day of God, a day which We have ordained to be the lamp of salvation..."*
> —Baha'u'llah

Monotheism can be visualized as a single linked chain entwined with wisps of mankind's additions and twists. We remake religion to reflect our personal thoughts, thinking this is more palatable than dealing directly with the Word of God. This night of darkness is followed by a New Dawn.

This book suggests that the addition of any factors to a solitary Supreme Being is more of an unraveling process for monotheism rather than a building process as proposed by say, Max Mueller, a respected philologist.

So there is a repetitive cycle for monotheism in each Age: Revitalization, Fading, perhaps Death and Renewal. The very essence of the phoenix! Since the time of Adam and Eve the destruction of purity in a revealed religion, begins with adding things to God.

The fading of a monotheistic Faith, starts as God – and something else. Perhaps it starts with the Prophet Himself, or some sort of evil antihero. Then elements of nature are added, like "moon" or "storm." These "spirits" soon become a list. Then it is God above the other gods, at least until the concept of a Supreme Being recedes into a pantheon.

When there is no guiding spiritual Force for civil discipline, virtues decay, and people, thinking only of themselves, are more apt to become greedy or indifferent and hurt one another or other creatures or even the earth.

Eventually animal or human figures are drawn, painted or molded. Icons are developed, which eventually become statues that need shrines. Some become etched into talismans, charms, or medals that may appear hanging from rearview mirrors.

Today we see monotheism strongly represented by at least nine living faiths, yet we see that praying to God alone, is not enough for many. Instead, multitudes of saints, angels, ancestors, deities and even the universe, are employed to cover our spiritual "needs."

"However sublime a spirit may be, once buried in flesh it temporarily loses the remembrance of its entire past"
—Empedocles as cited by Edouard Schure in *The Great Initiates*, p.428

ACKNOWLEDGMENTS

Although there are glimpses gathered from a lifetime here, it is safe to say this story of Ancient Ways could not have been told without vast assistance. I would dearly love to thank kindred spirits like Edouard Schure, who wrote *The Great Initiates* in 1889; and Muhammad ibn Jarir Al-Tabari, who wrote *The History of the Prophets and Kings* in 915 AD. He is still considered one of the world's greatest historical resources. A good translation was made by Franz Rosenthal in a thirty-eight Volume series called *The History of al-Tabari*; State University of New York Press 1989, the first volume of which; documents events occurring up to the flood, much like this piece. Thanks to all, who have previously walked this guided path.

I would also like to remember four mentors from the University of Montana. Dr. Frank Bessac, Dr. Charlene G. Smith, Dr. Dee C. Taylor, and Dr. Carling I. Malouf, who challenged me to think!

My thoughts have benefitted from listening to others, virtually everyone who has spoken with me on matters of spirit. This precious group includes my father Henry C. Mulberger, my mother Peggy, and my stepmother Eleanor and their many friends, who were great thinkers, like Russ and Gertie Walcher and Ellis Brown "Doc Rocks." Dozens of friends like Tom and Debbie, Mary, Petra, Misha, Ellen and Ragen stirred me to action. There are many others – I do not forget you.

My siblings and their spouses are very supportive; Val and Ditto, Fella and Pat, Peter and Heidi, Sandra and Bill. Sandy calls me regularly with interesting discoveries, many of which are included in this book.

I am thankful for my sons, my sons Andrew and Gavin, and 4 grandsons who converse with me often about sacred matters. I thank my husband, Penisimani I. Toutaiolepo, for his patience. My family, as families do, constantly stimulates my mind, and cause me to grow and strive.

Many of the citations here can now be found on the internet. I especially wish to thank Chad Jones for marshalling the extensive reference library of "Ocean." It is a free download if you wish to have it on your own computer. Many quotes of spiritual texts from the many layers of religions are found there. I am also tremendously grateful to Wikipedia, a great place to explore rare references.

I am humbly thankful to Gretchen Ames and Ragen Hart for editorial assistance.

A Present for my sister Valerie and Other Curious Souls

Diane Mulberger Olsen 2013

CONTENTS

Ancient Ways: A Holistic Treasury
Acknowledgements
Introduction i
Early People: Evolution of Body, Culture and Civilization through
Spiral Degrees of Unity, Art and Technology 1
    Ardipithecus 1
    Australopithecines 2
    Australopithecus Sediba 3
    Homo Naledi 3
    Homo Erectus 4
    Homo Antecessor 6
    Homo Heidelbergensis 6
    Homo Neanderthalensis 7
    Denisova 10
    Sima 12
    Modern Humans 13
    Summation 16
Symbolic Religion 17
Pre-Agricultural Religion 22
    Dawn of the Upanishads 22
    Gobekli Tepe 23
    Ainu/Jomon 24
Domestication and Religion 28
Early Cities 30
Revelation Advances Civilization 33
    Guiding Factors 34
Signs That the Holy Spirit Made Manifest, Has Returned to Earth .. 36
A WORLD OF FIRSTS: Antediluvian Accounts 41
Nu Wa 43
Fu-XI or Fo-HI (The Great Bright One) 44
    Fu-Xi's Event Line 44
Shennong 46
Huangdi (Yenti) The Yellow Emperor 47
Gayomart or Q-mers/Keyumers 51
    Primordial Creation 52
    Gayomart's Death 54
Siamak 55
Hooshang 56
    The Prophesy of the Return (Renovation) 56
Adam 58
Seth 61
Enoch/Hermes/Thoth/Idris: Before the Flood 62
The Esoteric and Occult Philosophies 64
    Science and Religion 68
    The Religious Science of Healing 70
    Magic, Sorcery and Divination 75
    Spiritual Contact 75

    Dealing With Negative Energies 76
    Components and Facets of Secretive Practices 77
    So Where are the Zombies? 81
    Removing Curses 83
    Folk Medicine 83
    Tortures and Torments 86
Osiris and Hermes 90
The Book of Enoch and The Book of Giants 93
Ram or Rama 95
    The Eden of Ram 95
    Desert Mummies 96
    First Dream 98
    Second Dream 99
    One Last Dream 100
    An Epic Journey 102
    Seasonal Festivals 102
Asclepius /Aesculapius /Abaris 104
    Homa and Early "Salvation" 104
Indo European Culture 107
Yima Xsaeta or Jamshed The Shining One 110
    Overpopulation and Tragedy 111
    Build A Vara! 112
    The Site of Derinkuyu 113
Adapa or Uan 115
    Melchizedek or Malki Tzedek 116
    The Firsts: A Summation 118
**Polytheism: The Matrix In Which Monotheism Is Born,
Flourishes and Dims** 120
Dualism, Pantheism, Syncretism, Henotheism 122
    Dualism 122
    Mehr/Mithra/Mitra (Vedic) 123
    Druids 125
Pantheism and Panentheism 127
Syncretism 128
    The Sikh Faith 128
Henotheism 131
    Norse Eddas and Sagas 133
    Baldr's Draumar (Dreams) 134
    Hamthesmol 135
    Reginsmol 135
    The Yazidi 136
    Melek Taus and the Seven 138
    Adam and Eve 139
    Unfortunately, Persecution Goes Both Ways 141
Idol Worship 143
    People of Noah 143
    People of Abraham and Moses 143
    How Did We Come to Worship Idols? 144
    Saints 145

- Great Disappointments: Justice and Mercy Two Edges of the Sword ... 146
- The Story of Noah (Nuh) ... 148
  - Noah's Epic Struggle ... 148
- Atrahasis and Gilgamesh ... 152
  - Atrahasis ... 152
  - Tragic Times ... 153
  - Gilgamesh ... 154
- Manu ... 156
- Deucalion ... 158
  - What Do We Think We Know About The Flood? ... 157
  - Summary of Flood Stories ... 157
- Hud/Heber/Eber ... 160
  - The 'Ad: People of the Towers ... 161
  - Rediscovery of Iram, Known by the Bedouin as Ubar ... 163
  - Sheba/Tubba ... 164
- Salih/Saleh: The Righteous One ... 166
  - The She-Camel ... 167
  - Other Tragic Attempts ... 168
  - The Dwellers of Ar Rass (Persia) ... 168
  - The Yasin People of Antioch ... 169
  - Sodom and Gomorrah; and Three Other "Cities of the Plain" ... 170
  - Uncovering Sites of Destruction ... 170
- Sho'aib/Shuayb ... 172
- Summary of Disappointing Times ... 174
- Resounding Successes ... 175
  - Migrations to India ... 175
- Krishna ... 178
- Abraham /Avram/Abram ... 196
  - A Fiery Youth ... 196
  - A Shocking Realization ... 197
  - Sabians ... 198
- Roots of One Planetary Faith ... 199
  - Moses: Zoroaster: Buddha: Christ: Mohammad ... 199
- Hosarsiph/Moses ... 200
  - Jethro and Salvation ... 201
  - Genesis ... 203
  - Akhenaten ... 206
- Zoroaster/Zarathushtra/Zardosht ... 208
  - Anguish ... 210
  - The Zend Avesta ... 212
  - Zoroaster's Teachings and Laws ... 214
  - The End of the World ... 216
- The Wanderings of Zoroaster: A Theory: The "Weeping God" Viracocha . 218
  - The Phoenicians ... 222
  - Tiahuanaco (Tiwanaku) ... 223
  - The People ... 224
  - Architecture ... 225
  - Agriculture and Aquaculture ... 225
- Whispers of Tiahuanaco: Chachapoya, Paracas, Diaguitas, and Calchaqui ... 227

The Olmecs and Mayans of Mesoamerica	232
South Sea Connections: Light Skins; Long Ears; Blonde-Red Hair and Beards	235
Tongan Giants	235
Long Ears and Ear Spools	238
Red Hair	239
Summation	240
Buddha	242
His Life	242
Reincarnation	243
God: All, or Nothing?	244
Wisdom	245
The Gospel of Buddha	246
Buddha's Pity	248
Christ	250
His Early Life	250
The Essenes	251
The Essenes – John the Baptist – the Temptation	254
The Messiah	259
Blessed are the Poor	260
Gospel of Christ	261
Days of Resurrection	262
Six Sightings:	263
A History of the Apocraphal and Gnostic Texts	265
The Cannonical Texts	266
Christianity and Islam	267
Mohammed the Seal of the Prophets	269
Early Life of the Apostle of God	269
A Dark Environment	270
The Friend	272
Anticipation of the Prophet	273
Mohammad's Mission	273
A Reckoning	274
Night Journey	275
The Road to Ultimate Victory	276
Momentum At Last	277
Betrayal	280
A Perfect Example	280
Submission to the Will of God: Islam	280
Laws and Duties	282
A New Dawn: The Baha'i Era	284
The Bab	287
Anticipation	288
Transfiguration	289
Baha'u'llah the Glory of God	292
Crisis and Victory	292
The Coming of the Glory of the Lord	295

"All Buddha's are glorious. There is not their equal upon the earth. They reveal to us the Path of Life. And, we hail their appearance with pious reverence."
– Attributed to Gautama Buddha

INTRODUCTION

During our exploration, we will encounter some of the rare early stories. They are tatters of human memory that seem at times bizarre, fun or entertaining. At other times they can be informative or utterly awe inspiring. In places where I cannot say it better I freely use the words of those whose accounts are expedient, or exquisite.

This is a discussion of some of the most ancient "Ways" or "Paths" humankind can recall. There are inclusions from the recent revelations of God's Word, because so much can be found about our past in the newer revelations. In fact Mohammad (Qu'ran) and Bahá'u'lláh (Kitab-i-Iqan) tell the most moving tales of what befell their Prophetic Predecessors.

It is good to remember two things throughout this read. First, it is the Word of God noble and eternal – that which can resonate in your heart – which is important, not what man *thinks* he knows or remembers about religion, or about the Beings of Light that have graced our planet.

Second, what people have chosen to remember about the Speakers might seem childish and trivial. Yet the names are still remembered because these Beings brought us the spiritual knowledge, social guidance, technology, science, crafts and arts that helped us prosper under dangerous and challenging conditions; and mature as a more virtuous species.

Many people would claim today, that monotheism began with Moses or Christ. Occasionally someone might add Zoroaster. Some point out that Abraham of Ur, and Ahkenaten of Egypt may have been the first to call on One God. There does appear to be a definite connection between the monotheism of Akhenaten and Moses. Righteous they all are, but no way are they the earliest. These examples range 3800 years ago on the outside, to 2000 years with Christ.

We used to characterize the beginnings of Faith as fear of the unknown. Meteors, eclipses, calamities, and pondering one's impending death needed explanations beyond the rational, or tangible physical realms. Those who sought reasons from the unseen world, were often ridiculed by those who thought this was simply a balm for the weak-minded masses.

It was speculated over time that animism and shamanism developed. Eventually religion progressed from worshipping gods, toward the fairly recent development of monotheism. Evidence to the contrary will be proposed in this study.

In the process of laying down the old creation story remnants, a theme developed unexpectedly during an early editing. So *Ancient Ways* actually became the story of the roots of monotheistic revealed religion and the "accretions" that inevitably occur as human memory fades over time and distance. I hope people will find bits of interesting information presented here not to change one's mind, but perhaps to suggest a change of perspective. Feel free to skip around the material, reading whatever interests you. It is not meant to be read cover to cover like a novel.

There are many names for God: Allah, Elohim, Great Spirit, the Lord of the Kingdoms of Heaven and Earth, Grandfather, Ancient of Days, Brahman, the Adored One, Adonai, the One, the Single, the Cause of All Being, the Peerless. There are hundreds for the Creator.

The force we interact with, and call on is not of the world of the seen. It does not have a face or hands, or a sex – obviously, since those are created things composed of atoms.

Our Creator stands alone, remaining entirely independent of the worlds of Creation. So how do messages get to us, so that we may be nurtured and grow? Many scriptures concur that an "Intermediary Force" was created to bear God's Word, and educative power to earth.

"That which is intended by 'Revelation of God' is the Tree of divine Truth that betokeneth none but Him, and it is this divine Tree that hath raised and will raise up Messengers, and hath revealed and will ever reveal Scriptures."
(The Bab, Selections from the Writings of the Bab, p. 112)

This divine Tree is a conduit, currently referred to as the HOLY SPIRIT. It returns in the darkest of times to bear God's messages to humankind. The Holy Spirit anoints a chosen one, who is then transfigured into a "Messenger" or "Manifestation of God's Word." That One renews the "Way" or the "Path" of the Ancient Faith, and helps us move forward as a civilization.

This is how we evolve socially, and spiritually. These Manifestations of God's Word, do have hands, faces, and unconditional love! And each brings a specific gift, different from the others.

For instance, Christ brought "personal salvation." For Baha'u'llah it was Unity through Justice because people who treat each other fairly have a better chance of building a lasting **world peace**. For Noah and Hud who had so few followers to remember them, we might speculate that they showed us that there are spiritual evolutionary dead ends, which are not selected to continue. Another Messenger would be sent another time – to another people, urging civilization forward.

"The Messengers of God are the principal and the first teachers. Whenever this world becomes dark, and divided in its opinions and indifferent, God will send one of His Holy Messengers."
(Abdu'l-Baha, Abdu'l-Baha in London, p. 44)

We were advised in Hebrews 13:15
"...for He hath said, I will never leave thee, nor forsake thee."

"For if Jesus had given them rest, then would he not afterward have spoken of another day."
(King James Bible, 4:8 Hebrews)

"All Buddha's are One Buddha."
Gautama Buddha – in The Avatamsaka Sutra

So, how far back does this evolutionary thread go? Well…
"The Primordial Buddha (dharmakaya) manifests countless glorious Forms (sambhogakaya) and material Forms (nirmanakaya), according to the place, time, and circumstance of sentient beings. This does not

imply that such diverse forms are identical. The Buddha's and Great Bodhisattvas are not identical in manifestation, and not different in essence. Every act of a Buddha or Great Bodhisattva is imbued with irresistible power." Tashi Nyima (posted 12/11/12 in greatmiddleway.wordpress.com)

"Verily He is the All-Possessing, the Most Exalted. When He purposed to call the new creation into being, He sent forth the Manifest and Luminous Point from the horizon of His Will; it passed through every sign and manifested itself in every form until it reached the zenith, as bidden by God, the Lord of all men." (Baha'u'llah, Tablets of Baha'u'llah, p. 101)

Do these last statements about the various forms of the Prophetic physical condition make you wonder? Baha'i writings continue to say that even though we humans were represented in the process of creation, and evolution of life on this planet. There was always the latent potential for us to evolve into a creature with a soul, so that we might remember and praise the Source of our being. Even though we might have shared similar evolutionary paths and characteristics with other creatures, we were always guided by a caring parental God.

If you doubt this possibility, you might want to take a long look at the developmental stages of a human embryo. How else might we explain the tadpole?

I like to think that I would fall in humble adoration at the feet of any of the better known Manifestations of the "Luminous Point," like Christ (The Anointed One), Mohammad (The Friend of God), the Bab (The Gate), or Baha'u'llah (The Glory of God); I would hope to have also recognized Moses, Buddha, Zoroaster, or Krishna, as well. But I ask you, how awesome would it be to stand awestruck in the presence of the Homo erectus incarnation, or even an Ardipithecus. WOW!

Okay, that may be too much! I'm just saying… keep an open mind when you pass from this stage of life. Who knows what you may be able to comprehend in the spiritual world, if you look with your soul!

Note: My sister Valerie has inherited a unique thanka (Buddhist educational painting), that came out of Tibet as a gift in the 1950's, when the young 14th Dalai Lama, His Holiness, Tenzin Gyatso was seeking outside assistance for the plight of Tibet, in the face of a Chinese onslaught. This thanka uniquely depicts a series of Buddha's receding to a past that could be considered H. erectus times.

Armed with divine power these Beings of Light have moved human civilization forward from its amazing yet vulnerable beginnings to the extraordinary times, in which we live.

If one takes the time to check out the dates for huge technological and social advancements in relation to the timing of a new Revelation, the relationship becomes apparent.

Back in the day in archaeology seminars, we would debate whether culture advanced by means of "technological determinism" or "social determinism." In other words, we examined which was the cause of human advancement. Did tools shape our bodies, vision, and our future, or was it evolution of society that was the primary causal factor? I would tease then and maintain now, that if one could just look with objectivity a few years ahead of each advance, he or she would find the Dawn of a new Day. Each of these events brought about an unfolding chain of spiritual, social and scientific knowledge to humanity. A return of the Holy Spirit, both precedes, and initiates each bloom.

If this is true, whether we are aware of it or not, all human knowledge comes from God. There is a conscious change in the world caused by each return of the divine Educator, and each Redemption more truly reflects the particular needs of a specific time.

**"These sanctified Mirrors, these Day Springs of ancient glory, are, one and all, the Exponents on earth of Him Who is the central Orb of the universe... The beauty of their countenance is but a reflection of His image... They are the Treasuries of Divine knowledge, and the Repositories of celestial wisdom. Through them is transmitted a grace that is infinite, and by them is revealed the Light that can never fade.... These Tabernacles of Holiness, these Primal Mirrors which reflect the light of unfading glory, are but expressions of Him Who is the Invisible of the Invisibles.
"** (Baha'u'llah, *Gleanings from the Writings of Baha'u'llah*, p. 47-48)

"No distiction do We make between any of His Messengers" (Qu'an 2:285)

"Thus hath Muhammad, the Point of the Qu'ran, revealed : 'I am all the Prophets.' Likewise, He saith: 'I am the first Adam, Noah, Moses, and Jesus.' ... Thou wilt behold them all abiding in the same tabernacle, soaring in the same heaven, seated upon the same throne, uttering the same speech, and proclaiming the same Faith." (Baha'u'llah, *The Kitab-i-Iqan: The Book of Certitude* Pp. 153-154)

"Nay, all the Prophets of God, His well-favored, His holy, and chosen Messengers, are, without exception, the bearers of His names, and the embodiments of His attributes. They differ only in the intensity of their revelation, and the comparative potency of their light." (Baha'u'llah, *The Kitab-i-Iqan: The Book of Certitude* Pp. 103-104)

"Hath not Muhammad, Himself declared: 'I am the first Adam, Noah, Moses, and Jesus? Why should Muhammad, that immortal Beauty, Who hath said : ' I am the first Adam' be incapable of saying also 'I am the last Adam'? " (Baha'u'llah, *The Kitab-i-Iqan: The Book of Certitude* p. 162)

" Similar statements have been made by 'Ali." and his son Husayn 'I was with a thousand Adams, the interval between each and the next Adam was 50,000 years...' "
(Baha'u'llah, *The Kitab-i-Iqan: The Book of Certitude* p. 167)

Most everything we think we know about the ancient Messengers is speculation based on fragmentary evidence, except that which is given by the great Prophets themselves.

As for the data, theories, and stories presented in this exploration – sometimes it is sufficient not to prove something, but rather to present the possibility, in hopes that it will help archaeologists and other researchers add credible pieces to the ancient quilt of religion.

EARLY PEOPLE:

Evolution of Body, Culture and Civilization through Spiritual Degrees of Unity, Art and Technology

"Revelation is as old as conscious humanity."
—Edouard Schure *The Great Initiates* 1889

Before we trace more recognizable spiritual paths, let's look back to what we might know about our primordial spiritual, physical, and cultural origins. Acknowledgements of spiritual guidance are present in oral traditions and some archaeological sites, which suggest recognition of something bigger than one's own life on this earth – **even in the earliest human forms**.

Humans evolved in Africa, primarily. Later developments took place in Asia and Europe. Although it is said our mitochondrial "Eve" is currently dated to around 152,000 to 234,000 years ago, we see other Primitive human forms developing much earlier. Ardipithecus date much earlier, nearly 6 million years!

There were several apparent cultural "explosions" of tool technology, which allowed early humans to prosper in a variety of tricky habitats. We tend to get excited about tools, because it is tough for any substance besides rock, to survive that long. *It is not* because the majority of their possessions was weaponry.

Technology improved chances for success, and led to a widening geographic range. Primitive humans burst out of Africa into Asia, then Europe, and beyond to the South Pacific and the Americas.

It is very exciting to note that two populations of ancient humans have been defined during the lengthy writing of this book! Denisovans and Sima were "discovered" in gene sequencing labs. We can only wonder how the information will advance in the next year or two.

A change of perspective might assist researchers to bring new evidence of early forms or religious practices to light, as was the case at Gobekli Tepe, Turkey. Let's take a brief look at this progression of early humans.

Ardipithecus

"Spirit sleeps in the mineral, breathes in the vegetable, dreams in the animal, and wakes in the man."
—Unknown, though it may be attributable to Rama

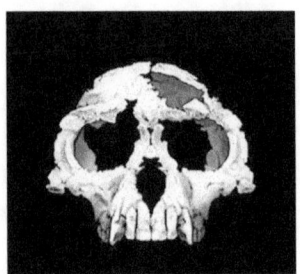

"Ardi" by T. Michael Keesey – Zanclean skullUploaded by FunkMonk. Licensed under CC BY 2.0 via Commons – https://commons.wikimedia.org/wiki/File:Ardi.jpg#/media/File:Ardi.jpg

We know very little about this human ancestral form, except that something caused a change in the way they lived. They dropped down from the trees to begin, at least partially, to walk bipedally on the ground. They probably couldn't cover great distances on two legs, because the ability to walk with ease was still developing. Their teeth were smaller, and their limbs had begun to change noticeably from early Anthropoid forms like Sivapithecus. Their teeth were their primary technology, if you will, and they were becoming redesigned to better adapt to changing times.

Smaller teeth could also suggest less aggression and fighting in the group. A change in the social fabric, might mean that infants were not killed as frequently, by interloping males. Two kinds of Ardipithecus are known from as early as the late Miocene. A kadabba dates back 5.6 million years and A. ramidus goes back 4.4 million years.

Australopithecines

These individuals walked upright and fashioned simple tools by knocking off a few flakes from river cobble stones, which is not as easy as it sounds. The result was a tool useful for chopping, sawing, digging and fighting. Oldowan tools may seem simple, but this change in vision and control helped impact their world more successfully, at least as far back as 4.2 million years ago. They were contemporaries of Ardipithecus, and Anthropoid forms like Sivapithecines. A. afarensis 3.9-2.9 million years ago, was moving down the path towards Homo naledi or Homo erectus.

In 1924, anatomist Raymond Dart found a skull of a juvenile primate in a box of fossil-bearing rocks, sent to him by the manager of a quarry at Taung, on the edge of the Kalahari Desert. The skull had holes which might have been made by the talons of a raptor or the teeth of a leopard, but the position of the opening at the base of the skull caught his attention. Dart concluded that the "Taung child" had walked upright like a human, even though it had a tiny brain and other apelike features. He labeled the find as *Australopithecus africanus* and thus a new branch was added to the human family tree.

PERSPECTIVE

It is from these early times, that shreds of ancient Guidance find their way to the present day. Certainly one of the earliest "recollections" comes to us through Asian tales of Nu Wa, a very early feminine Educator of mankind. Nu Wa came to a society which was exceedingly primitive; similar to what is seen in other mammals including great the apes.

There was no moral teaching. The only social organization, was that children relied on their mothers to teach them to survive and prosper amid the dangers that surrounded them. Childbirth was seen as surprising and not associated with male sexual contributions. So children did not know their specific fathers. The degree of unity here was pre-nuclear family, where the mother and available individuals, young and old, were responsible infant and child care.

When they were hungry they searched for food. When satisfied they threw away the remnants, with no thought to future need. They drank the blood and devoured their food with hide, hair, and whatever. They were probably hairy, but for additional climate protection they might have used skins and rushes. They may have built protected nests of leaves, grass and soft shrubbery.

Nu Wa was also known in Chinese literature as the "creator of all humans," but it seems more likely that She helped them begin the long, steady climb as cultural organisms, toward modern humanity. She gave them social, and perhaps, physical tools that they might adapt better to challenging environmental and social conditions than their vulnerable predecessors. Given the societal distinctions mentioned above, Nu Wa would likely have been remembered from remote, perhaps Australopithecine times. Certainly well before Primitive people moved out of Africa.

In Africa there are oral traditions of a Female, Mawu in some languages, who is related to the Creator, thought there are a variety of opinions on how that came about. (see vodun, under Occult Philosophies).

Australopithecus Sediba

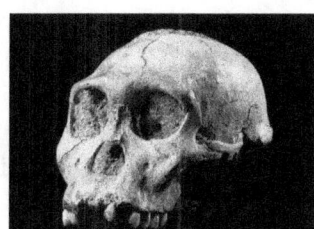

"Australopithecus sediba" by Photo by Brett Eloff. Courtesy Profberger and Wits University who release it under the terms below. – Own work. wikpediacommons

In a 2010 article in "Science," Dr. Lee R. Berger of Witwatersrand University, and a team of experts described the fossils of a boy and a woman, who were discovered near Johannesburg. The bones were a surprise because they displayed a mixture of primitive and modern human attributes, therefore qualifying as a distinct species. They have been named **Australopithecus sediba,** and lived about 2 million years ago.

These individuals travelled upright on long legs, with human-shaped hips and pelvis, but still climbed through trees on ape-like arms. They had the small teeth and more modern face of Homo genus that includes modern humans, but the relatively primitive feet and "tiny brain" of Australopithecus. Its primitive anatomy included a brain the size of an average orange. Other Australopithecines and early species of Homo, like H. naledi, were its contemporaries.

Dr. Berger indicated that the species evolved near or at the root of the Homo genus, about 2.5 million to 2.8 million years old. Geologists think the cave in which they were located is no older than three million years.

The Australopithecines in general, succeeded for millions of years in Africa. Then new experimental types developed, perhaps because of the influence of Nu Wa and other Great Teachers, who continued to offer better Ways. These more advanced forms hit the horizon under the genus label of "Homo."

Homo Naledi

Deep inside Rising Star Cave, explorers and scientists found a burial chamber for the dead of a previously unidentified species of early humans.

More than 1,550 fossil fossils make it the largest sample for any Primitive species, at a single site anywhere in the world. Amazingly, this is probably a small fraction of the fossils in this chamber. So far, parts of at least 15 individuals have been studied. Dr. Berger observed, "With almost every bone in the body represented multiple times, Homo naledi is already practically the best-known fossil member of our lineage,"

"(This) is quite different from anything else we have seen" said Ian Tattersall, an authority on human evolution at the American Museum of Natural History in New York.

According to Lee Berger, the anatomy of *H. naledi* suggests it originated at or near the start of the *Homo* genus, around 2.5 million to 2.8 million years ago, the exact same dates he proposed for Australopithecus sediba. "**They may have shaken each other's hands over the fence between Australopithecus and Homo!**"

The more modern-looking jaws, teeth and feet warrant placement in the genus Homo, not Australopithecus. William Harcourt-Smith a researcher at the American Museum of Natural History, led the analysis of the feet of the new species, which he said are "virtually indistinguishable from those of Modern humans." These feet, combined with its long legs, suggest that H. naledi was well suited for upright long-distance walking.

They had small skulls, with brains one-third the size of Modern humans, and the body was very slender. Dr. John Hawkes noted that an average H. naledi was about five feet tall and weighed almost 100 pounds.

Tracy Kivell of the University of Kent focused on the upper body. H. naledi had extremely long curved fingers, "more curved than almost any other species of early hominin, which clearly demonstrates climbing capabilities."

Paleoanthropologist Chris Stringer, from the Natural History Museum in London, found overall similarities between the new species and Homo fossils from Dmansi, in the republic of Georgia. The Georgian specimens were assigned to Homo erectus georgicus, and had been dated to about 1.8 million years ago, virtually a contemporary of Naledi.

Besides introducing a new member of the family, the discovery suggests that some Primitive **humans intentionally deposited bodies of their dead** in a remote underground cave chamber that did not have an outside access. This is a behavior previously considered limited to modern humans, Neanderthal and Sima, from pit caves like Sima de los Huesos in Spain.

Some of the scientists referred to the burials, which were apparently carried into the chamber intact, as **a ritualized treatment of their dead.** They clarified that by "ritual" they meant a deliberate and repeated practice, not *necessarily* a kind of religious rite. Yet, it would be very difficult to prove that religion played no part in this cultural practice.

"We think it is the first instance of deliberate and ritualized interment," says Hawks. "The only plausible scenario is they deliberately put bodies in this place." – See more at: http://news.wisc.edu/naledi/#sthash.gQYE8wHr.dpuf

By Thomas Roche from San Francisco, USA (Homo Erectus) [CC BY-SA 2.0 (http://creativecommons.org/licenses/by-sa/2.0)], via Wikimedia Commons

Homo Erectus

Just under 2 million years ago, there is another great shift: the control of fire! H. erectus (upright man), existed between 2 million and 300,000 years ago.

As users of fire, they could light and control flames, and transport coals to warm themselves and maybe cook some food. Furthermore, they used fire to hunt and fend off predators. It was even used to harden sharpened sticks into spears, or other tools, with which they could work flint.

They lived in family groups, and used fairly sophisticated

stone tools. A notable development in a crucial area of their brains suggests they communicated by language.

Some researchers claim that contemporary species in Africa, including: Homo erectus (Upright man) Homo rudolfenses, Homo ergaster (working man), and Homo habilis (handy man), are various representatives of just one group, Homo erectus.

Two non-African H. erectus offshoots are noteworthy. First, H. georgicus found in Dmanisi, Georgia, as mentioned above. It is viewed as intermediate between H. erectus and H. habilis, and dates from around 1.77 million years ago.

Secondly, the child sized Indonesian Islander, Homo floriensis, AKA the "Hobbit," who stood three feet tall and lived between 95,000 and 13,000 years ago. Sightings of short upright humanoid creatures are noted on Asian islands, and throughout the Americas and Caribbean. And cinema within the last century shows that the memory of such beings is quite widespread.

It is possible that H. habilis or "handy man," may actually have first developed the Acheulean tools from the more primitive Oldawan (Australopithecine) cobble tools; then shared them, and passed them down to their descendants. (Wood, B (2005). *Human Evolution A Very Short Introduction*. Oxford: Oxford University Press.)

One group, H. ergaster is called the "working man" because of the comparatively advanced Acheulean tools they developed. They lived in eastern and southern Africa about 1.8 million years ago. The distinctive oval and pear-shaped tools typically found with H. erectus remains are referred to as "Acheulean hand-axes." Some of them show remarkable crafting. They were used by people during the early Stone Age all across Africa and much of Southwestern Eurasia.

Basically, Oldowan and Acheulian tools were the standard technology for the vast majority of human history!

PERSPECTIVE

According to Avestan Scriptures Gayomart also known as Q-mers, became the first Shah (King) of the world. He may well have been the first Shah of a different stage of mankind. As a peaceful and pious King, he rendered the primitive world prosperous and habitable. It is said, He was the first human Ahura Mazda (God) created; and also, the first man who practiced Justice, so He was called the Lawgiver.

Some of His ancient teachings have coalesced into apothegms which are pertinent even today!

"Pay heed to what is said, not to the speaker. Look up to advice and wise words, no matter who says it. Acknowledge the truth, no matter of what provenance" – Gayomart/Q-mers

Gayomart's followers were cave dwellers, who like their Prophet wore the hides of animals. He wore the skins of leopards. Time wise, this could have been anything from Homo erectus times to Neanderthal, or even later Stone Age. He is referred to as the Gar-Shah or King of the Mountains, and said to have lived in caves of the Carpathian or Alburz Mountains. Or, some say around Ararat in the Lake Van area.

He was the first Great King to arise among humans, and ruled over men and beasts by His gentle and potent nature, and His unparalleled wisdom. The Avesta calls Gayomart the Pure, and Righteous. In the Avestan language God was known by the name "Ahura Mazda"; or simplified to "Ormuzd." He granted Gayomart/Q-mers the supernatural Farr, a radiant, shimmering Halo, an Aura shining white, and brilliant like the sun, which is reserved for spiritual Kings and Luminous Beings.

Homo Antecessor

Trickles of H. erectus began to leave Africa, and venture into Europe and Asia 1.8 million years ago, via a tiny strip of land known as the Levantine Corridor, across what would be known later as the arc of the Fertile Crescent, between the eastern Mediterranean and the Red Sea. Following game, or just moving from camp to camp gave these newcomers access to Europe and Asia, as well as the Middle East.

Homo antecessor, is one of the earliest known representatives of humankind in Europe. This form is now widely accepted to be the direct ancestor of Asian H. erectus, H. heidelbergensis, and therefore, Neanderthals, Denisovans and Sima.

Antecessor was a short, stocky European who stood a little over 5 feet tall and weighed around 200 pounds. He made a successful living for a very long time – 1.2 million to 800,000 years ago. It is almost certain that H. Antecessor, as described by Eudald Carbonell, Juan Luis Arsuaga and J. M. Bermúdez de Castro, influenced, or gave rise to the "giant" H. heidelbergensis.

Exactly how H. antecessor relates to other Homo species in Europe, is a topic of debate. Some suggest that he was an evolutionary link between H. ergaster and H. heidelbergensis. Others think it was, instead, a separate species that evolved from H. ergaster. Still other scientists say Antecessor was just a junior part of the H. heidelbergensis spectrum.

PERSPECTIVE

This chunky little ancestor has had a huge influence on modern humans, as well! Over a million years of hefty evolution is tough to slim down! From this point on we see some of the large – even gigantic human forms develop.

Homo Heidelbergensis

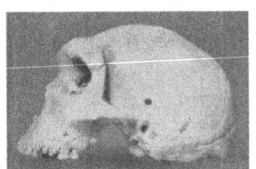

"Rhodesian Man" by J. Arthur Thomson. – http://www.gutenberg.org/files/20417/20417-h/20417-h.htm. Licensed under Public Domain via Commons – https://commons.wikimedia.org/

Homo heidelbergensis lived in Europe and Western Asia from *at least* 600,000 years ago, and may date in Africa, as far back as 1.3 million years. Rhodesian or Broken Hill man, was a Zambian counterpart dated from 300,000 to 125,000 years ago.

Homo heidelbergensis lived in families, communicated successfully with language, and practiced burial rituals with red ocher. Their stone tools resembled the Achulean toolkit of Homo erectus, with large bifacial, pear-shaped hand axes. They also used spears like H. erectus, and might have chosen to wear skin garments.

They survived until about 200,000 years ago, with cranial capacity and brains nearly as large as those of modern humans. These folks were huge and husky! They averaged over 6 feet, but many specimens towered well over 7 feet, and weighed several hundred pounds!

According to Lee R. Berger of the University of Witwatersrand, numerous fossils indicate some populations of heidelbergensis were "giants" routinely over 2.13 m (7 ft.) tall. They inhabited South Africa between 500,000 and 300,000 years ago.

PERSPECTIVE

They gave rise to several branches on the family tree, including Sima, Neanderthal, and Denisova. There are some who think that a version of this early human, or likely his large Denisovan descendants, are responsible for some of the current sightings of Yeti or Bigfoot in the woodlands of our present world. This would seem a good fit. Witnesses both recent and from tribal ancestors say it is not an animal, but a man.

It seems troubling that there is no noted use of fire! Any human form from the time of Homo erectus has the potential to use and control fire.

Also, there are no weapons or tools outside of wood knockers, and throwing stones. They are, however, credited with tree twists – not only branch twists, stick and branch aggregated "sculptures," and markers made from uprooted trees which are jammed upside down into the earth several feet.

Nests have been found in caves, abandoned dwellings, and in forest brush structures assembled in a way that reminds the observer of a wikiup.

One explorer pointed to the medicinal use of leaves. Willow leaves were stripped completely off overhead banches, presumably with grasping hands and fingers. The leaves and inner bark of willow contain salicylic acid, which is commonly acknowledged as a headache and pain remedy. Salicylic acid acquired the name "Aspirin" in the 1890's.

Perhaps most enigmatic, some believe they are capable in the use of telepathy, and can read the minds and agendas of those who seek them. This gives them a non-verbal heads up when humans approach. On the flip side, there are several reports that conversations between individuals have been overheard, though no specific words were identifiable.

Homo Neanderthalensis

Neanderthals developed in Europe and Asia, perhaps 300,000 years ago, and existed until 28,000 years ago. They were stocky like their ancestors, and shared with Homo erectus certain skull features like a prominent brow, receding chin, sloping skull and large nose, which helped them warm, and breathe frigid air.

Early anthropologists depicted the Neanderthals as primitive brutish, cave men. A few decades ago, they were thought to be mute hunter-scavengers who made clubs and crude tools. Frustratingly, they were seen as incapable of real language and symbolic communication, or thought.

Actually, they were highly intelligent, and able to adapt to a variety of climates stretching from parts of Europe, Uzbekistan, and south to the Red Sea. Some actually crossed back into Africa.

Living through two separate glacial advances, they mastered the harshest of climates. When plants were scarce, they relied heavily on meat, especially hooved animals like horses and reindeer which grazed the Steppe and Tundra.

Neanderthals lived in family groups of about 15 people judging from the size of modest rock shelters. Occasionally they built larger structures, rather than relying solely on natural rock shelters or caves. In France, Molodova, and eastern Ukraine holes in limestone rock remain where shelter poles made of trees or mammoth long bones, tusks and skulls, had once stood.

Ideal Neanderthal man 1875. [Public domain], via Wikimedia Commons

They were adept at communicating ideas and planning hunts. Communication between groups was necessary for gatherings, where they could trade products and materials, socialize, and find mates.

Strong collaboration skills allowed Neanders to encircle and hunt difficult prey like reindeer, and even much larger Pleistocene prey. Planning was critically important because they had to get up close enough to bash with clubs, poke with spears, and heave large rocks. This task would be difficult or possibly fatal, with only one or two people. They lived in dangerous times.

Neanders sustained a great number of injuries of the head and long bones, hazards of hunting and fighting gigantic Pleistocene fauna. Injuries also occurred from living in limestone rock shelters and caves, whose layers slough off crushing anything or anyone below.

PERSPECTIVE

Erik Trinkhaus, who worked with Neander skeletons 35,000 to 65,000 years old, from Shanidar Cave, stated, *"I have yet to see an adult Neanderthal skeleton that doesn't have at least one fracture. In adults in their 30's... It is common to see multiple healed fractures."* We know that these people suffered also, from pneumonia, predation and starvation.

"They did practice healing and burial rituals... They must have cared for the infirm as shown by a specimen from the Shanidar cave in Iraq, a 40-45 year old man with a variety of fractures... (he) had a blow to the left side of the head which crushed an eye socket and partially blinded him. The bones of his right shoulder and upper arm appeared shriveled as if his forearm had been amputated or severed. The right foot and lower right leg were broken while he was alive and the right knee, ankle and foot show that he struggled with injury-induced arthritis that would have made walking painful, if not impossible. He would not have survived without caring help from others." – Trinkhaus (http://archaeology.about.com/od/archaeologistst/g/trinkhause.htm)

Besides their Mousterian weaponry, they used refined tools similar to modern hunter-gatherers. They worked bone into awls or needles and wood into dishes and pegs. Flake tools whacked off rock such as chert or obsidian were employed for slicing meat off bones and scraping hides to make clothing, blankets or shelters.

Wood hafted knives or saws were embedded with rock chips. Large spear points were hammered from rock and attached securely to wooden shafts with tree pitch which had been brewed into a paste, in a bowl possibly made from a skull cap, which was nested in the ashes or coals. This was a complex process which required planning. The pitch was used heavily in the Middle Stone Age, but Neander used it, 40,000 years ago in Syria and Romania; and over 200,000 years ago in Italy. According to Dutch Archaeologist, Wil Roebroeks (http://www.pbs.org/wgbh/nova/evolution/defy-stereotypes.html)

A wide array of Neander arts have surfaced, suggesting a rich spiritual culture. They made physical adornments and ornaments of painted shells, bone, ivory and animal teeth; some of which are perforated or marked with grooves. They may have used face paints or tattoos. Surely they plied other crafts using feathers, twigs, hide, and rushes. These materials would not usually survive the ages, unless their castings were buried.

In Europe, Neanderthals were using red ocher as paint 250,000 years ago – least! They used yellow, brown and red ocher pigments, and even black manganese dioxide for paints and "crayons" to decorate skin, hides, statues and rocks. They probably gathered flowers and made pendants of feathers, shell and beads. Some of these items found their way into burials.

A nearly complete skeleton found in a cave pit inside a at La Chapelle-aux-Saints, in southwestern France, raised the possibility that these relatives of ours **intentionally buried their dead — at least 50,000 years ago.** These and at least 40 subsequent discoveries, from Europe, Israel and Iraq, suggest that Neanderthals actually had complex funeral practices.

They left behind beautiful funerary gifts. Several flutes like the Divja Babe flute, have been found. This one was drilled from a cave bear leg bone around 55,000 years ago. Stones, and beautiful spear points – perhaps even flowers decorated a grave site at a Shanidar Cave in Iraq 60-80,000 years ago. Another burial was bound in a precious bearskin 70,000 years ago in southwest France.

About the same time, a non-Neanderthal boy in southern Africa, was covered in red ochre, and buried with a seashell pendant. In Blombos Cave at the tip of South Africa, our Primitive ancestors worked red ochre as far back as 300,000 years ago! All this care suggests friends and family members practiced respect for the living and the dead, as well as love and artistry in their rather rugged existences.

In Malaga, Spain painted stalactites depict helix-like chains of swimming seals. These are among the animals that local Neanders would have eaten said, says José Luis Sanchidrián at the University of Cordoba, Spain. They have "no parallel in Paleolithic art." Charcoal remains found beside six of the paintings preserved in Spain's Nerja caves have been radiocarbon dated to between 43,500 and 42,300 years old.

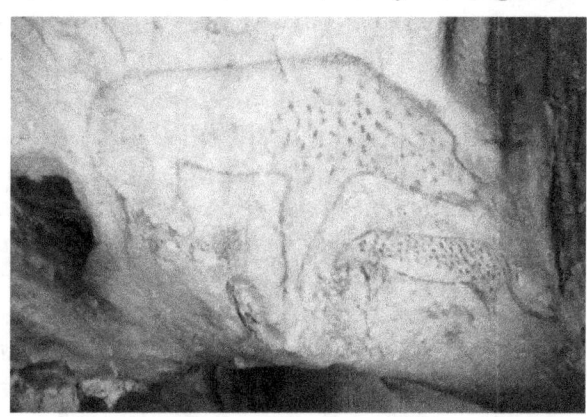
By Carla Hufstedler [CC BY-SA 2.0 (http://creativecommons.org/licenses/by-sa/2.0)], via Wikimedia Commons

The next dated paintings, 33,000-30,000 years ago, have been thought to be the work of Modern man. Pictures in Chavet cave in France reflect beautiful horses, aurochs, rhinos, bears and large cats, as well as other land and water creatures. These are not generally thought to be the work of our Neanderthal brethren, even though they did live in France at that time! They just had not been given credit for producing beautiful art until now. The Malaga seals may cause us to rethink the possibility of other Neander paintings in France.

At times ancestral peoples were overrun by competitive, modern neighbors who had more cunning technology and better hunting strategies. The newer arrivals had developed spear throwers and could attack from a safe distance. Neanderthals had to face their enemies or their prey, in much closer quarters to be successful. It seems the paths of these two human groups intertwined for at least 5,000 years before the noted disappearance of the Neanderthals.

Toward the end of their era, Neanderthals of pure lineage retreated to Spain, France and Croatia. They disappeared from the Iberian Peninsula 28,000 years ago. Yet there is evidence that Neanderthals may not all have been wiped out from conflict with more advanced neighbors, disease and starvation. Some have successfully interbred with their competitors. Recent DNA tests confirm that Neander blood is carried by a fair percentage of modern humans.

"Analysis of the skeletal remains of a four-year–old boy buried in a Portuguese rock-shelter 25,000-24,000 years ago shows a prominent chin, tooth size, and pelvic measurements that mark him as a Cro-Magnon, or fully modern human. His stocky body and short legs indicate Neanderthal heritage," says Eric Trinkaus, a paleoanthropologist at Washington University in St. Louis. 1990, Archaeological Institute of America http//www.archaeology.org/online/news/neanerkid.html

Denisova

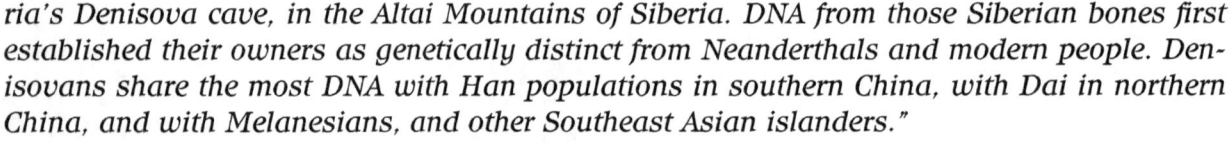

Denisovans were very large cousins of the Neanderthal. They were almost twice the size of many modern humans, standing well over 7 feet, and perhaps as much as 8 to 10 feet tall.

According to K. Kris Hirst, "*...present-day humans and Denisovans split apart about 800,000 years ago, and then reconnected some 80,000 years ago.*

Uncovered only in 2010, Denisovans are known solely from a pinky bone and a tooth found in 30,000 – to 50,000-year-old rock layers in Siberia's Denisova cave, in the Altai Mountains of Siberia. DNA from those Siberian bones first established their owners as genetically distinct from Neanderthals and modern people. Denisovans share the most DNA with Han populations in southern China, with Dai in northern China, and with Melanesians, and other Southeast Asian islanders."

Hirst continues, "*The stone tools in the layers in which the Denisovan human remains were located are a variant of Mousterian (used by Neanderthal), with the documented use of parallel reduction strategy for the cores, and a large number of tools formed on large blades. Decorative objects of bone, mammoth tusk and fossilized ostrich shell were recovered from the cave, as were two fragments of a stone bracelet made of a dark green chloriolite. The Denisovan levels contain the earliest use of an eyed bone needle known in Siberia to date.*" http://archaeologyinrussia.blogspot.com/2012/02/denisova-cave.html)

Beyond that, they must have been outfitted with a whole kit of fishing and boating gear, so early and sophisticated, it boggles the mind. Amazingly, they appear to have landed in the South Seas very early—well before the modern ancestors of the Australian Aborigines who arrived circa 55,000 years ago, possibly in a single wave of immigrants. Somewhere along the line they met Denisovans. "Dream Time" art displays both large and small humans! And DNA confirms the interbreeding of the primitive and modern humans.

PERSPECTIVE

Perhaps Denisovan travels could account for some of the sightings of giants referred to in prehistoric accounts and legendary encounters from all over the planet. We have literary references such as The Book of Giants (Enoch), the Nephalim of Genesis, the giants of the Norse Eddas and ancient Greek accounts, and those mentioned by Moses in the vale of Mt.

Horeb. They are sometimes noted as red-haired or cannibalistic. Gigantic skeletons have been found in the South Pacific Islands and the Americas.

American tales of red haired Giant skeletons may bear witness to successful Denisovan journeys. Some surprisingly enormous skeletons were buried with apparent respect, alongside modern humans in the mounds of the south central region in the United States. Abraham Lincoln was moved to say, "The eyes of that extinct species of giant, whose bones fill the mounds of America, have gazed on Niagara as our eyes do now."

Associated burial goods included copper axes, bracelets and crowns. For more on this topic, Jeff Solomon and Jim and Bill Vieira have organized a lot of interesting stories and records in "Search for the Lost Giants," a History Channel" series.

Denisovan DNA is found from Asia all the way down to Australia. For such world travelers it should have been no trouble for them to move to or from South America, fanning outward from there. Like the lost Atlanteans, these people had marine skills that weren't apparent anywhere else for thousands of years!

Denisovan Horns?
Though we know little about them other than their sailing, hunting and fishing skills were more than adequate, there may be things we could speculate about their culture.

Have you wondered about early musical instruments? Drumming seems rather easy after listening to primate tree knocks. But, how about the digeridoo and other deep-throated horns? Who else has such large instruments?

Eight to ten foot alpenhorns were used by mountain dwellers of the Alps and elsewhere. Similar wooden horns were used for communication in most mountainous regions of Europe, from France to the Carpathians. Smaller wooden and bamboo versions grace the Himalayas and Inner Asia. The use of horns became pretty much planetary, whether an oboe or trumpet, or the conch from an Island beach.

Perhaps it all started with the horns of rams and aurochs. Aurochs species date back at least 2 million years. Aurochs horns can be almost 8 inches wide and 31 inches in length. Their large horns, and those of various sheep and antelope, would have been available almost anywhere in Eurasia, an in parts of Africa.

Below are snippets of Greek and Norse legends concerning music and horns. To the Greeks "The Hyperborean (polar region) people were a musical race that also celebrated Apollon's divinity with a constant festival featuring music, song and dance. The hymns were joined by the sweet song of circling white Hyperborean swans. These gigantic kings, known as the Boreades, were sons or descendants of the north wind, Boreas." (Herodotus (4.13) 1996 Penguin Classics)

In Norse mythology Heimdallr is a god who possesses the resounding horn Gjallarhorn. Parts of the legend are colorful in that he owns the golden-maned horse named appropriately "Gulltoppr," he has gold teeth, and is the son of Nine Mothers. But some of this tale indicates that He may not have just been large and wonderful, but had the traits of a Manifestation of God.

His dwelling Himinbjorg (Heaven's castle or mountain) was located where the burning rainbow bridge (Bifrost) meets heaven. Heimdallr is said to be the originator of **social classes** (like Rama, Yima and Fu-Xi). He is possessed of foreknowledge, keen eyesight and hearing.

He like Enoch, kept watch for the onset of Ragnarok. A set of catastrophic events in which the lands would sink and most of the people and the gods will perish in water (flood).

This is corroborated by the Book of Enoch's foretelling the destruction of the giants in the coming flood. Very likely these Hyperboreans, and some of the Norse gods were large primitive humans or Prophets, perhaps in some cases both, as with Heimdaller. Their superhuman qualities made them stand out, so the stories were easier to remember.

They, like Neander and other archaic forms successfully interbred with more modern humans in certain parts of the world. Some think Denisovan men may have taken "modern" females, as their small boat loads arrived on Island shores. Contact between human types in general, were hopefully less violent in the areas where they co-existed for significant periods of time. DNA traces remain in Papua New Guinea, and in the Australian Aborigines, also in Filipino tribes like Mamanwa and Manobo. There are patches of Denisova remains in mainland Asia, and in Siberia. Skeletons of extremely large humans and legends of cannibals dot the islands of the South Pacific.

Sima

Karl Gruber's piece for National Geographic was published December 4, 2013. It defined Sima as an ancestor related to Denisovans and Neanderthals. Tests on bones hidden in a cave in the Atapuerca Mountains of Northwestern Spain set a new record for the oldest human DNA sequence ever decoded, from Western Europe. Samples belonging to 28 ancient humans who lived roughly 400,000 years ago preceded the earliest Neander sites by over 230,000 years, based on a recently uncovered Italian fossil.

Sima de los Huesos, or "cave of the bones" has been studied almost three decades and had produced more than 6,000 bone fragments of Spain's oldest known human remains, to date.

Sima people share certain features with Neanderthals, notably their thick-browed skulls. They also display features noted in Homo heidelbergensis. The bones were first thought to belong to European Neanderthals, but analysis showed they are genetically closer to the Siberian Denisovans.

"Could a natural catastrophe or carnivore activities explain the accumulation of so many bodies? Or were there hominins that accumulated the corpses of their relatives and friends in such a dark and remote place: a pit in a cave?" asked co-author and lead investigator, Juan-Luis Arsuaga.

Some scientists are stumped by the large bone pile. They find it difficult to think of the site in terms of intentional burial. A practice they pegged to a much later date. But Sima is not the first to entomb their dead. Such burial practice, is a key feature of H. naledi.

Matthias Meyer of Germany's Max Planck Institute for Evolutionary Anthropology in Leipzig, stated in an article for "Nature" that stable temperatures in the cave helped preserve the mitochondrial DNA. This allowed it to be unraveled by advances in gene-sequencing technology.

Paleoanthropologist John Hawkes of the University of Wisconsin, Madison, urges caution about regarding the Spanish genes and younger Denisovan ones as being closely related. *"The difference between Sima and Denisova (gene) sequences are about as large as the difference between Neanderthal and living human sequences…It would not be fair to say that Denisova and Sima represent a single population, any more than that Neanderthals and living people do."*

Mitochondrial DNA is generally transmitted through the female line, from mothers to offspring. For the full article see: National Geographic. (http://news.nationalgeographic.com/news/2013/12/131204-human-fossil-dna-spain-denisovan-cave/)

PERSPECTIVE

One reason for caution is that mitochondrial DNA results in the past have pointed scholars in errant directions. For example, early studies suggested that humans and Neanderthals did not share any common ancestry, which seemed very unlikely to many of us, from the get go.

A skull fossil found during exploration of a cave in Israel, tells of a transition 55,000 years ago. Some early humans who were leaving Africa, were interbreeding with Neanderthals.

Paleogeneticist Svante Pääbo of the Max Planck Institute for Evolutionary Anthropology in Leipzig, Germany, and his colleagues found that modern Europeans and Asians have inherited between 1 percent and 4 percent of their genes from Neanderthals. At this point, none are found in Africans, which might be expected. Even though some Neanders apparently moved into Africa, most were in Eurasia.

Time will tell what genes, beliefs or social culture Sima might have shared with their distant descendants. But the possibility of intentional and repeated burials, is intriguing!

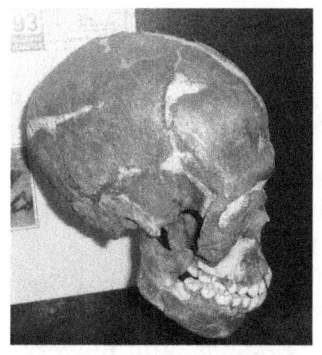

By Wapondaponda (Own work) [CC BY-SA 3.0 (http://creativecommons.org/licenses/by-sa/3.0) or GFDL (http://www.gnu.org/copyleft/fdl.html)], via Wikimedia Commons

Modern Humans

We think modern humans developed bit by bit from African H. erectus in various areas, but predominantly East Africa. Slowly brain capacity, chin slope angles and forehead alterations, brought about transformations that we are comfortable referring to as Modern.

The Levant, was a corridor which anatomically modern humans used as a bridge out of Africa. From there they spread across Eurasia, where they co-existed or replaced other forms of early human. Recent genetic evidence suggests that modern Homo sapiens and their Neanderthal cousins interbred in the Middle East 65,000-47,000 years ago. Anatomical features of the cranium indicate Neanderthal interbreeding occurred there before any encounters in Europe and Asia.

Modern humans likely co-existed with Neanderthals for up to 60,000 years in the Levant. Fossils like the one from Israel mentioned above, show physical traits different from the Africans they were leaving behind, as well as other human inhabitants along the corridor.

Recently, through the magic of gene sequencing, we are able to say that one fossil has a Neander ancestor only four generations back. Today we may have up to 20% Neander genes in Eurasian populations. Neander DNA differs from modern humans by 0.12%!

Interestingly, mitochondrial DNA points to **light colored skin** as being a later development from 6000-12,000 years ago.

Homo sapiens explorers passed through the Levant and entered the northern realm of Laos by 100,000, perhaps earlier. They were in Europe 50,000 plus years ago, living among the dwindling populations of Sima, Denisovans, and Neanderthals. They fanned into South Asia, and Pacific Islands, where presumably, they crossed paths with fleeting remnants of H. erectus and H. heidelbergensis. We have been the lucky inheritors of favorable genes from these various primitive populations, which have helped us fight diseases and adapt to rigorous changes in our world.

Tribes gradually spread across the Islands and continents. In North America valleys along the pacific coast were free of ice about 15,500-13,500 years ago, allowing migration into the interior of the Americas. Clovis and later, Folsom point and blade traditions were developed to hunt horses, mammoths, mastodon, extinct forms of bison and llamas, deer, pigs and other hoofed animals. Paleo-Indians also had to outfight dire wolves, giant cats, bears and winged carnivores. The degrees of social unity would include the family, clan and the tribe. It was difficult to survive alone. To be cast out of the group was usually a fatal, punishment.

In South America the Monte Verde culture predated the Clovis of North America by a thousand years! For this reason, many think that coastal travel was the primary route to South America, though technically, there could have been inland arrivals, shortly thereafter.

They dealt with giant sloths, teratorns, like Argentavis (Thunderbirds), and even a one ton giant rat! Truly a "rodent of unusual size." Huge flightless carnivorous birds, the Phorusrhacidae, which were nicknamed "terror birds," developed in South America and moved into North America.

Mostly they lived between 5 million and 2 million years ago. But, Titanis walleri who stood over 8 feet tall and weighed around 330 pounds, is thought to represent a significantly younger species of the lineage that may have survived until around 15,000 years ago. Recently, a younger species was reported in Uruguay. It is possible there were clashes with these and other extinct carnivorous South American predators.

By 55,000 years ago Australia was settled by Polynesian ancestors, who left Asia and Taiwan, expanding either by intention or by accident, into the various Pacific Islands, where they encountered Denisovan cousins in some areas.

They, like more recent tribes, were hunters of mammals, reptiles, amphibians, birds- even insects; as well as marine creatures like sea cucumber, octopus shell-fish and fish. Seasonally, they collected nuts, berries, fruits, roots and grains, stalks, leaves and flowers.

Life was not easy, and starvation haunted them always. Yet they were smart and ambitious enough to spread around the world. Fires were built outside or inside structures like rock shelters, teepees or huts. They wore animal hides, crafted extraordinary blades, fishhooks, and other delicate tools. There were designs and fashions expressed in bracelets and other jewelry, and hair and body decor like tattoos, face and hair paint; seed beads and feather ornaments.

Their improved weaponry included spear throwers and arrows. Flint points and feathers were regular improvements to wooden arrow shafts. Pitch and Ocher glue held points more securely in place.

The Middle Stone Age is associated with other behavioral innovations and expansions, both in and out of Africa. In places inhabited by layers of human settlements such as seen in a sequence at a Sibiu shelter near Blombos, South Africa. Comparisons of the artifacts show new developments over time.

One example is the cleaning of bedding material. Sometimes Primitive people burned their bedding for health reasons. But, by 77,000 years ago people constructed their bedding, from sedges and other plants, topped with aromatic leaves that contained insecticidal and larvicidal chemicals. The leaves were from Cryptocarya woodii. When crushed, they are aromatic and contain traces of chemicals that are effective against mosquitoes. Cryptocarya species, which are small evergreen shrubs of the laurel family are still used extensively in traditional folk medicine and magical preparations.

The use of Cryptocarya indicates that early use of **herbal medicines** may have been advantageous to Primitive people and implies a new dimension to the behavior of early humans at this time. (Science 9 December 2011: Vol. 334 no. 6061 pp. 1388-1391DOI:10.1126/science.1213317)

This is not a surprise since animals have been seeking medicinal plants for millions of years. So it is likely herbal remedies were used even back before Ardipithecus.

Another time-lapse focus is the use of ochre. Ochre is commonly found at archaeological sites world-wide, and it is generally assumed to be a coloring agent. It has accompanied burial offerings for our dearly departed, at least as far back as 95,000 years ago, when a boy in southern Africa, was covered in red ochre, and buried with a seashell pendant.

K. Kris Hirst relates that *"ochre is often associated with human burials: for example, the Upper Paleolithic cave site, Arene Candide, shows use of ochre at a burial of a young man 23,500 years ago. The site of Paviland Cave in the UK, dated to about the same time, had a burial so soaked in red ochre he was called the 'Red Lady.' A second 'Red Lady', this time actually referring to a female burial, was discovered at the Maya site of Copan."*

"Red ocher found at Blombos cave (rock shelter) on the Cape coast in South Africa, was used with a starchy plant resin to attach stone tools to wooden shafts or handles." Middle Stone Age occupation in sites like Blombos Cave, and Klein Kliphuis in South Africa, are 140,000 to 70,000 years old. Finds include examples of **ochre, slabs, engraved with patterns** carved into the surface." See K. Kris Hirst "Sibudu cave" archaeology.about.com/od/shthroughsiterms/qt/sibudu_cave.htm.

The earliest known use of ochre is nearly 300,000 years old, in the site of GnJh-03 in the Kapthurin Formation of East Africa, and at Twin Rivers in Zambia. Often associated with religious ceremonies, ochre was and still is, a popular pigment choice for artists. In Europe, **Neanderthals were using red ocher as paint 250,000 years ago** – at least!

Cro-Magnon artisans produced sculptures, and relevant murals and cave art, indicating prey animals such as seafood, gazelles, rhinos, aurochs, deer, bison and horses which they hunted.

Beyond middle and old Stone Age medical aid, hygiene, and ritual burials, we see hints of ritual caves. Used by cults whose foci tend to be represented by fierce animals like the cave bear in Europe 35,000 years ago, and a giant python ritual cave dating in Botswana back 70, 000. These may currently be the oldest examples of cultic ritual, but as the quality of achaeological work progresses, the diorama will undoubtedly expand.

The following passage from Rama's time corroborates interactions between such caves and the eariest Prophets. "He used magic spells against the priests of decadent cults, who kept enormous snakes and pterodactyls, rare survivors, which were worshipped like gods, and which terrified the masses. They made these snakes eat the flesh of captives... Sometimes Rama (also Krishna and others) appeared unexpectedly in these temples with torches, driving out frightening and subduing both serpents and priests." – Edouard Schure *Great Initiates* 1889

In French and Spanish caves like Lascaux and Altamira, we appreciate colorful, classic cave paintings and engravings. The leopard spotted horses on Pech-Merle cave walls along with black and bay coated horses from Lascaux and Altamira caves, were painted by ice age artists 25,000-33,000 years ago. They reflect actual horses they saw and interacted with. DNA studies of fossilized teeth and bone, in the vicinity, attest to the accuracy of the quarry paintings.

"Why they took the effort making these beautiful paintings will always remain a miracle to us...It's an enigma, but it's also nice to see that if we go back 25,000 years, people didn't have much technology and life was probably hard, but nevertheless they already endeavored in producing art. It tells us a lot about ourselves as a species." Says Michael Hofreiter, one of the authors of this study, who is an evolutionary biologist at the University of York in England. (Science 24 April, 2009 Vol 324 number 5926, p. 485).

Body "art" in the form of tattoos goes back at least 16-18,000 years, according to Aaron Deter-Wolf of the Tennessee Division of Archeology. The Iceman known as Ootzi bears the earliest physical evidence to date. A bone needle and "ink" made from charcoal punched through the skin for decortion, healing chronic pain, such as arthritis, or for cultural identity.

Summation

We know something about Primitive people's tools, their homes, decorations and their arts. They showed an appreciation of things that made life more beautiful. Undoubtedly many crafts and arts left little residue, and are not considered to be a part of a tool assemblage. Such things as baby slings and patterns swept into dirt flooring, as well as comforting woven goods – like mats, beds, basketry and fans. Yet, these things were likely a part of even the earliest Stone Age tradition.

Wherever they lived, our early ancestors faced difficult conditions. They survived two maximum glaciations and ice retreats, while living in crude shelters, teepees and caves. They hunted and fought Pleistocene mega fauna like: mastodons, mammoths, giant sloths, large teratorns and other carnivorous birds, reptiles, cave bears, lions and sabretooth cats.

The remains of Neanders and other cave dwellers show healing after traumatic accidents. Recuperative care suggests friends and family members did not give up on the victims. This suggests they practiced loving respect for both the living and the dead, and they also practiced healing arts, including tattoos & medicine and trephination.

Our ancient ancestors also expressed a desire for beauty, shown in a vast array of art forms, to brighten their otherwise rugged existences. People left behind funerary gifts like: ocher, flutes, animal skins, beads and yes, perhaps flowers, stones and beautiful spear points. The use of paints and colors expanded worldwide. We know that ancestors as far back as Neanderthal used red, brown and yellow ochre to paint, draw and to give the hope of life, to dead comrades.

As for spiritual development, we see traces that point to a belief in the existence of spirit in all things, life after death, and a spiritual Power greater than personal power.

With clues like those from Nu Wa, Gayomart/Q-mers, and the three snapshots which we will look at in a few pages on the Ainu, Gobekli Tepe, the Upanishads, we see glimpses of a primordial, spiritual mural.

SYMBOLIC RELIGION

Besides moving funeral displays; acknowledgements of passage to life beyond this stage; and healing rituals to cure and comfort the injured, sick and deformed; we have internalized symbolic remembrances of a creative Power, which precedes common Biblical interpretations. Examples of early symbolic spiritual activity that remain with us today include:

The Tree of Life and the general sacredness of trees: The Tree of Life is easily recognizable and nearly universal. The Tree of Life connects all life, and binds humans throughout our evolutionary forms. Spiritually, the Tree of Life is a border on the horizon between mortal and immortal realms. **Typically angels cannot even pass.** Here are references from various scriptures, ancient and new.

The Norse Oluf Bagge Edda tells of the Yggdrasil, an immense green ash in the middle of Aesir, which rises from a pure fountain of fate, also known as the well of Urd or Vurd. Yggdrasil joins nine worlds with its branches and roots, and Odin was said to travel up and down it on his horse, Sleipner.

In Egypt, they referred to the holy Sycamore which connected all life. Adam and Eve were familiar with the Tree of the Knowledge of Good and Evil. Gautama Buddha received His Revelation beneath the graceful "Bo," or fig tree.

Persian Creation mentions the Gaokerene or, the **World Tree**. Some say it is the Saenna, with effusive cascading yellow flowers and seed pods. In shape it would be similar to the Anisa, a broad-spreading tree which has been described as a **silver chord stretched from heaven to earth, and through all that lies between.**

"But Gabriel ascended with him (the Prophet Mohammed) for a distance above that, the distance of which only Allah knows, till he reached the Lote Tree (beyond which none may pass) and then the Irresistible, the Lord of Honor and Majesty approached and came closer till he (Gabriel) was about two bow lengths or (even)nearer." (Hadith, Bukhari Vol 9)

The Sidrah (short for Sadrat'ul Muntaha) or **Tree of Truth**. Sidrah means "of the stars" or "star-like" possibly referring to its cascading flowers. It is a holy tree at the end of the seventh heaven. It is a boundary.

In a Tablet Bahá'u'lláh states, "The Holy Tree [Sadrat] is, in a sense, the Manifestation of the One True God, exalted be He." (Baha'u'llah, Tablets of Baha'u'llah, p. 137)

In that light, the following quote from the Bab is a bit chilling: **"If thou art not a believer, the Tree of divine Truth would condemn thee to extinction."** (The Bab, Selections from the Writings of the Bab, p. 123)

"O MY FRIENDS! Have ye forgotten that true and radiant morn, when in those hallowed and blessed surroundings ye were all gathered in My presence beneath the shade of the tree of life, which is planted in the all-glorious paradise? Awe-struck ye listened as I gave utterance to these three most holy words: O friends! Prefer not your will to Mine, never desire that which I have not desired for you, and approach Me not with lifeless hearts, defiled with worldly desires and cravings. Would ye but sanctify your souls, ye would at this present hour recall that place and those surroundings, and the truth of My utterance should be made evident unto all of you." (Baha'u'llah, The Persian Hidden Words)

Enoch asks the Archangel Michael about the Tree:
And from thence I went to another place of the earth, and he showed me a mountain range of fire which burnt day and night. And I went beyond it and saw seven magnificent mountains all differing each from the other, and the stones (thereof) were magnificent and beautiful, magnificent as a whole, of glorious appearance and fair exterior: three towards the east, one founded on the other, and three towards the south, one upon the other, and deep rough ravines, no one of which joined with any other. And the seventh mountain was in the midst of these, and it excelled them in height, resembling the seat of a throne: and fragrant trees encircled the throne. And amongst them was a tree such as I had never yet smelt, neither was any amongst them, nor were others like it: it had a fragrance beyond all fragrance, and its leaves and blooms and wood wither not for ever: and its fruit is beautiful, and its fruit resembles the dates of a palm. Then I said: 'How beautiful is this tree, and fragrant, and its leaves are fair, and its blooms very delightful in appearance.' Then answered Michael, one of the holy and honoured angels who was with me, and was their leader.

And he said unto me: 'Enoch, why dost thou ask me regarding the fragrance of the tree, and why dost thou wish to learn the truth?' Then I answered him, saying: 'I wish to know about everything, but especially about this tree.' And he answered, saying: 'This high mountain which thou hast seen, whose summit is like the throne of God, is His throne, where the Holy Great One, the Lord of Glory, the Eternal King, will sit, when He shall come down to visit the earth with goodness. And as for this fragrant tree no mortal is permitted to touch it till the great judgement, when He shall take vengeance on all and bring (everything) to its consummation forever. It shall then be given to the righteous and holy. Its fruit shall be for food to the elect: it shall be transplanted to the holy place, to the temple of the Lord, the Eternal King.
(Other Apocrypha, The Book of Enoch, chapters 24 and 25)

"Then will aggression crumble away, and all that maketh for disunity be destroyed, and the structure of oneness be raised – that the Blessed Tree may cast its shade over east and west, and the Tabernacle of the singleness of man be set up on the high summits, and flags that betoken love and fellowship flutter from their staffs around the world until the sea of truth lift high its waves, and earth bring forth the roses and sweet herbs of blessings without end, and become from pole to pole the Abha Paradise." (Abdu'l-Baha, *Selections from the Writings of Abdu'l-Baha*, p. 36)

"Therefore it [the soul] is the Most Sublime Essence of God, the Tree of Blessedness, the Lote-Tree beyond which there is no passing, the Garden of Repose." (Baha'u'llah, Epistle to the Son of the Wolf, p. 110)

Throughout our evolution trees were our source of safety and food. They helped mold our grasping hands and keen eyes. People still find they are reverently attracted to the majestic beauty, peace and protection of trees. Sacred trees can be destinations, a place to leave offerings of ribbons and prayers. In most inhabited region's individuals, families and tribes honor sacred trees; and they are revived by the burning of fragrant or medicinal wood and herbs.

◎ **The sun:** Without it, all life on earth would quickly vanish. References both ancient and new, to our sun's warmth and nurturing brilliance, remind us of the parental care and endless spiritual light with which our Creator constantly bathes our souls, and the divine rays of bounties provided to all creatures. In a superficial sense, it can become worshipping the sun as an icon, or a god.

◎ **A brilliant halo or farr:** This applies to the bright transfiguration associated with the great Prophets and Manifestations of God's Word, when they are in the glowy revelatory state. References date from well back to Paleolithic texts like Avestan "Forest Books," and Vedic Aranyakas.

◎ **Stars with a variety of points, or other cosmic shapes:** These along with astrology, numerology, and visions of the seven "heavens" are recurring reminders of our universal aspect.

◎ **Angels:** The acknowledgement of angelic hosts and other great spiritual Beings who protect us against the whispers of evil, travels with us through the millennia. One belief is that loving angelic guides heal both physical and spiritual ills. Another, is that fierce warrior angels defend us against evil forces; Gargoyles are said to represent these warriors. As belief in angelic warriors fades, angelic icons, statues, and other representational forms, become more cutesy and inane.

◎ **Fragrant smoke and oils:** The use of smoke (incense) is another ancient unifying thread. Besides usually smelling "heavenly," smoke is used to purify material possessions, cleanse and bless homes and raise prayers heavenward, even today. It was especially important to the followers Rama, and reiterated by Zoroaster, and Viracocha, and others; who demanded fragrant smoke and oils rather than any kind of blood sacrifice.

◎ **Sacred Hands**: Prayerful, peaceful hands, palms up , palms down, humble hands folded, clasped, tucked under the thighs, clasped across the chest, finger outstretched gracefully, thumb and finger forming a ring. Hands are held up as a sign of non-violent or sacred greeting, a supplication, or sign of gratitude. Sacred hands.

◎ **Notched counting sticks, prayer wheels and prayer beads:** These kept our minds and hearts attuned to thoughts of God; and service to Creation.

◎ **Statues, crystals, pendants and amulets:** These symbolic representations, lower our eyes to material things, as far back as Neanderthals, or even further.

◎ **The thought that God is; and that God is in all things:** This primal edict, or "me," certainly preceded the Adamic Cycle. Yet a slight twist on seeing God in all things, such as seeing a "spirit" in all things can lead to idolatry.

A beautiful tree can catch our eyes, lift our mood and even put a smile on our face. Who does not like a peaceful walk in a park or forest? Some trees are almost like shrines. But if instead of praying to the One who made this tree and is in this tree, and is the source of its beautiful fruit; a person makes an offering to the tree itself; so it will bear fruit. Or worse, a person worships the god of the tree, perhaps in the form of an idol or an amulet. Or most distant the person prays to a random fertility deity so the tree will bear fruit. Such a digression, over time is common.

Animism can devolve from seeing God in all things, to seeing a spirit in all things. People leave the path and begin to worship a multitude of things, rather than God. This represents a huge materialistic departure from the original spiritual simplicity, and eventually leads us to the need for a "renewal" and regeneration of "The Word"

We see this today, cases where praying to God alone is not enough. Instead we employ multitudes of saints, angels, deities, or gods – even the universe. We remake religion in our image, so that it reflects personal thoughts, rather than accepting guidance from God. Such unravelling also happened throughout the ages.

This is not because primitive people weren't smart enough to grasp the concept of one God, a Single Creator, because they always were! We have many Paleolithic examples.

The verse below comes to us from the oldest Upanishads, the most ancient scriptures of India, which are similar in age to the most ancient root of the Avestan scriptures of Aryana Vaejah. This could put the shortened quote below, at the beginning of the last spiritual cycle or age, somewhere around, or even before 14,000 years ago, based on the commencement of the earliest religious complexes.

"Disciples inquire within themselves: What is the cause of the Universe? Is it Brahman [God]? Whence do we come? Why do we live? Where shall we at last find rest? Under whose command are we bound by the law of happiness and its opposite?

Time, space, law, chance, matter, primal energy, intelligence—none of these, nor a combination of these can be the final cause of the universe, for they are effects, and exist to serve the soul. Nor can the individual self be the cause, for being subject to the law of happiness and misery, it is not free." – Svetasvatara Upanishad from *The Upanishads Breath of the Eternal*, Pravabananda and Manchester Mentor Books Pg. 118. 1957

Not what you expected from a most ancient Stone age thought? The message is pristine even though it has been carefully handed down to us over the millennia.

Maybe the most ancient and deeply embedded teachings in our cultures are: apothegms, adages, maxims, quotes, proverbs and parables. We retell them as fables similar to tales of Aesop and Mother Goose. They contain shreds of verbal, spiritual wisdom, observations and guidelines; which have passed down orally through the generations of mankind.

Example: **"He who hesitates is lost."** Attributed to a cave-dwelling "first man" Gayomart, also known by Q-mers. If a person takes too long to think about an opportunity, it may vanish. Or, he may get eaten! Undoubtedly, you can think of other ties throughout the ages.

"And now regarding thy question, 'How is it that no records are to be found concerning the Prophets that have preceded Adam, the Father of Mankind, or of the Kings that lived in the days of those Prophets?' Know thou that the absence of any reference to them is no proof they did not actually exist. That no records concerning

them are now available, should be attributed their extreme remoteness, as well as to the vast changes which the earth hath undergone since their time." (Baha'u'llah, Gleanings form the Writings of Baha'u'llah, p. 172)

And perhaps a vast change in human forms, as well!

Individuals rose up to call on God and nature to help others seek understanding of various aspects of life. They called forth the powers of healing and sometimes its opposite. Karpans, priests, mediums, seers, witches and shamans, spoke out to contact God, and various spirits all over this planet. Their wisdom (and folly) pervades the human religious culture.

PRE-AGRICULTURAL RELIGION

Here are three pre-agricultural examples of religion. The Upanishads, Gobekli Tepe and the Ainu/Jomon tradition. All date roughly 12,000-14,000 years ago.

Dawn of the Upanishads

"Like radii of the same circle, all these traditions indicate a common center... long before the India of the Vedas, before the Iran of Zoroaster, in the early dawn..., one sees the first creator of the Aryan religion emerging from the forests of ancient Scythia."
(-Schure, *The Great Initiates*, 1889)

At least one of the Ancient Upanishads, Svetesvatara, is so hauntingly beautiful and clear that it awes the reader! These teachings were a part of an oral tradition protected by pure hearted Rishis, ancient sages who bore these Eternal Truths, until they could be placed on paper. Bless them forever! Here are excerpts of this poem which is perhaps one candidate for the world's oldest prayer:

"O Brahman Supreme! Formless art Thou, and yet (though the reason none knows)
Thou bringest forth many forms; Thou bringest them forth, and then withdrawest them to Thyself. Fill us with thoughts of Thee!
Thou art the fire, Thou art the sun, Thou art the air, Thou art the moon, Thou art the starry firmament, Thou art Brahman Supreme; Thou art the waters—Thou the Creator of all!
Thou art woman, Thou art man, Thou art the youth, Thou art the maiden, Thou art the old man tottering with his staff; Thou facest everywhere.
Thou art the dark butterfly; Thou art the green parrot with red eyes. Thou art the thunder cloud, the seasons and the seas. Without beginning art Thou, beyond time, beyond space. Thou art He from Whom sprang the three worlds.
Maya (material Creation) is Thy divine consort—Wedded to Thee...Many are her children—The rivers, the mountains, Flower stone and tree, Beast bird and man—In every way like herself.
Thou spirit in flesh, Forgetting what Thou art, Unitest with Maya—But only for a season. Parting from her at last, Thou regainest thyself.
Forgetting his oneness with Thee, bewildered by his weakness, full of sorrow is man; But let him look close on Thee, know Thee as himself, O Lord most worshipful, And behold

Thy glory—Lo this heavy sorrow is turned to joy.
Changeless art Thou, Supreme, pure! In thee dwell the gods. The Source of all scriptures Thou art; Yet what shall scriptures avail if they be smooth on the lip but absent from the heart?
To him who knows Thee comes fullness—to him alone!
The Source of all scriptures Thou art; and the Source of all creeds.
One Thou art, one only. Born from many wombs, Thou hast become many: Unto Thee all return. Thou Lord God bestowest all blessings, Thou the Light, Thou the Adorable One. Whoever finds Thee finds infinite peace.
Thou art Lord God of all gods, all the worlds rest in thee; Thou art ruler of the beasts, two-footed, four-footed: Our heart's worship be Thine! Thou art the blissful Lord, subtler than the subtlest. In Thee alone is there peace.
Thou, sole guardian of the universe, Thou lord of all. In the hearts of Thy creatures Thou hidest thyself. Gods and seers become one with Thee. Those who know Thee die not.
Of all religions thou art the Source. The light of thy knowledge shining, there is no day nor night, Nor being, nor non-being—Thou art alone.
Thou alone art—Thou the Light imperishable, Adorable; Great Glory is thy name. No one is there beside Thee, no one equal to Thee.
Invisible is Thy form, invisible to mortal eyes; the seers alone, in their hearts purified—They alone see Thee. They alone are immortal.
Neither male nor female art Thou, nor neuter; whatsoever form Thou assumest, that Thou art. Thou dost pervade the universe, Thou art consciousness itself, Thou art creator of time.
Thou art the Primal Being. Thou appearest as this universe of illusion and dream. Thou art beyond time. Indivisible, infinite, the Adorable One—let a man meditate on Thee within his heart, Let him consecrate himself to Thee, and Thou, infinite Lord, wilt make Thyself known to him.
Thou womb and tomb of the universe, and its abode; Thou Source of all virtue, destroyer of all sins—Thou art seated in the heart. When Thou art seen, Time and form disappear. Let a man feel Thy presence, let him behold thee within, And to him shall come peace, Eternal Peace—to none else, to none else!
Let a man devote himself To knowledge of thee: All his fetters shall be loosed.
OM . . . PEACE—PEACE—PEACE."
The Upanishads: Breath of the Eternal Prabhavananda and Manchester, 1948 Mentor Books, New York and Toronto; Pp 123-127 Translated from Sanskrit by Swami Prabhavananda and Frederick Manchester

AMAZING Purity! – Perfection! This Upanishad could have been revealed today, rather than several thousands of years ago. Certainly not all recollections are that exact.

Gobekli Tepe

In the June 2011 issue, "National Geographic" ran an intriguing article about the beginning of religion, by Charles C. Mann. And guess what? The exceedingly ancient, yet well designed temple, was reportedly built by hunter-gatherers wearing loin cloths, nearly 12,000 years ago. Some of the structures may even date as far back as 15, 000 years ago! This remote hilltop cathedral in southern Turkey precedes Stonehenge by 6000+ years! Obviously, people who wear animal skins can build surprisingly great religious monuments!

The article begins: *"We used to think agriculture gave rise to cities and later to writing, art, and religion. Now the world's oldest temple suggests the urge to worship sparked civilization."*

Wow! This vindicates those who believe civilization was always advanced by spiritual guidance! Thanks to the builders of Gobekli Tepe, who came from near and far to raise the beautifully carved pillars, build the mortared walls and bench seating, and engrave the art of this monumental complex – with flint and stone tools!

By Zhengan (Own work) [CC BY-SA 4.0 (http://creativecommons.org/licenses/by-sa/4.0)], via Wikimedia Commons

Ainu/Jomon

According to C. Loring Brace, an anthropologist at the University of Michigan in Ann Arbor. *"'The Jomon believed to be the original inhabitants of Japan, are the obvious ancestors of the Ainu but not of modern Japanese. They apparently migrated from the Northern Asian mainland at a time when the two regions were physically connected. When sea levels began to rise about 12,000 years ago, the Japanese archipelago became separate from continental Asia, and the Jomon were left to spread across the islands. Hunters, fishers, and foragers, the Jomon were also the world's first known potters. Indeed, their name-Japanese for cord marks-stems from the ropelike impressions found in their clay pottery."*

The study of "Kennewick Man's" skeletal remains shows the Ainu might well have been his relatives. Traces of that bloodline seem to pop up in other people on the Northwest Coast of the United States, as in the Lummi Nation in Washington State.

Below I have borrowed an excellent example from Stefan Anitei to put a flesh on the bones of prehistory. (http://archive.news.softpedia.com/news/9-Amazing-Things-About-the-Ainu-People-79277.shtml)

This example is so rich and descriptive of a life that really could represent elements of tribal life.

AMAZING THINGS ABOUT THE AINU PEOPLE

I In northern Japan, on the island of Hokkaido and a part of the Russian Sakhalin Island, lives a mysterious ethnic group, called Ainu... They are very distinct from the Japanese people and, before the Tungus invasion coming from mainland Asia (Korea and northern China), the whole archipelago was inhabited by the Ainu.

2 Ainu are shorter than the Japanese people, with lighter skin, robust body and short limbs. Unlike typical Mongoloids, their hair is wavy and the body hair is abundant; men wear large beards and mustaches, considered a sign of beauty, to the point that married women tattoo their lower face to mimic a beard...

3 Bears are considered powerful spirits which can... benefit... people. When Ainu capture a bear cub, a woman is charged to take care of it as if a child: the little bear lives and grows amongst the people of the village, getting accustomed to them. When it is 2-3 years old, the bear is sacrificed. The men drink its blood to get its power, and then they cut the head off and then fly the skin of the bear. Later, during family ceremonies, the bear skin occupies a prominent place, and food and drink is offered to it like to an honored guest. The bear was considered by the Ainu the mythological hero that taught them to fish, hunt, weave and so on.

4 Ainu lived in rectangular huts with walls and roof made of bundles of reed and rush. Ainu live in a clime where snowed winter can last 6-7 months annually, and the summer is extremely rainy; the heat source is the fire burning in a cavity dug into the ground. As these huts lack chimneys, the smoke filled the room and was released just through a small hole made on the roof. Over the fire, there was a kind of grill on which meat and fish were put for drying on time. Next to the door, the water bucket and the home tools were located.

5 The family slept over platforms made of wood covered with rush mats, and as they did not have bed linen, they slept dressed. As the house had just two windows, and one of them was sacred and never opened, the scents of the dry meat and fish and that of the human bodies mixed with the smoke and made those huts not very attractive.

6 The Ainu religion was animist: all the beings and many natural objects (rivers, volcanoes, fire, lightning, trees, etc.) were endowed with a spirit. When a living being dies, only the material part is gone; the spirit is freed and this spirit can be good or evil, harming living beings, including people. To avoid the actions of the evil spirits, Ainu used to work with wood, making coarse representations of the spirits, with a human form, called inaos. Today, inaos are simple sticks made with cuts of a knife. The inaos are thrust into the ground, inside the huts, close to the sea, on the cross of the roads, next to sacred trees and they are like prayers of the Ainu aimed to the superior spirits, asking for their protection.

7 Women were largely independent until marrying. After that, they were under men's will. But women went to war and could manifest their opinions during the councils of the village. Ainu women adorned their hands, forehead, arms and mouth outline with blue tattoos (as said, for mimicking mustaches).

8 Women worked the fields, gathered wood, cooked, span, wove, made clothes, cared [for] and educated the kids. Children were treated severely and even if crying, nobody gave them the least attention. Inside the houses, they were put into a wooden cradle hung on a beam. Outside, they were transported in a type of bag which the mother or a major sister hung at the back, using a fabric strip passing over the head.

9 The Ainu women weave mats, bags, nets and a type of fabric using elm bark. The bark is soaked and left until softening and large, thin threads can be removed. The women wind them in balls, later woven in coarse looms. This yellowish fabric is dyed with bright colors and from it women make large tunics with wide sleeves, adorned with beautiful embroidery motifs. The tunics are secured at the waist with leather girdles and brass appliqués. During the winter, over this tunic, a type of sleeveless jacket made of animal skins is worn. In the past, both women and men wore leather trousers, but now they use cotton pants. Bark leggings and leather moccasins completed the Ainu getup. For walking over the snow, they used skis and snowshoes.

10 The most important person in the Ainu village was the shaman, the person treating with the spirits. The shaman had, in his service, other animal spirits, which, at his will, helped him in his spells, and with whose help the shaman discovered the causes of the malfunctions of the villagers and took remedy against them. His main function was to cure the diseases.

When asked for help, the shaman waited for the sunset; in that moment, he approached the ill person, played a bass drum to call the evil spirits that produced the ailment, agitated his wand, with sound yells invoked the spirits of the animals that help him, danced in an uncontrolled way and, in the end, he fell in a trance; at his 'return', before the amazed eyes of the assistance, he extracted, out of the body of the patient (using a skilled trick), the cause of the disease: a stick, a stone, a small toad or an insect. Once this operation was executed, the healing was immediate. However, if the patient died (fact that often occurred), this was due to the subsequent intervention of an evil spirit.

11 When an Ainu dies, his family ignites a large bonfire inside his hut and sends messengers for informing his friends and remote relatives. When they have arrived, the burial is done. The corpse is exposed with its best clothes, but torn and cut in various places; at its side, his goods are disposed, all crumbled or broken. Sacrifices and libations are offered to the spirits, so that they will welcome the spirit of the dead; the family celebrates a great funerary banquet and, next day, the body wrapped in a mat is buried. The tomb is marked by a small mound and a wood and bamboo post crowned with a kind of an arrow, if the dead was a man, and with a rounded point, if the dead was a woman. Of which post, a frayed strip hangs. The strip was previously used by the defunct to hold his/her hair.

12 The base of the Ainu economy was represented by fishing, both in the sea and freshwater. On the beaches, they collected crabs, lobsters, scallops, mussels, oysters and even turtles. During the winter, fishing was made through holes in the frozen rivers. During the summer, fishing was made using nets, rods, hooks and harpoons, especially in the case of the salmons which ascended the rivers in large number for spawning. One fisherman thrusts the fish with the harpoon, and another finished it up at the bank of the river, with a mace. The harpoon's detachable tip was anointed with poison.

13 Ainu used monoxylon (made of one trunk) canoes, 8 m (26 ft.) long and 0.5 m (1.5 ft.) wide. The most peculiar Ainu fishing was with dogs. A great number of dogs were trained for this; they brought the captured fish to the shore. Usually, the Ainu employed two dog teams made of 20-30 individuals. At a signal, the dogs, found at a 200 m (660 ft.) distance one from the other, swam in columns into the sea and, at another signal, the two groups approached each other, heading to the shore. The fish caught in the middle were frightened by the noise made by the dogs. In shallow waters, the dogs captured them easily with their mouth. The dogs were recompensed with fish heads.

14 Ainu used to hunt seals, walruses and whales. They always cooked their food on embers. Traditional food consisted of chestnuts mixed with fish eggs. Dishes were made of tree bark and food was kept in wooden recipients.

15 For hunting, men use bow and envenomed arrows and a type of crossbow similar to the Medieval one used in Europe. The arrows are envenomed using a special substance kept in a bamboo quiver worn over the shoulder. These weapons and dogs are used for hunting deer and bears. Traps are used for catching birds and hares. Traps using venomous arrows are also used for killing bears and dears [sic].

16 Bear was the most appreciated game. Specially trained dogs approached the den where the animal spent the winter. The dogs forced the bear out, the moment when the hunters shot their arrows. The greatest trophy was a living cub, brought as described to the Ainu village, to be raised and sacrificed.

17 These people are kind and friendly; foreign visitors are welcomed as long as they follow their complex etiquette. When entering into an Ainu house, the visitor must emit a strong throat clearing and if invited to enter, he/she must leave the footwear before the door and, barefooted, he/she will go to seat next to the fire. The owner of the house will offer him/her a pipe tobacco and a cup of sake (a type of rice wine, similar to that processed by the Japanese). Sake drinking is a veritable ceremony, employing large painted wooden cups or bowls and, on a tray, they offer the guest finely cut sticks. The sticks are used by the Ainu for lifting their mustaches while drinking, because they are so large and dense that they enter into the dishes, fact considered to be bad manners.

DOMESTICATION AND RELIGION

"According to 'Baihu tongy' by Ban Gu of the Han Dynasty, in ancient times, people only ate animal meat. By Shennong's time, there were too many people and animals were insufficient. Thus Shennong taught people to do farming. People benefited a great deal from it. So they called him Shennong, which means the god of farming" http://chineseculture.about.com/library/weekly/aa_shennong02a.htm

Hunter-gatherer populations outstripped the ability of wild game and grains to support their numbers. Settling down to "farm" in a specific area impacted the material, social and the spiritual life of man.

People gradually encouraged popular species to stick around their settlements, to supplement hunting, fishing and gathering. Dogs, and perhaps other animals may have been domesticated as early as 30,000 years ago. By 12000-6000 years ago, in the Middle East and Asia, chickens, cats, horses, cattle, sheep, goats and pigs and some kinds of fish began to hang around settlements in exchange for handouts, or the favor of rooting through garbage piles for sustenance. Orphaned prey animals came to be tamed and then domesticated. Domestication of many staple vegetables, fruits and grains followed between 9000 to 6000 years ago. This process may have taken place earlier in Africa.

During this time man needed to learn to live in a civilized manner among a growing number of strangers and neighbors. Harmony between families necessitated advancements in social order. We needed direction whether we chose to follow it or not.

As people crowded together, spiritual, and later civic laws facilitated peaceful and just interactions.

People who left the path of God, and spiritual guidance were generally not as careful about how they treated the animals who served them, or the people around them.

Agriculture was flourishing by Cain and Abel's time, giving us a cultural backdrop for the conventional story of Adam and Eve. Their sons were farmers and herdsmen.

Sheep, goats, and other farm crops were already domesticated say around 14,000 – 9,000 years ago. Yet human forms have existed for 5.6 million years. This suggests that Adam was not the first human ever – even though we read in the Torah or Old Testament that He is the first! The sacred text seems to conflict with itself. There are explanations.

When the Torah was composed, certain portions of Hosarsiph's (Moses') texts were unavailable due the loss of the code keys for the higher Egyptian languages. The Hebrews did

the best they could with what was available to them at the time. More on that later.

A second possibility is that each spiritual epoch has a beginning and an end. The appellation of "Adam" can mean "First Man" or "Spirit," a new cycle for the spiritual and physical development of humanity; and the end or closing of the older age. **Perhaps Adam was the "first" for a newer version of mankind.**

Since God has promised us that he never would leave us alone without His nurturing guidance, and the Adam of the Bible is only several thousand years old culturally, why do we see remnants of spiritual activity far before that? It's a fair question. How many "Adams" initiated previous spiritual ages?

"There have been a thousand Adams. Nay, a thousand times a thousand!" (–unknown)

So with this new perspective, we see that revealed religion goes further back than we may have thought. It also trails off into the unforeseeable future – 500,000 years, at the very least according to the Baha'is. Each stage will bring its page of Redeemers and Guides for the beloved Creation of God.

"Witness, therefore, how numerous and far-reaching have been the changes in language, speech, and writing **since the days of Adam. How much greater must have been the changes before Him!"** (Baha'u'llah, Gleanings from the Writings of Baha'u'llah, p. 173 & 174)

EARLY CITIES

Many aspects of life necessary to build the early cities were put into play by Prophets whose names are unremembered. So even the earliest Stone Age cities of around 12,000-10,000 years ago, demonstrate advanced building design, markets and sewers, etc. Phenomenal examples of architecture can be found in lands of the Middle East and India. The presence of cities will be mentioned in the stories of Yima and later, Sri Krishna, and others.

Jericho 12,000 years ago, Jarmo 9,000, and Catal Huyuk 8,500 years ago, are long term settlements which predate Sumer at 7,500-6000 years ago. The later sites Mohenjo Daro and Harappa are mentioned in the preface to the piece on Lord Krishna.

Jericho shows evidence of settlement dating back to 12,000 years ago during a period of cold and drought. Permanent settlement at a single location was not yet possible. However, a spring at what would become Jericho was a popular camping ground for **Natufian** hunter-gatherer groups, who left crescent microlith tools behind.

Circa 11,960 years ago, the droughts and cold came to an end, making it possible for the Natufians to extend their stays. This eventually led to year-round habitation and permanent settlement. The first permanent settlement on the site of Jericho developed near that spring.

As the climate warmed, a new Stone Age culture, based on agriculture became possible. Sedentary villages of small circular dwellings emerged. Houses were built of adobe bricks, made from clay mixed with straw and animal dung. These bricks were left to dry in the sun, then plastered together with a mud mortar, as they are even today.

Each house measured about 16 feet across, and was roofed with mud-smeared brush. Hearths were located within, and outside the homes. The bones of the dead were placed within the floors. These people relied on harvesting wild game, and plant foods. Now they were transitioning to the cultivation of wild or domestic cereals. They had not yet used pottery.

By about 9400 years ago, the town had grown to more than 70 modest dwellings which housed up to three thousand people. There was a massive stone wall over 12 ft. high and 5'11" wide at the base. Inside the wall, stood a tower over 12 feet tall that housed an internal staircase with 22 stone steps. The wall may have defended the tower so it could be used peacefully for ceremonial purposes.

After a few centuries the first settlement was abandoned. A second settlement established 6800 years ago was perhaps the work of invaders who had absorbed the original inhabitants into their culture. Artifacts dating from this period include ten skulls, plastered and painted, to reconstitute the individuals' features. These "portraits" were kept in people's homes, and the bodies were buried.

Jarmo was a small permanent village, approximately three to four acres of oak and pistachio woodlands, located in northern Iraq, in the foothills of the Zagros Mountains. As one of the oldest agricultural sites in the world, it dates by carbon-14, back to 9,090 years ago. There were twelve levels. Two older permanent Neolithic settlements, were contemporary with Jericho in the southern Levant, and Catal Huyuk in Anatolia.

That period was represented in Shanidar Cave, Israel. Shanidar not only contained the remains of ten Neanderthals dating from 35,000 to 65,000 years ago, but also contained two later cemeteries. One of these contained 35 individuals dating to about 10,600 years ago.

The high point for Jarmo seems to have been between 8,200-7800 years ago. This small village consisted of approximately twenty five permanent mud-walled houses, which rested on stone foundations. The population was estimated to be 100-150 people. The adobe walls supported sun-dried mud roofs that probably served as walking areas.

A simple floor plan was dug from the earth. Inside, residents reclined on reed bedding. Even in the oldest level baskets have been found. They waterproofed with pitch which is readily available in the area. Early phases of Jarmo contain objects made from stone and obsidian from the Lake Van area of 200-300 miles away. The presence of obsidian, and ornamental shells from the Persian Gulf show us that organized commerce existed. The presence of stone sickles, cutters, stone bowls and receptacles of engraved marble, for harvesting, preparing, and storing food, attest to agricultural activities.

Villagers grew emmer and einkorn wheats, primitive barley and lentils. In addition to farming they still foraged for wild plants such as the field pea, carob seeds, acorns, pistachio nuts, and wild wheat. There is evidence that they domesticated goats, sheep and dogs. They may have collected snails, which were found at the site, to use for food, as a dye for cloth, or something else altogether.

In later layers bone tools were found in abundance. Awls, carefully made bone spoons, buttons and beads were found. On the higher levels of the site bones of domesticated pigs, and early examples of clay pottery were recovered. Jarmo is one of the oldest sites to contain pottery. This pottery was handmade from 9,000 years ago. It has a simple design and thick sides, and it was treated with a vegetable solvent.

There were clay figures of animals and people including figures of pregnant women, which are taken to be fertility goddesses, similar to later Stone Age cultures in the same region. Their ancestors may have acknowledged Lord Rama, but the religion had faded significantly.
– (Ralph S. Solecki, Rose L. Solecki, and Anagnostis P. Agelarakis (2004). *The Proto-Neolithic Cemetery in Shanidar Cave*. Texas A&M University Press. pp. 3–5. ISBN 9781585442720.); (http://en.wikipedia.org/wiki/Jarmo)

Tim Lambert gives a concise recap of **Catal Huyuk**, built in what is now central Turkey about 8,500 years ago, not long after farming began. The town had a population of about 6,000 residents. Houses were made of mud brick, and were built touching against each other. Walls did not have doors or windows, so entry was through roof hatches which also vented the smoke.

Perhaps the united buildings protected the settlement. This is why Catal Huyuk was not surrounded by external walls. Since houses were built touching each other, the roofs must have become streets. People were able to walk across them to other home entrances. This architecture is common throughout the arid lands of Eurasia all the way to the Tibetan Plateau. It is also seen in the log and adobe apartment-communities of Southwest United States.

Inside walls were plastered and often featured painted murals of people and animals. Beds were laid on platforms. The dead were buried in the floor, although they may have been exposed outside for vultures to clean the bones, first.

These sedentary people were generally farmers. They grew wheat and barley, and they raised flocks of sheep and herds of goats. They also kept dogs, who may have helped in hunts for animals like aurochs, and chased away predators like wolves, foxes and leopards.

The people of Catal Huyuk wore clothes woven from wool. They also wore jewelry made of stone, bone and shell. They wove baskets of reeds, made pottery and they used obsidian, for tools and weapons. Craftsmen made dishes of wood, and carved wooden boxes for storage.

They made figurine idols of clay and stone, which may have been gods and goddesses. They also mounted bull's skulls on the walls of some buildings and covered them in plaster to resemble living heads. It is believed these buildings were shrines, perhaps to Mithraic practices.

Catal-Huyuk was abandoned about 7,000 years ago. Nobody knows why, but it may have been due to climate change. It is probable that destruction of the lush forests, around these cities played a role in their demises. (http://www.localhistories.org/catalhuyuk.html)

Sumer was a collection of farming villages which became city-states in what is now southern Iraq along the lower Tigris and Euphrates rivers 7,500-6000 years ago. It had a thriving agriculture and trade industry. It developed a religion and society that influenced both its neighbors and conquerors, and even early Biblical history.

In matters of justice and mercy a person might lament, wail or tearfully confess sins and failings. They may plead with a family member, or specific god or goddess to intercede on their behalf.

Each city had its temple with a powerful patron deity selected from a pantheon. There was a priesthood which strongly influenced even their secular kings, many of whom claimed divine right. The clergy also acted as soothsayers interpreting omens and dreams.

Sumerians built temples and ziggurats. Their walls were finished in mosaics and frescos. Here they celebrated the monthly feasts and seasonal events like the New Year. Ziggurats enclosed a rectangular central shrine called a "cella" which contained a mud brick altar or offering table in front of the statue of the temple deity. The cella was lined with rooms along the side for priests, priestesses, musicians, singers and castrates or other attendants. Cellas were still fixtures in holy places at the time of Christ, and by a variety of other names, are seen even today.

Sumerian cuneiform is one of the earliest written languages. We have bits of many recorded business transactions and lessons from schools. Sheep, goats, pigs, grain and veggies along with pottery and processed goods, were traded for fruits, cedars from the Levant, and other raw materials which were ferried up and down river, and around the Persian Gulf.

REVELATION ADVANCES CIVILIZATION

"Shri Rama...Prophet of Peace is an Avatar of Mahavishnu (God). He is the Adi Purush – the Ancient One – who, out of compassion for humankind, descends to earth in human form, taking upon himself the trials and tribulations of human existence, willingly suffering ordeals to protect the virtuous and annihilate the wicked... whenever virtue decays and evil causes misery to the good and the virtuous, and the earth itself"
– Saint Tulsidas (treatise on Lord Rama) Saint Tulsidas 1532-1623
author of the Ramayana.

The Holy Spirit descends again and again, to check the progress of mankind's civilization, and to encourage new growth. Each Prophet marks the re-establishment of monotheism, praises the Single Creator, banishes evil and fosters virtuous behavior.

"Thus hath Muhammad, the Point of the Qur'án, revealed: "I am all the Prophets." Likewise, He saith: "I am the first Adam, Noah, Moses, and Jesus." (Baha'u'llah, The Kitab-i-Iqan, p. 152-153)

Prophets have been sent into this world to teach and enlighten mankind, to explain to them the mystery and the power of the Holy Spirit; and to enable them to reflect the light of God. And so in turn, they may become the sources of guidance to others. The Heavenly Books, the Avesta, the Bible, the Qur'án, and the other Holy Writings have been given as guides to the Path of divine virtue, love, justice and peace.

Revealers including Adam, Noah, Hud, Salih, Krishna, Abraham, Moses, Zoroaster, Buddha, Christ, Mohammad, the Bab and Baha'u'llah; as well as the countless dozens of prophets and Visionaries of tribal memory like Star Child, Wovoka and Black Elk seek to inform humanity about a single loving Creator above, alone and unknown, by Its creation.

All the Manifestations selflessly praise the one who came before them. They tell of the next to come, and all tell of a special One who will come at the end, the Promised One of all Ages and of all Faiths.

"Ye have heard how I said unto you, I go away, and come again unto you. If ye loved me, ye would rejoice," – Christ (*King James Bible, John 14:28*)

"Nevertheless I tell you the truth; It is expedient for you that I go away: for if I go not away, the Comforter will not come unto you; but if I depart, I will send Him unto you. And when He is come, He will reprove the world of sin, and of righteousness, and of judgment: 16:9 Of sin, because they believe not on Me; 16:10 Of righteousness,

because I go to my Father, and ye see Me no more; 16:11 Of judgment, because the Prince of this world is judged.

...I have yet many things to say unto you, but ye cannot bear them now. Howbeit when he, the Spirit of truth, is come, He will guide you into all truth: for He shall not speak of Himself; but whatsoever He shall hear, that shall He speak: and He will shew you things to come. He shall glorify me: for He shall receive of Mine, and shall shew it unto you." – (*King James Bible, John 16:7-16:14*)

Likewise: **"When the Buddha was about to pass away, Ananda and many other disciples wept. The Buddha said 'Enough Ananda. Do not allow yourself to be troubled. Do not weep. Have I not already told you that it is in the very nature of things that they must pass away? We must be separated from all that is near and dear to us.'**

The Buddha continued again: 'I am not the first Buddha to come upon earth: nor shall I be the last. In due time, another Buddha will arise in this world, a Holy one, a Supremely Enlightened One, endowed with wisdom, in conduct auspicious, knowing the universe, an incomparable leader of men, a master of devas and men (angels and mortals). He will reveal to you the same Eternal Truths which I have taught you. He will proclaim a religious life, wholly perfect and pure; such as I now proclaim..." – Maha-Parinibbana Sutta (*Last Days of the Buddha*)http://www.accesstoinsight.org/tipitaka/dn/dn.16.1-6.vaji.html

Guiding Factors

Back in the day, in archaeology seminars, we would debate whether culture advanced by means of "technological determinism" or "social determinism." In other words, we examined which was the cause of human advancement. Did tools shape our bodies, vision, and our future? Or was it the evolution of society that was the primary causal factor? I would tease then, and maintain now, that if one could just look with objectivity a few years ahead of each advance, one would find the Dawn of a new Day, in an unfolding chain of spiritual, social and scientific knowledge to humanity.

There is a conscious change in the world caused by each return of the divine Educator, and each Redemption more truly reflects the particular needs of a certain time.

"These sanctified Mirrors, these Day Springs of ancient glory, are, one and all, the Exponents on earth of Him Who is the central Orb of the universe... The beauty of their countenance is but a reflection of His image... They are the Treasuries of Divine knowledge, and the Repositories of celestial wisdom. Through them is transmitted a grace that is infinite, and by them is revealed the Light that can never fade...." (Baha'u'llah, Gleanings from the Writings of Baha'u'llah, p. 47-48)

If one takes the time to check out the dates for huge technological and social advancements, and the timing of a new Revelation, the relationship becomes apparent.

For a number of years, eager scientists like Tesla, Edison, Bell, Marconi and other inventors struggled with ideas and experiments which led to the successful long distance transmission of magnetic forces, electronic signals and wave modulations. These efforts were punctuated by an occurrence on May 24, 1844, with the message, "What hath God wrought?" that was sent by "Morse Code" from the old Supreme Court chamber in the United States Capitol, to Samuel Morse's partner, Alfred Vail in Baltimore. Annie Ellsworth, daughter of a friend, chose a verse from Numbers XXIII, 23: "What hath God wrought?"

which was recorded onto paper tape with raised dots and dashes, then translated later by a devise operator.

That very night the communicative power of humanity advanced through the use of Morse code, so that the whole world might hear messages in a shorter time than by word of mouth or writing, alone. On May 22, 1844 the Bab had announced He was the Promised one of a new age.

Scientists had successfully brought advanced communication into this world. How has communication advanced since 1844? What could be the underlying reason and cause for the timing of this?

Followers of God's newest Manifestation had a need for mass communication, to spread the news: of the massive change in technological and social history and —the imminent coming of the Promised One, the Glory of God, who would bring guidance for the unification of an entire planet!

"The inner ethereal reality grasps the mysteries of existence, discovers scientific truths and indicates their technical application. It discovers electricity, produces the telegraph, the telephone and opens the door to the world of arts. If the outer material body did this, the animal would likewise be able to make scientific and wonderful discoveries, for the animal shares with man all physical powers and limitations. What then is that power which penetrates the realities of existence and which is not to be found in the animal? It is the inner reality which comprehends things, throws light upon the mysteries of life and being, discovers the heavenly Kingdom, unseals the mysteries of God...Of this there can be no doubt." (Abdu'l-Baha, Foundations of World Unity, p. 109)

SIGNS THAT THE HOLY SPIRIT MADE MANIFEST, HAS RETURNED TO EARTH

Renewal of Monotheism: Eventually, in each cycle, humanity will stray from the worship of one God, to seek extra assistance from animals, human icons, statues, sainted beings, angels, ancestors, gods, etc. This is not necessarily bad, unless one forgets to acknowledge the Single Creator. Unfortunately, that happens quite a lot. If there is no guiding Force, virtues tend to decay, and people, thinking only of themselves, are more apt to hurt one another, and are less affected by the suffering of other beings, or the planet.

God transmits the Holy Spirit to us through a chosen one, who will deliver the Word of God, and thereby nourish and refresh humanity, for another age. It is clear that the return of the Holy Spirit bears no resemblance to "reincarnation" as humans choose to apply the concept. Human reincarnation is a corruption of the "return." It is better we look to a long ascent towards a parental Creator than putting hopes on becoming a bug or another person. What is the point? Such thoughts may block our forward movement on a path, which is already rife with perils. We aren't meant to be perfect, just to be humble servants.

Deadly Resistance and Courageous Collaboration: Unfortunately, one tradition that stays fairly constant is the deadly resistance against recognizing the Return of the Holy Spirit in a different human form and with a new name.

A newly revealed religion, however gentle or firm, meets with an outcry from the masses of people who refuse to believe there can be anything newer than what they were taught to believe by their parents. God's precious Educator is often, ridiculed, humiliated, beaten, exiled, betrayed, harmed or even killed.

Passionate "believers" who have lost the ability to see with their own eyes and hear with their own ears, manifest a desperate need to crush and annihilate the tiny new flame of Faith. A sad passion that recurs in every age. A play of innocence and fiery vengeance in front of a bloody sacrificial backdrop unfolds time and time again.

Luckily for humanity, in a paired action, new believers arise and become the Apostles of the new Prophet. His Revelation is almost always triumphant, eventually. This is the supreme example of the fight of evil against good. Sadly, there are a few accounts of complete devastation; which follow under the topic of "The Great Disappointments."

Additional Spiritual Knowledge is revealed from the "MOTHER BOOK": During the state of "Revelation" these divine Beings become transfigured and wreathed in glowing bright light, referred to as a halo by some, a farr by others. The impact affects onlookers to the point they are awe-stricken. The bright glow might prevent them from seeing physical details of the Holy Spirit incarnate.

Spiritual information comes from a source referred to as the "Mother Book." I with my limited mind picture it scrolling, like the prelude to a Star Wars movie, but that is ridiculous by comparison. During the process of revelation the Speaker's voice may become quite loud.

"I have yet many things to say unto you, but ye cannot bear them now."
– Christ

There is never a contradiction between the Messages revealed by the Manifestations of Light. Any differences are due to misunderstanding or misinterpretation, or people editing information to coincide with what they wish to hear.

What does change is the addition of new information each time a Messenger comes. We may seek out the newer Revelations, even if we are quite comfortable with our chosen Faith, to become aware of the additional chapters of spiritual guidance; similar to the way people accept the various layers which appear in the Bible from pre-Sumerian times, to 1700 years ago.

Physical, Scientific and Technological Bursts: Technological bursts certainly contribute to the advancement and evolution of human civilization, but they do not generate it. Major achievements that come to mind include the use of sticks, lithic tools, fire, domestication of animals, agriculture, aqueducts, wheels, metallurgy, architecture, medicine, astronomy, magic, alchemy and writing. Most of these processes were accretions of knowledge dosed out through the ages. Some inventions such as writing (Enoch/Hermes/Idris/Thoth) and medicine (Ram/Rama/Asclepius) are easily attributed to more specific sources.

We are astounded by great leaps and bounds in the fields of transportation, and communications. These have been developed to unite the peoples of the whole world. People can communicate with nearly all the points of the earth in a split second. Some of the bounties this will bring to the planet are that tragedies and injustices can be spotted quickly and corrected, and that education can reach everyone. A common language and monetary base will arise so we can travel more easily and *appreciate* the differences in the peoples and places of the world. This will help foster a stronger unity. Now with so many travel and adventure shows on television and the internet, we really can just watch and learn.

Burgeoning of the Sciences, Arts, and Crafts: We can look at the tremendous flourish of sciences, and revitalization of arts, skills and crafts over the last 172 years. This is nothing short of an explosion of information and growth, the like of which has not been seen before. Look at the invention of plastic, and how it has eased the everyday chores of life. Plastic bags and jugs, for example, have made carrying just about anything easier. We must ask ourselves, "How does this influence human civilization? What might the Creator want us to learn from all of this?" It is like we have to get our act together as a planet; for the next step, whatever that may be. It might be appropriate to reflect on some reasons we need a united planet.

Laws and Social Codes: Coincident, with a new Revelation of advanced spiritual knowledge, we are given pertinent guidance in the form of social codes of conduct or "laws"; like avoiding non-prescribed drugs and alcohol, or avoiding casual sex. The new laws may replace, outdated laws, as when Christ chose to heal on the Sabbath, or the lifting of the ban on eating of pork, now that diseases of the past can be controlled with care and refrigeration.

The making and abrogation of such laws help us walk the challenging "Path" of in this world, and prosper as spiritual beings. And it is the sole right of the Manifestation of God for each specific age. Many beneficial laws remain unchanged for millennia. It is this very point which gives most of the religions we know today, the title of the "Path" or the "Way."

Laws are meant to guide rather than punish or debase people. A trip through this world can be tricky and treacherous. In fact, it is meant to be. Guidelines are a gift to keep us moving forward, in a good way. Unfortunately, self-righteous or fearful humans think it is their duty to shun or debase others, citing God's guiding laws as accusations.

"... social laws and regulations (are) applicable to human conduct. This is not the essential spiritual quality of religion. It is subject to change and transformation according to the exigencies and requirements of time and place. For instance, in the time of Noah certain requirements made it necessary that all sea foods be allowable or lawful. During the time of the Abrahamic prophethood it was considered allowable because of a certain exigency, that a man should marry his aunt, even as Sarah was the sister of Abraham's mother. During the cycle of Adam it was lawful and expedient for a man to marry his own sister, even as Abel, Cain and Seth the sons of Adam married their sisters. But in the law of the Pentateuch revealed by Moses these marriages were forbidden and their custom and sanction abrogated." (Abdu'l-Baha, Baha'i World Faith – Abdu'l-Baha Section, p. 274-275)

By comparison, the code of Ur-Nammu is the oldest surviving written civil law code. It is from Mesopotamia and is written on tablets, in the Sumerian language, c. 2100–2050 BC. These civil laws were harsh and cruel, and they were meant to favor the wealthy.

Advancing Degrees of Unity: Each time a sanctified Being returns, an additional degree of unity is achieved. At one time it may be the union of body, mind and soul (yoga). Another time, the social unity of the family evolving from just a female and child (Nu Wa) to a state of marriage (Fu-Hi), thus encouraging the active participation and protection of a male. Later on, the progressions of unity included the extended family, clan, tribe, city-state, nation, and now the world. It might be wise to begin thinking about what the next degree of unity could be.

New Calendar System: Among other things associated with the coming of a Manifestation there would likely be a changing of holy days, and even a new calendar. The calendar may change from lunar base to a solar base. The most recent example is the Badi calendar brought to us by the Primal Point known as the Bab (Gate). It is a solar calendar with 19 months, each with 19 days; each of those represents a name of God, like: Splendor, Beauty, Dominion, and Loftiness. The Islamic, Chinese, Hindu, Zoroastrian, Hebrew and Gregorian, are examples of other calendars still in use today.

Sacrifice, Purification and Inspiration: We benefit when we sacrifice a material choice for a spiritual one. The opportunity for this arises every single moment. This offers us a variety of sacred choices, sort of like the cartoon angel and devil characters on "Goofy's" shoulders. We can choose for example; to spend a little less time and money on ourselves and to give to our Faith, help the poor, or befriend the fallen. We may not always make a good choice, but guess what? Before long we get a chance to make a better choice.

Sacrifices and purifications; can lead us to inspiration. Fasting, meditation, prayer and reading sacred texts, coupled with items which remind us to focus on spiritual matters like: incense smoke, prayer wheels, sound prayers and mantras calm us. They replenish and protect our souls. Ancient wonders like astral bodies, fire, dance, song, waterfalls, trees and lofty places still inspire awe. We can feel and recognize that which is sacred, and it reminds us that we too, are sacred beings.

New Sound Prayer: There are many "sound prayers," a term I picked up from a friend, Steve Allen. The gift of God's name has been given since the first cry of the first human baby "alla." More recently it has accompanied us through the years in words like Elohim, Hallelujah, Aum or Om, Ojala!, Allah'u'akbar, Hello, and Allah'u'abha.

PERSPECTIVE

Hello! When I hear the word Allah spoken by my Persian friends, it sounds very much like the word "hello" or "allo," with a soft "H," and that is no coincidence. The Primary Canaanite God was El, and carries into the Bible as El or Elohim, in newer Faiths, it is Allah.

Likewise many familiar names such as: Michelle (Who is like God), Elijah (the Lord is my God), Gabriel (strong man of God), Samuel (his name is God), Jorel (God will uplift), Isabelle (consecrated to God), Daniel/Danielle (God is my judge), Bethel (house of God), and Michael (like God) bear this mark.

It seems that "ell" and "all" are almost interchangeable since written vowels aren't important in many languages, or are generalized like the schwa, which is an unstressed or neutral vowel in our language.

So the term "Allah" will crop up often as a term for God, in the following accounts. Don't be afraid—Allah really is God.

The Arks: Much is written about how Moses freed his beloved wanderers, and taught and protected them. What about the powerful Ark of His Covenant?

All revelations include a Covenant, often associated with an Ark/Arc of one kind or other; between God and His people. Moses borrowed the idea of a golden Ark from the Egyptians. However the figures on top were not sparrow hawks as before. The Ark of Israel is topped by four sphinxlike cherubim, who have heads of a bull, a lion, an eagle, a man, after Ezekiel's vision; and they represent four universal elements: earth, water, air and fire. With their wings, they cover the mercy seat or throne of God. It is said to contain the Sepher Bereshith, or Book of Cosmogony, written by Moses in Egyptian hieroglyphics, and the magic wand or "rod" of Moses, and the Book of the Covenant, known as the Law of Sinai.

The Ark of Noah was a last plea for people to save themselves, and the arc of the rainbow, was a sign of forgiveness and hope.

The Arc on Mount Carmel, houses several key structures above the Shrine of the Bab, encased in 19 elegant terraced gardens. The administrative buildings of the Bahá'í World Center form the sides of the arc. From left to right include: The International Teaching Centre Building, the Seat of the Universal House of Justice, the Centre for the Study of the Texts, and the International Archives Building. They are not only central to the Bahá'í Faith, thousands of all faiths walk the gardens, and visit these buildings.

Perhaps one could push the ark theme to the extreme and talk about the arc of the Levantine Corridor known as the "Fertile Crescent." That passage was the cause of great advancements in knowledge, new technologies, changes in society, and even changes in physical human forms.

Watch for some of these signs as we bring on our earliest known candidates, referred to as the "First."

By Pierre5018 (Own work) [CC BY-SA 4.0 (http://creativecommons.org/licenses/by-sa/4.0)], via Wikimedia Commons

A WORLD OF FIRSTS:
Antediluvian Accounts

In the earliest pre-flood accounts there are tatters of sacred memory that appear to precede Adam as He is presented in Genesis. The story of Adam is not unique. There are other stories about Creation and the "First Man," which are truly amazing. All have similarities. Differences arise from the passing of vast ages, and rumors which spread across vast spaces.

The beginning of the last Age was a long, long time ago. And that "First Being" or quite probably multiplicity of Beings is referred to by people from all over this planet. There are threads which connect all of the names we will explore, to the title "First"; but it is quite obvious that most of the stories contain combinations of three or more unique Manifestations. The tales are somewhat woven together, and one remembered name is applied to the actions of several. Since all bear the Word of God by means of the Holy Spirit, the teachings really are a continuum.

These several Prophets combined, appeared to live many thousands, or even millions of years. Obviously there are several separate times and events involved, but the individual accounts get blenderized into a Saga.

One example is the story of Yima, whose tale spans well over 3,600 years. A succession of At least three Great Prophets were combined so Yima appeared to live for thousands of years.

Or consider Adam, said to be the first man, so of course He preceded the domestication of plants and animals. Yet He is credited with siring offspring millions of years later, in agricultural times. Adam might have been the reference given to the first Man of a new Age. Perhaps there is an "Adam" at the outset of every Age of man.

The name Adam, as given in the Bible likely refers to His entire lineage instead of a single man in a single time or place. When we read that Adam begot Seth it could actually mean that Seth came from the line of Adam. So confusion concerning timing and lineage surrounds Seth, Enoch, and the other "begats." Yet the sequence of names was an effective verbal, then written historical aid, which allowed men to recall the Prophets of old.

A very similar case involves Gayomart (Q-mers in Persian) in the pre-Zoroastrian, Avestan Bundahishn. The tale includes a son Siamak, and a "grandson," Hooshang. They may not be a child and grandchild, but actually successive Prophets, especially in the case of Hooshang.

Blending also crops up in Egyptian and Greek philosophical texts. Some of the original names and individual divine purposes have faded, or been destroyed by crises like the flood. They have blended over time, devolved with forgetfulness, or worse, have been re-explained in terms that made sense to the tellers. Some elements were dumbed down to the point or they bore little, if any relation to the Revealer or the Message. Nobody remembers which one of three said what, and is it really important? They become like a Janus figure, with multiple faces. In the end it is only what is given to the world of humanity that is relevant.

As was suggested at the beginning we have never been without guidance, nor can we know the exact names and times of all of God's previous Messengers. So – now we can relax.

Speaking of names, there is another problem (well, at least one more). People of different regions refer to the same Prophet by different names. So a prophet like Enoch may have several names, identities, and attributes, depending on how far away the story is from its source.

Although the Hebrews refer to Enoch," Baha'u'llah and Mohammad refer to the same Prophet as "Idris." The Greeks called Him "Hermes," and He is also "Thoth" the Egyptian Scribe.

You catch the drift. These distractions can make identities muddy at first, but remember why they came, it's not just their names and what people chose to remember about them that matters. This way we might not get so bogged down in the differences. Taken together, remembrances of these primal Heavenly Kings gives us an accumulated history of our beginnings, which have built up in layers of traditional lore like Shrek's onion.

Today, these prophets have been demoted, dumbed down, and nearly forgotten. Some are labeled, and re-labeled as gods, goddesses, titans, demi-gods, and heroes. But if one takes the time to peel the onion, a special unicity becomes apparent. There are similarities between various recollections of events or people, yet there are some very surprising dichotomies which I am sure you will appreciate in the following renditions. Most of them explain the overall period of time before the flood.

Now let's enjoy exploring the picture of the "First" Manifestation of the last Age, as pieced together from many peoples, languages, and backgrounds. In order of presentation:

1. Nu Wa
2. Fu-Xi, Shennong, Huangdi
3. Gayomart, Siamak, Hooshang
4. Adam, Seth, Enoch
5. Ram or Rama, Asclepius/ Aesculapius and Abaris
6. Yima/Jamshid
7. Adapa or Uan and
8. Melchizedek

"Creation" Stories share four concepts: 1) Creation of heavens and earth 2) proto-human or pre-physical existence 3) man becomes embodied on the earth as some sort of human, to begin the fight of good versus evil, light and darkness and 4) the rise of agriculture helping to stave off famines, and increase health and prosperity.

Human groups that *did not* remember previous times because the area was wiped clean, generally start with "At first there was water."

Please keep in mind that these revealers of God's word came to a variety of human branches – not just Homo sapiens.

NU WA

"Three things come into existence at the same time God light and freedom."
– attributed to Sri Krishna

Here is a unique bit of human prehistory which begins with a social order not much different than some of the great apes or even non-primate mammals. The Remote One called Nu WA would most likely have nurtured mankind from primal human memory, perhaps even back to Ardipithecus or the Australopithecines 4 – 6 million years ago in Africa.

In the beginning there was as yet no moral or social order. This was the time of a pre-nuclear family. Children only knew their mothers as immediate parents, not specific fathers. Childbirth was not usually associated with the attentions of one male and children were raised by the mother and other available individuals.

When hungry, Nu WA's people searched for food. When they were sated, they threw away the remnants without regard for the next meal. Like many animals they devoured their food, hide, hair, blood, and whatever they had in their possession.

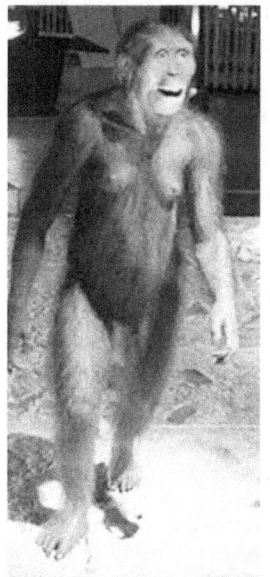

Australopithecus afaresis female image via Wikimedia Commons

If needed, they made nests, beds, or simple shelters, and occasionally used leaves, bark, mud or rushes to cover parts of their bodies. (Fu Xi http://history.cultural-china.com/en/46H5031H11121.html)

This is the most ancient specific religious reference to the early human condition I have yet seen. In some ways it is more primitive even than the much sought after Bigfoot, who probably eat in a similar manner and don't need much "clothing." Yet one Siberian sighting described an individual wearing animal hide draped, like a shawl over the shoulders. They are said to live in structured family groups including fathers.

According to some texts, Nu Wa was also Fu Xi's wife and/or sister. Some think these two were the only survivors of a great flood. Yet that makes little sense given Nu Wa's primitive event line. Fu-Xi's time was far more sophisticated. Still, some Taoist depictions show the lower bodies of Nu Wa and Fu Xi, which resemble serpents, intertwined like a double helix, or caduceus.

FU-XI OR FO-HI (THE GREAT BRIGHT ONE)

By Farm (Own work) [GFDL (http://www.gnu.org/copyleft/fdl.html), CC-BY-SA-3.0 (http://creativecommons.org/licenses/by-sa/3.0/) or CC BY-SA 2.5-2.0-1.0 (http://creativecommons.org/licenses/by-sa/2.5-2.0-1.0)], via Wikimedia Commons

"Then came Fu Xi and He looked upward and contemplated the images in the heavens, and looked downward and contemplated the occurrences on earth. He united man and wife, regulated the five stages of change, and laid down the laws of humanity." – Ban Gu, Baihu tongy (http://en.wikipedia.org/wiki/Fu_Xi)

A sizeable number of Fu-Xi's contributions cluster in the an area of 5000 years ago. This time period, and personal information about this Being resemble information we have for another Prophet, Krishna. Krishna's tale as you will see later does suggest contact with Chinese people.

Fu-Xi is known as the first Supreme Ruler and God-Emperor of China. He was born around 4952 to 5,468 years ago. What is known about His birth shares details with the virgin birth of Devaki, Lord Krishna's, mother. Fu Xi's mother was made pregnant by a rainbow and a white elephant. It would seem that three nymphs came to do some washing in a river and suddenly a garment bore an image of a lotus in full fruit. The child born of this virgin was a boy, radiant as a rainbow. http://www.godchecker.com/pantheon/chinese-mythology.php?deity=FO-HI

In the tale of Krishna, also called the Radiant One, it is said the land in which He lived, the Himavat, was visited by yellow-skinned people. Even the archers who shot Krishna were of yellow and black skins. So it is highly conceivable that East Asian disciples graced their homelands with tales of Krishna as the mighty Fu-XI.

Fu-Xi also shared with us events from His times, and those of His predecessors. So an extraordinary stream of events came to be associated with the name and line of Fu-Xi; similar to the successions in the Bible and the Persian story of Creation.

Fu-Xi's Event Line

He taught the people to:
1. Cook with fire – Homo erectus 1.8 million to 300,000 years ago.
2. Offer the first sacrifices to heaven – earliest date unknown.

3. Use medicinal plants – nearly 80,000 years ago. Known to be used by Rama, Abaris and Asclepius. But even animals seek out herbal remedies.
4. Fish with nets – evidence of fishing goes back to Paleolithic times 40,000 years ago, but nets made of willow wands date to 10,300 years ago and sinkers have been found at several sites 10,000 to 5,000 years ago. History of fishing http://en.wikipedia.org/wiki/History_of_fishing
5. Tame wild animals – 30,000 to 6,000 years ago.
6. Marry – Fu Xi is said to have instituted the one hundred Chinese family names and decreed that marriages may only take place between persons bearing different family names. As the reproductive process became better understood parents became bonded. The degree of unity advanced and some ancient societies, like Fu Xi's, moved toward a patriarchal system, which predates recorded history.
7. Use fasting for physical and spiritual cleansing – earliest date unknown
8. Cast oracles by the use of yarrow stalks – earliest date unknown, though divination is associated with Enoch.
9. Farm silk worms – 5500 years ago
10. Use of the eight trigrams of the I Ching or Pakua, which are said to be the basis for Chinese writing. – Possibly around 5000 years ago.
    "He devised the eight Trigrams of the I Ching" The origin of the trigrams is attributed to his reading of the He Map (or the Yellow River Map). According to this tradition Fu Xi had the arrangement of the trigrams revealed to him supernaturally, perhaps on the shell of a turtle's back, in order to gain mastery over the worlds. – Ban Gu, Baihu tongy http://en.wikipedia.org/wiki/Fu_Xi
11. Play a stringed musical instrument that looks like a short clarinet with 7 strings – Known currently as the guqin zither, originating about 5000 years ago.
    The arched harps also date to 5000 years ago, as noted in Egyptian funerary art and relics. Players are depicted as kneeling and using both hands to pluck the strings. The arched harp was universal in all early cultures across Asia, Africa and Europe. It is still used to accompany the performance of oral history and myth in Africa. It consists of a broad wooden or hide-covered sound box, joined to a curved branch. The number of gut strings varied anywhere between three and ten. *String family history* (http://www.classicol.com/classical.cfm?music=instrumentInfo&section=StringHistory&title=String%20Family%20History)
    It is Likely the earliest stringed instruments were developed from plucking the string of a bow.

12. Hunt with weapons made of iron – 3200 years ago, after the Stone Age and Bronze Age. People lived in thatched huts, or castles, some made pottery and iron jewelry as well as a wicked assortment of weaponry.

Obviously Fu-Xi is the name remembered for most of Chinese prehistory. There are many parts to His story, beginning as far back as humanity itself, or even before. Clearly the story of Fu-Xi is an intricate accumulation of divine Manifestations, and Their revelatory gifts. These Beings endowed humanity with social laws, art and inventions to move civilization forward over the millennia.

SHENNONG

According to 'Baihu tongy' by Ban Gu of the Han Dynasty, in ancient times, people only ate animal meat. By Shennong's time, there were too many people and animals were insufficient. "Thus Shennong taught people to do farming. People benefited a great deal from it. So they called him Shennong, which means the god of farming"

Fu-Xi is succeeded in mission by Shennong the next of the noble emperors. He is said to be an ancient forbearer of the Chinese. He gave humans a mass of medicinal lore, and farming advice.

Agriculture allowed humans to have some control over periodic horrifying famines. Shennong (like Yima) taught humans the use of the plow, an ard used prior to 3000 years ago. Oxen hooked to a simple shaft dragged an angled stick through the soil to loosen it. The farmer grasped another stick, projecting from the top of the shaft for guidance control. Shennong graciously shared other aspects of basic Mesopotamian types of agriculture, as well. He is associated with the growing of barley, beans, hemp, millet, oats, peas, rice, sesame and soy beans. Shennong's descendant, Huangdi is also acknowledged for farming lore. http://chineseculture.about.com/library/weekly/aa_shennong02a.htm

"Shennong3" by Li Ung Bing – Li Ung Bing, Outline of Chinese History, Shanghai 1914. Licensed under Public Domain via Wikimedia Commons – https://commons.wikimedia.org/wiki/File:Shennong3.jpg#/media/File:Shennong3.jpg

"Shennong2" by mural painting from Han dynasty – Li Ung Bing, Outlines of Chinese History, Shanghai 1914. Licensed under Public Domain via Wikimedia Commons – https://commons.wikimedia.org/wiki/File:Shennong2.jpg#/media/File:Shennong2.jpg

HUANGDI (YENTI) THE YELLOW EMPEROR

Huangdi was known as the originator of the degree of unity known as the centralized state and He is regarded as the initiator of modern Chinese civilization. His homeland is thought to be the Sheep's Head Mountains just north of Goaoping in Shangxi Province. He was a Cosmic Ruler, and a Lord of the underworld. He is known for numerous inventions and innovations and was a patron of esoteric arts.

His teachings are said to be the basis for Five Phases or the Five Elements (wood, fire, earth, metal and water), the Five Virtues, and also Five Cardinal Points (North-black, East-green, South-red, West-white and Center-yellow) which are used for describing interactions and relationships between phenomena. They are employed in many fields of early Chinese thought, including geomancy or Feng Shui, astrology, traditional Chinese medicine, music, military strategy and Shao Lin martial arts. (Wu Xing (the Five Phases) http://en.wikipedia.org/wiki/Five_Phases

According to an inscription on a bronze vessel accounts of Huangdi also known as the Yellow Emperor after the yellow Phase which represents the earth, dragons, center, up and down; started to appear in Chinese texts of the Warring States period prior to 2475 years ago.

Huangdi is reluctantly associated with an epic war, like Krishna. According to traditional accounts the Yan Emperor fought the evil force of the Nine Li tribes under their leader Chi You, who is described as bull-headed, sharp-horned, bronze-foreheaded, four-eyed, iron-skulled man, with six arms and a human body! He was unbelievably fierce. A cruel and greedy tyrant, a corruptive force who was Shennong's descendant, and a cousin of the Emperor.

The good Yan emperor was decisively defeated by Chi You. He fled to Zhuolu and begged the Yellow Emperor, Huangdi, for help. During the ensuing Battle of Zhoulu, the Yellow Emperor employed his tamed animals, but the evil Chi You darkened the sky by breathing out a thick fog which confounded the enemy.

Huangdi then invented the South Pointing Chariot, a compass of sorts. It was actually a small two-wheeled vehicle that carried a movable figure with outstretched arm as a pointer to indicate the direction of "south." No matter how dark the skies, the chariot turned to lead His army out of the fog. ("Yan Emperor" http://en.wikipedia.org/wiki/Yandi)

In traditional Chinese accounts the Yellow Emperor invented carts, boats, and elaborate clothing. Other inventions credited to Him include the Chinese diadem, throne rooms, early astronomy, math calculations, and "cuju," an early Chinese version of football. And – as is

His right as of a Manifestation of God, He invented the Chinese calendar and a sound code of laws.

Huangdi is regarded as father of Chinese characters, said by some to be the oldest continuously used system of writing in the world; and the oracle bone script found on animal bones or turtle shells used in divination during Bronze Age China. His principal wife, Leizu taught people how to weave silk and dye clothes. This has also been attributed to Fu-Xi above.

The Yellow Emperor was said to have lived for over a hundred years before meeting a "phoenix," a symbol of high virtue and grace, and a "qilin," a mythical hooved lion-headed, horned horse creature sometimes depicted as a giraffe. They are said to appear with the imminent arrival or passing of a wise Sage or an illustrious ruler. Then – Huangdi died. ("The Yellow Emperor" http://en.wikipedia.org/wiki/Yellow_Emperor)

Shennong and Huangdi were considered to be friends and fellow scholars, despite the 500 years and seventeen or eighteen generations between them.

It is said that the Manifestations know each other intimately and sympathize with the sufferings, the others must bear as a result of their own exalted stations.

Shennong and Huangdi who is known as "the Yellow Emperor" are said to be Fu-Xi's spiritual descendants. Together the three are called **The San Huang Trio**.

The San Huang Trio shared with humanity alchemical secrets like the making of gold, the improved practice of medicine, and of course the search for immortality. Each is credited with improving the livelihood of the nomadic hunters of His tribe, teaching them how to build shelters, and tame wild animals. The Han Chinese regarded both Shennong and Huangdi as their ancestors.

These three legendary Emperors Yao (Fu-Xi), Shun (Shennong), and Yu (Huangdi), all ruled by virtue. **Their sagacity, xiao (filial piety), and dedication to work enabled them to create a remarkable political culture based on responsibility and trust**.

("Fu Xi" http://www.pantheon.org/articles/f/fu_xi.html); Fu Xi Article "Fu Xi" created on 03 March 1997; last modified on 16 January 2004 (Revision 2).

The San Huang Trio along with Nu Wa paint for us a tremendously long history and bring a richness and noble beauty to the development of Asian Religion. This, along with the teachings of the Tao of Lao Tzu, and organizational wisdom of Confucius, weaves a tapestry of human development guided by these Beings that is one of the most intriguing in the house of civilization.

Interestingly, during the late 1500's and early 1600's Jesuit missionaries, most notably Matteo Ricci, tried to find common ground between Christianity and traditional Chinese spirituality. These Jesuit Figurists viewed Fu-Xi as Enoch the biblical descendant of Adam. In part, such as the source of writing and divination, they were quite probably correct.

They considered Confucianism's moral teachings as compatible with Christian beliefs. Viewing Confucian rites such as the veneration of the dead, who truly continue to live and influence the fortunes of earthly inhabitants as essential moral basics rather than conflicting religious doctrine.

When addressing the European public the China-based Jesuit missionaries strove to present Confucianism as represented by its Four Books 1) The Great Learning and 2) the Doctrine of the Mean (which were originally chapters in the Classic of Rites); as well as 3) the Analects and 4) the Mencius; and the Five Classical Chinese texts of Confucius in a favorable light. (Matteo Ricci) S.J. http://faculty.fairfield.edu/jmac/sj/scientists/ricci.htm

Though Confucius was not himself a manifestation of God's word, he summed up the laws and practices of Chinese Faith. The Five Classics can be described in terms of five visions: metaphysical, political, poetic, social, and historical; as told by Tu Weiming.

The Yijing (I-Ching) "Classic of Changes" – is a metaphysical vision which combines divination, numerology and ethical insight. The cosmos changes from the constant interaction of yin and yang. Two complementary as well as conflicting forces, dark and light energies. The world as a result of this ongoing chaos, exhibits both organic unity and dynamism. The exemplary person, inspired by the harmony and creativity of the cosmos, must aim to **"realize the highest ideal of 'unity of man and heaven' (tianrenheyi) through ceaseless self-exertion."**

Shujing – a political vision of a kingship ruled from an ethical foundation, and a humane government. The legendary Three Emperors Yao (Fu-Xi), Shun (Shennong), and Yu (Huangdi) all ruled by virtue. Their wisdom, xiao is sometimes referred to as filial piety. " ...*dedication to work enabled them to create a political culture based on responsibility and trust. Their exemplary lives taught and encouraged the people to enter into a covenant with them, so that social harmony could be achieved without punishment or coercion. Even in the Three Dynasties (Xia, Shang, and Zhou) moral authority, as expressed through ritual, was sufficient to maintain political order. The human continuum, from the undifferentiated masses to the enlightened people, the nobility, and the sage-king, formed an organic unity as an integral part of the great cosmic transformation. Politics means moral persuasion, and the purpose of the government is not only to provide food and maintain order, but also to educate.*" (Weiming)

Tomb of Huangdi. [GFDL (http://www.gnu.org/copyleft/fdl.html) or CC BY-SA 4.0-3.0-2.5-2.0-1.0 (http://creativecommons.org/licenses/by-sa/4.0-3.0-2.5-2.0-1.0)], via Wikimedia Commons

The Shijing "Classic of Poetry" – "*The poetic vision... underscores the Confucian valuation of common human feelings. The majority of verses give voice to emotions and sentiments of communities and persons from all levels of society expressed on a variety of occasions. The basic theme of this poetic world is mutual responsiveness. The tone as a whole is honest rather than earnest, and evocative rather than expressive.*" (Weiming)

The Liji "Record of Rites" – a social vision, depicts society, not as an adversarial system based on contractual relationships, but as a community of trust with emphasis on communication. The structure of society is the four functional occupations (Seen also in Yima/Rama's time)—scholar, farmer, artisan, and merchant. ..."*(in) the true sense of the word, a cooperation. As a contributing member of the cooperation each person is obligated to recognize the existence of others and to serve the public good. It is the king's duty to act kingly, and the father's duty to act fatherly. If the king or father fails to behave properly, he cannot expect his minister or son to act in accordance with ritual... (A) Chapter entitled the 'Great Learning' specifies, "From the son of heaven to the commoner, all must regard self-cultivation as the root. This pervasive consciousness of duty features prominently in all Confucian literature on ritual.*"

Such a high aspiration for Civilization!

The Chunqiu –*"the 'Classic of History' is a historical vision, also called the "Spring and Autumn Annals" – this refers to pre-Confucian texts, which emphasize the significance of collective memory for communal self-identification. Historical consciousness is a defining characteristic of Confucian thought, though he was not the author. Yet he applied moral judgment to political events in China proper from the 8th to the 5th century B.C., By defining himself as a lover of antiquity and a transmitter of its values, Confucius made it explicit that a sense of history is not only desirable but is necessary for self-knowledge."* (Weiming) Reanimating the old is the best way to attain the new. http://www.britannica.com/EBchecked/topic/132104/Confucianism/25461/The-Five-Classics

According to Mirza Tahir Ahmad, the fourth Caliph of the Ahmadiyya Muslim Community, all Chinese religions are derived from the teachings of Fu-Xi. This is undoubtedly true, since all revealed religion is the single path toward one Creator, and all the Manifestations are related, in fact, they are unified by the Holy Spirit.

So religion as a whole, shares a larger vision. Ancient wisdoms return time and again. For example: "Hear no evil, speak no evil and see no evil," clearly we could add "think no evil" and of course "do no evil." This is a pre-flood teaching, which goes back to a very early layer of Fu-Xi, or even back toward the Nu Wa times. Either way it is reminiscent of the Golden Rule, which is repeated again in every revealed religion throughout history.

"O COMPANION OF MY THRONE! Hear no evil, and see no evil, abase not thyself, neither sigh nor weep. Speak no evil, that thou mayest not hear it spoken unto thee, and magnify not the faults of others that thine own faults may not appear great; and wish not the abasement of anyone, that thine own abasement be not exposed. Live then the days of thy life, that are less than a fleeting moment, with thy mind stainless, thy heart unsullied, thy thoughts pure, and thy nature sanctified, so that, free and content, thou mayest put away this mortal frame, and repair unto the mystic paradise and abide in the eternal kingdom for evermore." (Baha'u'llah, The Persian Hidden Words, number 44)

GAYOMART OR Q-MERS/ KEYUMERS

"Pay heed to what is said, not to the speaker. Look up to advice and wise words, no matter who says it. Acknowledge the truth, no matter of what provenance" – Gayomart/Q-mers

Gayomart, *The Protoplast of Man,* http://www.cais-soas.com/CAIS/Mythology/gayomart.htm (as in the translation of Tabari, Bal´amî, ed. Bahâr, p. 123).

This piece on Gayomart or Keyumars (pronounced Q-mers) is inspired by information gleaned from Ferdowski's epic poem the Shahnameh; the Avestan Yasnas, and the Bundahishn, a collection of pre-Zoroastrian beliefs regarding "Primordial Creation."

Gayomart's followers were cave dwellers, who like their Prophet wore the hides of animals. He wore the skins of leopards. Timewise, this could have been anything from Homo erectus times to Neanderthal, or even later Stone Age. He is referred to as the Gar-Shah (King of the Mountains) and He lived in caves possibly in the Carpathian or Alburz Mountains; others say around Ararat in the Lake Van area. The truth is, He could have been in Africa or the Levant.

He was the first Great King to arise among humans and ruled over men and beasts by His gentle and potent nature and His unparalleled wisdom. The Avesta calls Gayomart the Pure and Righteous.

God, known by the name "Ahura Mazda" or simplified to "Ormuzd," granted Gayomart the supernatural Farr. This is a radiant, shimmering Halo. An aura, shining white and brilliant like the sun. It is reserved for spiritual Kings and Luminous Beings.

Gayomart became the first Shah or King of the world. He was peaceful and pious and rendered the primitive world prosperous and habitable. He was the first human Ahura Mazda (God) created. He was also the first man who practiced Justice. He is called the Lawgiver.

In fact, Gayomart/Q-mers is celebrated as the first Righteous man who embraced the Will and Commandment of Ahura Mazda (God); and from whom developed the family of Aryan lands; and all ancient Teachers of Faith.

Muhammad ibn Jarir al –Tabari, a pure hearted 10th century Persian scholar, ascribed to Him a Collection of Apothegms: or "wise sayings." This verbal tradition allows people to easily remember bits of wisdom, since there was no form of writing. **"Know thyself"** is one such gift from Gayomart.

Tabari wrote the History of the Prophets and Kings around 915 AD, 1, 099 years ago. **"This is a** universal history from the time of Qur'anic Creation and is renowned for its detail and accuracy concerning Muslim and Middle Eastern history. Tabari's work is one of the major primary sources for historians, even today." http://en.wikipedia.org/wiki/Muhammad_ibn_Jarir_al-Tabari

As with most of the early Prophets there is a Creation piece. The Creation as told by Gayomart and other Prophets, precedes the coming of mankind to earth. This account is rare and not easily found by most of us. Here is a blending of two ancient versions; one Persian one Indian.

Even if elements of this story make no sense by modern standards, remember, this is a collection of extremely ancient human memories, and perceptions about the First King from the Yasnas and elsewhere. We are very lucky to have it.

Primordial Creation

First the sky was created from rock crystal in the shape of a hollow sphere so that it was both above and below where the earth would be. First water was created and then earth. The first tree grew, the Saena-mother of all trees. Its crown provided a place for the first nest for the first bird, a falcon. When he beat his wings the dropping tree leaves became the first plants.

The Saena or Gaokerene is an "ox-horn" physically, but the "Tree of Life" spiritually. It had healing properties when eaten, and gave immortality to bodies resurrected from the dead. This is likely a reference to a spiritual resurrection.

The Tree of Life is often a reference to the Manifestation, whose knowledge humans cannot surpass. In a Tablet Bahá'u'lláh states,

"The Holy Tree (Sadrat) is, in a sense, the Manifestation of the One True God, exalted be He." (Baha'u'llah, Tablets of Baha'u'llah, p. 137)

After some plants were created, then animals began to appear, then south of the Caspian Sea the first Alburz mountain, also known as Mount Hara or Harbatz, grew. The first animal that came into existence was a white bull a primeval ox or Aurochs as bright as the moon. It lived on the banks of the Vah (River) Daiti in Airyanem Vaejah also known as Ērān Wēj or Eran Vaeja, the ancient homeland of the Aryans, well before they had lighter colored skin.

Airyanem Vaejah is thought to be the Polar or Siberian homeland prior the advance of ice. Maximum glaciation was approximately 18,000 years ago. So this could have been roughly any time before 20,000 years ago.

Across from the bull's home on the left bank of the Daiti River was the first man, Gayomart. The Primal Man was created immediately after the Primal Bull that was to supply him with food and help him fight evil. These two beings stood on opposing banks of the river, the good Daiti, which flowed from the center of the world.

Gayomart in His radiant beauty, was created spontaneously by the Force of Creation to assist Ahura Mazda in his fight against the Evil Spirit, known as "Ahriman" or "Angra Mainyu." This took place in the middle of the world on the sixth 'Gāh (Like Day) of the Creation similar to Genesis.

He came as a 15 year old boy. Sometimes He is said to be created from mud, with physical features similar to men later born

Tree of Life symbol
counrtesy Wikipedia Commons

of his seed. Perhaps He, Himself was a pre-modern form of man. His body was created from earth, its divinity and sperm were fashioned from the light and brightness of the sky.

He measured four medium reeds in height and in breadth. He was round, white and brilliant, and shone as the sun because of the supernal Farr.

Gayomart was the representative of God on earth so He took it upon himself to contend with the evil Ahriman. When Gayomart and the bull appeared, Ahriman, the source of evil and darkness was laid low in awe.

Gayomart lived for 3000 years in peace and did not pray, did not eat, and did not talk but he was thinking the whole time. (Note: The fact that Gayomart did not talk or pray for the first 3000 peaceful years before Angra Manu, the Evil one who took the form of a fiery dragon was awakened; may mean **the people did not yet pray to personal idols** for that length of time; as noted in the Atrahasis/Gilgamesh Epic.)

At the end of the 3000 year period in which Ahriman was stunned and could not do anything, Jeh or Jahi (similar to Lilith – Hebrew and Lilitu-Babylonian) the arch demon whore yelled, which woke him up! She promised to help him destroy Gayômart and the creatures of God. Ahriman (Satan) and his minions the Divs (demons) fought with the Light, and on the first day of the spring, Naw Ruz the Iranian new year, the Evil One himself leaped onto the earth as a dragon (a snake with legs). He started to create death, illness, lust, thirst, and hunger among the life forms. He also spread the Kyrm, a category evil beings, men interpreted as including reptiles, insects and rodents in the world. (Perhaps the latter was a human addition, to explain what the evil beings were.)

Commencing the second cosmic stage, Gayomart and the bull were attacked by Ahriman because they had withstood his attempts to spread world-wide destruction by introducing Want, Sloth, Lust, and 1000 diseases. But that was not enough to defeat the forces of good. So Angra Mainyu sent the demon of death, "Astovidat" to spy on Gayomart, but he could not kill the Prophet because His fate had not yet come.

The ensuing combat between the forces of Light and Darkness came to an end by the arbitration of angels, but the bull had been mortally wounded. Foreseeing the Bull's death God administered a soporific to ease its pain. From the dying Bull's blood sprang forth all vegetation. From its seed, which was carried to the Moon then fell back to earth, came all the animals we see today.

At first Gayomart had no flock to preach His Revelation to. Later the Word of God and prophetic counsels addressed to his mind were subsequently revealed to Masia, His wife, then later through their son or descendant Siamak and thirdly, through Hooshang a grandson or descendant to all mankind. These revealers are almost certainly different human forms than Gayomart.

Time had destined Gayomart to live for thirty more years. When Ahriman, also referred to as Angra Manu finally killed Him. Gayomart left his "throne" to Hooshang, a powerful Manifestation of God, perhaps no less than Enoch, Who then became the Leader or King of men.

Gayomart's Death

He foretold as He died, that despite His death the modern human race would be born. Where He was slain His seed fertilized the earth, and forty years later a rhubarb plant shot up. Splitting into two branches it gave forth two persons, a male Mashya and a female, Mashyana. They became the first modern mortal couple and are known as Ask and Embla in Norse

Mythology. Some call them Adam and Eve. Okay! Rhubarbs yes! But is that any weirder than coming from a rib, earth, or mud? There were no classes on evolutionary development at that time.

Later Angra Manu, the Evil one who took the form of a snaky, fiery dragon (AKA: Ahriman) tricked Mashya and Mashyana into worshipping him as their creator. This was the first sin. You could say it was the tasting of the fruit of the Tree of the Knowledge of Good and Evil. Given a choice, they put something or someone before God and it filled the world with corruption and evil.

SIAMAK

Siamak was beloved of all except the devil Ahriman, who raised an army under the command of his own demonic son to kill Siamak. An angel named Sorush warned Gayomart. But the noble Siamak led an army of His own and accepted the challenge of hand to hand combat with the evil son of Ahriman. So it was, that the beloved Siamak died at the hands of that demon. (Cain and Abel? Here also, two sons carry on the fight between Evil and good, as in the case of Adam and Eve).

HOOSHANG

Siamak's son or descendant, Hooshang was grown by this time and led the army that defeated Ahriman's son who was eventually bound and beheaded. Perhaps this story is a parable about the evil of that age being defeated with a renewal.

After 50 years the first humans of a newer age, Mashya and Mashyana bore twins. But because their sin caused a horrible famine (similar to Adam and Eve) they were forced by starvation to eat their precious children.

There are memories of tremendous starvations which included the eating of children. See Atrahasis, Yima and Adam.

After a long, long time Mashya and Mashyana were able to bear another set of twins **from which humanity developed.** Finally when humans, the most perfect of all creations were born in the seventh creation fire, all was done and the Creator rested. "The Persian Creation story" (http://www.oocities.org/west_johnny2001/Persia/Persian_Creation.htm) ("Keyumars" http://en.wikipedia.org/wiki/Gayomart)

The Prophesy of the Return (Renovation)

Gayomart shares with us an account of Ahura Mazda's Creation, and of First Man, actually several kinds of First Men. As bearer of divine prowess, He is a loving Caregiver of the whole of Creation. He is granted the perfection of the Holy Spirit, and thus immortality. This allows Him to return to us at the time of the "Renovation," a period, which marks the end of one age and the Dawn of the next.

The "Return" or "Saoshyant" is a term used in the Avestan Gathas referring to One who will renovate the world and bring salvation again, to mankind. There are three Saoshyans named in the Avesta: Hushydar, Hushydar-Mah and The Saoshyant who may also be called Sushyant, or Sorush. These redeemers will come in succession of periods, each lasting at least one thousand years. (Bundahesh, Pg 32)

Gayomart, will at least in the Holy Spirit be raised at this Resurrection to bring about the "Renovation."

The Saoshyant is the "Hidden Savior," or "Whole World's Savior," also referred to as the "King of Kings" (the Shah han Shah)! The Baha'is feel that these names and attributes apply to their Prophet, Baha'u'llah)

New names and faces must not deter vigilant seekers! Many of us are familiar with this concept of The Return of the Holy Spirit – even if the body and name it wears are different. The Word brought by the many Luminous Points is the same eternal truth from One Single God.

Here follows a precious and rare example from the antiquity of Gayomart, and also from

Indian Peafowl. This picture was taken by Richard Bartz by using a Canon EF 70-300mm f/4-5.6 IS USM Lens (Own work) [CC BY-SA 2.5 (http://creativecommons.org/licenses/by-sa/2.5)], via Wikimedia Commons

very recent revelation, which demonstrates that the same spiritual teachings pass from age to age, as a constant gift to humanity, as they develop and mature. These two quotes are separated by many thousands of years.

"Pay heed to what is said, not to the speaker. Look up to advice and wise words, no matter who says it. Acknowledge the truth, no matter of what provenance" – Gayomart/Q-mers

And **"Likewise the divine religions of the holy Manifestations of God are in reality one though in name and nomenclature they differ. Man must be a lover of the light no matter from what day-spring it may appear. He must be a lover of the rose no matter in what soil it may be growing. He must be a seeker of the truth no matter from what source it come. Attachment to the lantern is not loving the light."** (Abdu'l-Baha, Foundations of World Unity, p. 15)

ADAM

As one to whom God spoke directly, Adam is seen as a great Prophet and Bearer of God's Word by many on earth. The following information comes from the Qu'ran, the Torah or Old Testament, also some Gnostic references like the Book of Enoch.

2:23 And Adam said, This is now bone of my bones, and flesh of my flesh: she shall be called Woman, because she was taken out of Man. 2:24 Therefore shall a man leave his father and his mother, and shall cleave unto his wife: and they shall be one flesh.

2:25 And they were both naked, the man and his wife, and were not ashamed.

3:20 And Adam called his wife's name Eve; because she was the mother of all living. (Modern Humans?) -King James Bible, Genesis

Occasionally, today a person is born with 11 ribs rather than 12. Some see this as a remembrance of this early event.

Eve, wanting to please God gained knowledge of the difference between good and evil. Only later finding that such knowledge, or rather the choice of good or evil was a distraction from knowing God alone. In Genesis, Adam and Eve ate of the fruit offered by the dragon, a snake with legs which were later taken away as God's punishment, so he had to crawl on his belly.

"And the great dragon was cast out, that old serpent, called the Devil, and Satan, which deceiveth the whole world: he was cast out into the earth, and his angels were cast out with him." (King James Bible, Revelation)

Sounds just like the snaky dragon, Angra Manu in the Persian story.

In the Qu'ran it is claimed Adam gave Eve the forbidden fruit from the Tree of Knowledge of good and evil. In this way she and Adam became aware of the conflict between Good and Evil. Perhaps historically, humankind had become more consciously aware of themselves at this point in evolution. And they became aware of the consequences of their actions.

Most stories say they turned away from God and towards something more worldly for a time. They were grieved when they realized their mistake and saw God's great disappointment and displeasure. Both were punished and sent from Eden.

"Unto Adam also and to his wife did the LORD God make coats of skins, and clothed them. Therefore the LORD God sent him forth from the garden of Eden, to till the ground from whence he was taken. So he drove out the man; and he placed at the east of the garden of Eden Cherubim's, and a flaming sword which turned every way, to keep (safe) the way of the tree of life." (King James Bible, Genesis 3:21-3:24)

Some renditions say that means they had to leave Heaven to become mortal earthly Beings. The Quran says that Allah (God) sent both of them away from heaven, down to earth where they became His representatives. In the Torah, God banishes Adam and Eve from Eden (heavenly state) and sends them to earth. Others say they moved elsewhere on earth, but in the end they were forgiven by their Creator. After they left Eden, they suffered a famine very similar to the horrible famine of Mashya and Mashyana. Agriculture became a necessary occupation.

"When they were driven out from paradise, they made themselves a booth, and spent seven days mourning and lamenting in great grief. But after seven days, they began to be hungry and started to look for victual to eat, and they found it not. Then Eve said to Adam: 'My lord, I am hungry. Go, look for (something) for us to eat. Perchance the Lord God will look back and pity us and recall us to the place in which we were before.' And Adam arose and walked seven days over all that land, and found no victual such as they used to have in paradise." (King James Bible, Genesis)

Some texts opt to place Eden in an earthly abode and go to lengths to try to name its rivers. There are geographical problems that need to be considered. The rivers, such as the Euphrates, change their paths – not to mention that the whole region was covered in glaciers and later, several feet of flood debris. Layers of rock containing a mass of remains of creatures that died during those times, cover the stricken sites. The Tigris and Euphrates of today might be named after large antediluvian rivers, but are not likely to be the same rivers, on the same paths.

It is also interesting that the head of the Persian Gulf has vacillated. At times it reached up to the current location of Ur. It has also receded down past the Isle of Bahrain. It is for this reason that some people think the Garden of Eden was once on al-Bahrain. On an Island which is now mostly submerged – called Dilmun. There is a fort, a large temple and thousands of burial mounds, but they are dated to only 5000 years ago. Dilmun is known for water palms and **forbidden** sacred trees.

Perhaps if there is a specific physical place, Eden is buried in the Persian Gulf, or north by Ararat; but surely the exact location is unimportant. Finding it, as if one could, is really only a diversion from the importance of the spiritual history.

There are beautiful renditions of the story of Adam and Eve, one of which was supposedly related by Seth known as Sith or Shiith in the Qu'ran. But sadly, these embellished pieces were examples biographical writing, art, or pseudopigrapha that was made popular around the time of Christ. Still, it is very beautiful and traditional.

In the Book of Enoch, which is used in Oriental Orthodox churches, when God announces his intention to create Adam, some angels express dismay. They ask why He would create a being that would do evil. Yet some Gnostics felt that Adam and Eve were created to help defeat Satan, who made of fire, was prideful and refused to bow before Adam, who was made of clay.

According to the early Islamic commentator Muhammad ibn Jarir al-Tabari's account, after receiving the breath of God Adam remained a dry body for 40 days. Then gradually came to life from the head downwards. He came back to life as an embodied, anointed Being saying "All praise be to God, the Lord of all beings!"

The rush of Life Force from the head downward is familiar as the transformational power that flows into the Manifestation at the anointment. This is symbolized by John baptizing Jesus by pouring water over His head.

Baha'u'llah shares with us His feeling at the time of His anointing with the Holy Spirit. He sat sunken in the infested muck of a dank prison with His feet in stocks and weighed down by over 200 pounds of chain clamped around His neck.

"During the days I lay in the prison of Tihran, though the galling weight of the chains and the stench-filled air allowed Me but little sleep, still in those infrequent moments of slumber, I felt as if something flowed from the crown of My head over My breast, even as a mighty torrent that precipitateth itself upon the earth from the summit of a lofty mountain. Every limb of My body  **would, as a result, be set afire. At such moments My tongue recited what no man could bear to hear."** (Baha'u'llah, Epistle to the Son of the Wolf, p. 22)

Having been created, and being sentient with the knowledge of good and evil, Adam is given domination over all the lower creatures which are His to name. He and Eve bear two sons and probably several other children including daughters. Like Cain and Abel, they were probably employed in agricultural occupations. These people later bear other children and descendants, which ensure the propagation of more modern humans.

SETH

In *Antiquities of the Jews*, Josephus refers to Seth as virtuous and of excellent character. He states that *"his descendants invented the wisdom of the heavenly bodies, and built the 'pillars of the sons of Seth', two pillars inscribed with many scientific discoveries and inventions, notably in astronomy. They were built by Seth's descendants based on Adam's prediction that the world would be destroyed at one time by fire and another time by global flood, in order to protect the discoveries and be remembered after the destruction. One was composed of brick, and the other of stone, so that if the pillar of brick should be destroyed, the pillar of stone would remain, both reporting the ancient discoveries, and informing men that a pillar of brick was also erected. Josephus reports that the pillar of stone remained in the land of Siriad in his day."* William Whiston, a 17/18th century translator of the Antiquities (http://en.wikipedia.org/wiki/Seth)

Here is an Islamic view of the Prophet Seth (Shiith).

"Years and years passed, Adam grew old, and his children spread all over the earth. Muhammad Ibn Ishaq related: that when Adam's death drew near, he appointed his son Seth (Shiith) to be his successor, and taught him the hours of the day and night along with their appropriate acts of worship. He also foretold to him the flood that would come.

After Adam's death, his son Seth (Shiith) took over the responsibilities of prophethood, according to a hadith narrated by Abu Dhar. (The) Prophet Muhammad said: 'Allah sent down one hundred four psalms, of which fifty were sent down to Seth.' When the time of his death came, Seth's son Anoush succeeded him. He in turn, was succeeded by his son Qinan, who was succeeded by his son Mahlabeel.

He (Mahlabeel) reigned for a period of forty years. When he died his duties were taken over by his son Yard, who on his death, bequeathed them to his son Khonoukh (Enoch), who is Idris according to the majority of the scholars (Ulama)." http://islamickids.tripod.com/id108.htm

The Persians claim that Mahlabeel was the King of the Seven Regions. They said He was the first one to cut down trees to build cities and large forts. It was he who built the cities of Babylonia. Sadly, this may have contributed to droughts and famines.

Unfortunately in Egypt, Seth's or Set's distant memory no longer bears any ties to reality only fanciful tales. Sadly, he was debased to a mischievous composite animal creature. Or, perhaps forgotten altogether.

ENOCH/HERMES/THOTH/IDRIS: BEFORE THE FLOOD

"None of our thoughts can conceive of God, nor can any language define Him. The incorporeal, invisible and formless cannot be comprehended by our senses...God is ineffable. God indeed can transmit to a few elect, the ability to rise above natural things in order to perceive some radiation of His supreme perfection, but these elect find no words to translate into every-day language the non-material vision which has made them tremble...the First Cause remains hidden..." – Hermes (Stone-age Prophet)

In Neolithic times there was a bold and brilliant pre-flood Messenger called by many names including Enoch. He was a spiritual and literal King, a Messenger of God. He called the Babylonian people back to His forefather, Adam's religion. Only a handful listened while the majority turned away. He was forced to abandon the land of His birth where few wished to hear the Word of One God. Later He was called Hermes Trismegistus, or 'thrice great'; excellent as a great king, a legislator, and priest.

We humans remember an immense amount of information about Enoch! Details like whether He was fifth, seventh or ninth in succession after Adam; may become confused and conflicted; but it is what He said and did that really sets Him apart. **A supreme Manifestation of an ancient age, whose every word has impact for us today.** Enoch was born of the line of Cain and was the first of the Children of Adam to be given prophethood after Adam and Seth. Most interesting, is the mention of a major pre-flood city named after "Enoch."

"And Cain knew his wife; and she conceived, and bare Enoch: and he builded a city, and called the name of the city, after the name of his son, Enoch." (King James Bible, Genesis 4:17)

Although Enoch's first people failed to grasp His revelation and are pretty much lost to us; His teachings did succeed famously in other parts of the world.

"Leading his brave followers out of Babylon, he headed for Egypt. There as Thoth to the Egyptian, and Hermes to the Greek, He carried on His mission. Hermes or Thoth had His greatest effect on mankind from Egypt, where the effect of His Illumination was gargantuan and mysterious.

Beneath the seeming idolatry of its external polytheism, Egypt preserved the ancient foundations of esoteric theology and its priestly organization. In Assyria royalty controlled and crushed the priesthood. ...whereas in Egypt the priesthood disciplined royalty and never abdicated even in the worst times, standing up to kings, driving out despots and always governing the nation...for a period of over 5000 years Egypt was the stronghold of pure and exalted teachings..." – Edouard Schure

"In Egypt, Thoth is considered to be Ra's Will, translated into speech. He is associated with the arts of magic (dealing with Angels and Demons) and a system of writing, as well as, the development of science. He became associated with the judgement of the dead." – The Gods of the Egyptians 1899, Vol 1 pp 405-415, by E. A. Wallis Budge.

He bade people to do what is just and fair. He also taught them prayers, and to fast on certain days, and to give a portion of their wealth to the poor. He shared a vast amount of divine knowledge. According to Baha'u'llah, He is the first great human philosopher, Idris!

Enoch, the Shepherd of men is often shown in the company of a lamb, or ram. He is a Healer with Neolithic roots and His head in space.

"The first person who devoted himself to philosophy was Idris. Some called him also Hermes. In every tongue, he hath a special name. He it is who hath set forth in every branch of philosophy thorough and convincing statements. After him Balínús derived his knowledge and sciences from the Hermetic Tablets and most of the philosophers who followed him made their philosophical and scientific discoveries from his words and statements...."   (Baha'u'llah, Tablets of Baha'u'llah, p. 148)

"From one Soul of the Universe are all Souls derived. . . Of these Souls there are many changes, some (move) into a more fortunate estate, and some quite contrary. . . Not all human souls, but only the pious ones, are divine. Once separated from the body, and after the struggle to acquire piety, which consists in knowing God and injuring none, such a soul becomes all intelligence. The impious soul, however, punishes itself by seeking a human body to enter into, for no other body can receive a human soul it cannot enter the body of an animal devoid of reason. Divine law preserves the human soul from such infamy...The soul passeth from form to form and the mansions of her pilgrimage are manifold. Thou puttest off thy bodies as raiment and as vesture dost thou fold them up. Thou art from old, O Soul of Man yea, thou art from everlasting." –Hermes

In Egypt He was known as Thoth the Scribe. It is reported that He was the first to invent a basic form of writing. There have been subsequent inventions and improvements in the various scripts and types of communication coincidental with the arrival of other Manifestations. Yet Hermes/Thoth is credited with filling several halls in Egypt with collected spiritual wisdom, science and magic. That's a lot of writing!

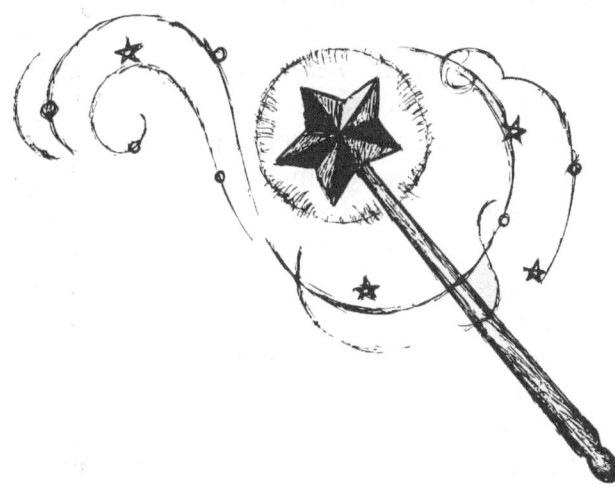

The Egyptians attributed to Hermes forty-two books dealing with esoteric science. The doctrine of the fire-principle, and words of light contained in the Vision of Hermes, which is the climax of Egyptian priestly initiation. His esoteric work is the base of much of the occultic philosophy and ritual from around the world.

THE ESOTERIC & OCCULT PHILOSOPHIES

"God is subtle not malicious"
– Albert Einstein http://www.spaceandmotion.com/Albert-Einstein-Quotes.htm

To begin: it is important to realize that the word occult does not mean a cult. Esoteric and occult simply mean secret or hidden **"inner" knowledge**. It is **self contemplation**. The esoteric/occult practitioner studies the inner nature of things, the divine, and human spiritual nature, as opposed to outer characteristics, which may be studied and defined by science.

Esotericism is the term which will be used here forward, but please know that occult studies were every bit as noble and peaceful, and hopefully when you see that term in your own studies you will weigh its merit, before you toss it away, as I did before deepening my understanding. Any word or term can be perverted, examples of that appear at the very end of this section before the piece on "Osiris and Hermes."

Mr. Einstein's quote above could represent the vast majority of esoteric studies. Such thinking stretches back at least into Neolithic times.

Esoteric concepts can be found in religious philosophies such as: Shamanism, Hermeticism and Kabbalah (both the Hermetic and later Jewish versions), Gnosticism, Rosicrucian, Theosophy, Wicca, Thelema, Paganism, Chaos magic, and Druidic thought.

Esoteric seekers refer to paired theories of correspondences, which link the states of the sacred with the mundane. Relationship is found between two levels of existence, the divine and the earthly aspects of human life. What ties bind the human soul to the invisible, and the visible cosmos. This mystical knowledge would reward the seeker with personal and spiritual transformation. Since the massive bloom of sciences in the 1800's and early 1900's, esotericism is evident in the New Thought Movement and Christian Science practices.

Early esoteric topics included many aspects of divination, magic, alchemy, astrology and various paranormal unknowns. Later seekers of the divine worlds employed astral travel, spiritualism, and extra-sensory perception. The term esoteric also encompasses several categories of secretive practices which often required some sort of initiation, as was the case with the Egyptian priesthood.

For thousands of years **Hermetic esotericism** has streamed through our religious thought, and influenced human contemplation. It was prevalent in Ancient Pagan traditions and cults from well before the time of Christ, and it often vied with the strict man-made dogmas prevalent in some monotheistic religions at the time. It pervaded our excursions into the unknown, and was the cause of secretive societies, many of which were based on Kabbalah, such as Neo-Platonism, and the mystery religions, and well-known lodges.

For millennia occult qualities were those properties that had no visible or rational explanation. In the Middle Ages the unseen properties of magnetism and gravity were considered occult. Newton's contemporaries severely criticized his theory that the unseen force of gravity could affect matter from a distance. As if by magic! Since "magic" in general was practiced in isolation and secrecy, it was viewed with suspicion by the wider community.

The Hermetic Order of the Golden Dawn was considered a magical order which delved into the study and practice of spiritual wisdom, science and magic as laid down by Hermes/Thoth in Egypt. During the late 19th and early 20th centuries the Order studied hidden knowledge, also paranormal and natural unexplained phenomena, like the psychic abilities employed by spiritual guides and mediums, also people with extra-sensory perceptive gifts of clairvoyance and clairaudience. They like many of us, were curious about cryptid creatures, ghosts, extraterrestrials and UFO's.

The three founders were Freemasons, and members of Rosicrucian Societies. Freemasons were open to followers of any Faith who believed in a "Supreme Being". This was not limited to Christianity, but also included Native Americans, Buddhists, Hindus, etc. who believed in one Causal Force, above all else. Many of the founders of the United States were Freemasons. So it would not be accurate to say that the basis for United States doctrine was Christian. Indeed it had a much broader scope.

The structure and grade system of the Order of the Golden Dawn was derived from the 18th-century **German Order of the Golden and Rosy Cross.** These "Rosicrucian's" were a German secret society "built on esoteric truths of the ancient past". The Golden Dawn was officially founded in the 1750s, but Frater U.D. believes that in 1710 the idea for the order was born with the alchemical publication of Sincerus Renatus' *"The perfect and true preparation of the Philosophers Stone according to the secret of the **Brotherhoods of the Golden and Rosy Cross.**"* By the 1770s the Golden Dawn had centers in Germany, Austria, the Czech Republic, Poland, Hungary and Russia. It slowly began to decline after the death of Prussian King, William II in 1925.

The Golden Dawn hierarchy included an initiation similar to the Masonic Lodges except that women were admitted on an equal basis with men. Progress within the order was based on achieving nine sequential grades: Zelator, Theoricus, Practicus, Philosophus, Adeptus Minor, Adeptus Major, Adeptus Exemptus, Magister, and Magus.

There were three developmental stages. "Golden Dawn" was the first, although all three are often collectively referred to as the "Golden Dawn". The First Order taught esoteric philosophy based on the Hemetic Kabbalah, and personal development through the study and awareness of four classical elements: Earth, Water, Air and Fire. The Second or "Inner" Order, the *Rosae Rubeae et Aureae Crucis* (the Ruby Rose and Cross of Gold), taught alchemy and astral travel, as well as proper magic and divination, including: scrying, astrology, tarot, and geomancy, etc. The Third Order was that of the "Secret Chiefs", who were said to be highly skilled. They directed the activities of the lower two orders by telepathy, or "spirit communication". Secret Chiefs were transcendent cosmic authorities who oversaw the actions of the Golden Dawn's spiritual organization, which manifested itself outwardly as a magical order, or lodge. The Chiefs exist on higher planes of being, or dwell among the living. They might gather at some special location such as Shambhala, or they may scatter through the world assisting souls anonymously. Shambhala is a myth which is likely based on a real place, hidden in Inner Asia.

Gnosticism, "having knowledge" refers to a collection of ancient religions whose adherents shunned the material world and embraced the spiritual world. Gnostics viewed the world of the demiurge as the lower material, world. The world of God was represented by the upper world and is associated with the soul and perfection. That world is eternal and remote. Gnosticism as a unique and recognizable belief system was considered to be a second century development until it was changed radically by the discovery of the Nag Hammadi scrolls after the time of Christ."

Neo-Platonism was a "Pure form of Idealism" from the early 2nd century. It was an Ancient Pagan development of the late Roman Empire which sought to find the central threads of wisdom given to us by the various god's and goddesses. Even though it was not "Christian" it was most definitely a noble renewal.

Elements of this line of thought included an "Unknowable Essence" known as the "One", and an imperfect Demiurge (the self) which must be banished for being separate from the "One" and therefore imperfect. A human spirit must rise above this imperfection of worldly matters by contemplation and by the acquisition of virtues.

Hermeticism is a religious and philosophical tradition based primarily on the Hermetic tablets. The search was for esoteric meaning, that which is hidden or innermost. It is based on a doctrine that affirms the existence of a single belief that is present in all religions, and was given by God to man even in the most primitive times. This doctrine asserts that a single theology exists. A "ONENESS" which threads through all religions, given by God to humankind from deepest antiquity.

Adepts attempted to access esoteric knowledge via a variety of processes which might include: meditation, sacred symbols, rituals, calling on angels, mediums or guides, and personal visions; rather than empty magic or ritual which might be used by some for show, and to impress others. Mystery Religions may have favored the latter.

"Mystery Religions," "Sacred Mysteries" or simply "Mysteries" were Greco-Roman religious schools. The most famous were the Eleusinian Mysteries from the cults of Demeter and Persephone. The initiation and ritual practice was secret and not to be revealed to outsiders. Each of the cults passed a particular "secret" on to the initiates regarding a particular god or goddess. The mystery schools flourished until the mid-4th century, but they never really ended.

The initiation described above seems to be an almost perfect description of initiation into a sorority I once joined. Pledges were wakened during the night and led downstairs by candlelight to learn a secret about a particular saint. Afterwards, we were welcomed as sisters. So "Greek" sororities and fraternities have carried on the tradition of secrecy, and sometimes debauchery.

Secret societies and esoteric philosophies greatly impacted Middle Age thought from the 13th to the 17th centuries. The scientific and philosophical writings of Hermes Trismesgitus greatly influenced the Reformation and Renaissance in Europe, as well as Asia, India, Europe, Africa and America. Planet-wide traditions are described collectively as Western Esotericism even though participation was actually much more universal. The European branch peaked about 1770 due to a renewed desire for mysticism.

Today the tradition of secret initiations continues with sororal and fraternal organizations, men's clubs, mystic lodges like the Freemasons, and social service clubs. They all have that little "secret", or spiritual orientation, which distinguishes and guides them. God or in some cases, gods or saints are invoked during gatherings or meetings.

Some organizations don't even pretend to be motivated by purity or good intentions as might be the case with Bohemian Grove, and several other social orders which today are basically drinking clubs.

Others like the Lions, 4H, Shriners, Rotary and Rotaract, are a blessing to the communities they serve. The Rotaract motto sums it up. "Be a gift to the world."

The Esoteric & Occult Philosophies

Madame H.P. Blavatsky. By Internet Archive Book Images Wikimedia Commons

In the last three hundred years U.S. secret societies and lodges, and supportive organizations were and are an integral part of the social fabric.

The Theosophical Society was founded in New York City in 1875. Co-founder Madame H.P. Blavatsky claimed to be in contact with mystics of a Himalayan Great White Lodge. She mentioned Shambhala several times, but without special emphasis. Later esoteric writers elaborated on the concept of a pure hidden land inhabited by an elusive mystic great white brotherhood whose members labored for the good of humanity, much like the "Secret Chiefs" mentioned above. https://en.wikipedia.org/wiki/Shambhala

Theosophy is a field of esotericism referring to hidden knowledge or wisdom that offers the individual enlightenment and salvation. Here one seeks direct knowledge of the mysteries of being and nature, in relation to divinity. Practitioners not only hope to understand the mysteries of the universe, but also the bonds that unite the universe and humanity, with respect to the divine.

Based on his research into the modern German Occult Revival (1890–1910), Goodrick-Clarke proposed that the driving force behind occultism is:

"A strong desire to reconcile the findings of modern natural science with a religious view that could restore man to a position of centrality and dignity in the universe."

Unfortunately his work and that of Madame Blavatsky inspired Hitler and early Nazis to attempt to restore an imaginary and twisted, German Aryan brotherhood, even though Aryans were not Germans, but residents of the northern Eurasian lattitudes, and were brown skinned until fairly recent times.

The astral plane is an intermediate world of light between Heaven and Earth, composed of the spheres of the planets and stars. These astral spheres are populated by angels, demons and spirits. **Astral projection** or travel, assumes that the astral body can separate from the physical body, and is capable of travelling outside it in an astral plane. The soul's journey or "ascent" is an out-of-body phenomenon. This is very similar to what people today refer to as a Near Death Experience, or NDE. The spiritual traveler leaves his or her physical body and travels in a subtle astral body. Occurrences are often associated with sleeping, dream, or meditation. Or in one case hypnosis (See Cayce, below).

According to classical, medieval and Renaissance Hermeticism, Neoplatonism, and later Theosophist and Rosicrucian thought; the **astral body** is an intermediate body of light linking the rational soul to the physical body. Often astral bodies and their planes of existence are depicted as a series of concentric circles or nested spheres, with a separate body traversing each realm.

Astral planes were adopted by and further developed in *The Aquarian Gospel of Jesus the Christ: The Philosophic and Practical Basis of the Religion of the Aquarian Age of the World and of the Church Universal*. It was written by Levi H. Dowling and first published in Dec 1908. Dowling transcribed what he referred to as the **"Akashic" records.** From these he was able to access an ethereal knowledge encoded in a non-physical, astral plane of existence. This Book, and other Theosophical concepts have experienced a recent revival among New Age mystical, and spiritual groups.

"Listen to your inner selves and look into the infinity of space and time. There reverberate[s] the song of the stars, the voice of the numbers and the harmony of the spheres.

Each sun is a thought of God, each planet a mode of that thought. In order that you may know divine thought, O souls, you painfully descend along the paths of the seven planets and their seven heavens and ascend once again.

What do the stars do? What do the numbers say? What do the spheres revolve? O souls that are lost and saved, they relate, they sing, they revolve – your destinies!"
–Fragment from Enoch/Hermes in *The Great Initiates.*

Science and Religion

According to Albert Einstein,
"Science without religion is lame. Religion without science is blind."

Many sources have depicted science and religion as equivalent counterparts. The branch of Esotericism known as the New Thought Movement and the Baha'i Faith insist that science and religion must work together "like the wings of a bird" to lift our understanding.

PERSPECTIVE

The following thoughts on the substance of God by Walter Russell and a piece on Spiritual healing are two culminations of the "paired thoughts" of the divine and the mundane. Most esoteric organizations sought out ways to discover a coherent purpose and origin of the universe, especially regarding the nature of what is sacred and holy and how it applies to humans. What better way to do this than by *personally experiencing* the sacred realms. The following examples demonstrate two facets of the unity of science paired with religion. First, a mind popping scientific description of the God-force. Second, the realization that human perfections and healing are achievable through awareness of our identity with God.

Walter and Lao Russell: Walter 1871-1963 was born in Boston. Some refer to him as a "modern Leonardo DaVinci." His careers included illustrator, correspondent in the Spanish–American War, and child portrait painter. He also attracted widespread attention with his allegorical painting "The Might of Ages" which won several awards. He published three children's books by 1903, and made his mark as a builder by creating $30 million worth of top-quality cooperatively owned apartments. At IBM he was a motivational speaker, and later sculpted busts of a number of influential individuals like Thomas Jefferson and General MacArthur. He added several substances and isotopes to the Periodic Table. He communed with Nicola Tesla in the 1930's regarding these changes. Walter Russell is mentioned *Who's Who in America, 1976.*

But mostly he is remembered for this theory of "Cosmic Consciousness" a result of a "cosmic illumination" which he is said to have experienced, during the 1940s. He debated with other scientists about a "Two-Way Universe" reflecting the paired forces of gravitation and radiation, which perpetually void each other by mutual giving (The Voidance Principle, the Law of Balance).

In *A New Concept of the Universe*, (1953) he explains the universe in the relationships of matter and energy, electricity and magnetism, which emanate from LIGHT. Russell describes the process of Creation, the nature of atomic and stellar systems, the Natural Laws that govern the universe, and man's relation to God and the universe – in terms of Light. Light is all there is. "If science knew what LIGHT actually [IS], instead of the waves and corpuscles of incandescent suns which science now thinks it is, a new civilization would arise from that fact alone." (from the introduction). "The locatable motionless Light which man calls magnetism is the Light which God [IS]" and therefore "God is provable by laboratory methods," (P.4)

"The cardinal error of science" is "shutting the Creator out of his Creation." He refered to God as "invisible, motionless, sexless, undivided, and unconditioned white Magnetic Light of Mind which centers all things." - Russell "Atomic Suicide", 1957, 106.

Russell wrote in 1947, *Secret of Light* Pp. xi, xiii "For within the secret of Light is vast knowledge not yet revealed to man." And, "Revelation of the nature of Light will be the inheritance of man in the coming New Age of greater comprehension." He saw a New Age coming in human relations, as a result of the marriage of Religion and Science.

"Religion and Science must come together in a New Age." – The Message of the Divine Illiad, P. 95

An engineer, C. W. Kelsey, wrote a letter to the *New York Sun* March 5, 1930 entitled "Walter Russell and the Atom", in which he stated, "If Russell's theories are sound, they will be of utmost value, as he shows that there can be but one substance, and that the difference [among the elements] is a dimensional difference and not a difference of substance. In other words, if Russell's theories are right, transmutation can be reduced to a practical reality."

Russell among others felt that not only the human body, but also human consciousness, had evolved in stages, making periodic leaps, such as that from animal awareness to rational self awareness. Humankind was, Russell believed, on the brink of making another key, evolutionary leap in consciousness.

The next cycle of human evolution would be from rational self-consciousness to spiritual super-consciousness on the order of that experienced by sages, artists and illuminates of the past 2,500 years. This would include The Buddha, Confucius, Lao-Tzu, Mohammed, the unknown author of the Bhagavad-Gita, Moses, Jesus, Zoroaster, Leonardo da Vinci, Shakespeare, Michelangelo, Emerson, Whitman etc., according to Richard Maurice Bucke, in *Cosmic Consciousness (1901),* introduction' and Pp. 65-66

"Without these few illuminati, the world of man would still be primate." Russell, Walter and Lao *Home Study Course*, p. 106.

"This New Age is marking the dawn of a new world-thought. That new thought is a new cosmic concept of the value of man to man. The whole world is discovering that all mankind is one and that the unity of man is real – not just an abstract idea. Mankind is beginning to discover that the hurt of any man hurts every man, and, conversely, the uplift of any man uplifts every man." Russell, Walter, *Message of the Divine Iliad, vol. 2,* 1947–48, p.69

"The sole purpose of man on earth is to manifest his Creator. He has no other purpose." A New Concept of the Universe, P. 139

I remember as a young child that our family travelled from Colorado Springs to Swannanoa, near Waynesboro, Virginia, to visit Walter and his wife Lao. I remember a tall lady in a gown and several sculpted busts. My dad attempted to build a mock-up of one of Nicola Tesla's ideas for concentrating light by means of a telescoping series of lenses, laser like, to heat water to steam. My brother Peter Mulberger, says the water tank metal was melted in the process of their experiment.

Many of our family friends back then focused on "Atomic research", which was actually the name of a corporation our parents started. We children grew up helping to make geiger counters and black lights in our basement laboratory. Ted and Fritzi Tetman, Jack and Ella Morrison, Robert Hilgendorf, Bob Heiburger, Ellis and Hallie Brown and Gertrude and Russell Walcher and a number of others were also influenced by Mr. Russell' "Atomic Suicide" I remember Gertie showing my dad a paper she had written regarding the chain-reactive, destructive force of mu-masons, which were released by atomic activity. She feared they may cause exponential harm to the earth. There is no doubt that all of these people believed in the inescapable union of science and religion.

The Religious Science of Healing

It is likely that the sacred duty and arts of healing began at the start of conscious humanity. Shahmans and Folk Healers have attempted to prevail over discomfort and despair since at least Neanderthal times. However knowledge, resources and methods were limited. Prayer as a cry from the heart became coupled with the attempts, and it has been incorporated ubiquitously into the healing arts, from long before the time of Ram. In the 19th and 20th centuries a scientific component was expanded.

"Healing is based on universal mental and spiritual laws which anyone can utilize who will comply with the conditions involved in these laws." Fillmore, Charles Jesus Christ Heals, 19th ed 1999, p. 79

Mary Baker Eddy (1821 – 1910) founded the Church of Christ, Scientist in 1879 based on her book *Science and Health with Key to the Scriptures*, 1875. In her book she states "It has been said, and truly, that Christianity must be science, and science must be Christianity, else one or the other is false and useless; but neither is unimportant or untrue, and they are alike in demonstration. This proves the one to be identical with the other."

Charles Sherlock Fillmore (1854-1948) with his wife, **Myrtle** founded **Unity School of Christianity** in 1891. He became known as an American mystic for his contributions to spiritualist interpretations of Bible text. He was born on a Minnesota Indian reservation in 1854. Before age 2, Fillmore was kidnapped by Sioux Indians and might have experienced a mystical ceremony. As a teen, he was intrigued by metaphysics and mysticism and he became a devoted student of American writers of the time, of Spiritualism, and Eastern Religions.

He moved from Texas to Gunnison, Colorado where he worked at mining and real estate. Myrtle was suffering from TB when they married in 1981, and moved to Pueblo, Colorado. She sought help from the "New Thought" healing ideas of **Phineas Parkhurst Quimby** (1802 – 1866). Quimby was a philosopher, magnetizer, mesmerist, healer and inventor from Maine.

Phineas Parkhurst Quimby: Quimby's work is widely recognized as leading to the New Thought Movement. Mary Baker Eddy was a patient of Quimby's and shared his view that disease is rooted in a mental cause. This interested Charles who then studied "New Thought" intensively.

Quimby refers to the practice "animal magnetism." Though definitions are somewhat confusing, perhaps it is a charismatic hypnosis. He explained that the practitioner has the power to manipulate the "magnetic fluid" inside a body, in order to hold the patient's attention. Some magnetizers attempted to channel what they thought was a magnetic "fluid", and applied it to the client with a "laying on of hands." Effects included: intense feelings, heat, trembling, trances, and seizures. British magnetizers were eager to distance themselves from the theoretical orientation of animal magnetism that was based on the concept of "magnetic fluid." Yet some felt that "The magnetizer is the imam of vital energy." Gorsas, Antoine-Joseph, *L'Ane promeneur*, 1784, p. 41 and p. 342.

Quimby spoke vedic thoughts of "Infinite Intelligence", meaning God is everywhere. Spirit is the totality of all things real. True human selfhood is divine. Divine thought is a force for good. Sickness originates in the mind and "right thinking" has a healing effect. He taught that Infinite Intelligence is "supreme, universal, and everlasting", and it dwells within each person, therefore all people are spiritual beings.

"the highest spiritual principle [is] loving one another unconditionally... and teaching and healing one another", and that "our mental states are carried forward into manifestation and become our experience in daily living." https://en.wikipedia.org/wiki/Phineas_Quimby

Shortly after studying Quimby's work, an E. B. Weeks lecture grabbed the Fillmore's attention. **"I am a child of God and therefore I do not inherit sickness."** With what she had learned from her studies on self hypnosis and affimative prayer Myrtle healed herself from her chronic tuberculosis and Charles began to heal from his childhood ice skating accident. They were elated and inspired to share their healing experiences with others.

If God is love and intelligence, and is the ubiquitous source of all good, it is not necessary for people to be in the same room in order for them to unite in thought and prayer. An extreme case of long-distance healing was the master of hypnotic astral travel.

Edgar Cayce (1877-1945) "had more near-death experiences than anyone ever documented. Cayce learned that when he was hypnotized, he could leave his body and journey into the afterlife realms. Cayce made over 14,000 otherworldly journeys in his life and the information he gained from these journeys has astounded people all over the world... Cayce was swamped with an avalanche of 25,000 requests for medical help. President Woodrow Wilson sought the services of Edgar Cayce for healing and guidance while... conceiving the idea of the League of Nations. In 1954, the University of Chicago accepted a Ph.D. thesis based on a study of his life and work. Cayce is also considered to be the father of holistic medicine by JAMA, the prestigious medical journal. Cayce was a wonder to the medical community because of his ability to diagnose and specify a treatment for gravely ill people often hundreds of miles away through his out-of-body journeys. Cayce was able to gain a tremendous amount of information through his frequent NDEs. Much of this information solved some of the greatest mysteries of humanity." – Kevin Williams http://www.near-death.com/paranormal/edgar-cayce.html

"Cayce 1910." Licensed under Public Domain via Wikimedia Commons - https://commons.wikimedia.org/w

In 1889, the Fillmores founded **Unity** on principles of prayer and healing as a development within the New Thought movement. In 1889 The Fillmores started the magazine "Modern Thought" and published the work of New Thought pioneer William Walker Atkinson. In 1890 they announced a prayer group that would later be called 'Silent Unity'. Several of the Fillmore's societies, including Silent Unity, and various literature pieces merged into "Unity School of Christianity."

In 1891 Fillmore's 'Unity" magazine was first published, and in 1893, Myrtle began *"Wee Wisdom"* a children's magazine. She served as the editor for 35 years. Another prominent publication was the "Daily Word." It was a kindly application of the positive principles of Truth as taught and exemplified by Jesus Christ. Both "Wee Wisdom" and the "Daily Word" were staples of our childhood home in Colorado Springs in the 1950's and 1960's.

Charles Fillmore's teachings are the basis of the Unity religion, especially the *Metaphysical Bible Dictionary* and *Talk on the Truth*. He taught that people have problems due to false thinking and if everyone would be content and happy if they could reverse their thinking. In his Talks on Truth Fillmore explains the true "Church" is a "state of consciousness in mankind." Each person is a unique expression of God, that each person is sacred, and each person is worthy. We must take personal responsibility to choose life-affirming thoughts, words and actions, to experience a more fulfilling and abundant life.

The Bible is a spiritual resource studied as history and allegory. It is a metaphysical representation of each soul's evolutionary journey toward spiritual awakening. It is a reflection of the comprehension and inspiration of the writers and their times. Followers of Unity believe in the divinity of Jesus, but only in the sense that all humans are the children of God and share that divine potential. They believe that Jesus was a master teacher of universal Truth. He expressed divine potential and sought to show others how to do the same by following him. The term "Christ" refers to the divinity in all people. For them Jesus is the great example of the Christ in physical form.

In his later years, Fillmore felt so young that he thought that he might be physically immortal, through the control of his mind, and perhaps because he was a reicarnation of Paul of Tarsus. Fillmore believed he could never die because he was in true harmony with universal law.

Charles had no intention of making Unity into a denomination but his students wanted a more organized group. He and his wife were among the first ordained Unity ministers in 1906. Although Charles Fillmore died in 1948, Unity continued and grew into a worldwide interdenominational movement.

The Unity Church demonstrates Our purpose in life is to express divine potential as taught by Jesus. God is the source and creator of all. There is no other enduring power. God's spiritual energy is present everywhere and available to all. God is Spirit, infinite Mind, the immanent force and intelligence everywhere manifest in nature. "We are Spiritual Beings created in God's image. The spirit of God lives within each person; therefore, all people are inherently good." "We create our life experiences through our way of thinking."

"There is power in affirmative prayer which can increase a person's connection to God." Prayer is not a way to inform God of one's troubles or to change God in any way, but rather, prayer is properly used to align with the power that is God. Affirmative prayer means praying with the belief that we have already received all that we need. It is understood to be the highest form of creative thought. Through prayer the mind is renewed and the body transformed.

One must first release any negative thoughts, and hold onto statements of spiritual truth. Prayer and meditation are ways of attaining the presence of God, which are best experienced out of doors in nature. This heightens our awareness of truth and transforms our lives. Prayer is valuable not because it alters the circumstances and conditions of life, but because it alters the seeker. Freeman, James Dillet, "Life is a Wonder" Unity Magazine, Mar–Apr 2001, pp. 18–19

Unity considers itself to be a non-sectarian educational institution although Unity ministers do complete a prescribed program of courses, training and ordination. In 1896

H. Emilie Cady wrote *Lessons in Truth, A Course of Twelve Lessons in Practical Christianity* which is considered a core text of Unity. It offers an approach that is scientifically sound, psychologically healthy, intellectually challenging, and spiritually satisfying. Unity:

- Gives you freedom to grow spiritually at your own pace and to evolve your own working philosophy of ideas and beliefs.
- Has no creedal requirements; never asks you to profess something you do not believe.
- Has little concern for dogma, ritual, ecclesiastical garb, and other trappings of religiosity
- Does not impose any financial burden on its adherents; is supported by freewill offerings, and looks upon tithing and other forms of giving as the joyous response of a generous, Spirit-filled soul.
- Sees religion as an open-ended search for Truth rather than a closed system.
- Sees worship as serving God by uplifting and glorifying God's spirit in man in a positive, joyous way.
- Offers more than a once-a-week religion; gives you positive ideas to think on and apply seven days a week.
- Feels it has no exclusive right to or "corner" on truth.
- Emphasizes the spiritual unity of all churches, faiths, man, and truth.
- Welcomes in dignity and love, people of all races, colors, religions, social backgrounds, and economic levels.
- Is dedicated to loving service to individuals, society, and the world at large.
- Proclaims the divinity of Jesus, but goes further and assures you that you, like Jesus, are a child of God and therefore divine in nature.
- Declares that as a child of God, you inherit His goodness, His spiritual qualities, His spiritual and material abundance.
- Stresses your dominion, as a child of God, over every challenge.
- Believes no negative condition of mind, body, or affairs is incurable.
- Believes the body of man to be the holy temple of God, created to express harmony, life, and perfection of Spirit.
- Sees prayer not as technique for changing God, but as a technique that expands and transforms your mind, and thus changes you.
- Assures that you can commune with God directly without intercessor or intermediary.
- Acknowledges Jesus as Savior, Teacher, Way-Shower, and Elder Brother
- Describes God as Spirit, Creator, Source, Sustainer, Divine Mind, Life, Light, Love, Energy, Principle, Divine Law, Omnipresent, Omnipotent, Omniscient, Our Father, Mother.
- Denies the existence of any power or presence opposed to God. There is no personal "Devil" or place called "Hell," Unity sees there are evil appearances and suffering in the world, but ascribes these to man's ignorance and erroneous use of God's laws of life.

The preceding information is courtesy of Unity Institute.

Ernest Shurtleff Holmes (1887 – 1960) was the founder of "Religious Science", a part of the New Thought movement known as "The Science of Mind." He was the author of The Science of Mind book and magazine, and numerous other books which inspired and influenced many generations of metaphysical students and teachers. Holmes had previously studied another New Thought teaching, "Divine Science" and he became an ordained Divine Science Minister. Some of his offerings appear below.

1. Since the only life you can have is the life of the Spirit within you, you need but permit Its radiance to flow through your thought into self-expression. You are surrounded by a dynamic force, a great surge of living power. You are immersed in and saturated with the vital essence of Life. Its presence permeates everything, binding all together in one complete whole.

2. You have discovered the spiritual universe. Many others have discovered this same world, but each must make the discovery for himself. You are going to have a lot of joy sailing around this world of yours. Don't fight the opinions of others, or waste your time arguing over these things. Follow the inward gleam of your consciousness and you will arrive.

3. You are an eternal being now on the pathway of endless unfoldment, never less but always more yourself. Life is not static. It is forever dynamic, forever creating not something done and finished, but something alive, awake and aware. There is something within you that sings the song of eternity. Listen to it.

4. Trust in your own self more than all else.

5. You are more than you appear to be - Life is greater than you have ever known it – The best is yet to come.

6. Spirituality is natural goodness. God is not a person; God is a presence personified in us. Spirituality is not a thing; it is the atmosphere of God's Presence, goodness, truth, and beauty.

7. The universe must exist for the self-expression of God and the delight of God. Read more at: http://www.azquotes.com/author/6840-Ernest_Holmes

Ernest also stated: I believe in God, the Living Spirit Almighty; one, indestructible, absolute and self-existent Cause. This One manifests itself in and through all creation, but is not absorbed by its creation. The manifest universe is the body of God; it is the logical and necessary outcome of the infinite self-knowingness of God. I believe in the incarnation of the Spirit in all, and that we are all incarnations of the One Spirit. I believe in the eternality, the immortality, and the continuity of the individual soul, forever and ever expanding. I believe that Heaven is within me and that I experience It to the degree that I become conscious of it. I believe the ultimate goal of life to be a complete emancipation from all discord of every nature, and that this goal is sure to be attained by all. I believe in the unity of all life, and that the highest God and the innermost God is one God. I believe that God is personal to all who feel this indwelling Presence. I believe in the direct revelation of Truth through my intuitive and spiritual nature, and that anyone may become a revealer of Truth who lives in close contact with the indwelling God. I believe that the Universal Spirit, which is God, operates through a Universal Mind, which is the

Law of God; and that I am surrounded by this Creative Mind which receives the direct impress of my thought and acts upon it. From a paper by Dr Ernest Holmes, "What I believe." https://en.wikipedia.org/wiki/Ernest_Holmes

The thoughts and beliefs of all of the leaders of New Thought mentioned in this chapter have profoundly impacted society's evolution and understanding of the universe and its laws. Some of the main tenets common to all of them are that 1. All is Oneness, everything and everyone are intrinsically connected. 2. There is one God and all paths of faith are honored. 3. We are eternal beings, as is all life. 4. Love is the ultimate power. – Deborah Perdue, RScP

Magic, Sorcery and Divination

I cannot know what Enoch discussed in His volumes on science and magic, which have been associated with Rama, Krishna, and Moses. Many Prophets performed "miracles" whose effects on dull audiences were only temporary entertainment. All of the embodiments of the Holy Spirit have such "powers". They are privy to the secrets of created matter. They stun humans with the self emanation of the Farr or Halo, and their unconditional love which melts frozen, dark hearts. They have no need for drugs or parlor tricks.

Magic has facinated us in our attraction to these mighty Kings of earth. In the last few thousand years our magicians have emulated them for purposes of entertainment, dealing with spirits, entities, and energies; and for spiritual growth.

Divination, also associated with various Manifestations, is subjective, ineffective and when misused, is spiritually and physically cruel and dangerous to humanity and other living beings.

Spiritual Contact

Spiritualism assumes that the spirits of the dead continue to evolve in the spiritual realm. Spirits can if they wish to communicate with the living. The spirit world is seen not as a static place, but as one in which spirits continue to evolve. They are capable of providing useful knowledge about moral and ethical issues and information on aspects of the nature of God. Spiritualists will speak of their "spirit guides" on whom they rely for guidance and assistance.

Spirits which are more advanced can choose to contact us through dreams or visions, the aid of accomplished psychic mediums, through spiritual telepathy, or leaving signs like coins to validate their support.

The downside to this is, of course, that the spirits who are contacted may not be helpful and could be harmful, as many who have been to séances or used an Ouija board can attest. Spirit energies can affect the physical world and the living either through people who are unaware they have psychic "abilities," or active mediums. And they are capable of **producing positive or negative effects in both worlds.**

The Spiritualist movement reached peak popularity between the 1840s to the 1920s. Ideas and cohesion were transmitted through books or periodicals, and were passed along by trance lecturers and camp meetings. By 1897, Spiritualism had eight million followers in the in the middle and upper classes of the United States and Europe. Many adherents were prominent women who supported causes like abolition and women's suffrage.

By the 1900's the credibility of mediums plummeted as frauds were exposed. In the 1920s, **Harry Houdini** began focusing his energy on debunking psychics and mediums. He found that the mediums he met while trying to contact his deceased mother during séances, were often frauds. He began investigating their methods and reproducing their results to prove they were conning people. Spiritualism is currently practiced in spiritualist churches of the United States.

Spiritism, a branch of Spiritualism was developed by Allan Kardec, and today is found mostly in Europe and the Americas. Mr. Kardec postulated that **humans are immortal spirits that temporarily inhabit physical bodies** for several necessary incarnations while they attain moral and intellectual improvement. The reincarnation here is likely borrowed from Pythagorean thought from 2700 years ago. Pythagorus' philosophy influenced Plato and many others, including the Freemasons and the Rosicrucian's.

Dealing with Negative Energies

A **devil, demon, imp** or **fiend** is a malevolent presence which could be described as a dust bin of accumulated negativity relevant to a particular place or person. Any negative entity continues to produce, attract and "feed on" negativity until it ramps up to become a more dangerous entity or persona. These are referred to as non-human, or elemental things. This is different than a negative human spirit who scares, pesters and controls others out of spitefulness.

But the fiend can of course influence the behavior of a spirit so that it can derive benefits from the negative outcome. This can result in an entity becoming a "soul collector." "We are legion" a demon might say after it has destroyed many human souls, and binds pieces of them in its evil dustbin.

This is a very good reason for people to learn to control their anger, fear, anxiety and other negative emotions. **Our emotions truly are always feeding something - good or bad.**

"One evening an old Cherokee Indian told his grandson about a battle that goes on inside people. He said, 'My son, the battle is between two 'wolves' inside us all. One is Evil. It is anger, envy, jealousy, sorrow, regret, greed, arrogance, self-pity, guilt, resentment, inferiority, lies, false pride, superiority, and ego.

The other is good. It is joy, peace, love, hope, serenity, humility, kindness, benevolence, empathy, generosity, truth, compassion and faith.'

The grandson thought about it for a minute and then asked his grandfather: 'Which wolf wins?'

The old Cherokee simply replied, 'The one you feed.'

The Evil wolf or the Good Wolf is fed daily by the choices we make with our thoughts. What you think about and dwell upon will in a sense appear in your life and influence your behavior.

We have a choice, feed the Good Wolf and it will show up in our character, habits and behavior positively. Or feed the Evil Wolf and our whole world will turn negative: like poison, this will slowly eat away at our soul." https://wizdompath.wordpress.com/2008/03/05/an-old-cherokee-tale-of-two-wolves/

Within the last decade, we have been blessed with the televised actions of excellent, dedicated **psychic mediums** like Amy Allen, Kim Russo, Teresa Caputo, Chip Coffee, Sylvia Brown, the cinematic "ParaNorman" and a dozen others who deserve mention though their names have escaped me.

They have helped us tremendously by explaining what we may feel but can't see – or understand. They are able to inform us that not all spirits or entities are scary or evil, many are family or friends, and some are protectors. This will empower us to be less afraid of the unseen and more compassionate to spirits who are experiencing difficulties in this world *and* the next.

They also make us painfully aware attachments can keep us from moving on. Honestly is a certain dresser, an artifact or an especially nice bathroom – is that a reason to stay behind?

Attributes that mark ghosts or entities as "negative" are seen in this world every day! We find them in our neighbors and ourselves. So we might as well try to heal ourselves by honing virtues in this world so we can avert problems in both worlds!

The travel Channel programs, "The Dead Files" and "The Dead Files Revisited" show us that almost any approach can be effective in removing negativity from a person or a locale, *if* the living and/ or the dead individuals believe it works. In most cases we just have to make a strong effort to bring things back to harmony. (Example below)

About a decade ago a young woman from Costa Rica told me that her younger sister who was about 4 years old at the time was under attack. She was being choked by something, maybe a bruja. My friend who then was about 8 years old took action since the girls were apparently alone in the house. The older sister ran downstairs to make some holy water with salt, which she then sprinkled on her sister and in every corner of the house. When she was finished there were bruises around the little sister's neck, but the bruja was gone, having fled outside and up into a tree. It never bothered them again!

Even the worst evils can be repelled by fervent prayer to the Concourse on High and to ones ancestors for immediate and emphatic help. Various prayers and "sound prayers" work. "Ya Baha'u'llah!" has cleansed many a home, and the Protection Prayer revealed by the Bab is quite effective, as is Christ's "Our Father." The choices are many, and they include whatever words are in your heart at the time. A common phrase is "All negativity is banished. Only love, light and peace may enter!"

Gear like sage or sweetgrass bundles, abalone shell and feather, salt, tar water or brick dust, candles and crystals may help build our confidence.

Humility with strength and utter confidence, rather than boisterous fear are essential. A final note. Be very careful not to chase away kindly or protective spirits, because you might cause them harm. Just let them know they can leave whenever they are ready.

Components and Facets of Secretive Practices

Theurgy, magic or sorcery is the beseeching of God or other supernatural being, by the use of prayers, rituals, symbols, actions, gestures and words, which is believed to effect or affect supernatural forces. Sorcery has long been practiced by shamans, "witch doctors", cunning folk and tribal medicine men who used it to "find" the source of disease or other problem. Usually this is achieved by a slight of hand maneuver, with a physical object representing the causal factor. If a victim of illness believes strongly enough that they have been blessed by this ceremony, and that the "source" of the trouble has been removed, the ritual may assist in their recovery. If this doesn't work, a "plan B" is usually cited for the failure.

Forms of shamanic contact with the spirit world seem to be nearly universal, and their supplications to God, particular spirits and the ancestors awe the audience with magic ritual expressed in visual and eerie, audible display. It can be mesmerizing, even a bit frightening!

Unusual Voices
Early necromancy was related to shamans who "raised" the spirits of ghosts and ancestors, with whom they communicated. Necromancers, and Shamans called the dead in a voice which combined high-pitch beathy squeaking, wailing and low droning interspersed with trance-state mutterings.

These vocalizations stick with the hearer, as they are quite eerie, like the Eskimo wind witches featured in the movie "The White Dawn." These witches exacted punishment on three stranded fishermen, who had spread vice among the native people who had offered them sanctuary.

Throat singing began in Mongolia and Siberia as a way to harmonize with nature, particulary with the harmonious sounds produced by waterfalls. Waterfall music attracted deer to bask in or near the water. Throat singers, wind witches and shamans produce "music" the hearer never quite forgets. Perhaps the Norse tree singers derive from a similar background. Like living ents they also produced haunting multitoned sounds.

"**Magical thinking**" refers to the ability of the human mind to affect the physical world. Moses and His serpent staff provided us with several key examples.

Fascination with magic, and references to acts of magic, are a part of recorded history and religions. A belief that one can influence supernatural powers, by prayer, sacrifice or invocation of ancestral spirits dates back to prehistoric times.

Belief in magical realms and creatures like hobbits, fairies, or Santa Claus can also bring us joy and hope, and even inspire healing! Facination with magic and fantasy in diverse forms has pleased or awed us since Primitive times. Rituals are performed with the intention of invoking the action or presence of God or supernatural beings, with the goal of uniting humans with the divine, in a state called "henosis", a mystical oneness.

Ceremonial Magic also referred to as high or learned magic is basic to Western esotericism. Typically this is expressed in long, elaborate and complex rituals performed for certain occasions. Special gear like candles and crystals, wand or staff; even special vestments such as cloaks or hats aid practitioners in a sequence of activities involving gestures, words and symbols. The ceremony heightens the magician's power by increasing his or her confidence. This encourages both the speaker and the audience to achieve a desired result. Ceremonies are usually performed in a sequestered place.

Ceremonial magic is often synonymous with ritual magic. It draws from the Hermetic Kabalah, and Enochian magic. The source is the same. It is a system based on the invocation and commanding of various spirits.

Dr. John Dee and Edward Kelley claimed in 16th-century writings, that they received information via the so-called Enochian language, from various angels. Kelley was a medium who believed their visions gave them access to secrets contained within the apocryphal (if unreadable) Book of Enoch.

Wicca and other **contemporary pagan** religions enthusiastically embrace the occult as an integral, esoteric aspect of their mystical religious experience. Aspects of Hermeticism and Ceremonial Magic are practiced by Neopagans and Wiccans, who might see themselves as good white witches or wizards. Through prayers, rituals and spells, they act to bring good fortune to those in need. By acknowledging a strong harmonic connection to the earth, the moon and the seasons, along with the potency of crystals, talismans, charms, herbs and candles, they work to harness supernatural forces for achieving good results.

A **grimoire** is a magic textbook, a book of spells. Grimoires have long been used in Europe, by ceremonial magicians and cunning folk. Similar books can be found all across the world, including the Near East, Jamaica and Sumatra.

Typically such a book would include instructions on how to create magical objects like **talismans, charms or fetishes** which are objects believed to contain certain magical properties. They may attract good luck like a rabbit's foot, or offer protection like a Catholic medal. Conversely, an **amulet** contains natural magical properties like a crystal, or an herb that can be used for averting evil, or attracting good luck.

A talisman is made for a specific reason and must be charged with magical properties, perhaps in the presence of prayer and ritual, as in the making of holy water, to be effective.

The grimoire would also indicate how to perform magical spells and various forms of divination. It provides information on how to summon or invoke supernatural entities such as angels, spirits and demons. In many cases the books themselves are also believed to be charged with magical powers. The sacred scriptures of any monotheistic Faith are also charged with power.

Chaos Magic is a highly individualistic Neoshamanic practice, in which the individual magician borrows pieces from other belief systems, or science to suit a need. The use of a sigil is basic to chaos magic. Historically a sigil has referred to a pictorial signature of a demon or other dark entity. These days it is a symbolic representation of the magician's desired outcome. For instance a pentagram may be drawn for the purpose of protection, so the magician can focus on the battle with evil.

In much of the world a demon is considered "unclean." It may cause demonic possession. Removal often calls for the exorcism of a person or a location - by a Catholic priest, a vodun priestess, a chaos magician, or Wiccan who may be able to conjure, and control the entity.

Less intense cases may be removed by a cleansing, or a house blessing, which can be performed by a chaos magician, priest, Wiccan, a psychic medium, or any confident, dedicated spiritual human being. This was exemplified by the Costa Rican girl mentioned above under "Dealing With Negative Energies" above.

Computers connect chaos magicians, and store virtual knowledge libraries. They can test skills with simulations of ritual environments. Other sources of inspiration include ceremonial magic, eastern philosophy and world religions, science and even science fiction. Choosing one's path requires experimentation. Some chaos magicians use psychedelic drugs, "chemognosticism", so that they may view the problem from an altered state.

Chaos magicians are frequently successful in clearing up negativity because they use whatever they deem necessary to achieve the desired outcome.

Black magic has traditionally referred to the use of supernatural powers or magic for evil and selfish purposes. Its intent is to injure, intimidate or control frightened people or creatures. Controlling others with fear is a type of enslavement used by the military, or political regimes, or terrorists. Even a dead person or living person who is acting like a jerk, can become a "soul collector", in either world. This is practicing evil or sorcery of the worst kind!

Black magic is the malicious, counterpart of the benevolent white magic. Any person using a form of control, manipulation or coercion is not walking a positive spiritual path in that regard. Even jaded people who consider themselves to be "nice" should be very aware of the times they attempt to get others to do things for them.

We should be wary of people who "lord it over others" or bully the timid or weak. Control or manipulation of others is harmful to the living and to the dead. It can derail, or stop spiritual progress altogether. Negativity can well up causing victims to rebel in an outburst, sometimes quite dramatically. A good example of pernicious bullying is the making of zombies.

Magical attack is sometimes the cause of grief or misfortune. The deliberate attempt to place curses is part of the practice of dark magic. The study of curse ritual formats comprises a significant portion of witchcraft lore.

A **curse** is a magical wish that adversity, misfortune or devastating harm will befall a victim. The curse may be placed by means of a magic spell, incantation, imprecation or execration beseeching God, a natural force or a negative entity to bring about the woe.

Curses might be blocked or averted. In order to be protected from the evil eye in the Middle East a protection talisman is made from dark blue circular glass, with a circle of white around the black dot in the middle, reminiscent of a human eye. In the USA we use "God's Eyes" to protect our dreams. How ever far this evil art goes back, it is time for it to end.

A curse can also affect a location or a specified object. There are a number of places where so much blood has been spilled in hatred or warfare, that the land is actually considered to be cursed. Such a curse can remain on the land indefinitely, until it can be healed. An early written curse rests in the Archaeological Museum of Athens. It was written on a sheet of lead 2400 years ago.

Vodun in Fon and Vodu in Ewe, is a fine example of polytheism from West Africa. There are local variants but this is a basic outline. A divine female Creator called Mawu, bears similarities to Nu Wa the female Guide sent to the earliest level of human society in Africa. This may be an incredibly old remnant of "monotheism."

There is some disagreement as to whether the Creator is Mawu, or gave birth to Mawu the moon and Lisa the sun. Male and female, sun and moon are perfect examples of oppositional "duality." Other versions contend that Mawu is a combination of created and Creator, in the way Christ can be referred to as God and man. In some places Legba is seen as her male consort. Mami Wata is another remembered name for a powerful female ancestor.

Either way, Mawu bore seven children and gave each a realm of nature like plants, animals, earth and sea. Their names and prototypes may be based on prehistoric or historical individuals, or other Prophets.

Divine essences govern the forces of nature and society, while individual spirits inhabit streams, trees and rocks. Dozens of ethnic vodun spirits live side by side with, and act as defenders of, the clan, tribe or nation. This constitutes a perfect definition of "henotheism", where one God expands into a dazzling array.

Vodun practitioners found a "syncretic" relationship with Catholics, who also believe in the intercession of supernatural spirits like angels and saints.

In Haitian Vodun each family of spirits has its own female priesthood. Queen Mothers and High Priestesses officiate various activities, often by oracle. There is occasional sorcery, where harm is the goal, but this is not performed by the priestesses. This evil sorcery is the dominion of bokors.

So where are the Zombies?

There is no joke in this! It seems that the origin of zombies may have been in Africa. The practice eventually spread to Europe via Egypt and India, perhaps in the time of Hermes/Thoth. But it has been practiced more recently in Haiti and the Southern United States of America.

Bokors are sorcerers with evil and greedy intentions, who create zombies. One bokor known as Dr. John was said to use the zombies he created as his personal slaves. Yet for the most part his bread and butter came from making love potions, remedies, and protection charms of brass with loops of beads hanging from the base, mostly for children. He also held seances and did fortune telling.

In the 1900's Marie Laveau was famed for her powers. She had a dark reputation but she was devoted to healing. The people of New Orleans feared her because of wild voodoo rituals, where she danced with a large snake around her neck. The serpent was known as Li Grand Zombie.

But there were many bokors who kept zombie slave crews on hidden, outlying farms where crops like sugar were tended only at night, to keep away prying eyes. The night made it easier for the zombies, because their eyes could not tolerate the sunlight.

According to Canadian Ethnobotanist Wade Davis the main drug was derived from the poisonous tetrodotoxins of puffer fish. He mentioned one concoction which contained that toxin along with bufo toads, a crushed human infant skull, sea worm, blue lizards, mimosa and itchy peas. The ingredients were powdered and perhaps ingested, or blown into the face of an intended victim. As it entered the blood stream it caused "death" in about a half hour. The death is permanent if the toxin dose is slightly too large. Otherwise it simulates death with a deep suspended coma. Either way the victim is buried.

One Zombie named Clairvius Narcisse returned to his home town in Haiti 18 years after his burial in 1962. He told of being drugged and made a zombie. In his suspended animation Clairvius remembered his burial, and that a bokor took him from his coffin. He was revived with an antidote which caused violent spasms during the "awakening." He was then given another drug made from the zombie cucumber which put him into a trance like stupor. It is easy to see how bokors would also be referred to as necromancers, who were thought to have the power to raise the dead.

Clairvius was forced to work on a sugar plantation as a slave. Every movement was painful and difficult in his semi-comatose state. After 2 years the bokor died and Mr. Narcisse became conscious. He did not feel it was safe to return home until his brother died in 1980, since he suspected his brother betrayed him to the bokor. His senses and depth perception

were permanently damaged and he could not see straight. He said it was like his eyes were "turned in."

Some other names given to the zombie cucumber, a member of the deadly nightshade family include jimson weed, loco weed, devil's snare and thorn apple, are readily recognizable. A single purple flower on a branch bears a burr. The whole plant is poisonous and it causes delirium and photophobia, amnesia and bizzare behavior. Symptoms of one dose may last from 24 hours to two weeks. The drugs are sodium blockers. Sodium and potassium are both necessary for normal muscle function. It sounds like the poor victims were better suited for hospital recovery, than toiling in the fields at night, with creepie-crawlies, and greedy, evil bosses.

To end a zombie state the victim would need to ingest either salt or meat. There is a story of a bokor's wife who thought it would be safe to give the zombie slaves a sweet treat. But salt was one of the ingredients, and the slaves became unstupified. They then walked back towards the town. Most of them walked right through it to the grave they last remembered. I do hope the bokor's wife fled before he found out!

Salt might free them to go home, but not from the torment of residual damages. Victims' eyes may be white, with no visible pupil. They may be described as having "dead" or "unseeing" eyes because of neural and light damage. Some cannot speak but make strange noises in their throats. Zora Neale Hurston, who traveled through Haiti described a woman who had returned after 30 years of death. "She was a permanent wreck, hiding in the hospital room corner with a blank face and dead eyes."

There is now a Hatian law forbidding zombie making. Using a substance capable of mimicing death, or inducing a prolonged lethargic coma is attempted murder. If a victim is buried after receiving the drug, it is considered an act of murder no matter what the result. Thankfully many bokors have been discouraged. (Ref. *Zombies in America*, by Diane Bailey 2011)

Still drugging people into a stupor has not ended. Most recently gunpowder has been associated with sharpening aggression in animals and humans. It was said to be given to youths in Ruwanda's genocide. It was given to elephants in India who would then crushed Sikhs and other prisoners. It may also be used to enrage berserkers and fighting dogs. In all cases its ingestion is deleterious, crippling and even fatal.

Sorcery is most often associated with the secretive practices of Hoodoo in the southern United States. Known Hoodoo spells date back to the 1800s. Back in the 1700's and early 1800's **Obeah** was the word used to describe these practices.

Hoodoo jinxes and crossed conditions, assail victims, as well as a form of foot track magic where cursed objects are laid in on a path or step. They are activated when the victim walks over the object. At other times, one could leave or deliver an object to the victim after it was charged with "power" to threaten, harm or kill as in voodoo. Synonyms for hoodoo include conjuring, witching, or "rootwork." Conjuring is believed to have evolved among the slaves concentrated in the Mississippi Delta. The practice was first documented in America in 1875. It spread up the Mississippi as people left the Delta beginning in the 1930s. Practitioners integrated hoodoo with their Christian faith; so Icons of Christian saints are often found on hoodoo shrines or altars.

Spells are dependent on the intention of the practitioner and a correct "reading" of the client. Priests or sorcerers would "hoodoo" someone with potions, parapsychological power, or objects such as charms intended to bring good luck, or to cause harm. A recipient of a spell may find themselves in an altered consciousness or spiritual hypnosis, as if "under a spell." A fear reaction is usually a major component of this hypnotic effect but drugs are used, as well.

Healing and protective folk magic is the dominant focus in Vodun and Hoodoo. But because of the frightful nature of the harmful magic, there has been a great deal of misunderstanding and undeserved prejudice, which is heightened by the media including T.V. and cinema.

Germanic people used a curse form called hexing. A common hex laid by a stable-witch caused milk cows to go dry, or horses to go lame.

Removing curses

Actual curse removal or breaking is believed to require elaborate rituals and prayers. Help may come in the form of a medium who will counsel or convince the spirit who laid the curse on the person, place or object—to knock it off, and break the curse because it harms everyone—especially the one who cast it.

Folk Medicine

In England, Folk healers, also known as cunning folk or white witches practiced folk medicine, divination and healing, at least from the 1400's in literature, but in reality, from very early times. Diagnosis is reached through spiritual means and a treatment is prescribed, usually consisting of a herbal remedy, or potion. The belief is that illness is not derived from chance occurrences, but through some specific physical, spiritual or social imbalance.

Traditional African folk medicine is a holistic discipline involving spirituality, diviners, midwives, and herbalists. Practitioners are able to cure just about anything. They are effective for common conditions such as urinary tract infections, psychiatric problems, high blood pressure, epilepsy, asthma, eczema, fever, anxiety or depression, They also are noted to be effective against cholera, most venereal diseases, many cancers, benign prostate trouble, gout, wounds, burns and even ebola.

Alchemy played a significant role in the development of modern chemistry and medical science, but it differed in its inclusion of Hermetic principles. Alchemists believed in the observation of natural causes as well as the four Elements, cryptic symbolism, and mysticism as integral parts of their work.

Alchemy was socially accepted, and it was included in "The Encyclopedia of Diderot an Encyclopaedia, or a Systematic Dictionary of the Sciences, Arts, and Crafts" published in France between 1751 and 1772. Alchemists may not have understood atomic theory like modern chemists, but they developed other lines of theory and laboratory techniques, as well as pertinent terminology and experimental methods which are still in use today. Alchemy was chemistry of the subtlest kind. It allowed one to cause and observe chemical reactions, rather than waiting to observe natural chemical occurrences.

The **Emerald Tablet**, also called Smaragdine Table is a cryptic alchemic text associated with the creation of the **philosopher's stone**. The original source of the Emerald Tablet is unknown, although Hermes Trismegistus is the authority named in the text. It was translated into Latin in the twelfth century, from a book written in Arabic between the sixth and eighth centuries. Highly regarded in Europe, it was the foundation of the alchemic art and was reputed to contain the secret of "**prima materia**" the primitive formless "base" of all matter. Prima materia was considered to be the substance which fills the universal void and separates heaven and earth. It was also referred to as quintessence, or ether.

The legendary philospopher's stone was thought to be capable of turning metals like lead into gold or silver. It was also deemed capable of extending one's life, hence the name "elixir of life." It could be used for rejuvenation as well as achieving immortality.

For many centuries the philosopher's stone was the most sought after goal. It became the central symbol of the mystical terminology of alchemy, symbolizing the perfection and heavenly bliss. Efforts to discover the philosopher's stone were known as the Magnum Opus ("Great Work"), but, in the end, all efforts were unsuccessful.

By the eighteenth century alchemy and all unorthodox religious, philosophical, even some scientific ideas were under attack as being occult. Even seventeenth-century scientists, such as Sir Isaac Newton felt the sting of being labeled, when he discovered the unseen, almost "magical" force of gravity.

Ironically, some of the cruelist perversions of occult traditions were perpetrated by the church, and by civil law (see divination) below, institutions that were believed to protect human rights. Their sadistic folly bore no relationship whatsoever to the noble aspirations to find esoteric knowledge of the divine.

Astrology is based on a relationship between astronomical phenomena and events in the human world. Prophets like Ram, Abraham and Hermes spoke of our relationship to aspects of the universe, like stars, sun, moon and planets. The Indians, Chinese, and Mayans had elaborate systems for predicting terrestrial events from celestial observations.

Today, astrology affects us most often in the form of horoscopes. This method seeks to explain aspects of a person's personality, and predict future events in their life based on the positions of the sun, moon and other celestial objects present at the time of one's birth.

Throughout most of its history astrology was considered a scholarly study, and was accepted in political and academic contexts. It enjoyed a popular study like its contemporaries: astronomy, alchemy, meteorology, and medicine. At the end of the 17th century newer scientific concepts called astrology into question. It has since lost its academic appeal and declined.

Divination originally was the attempt to gain insight into a question or situation by way of a standardized process or ritual. Divination in its many forms suggested how a person should proceed with tricky matters. Diviners read signs and received oracles or omens through alleged contact with some supernatural agency. Sometimes it was a somewhat more scientific process, as with the use of gear like "water witching" or "dowsing" with divining rods made of copper.

Divination is a system which draws order from disjointed or random information like reading tea leaves so that one might gain insight into a problem at hand. It is more formal and ritualistic than regular fortune telling, but it is very subjective. Usually results are determined in a religious context as seen in traditional African folk medicine. But some types of divination were twisted into cruel, punishments, torture and even death. It is hard for

skeptics to envision a time when these practices could have been taken seriously enough to cause killing and death,

Tarot reading or **cartomancy** employs cards to gain insight into past, current and future situations, by posing a question to the cards dealt. The cards become instruments used to tap knowledge given by a spiritual guide, the collective unconscious, or the practitioner's own creative subconscious. The belief in the divinatory meaning of the cards is associated with a belief in their hidden mystical properties. A belief in cartomancy was supported suprisingly, by prominent Protestant clerics and freemasons of the 18th century.

Scrying is the practice of looking into a translucent ball or other material with the belief that one might see spiritual visions. These pictures can predict past, present, or future events. Although scrying is most commonly done with a crystal ball or mirror, any smooth surface such as a bowl of liquid, a pond, or a crystal will do.

Alternative media must be reflective, translucent, or luminescent such as stone, glass, fire, or smoke. The visions might appear when one stares. Results are thought to come from spirits or other entities, or from the reader's psychic mind. Today visions are mainly thought to come from one's subconcious or imagination.

Like other aspects of divination scrying is not a scientific method of predicting the future. A related form of "seeing" is a Ganzfeld experiment which involves sensory deprivation. Here blankness becomes the screen for scrying.

In Renaissance times, seven categories of divination were considered "forbidden arts",- geomancy along with necromancy, hydromancy, aeromancy, pyromancy, chiromancy or palmistry, and scapulimancy, which divines by oracles from scapulae and turtle plastrons. Yet these were not the worst.

Geomancy, or "earth divination" is a method that interprets markings on the ground or patterns formed by tossed handfuls of soil, rocks, or sand. A prevalent form of geomancy involves the interpretation of a series of 16 figures formed randomly by a series of throws, followed by analysis and interpretation. Geomancy was practiced by people from all social strata, and it was one of the most popular forms of divination throughout Africa and Europe during the Middle Ages and the Renaissance. Books and treatises on geomancy were published up until the 17th century when, like other occult traditions it fell out of popularity. It is dismissed by scientists and skeptics today as superstition.

Necromancy is considered to be a form of black magic or witchcraft in general. More typically it refers to summoning a spirit to appear – for the purpose of divining future events as in shamanism, or disseminating hidden knowledge or weirdly, to use the deceased as a weapon. A prime example of the latter was depicted in the movie "The Return of the King" when Aragorn called warrior spirits to honor an ancient pledge.

Necromancy was prevalent throughout antiquity with records of its practice in Babylon, Egypt, Greece and Rome. In his Geographica, Strabo refers to "diviners by the dead" to be prevalent in Persia. It was widespread among the Sabians, or "star-worshipers", and the Etruscans; and as mentioned before by bokors who stupify zombies. Today we use Medical Examiners to divine information from the dead.

Pyromancy derived visions from flames and trailing smoke wisps. Use of pyromancy probably began in prehistoric times since staring at flames was likely a mesmerizing form of entertainment.

Aeromancy used cloud formations, wind currents and cosmological events such as eclipses or comets to divine the future. Sub-types include: austromancy or wind divination, ceraunoscopy, an observation of thunder and lightning, chaomancy or aerial visions, meteors, shooting stars and nephomancy was a type of cloud divination.

Hydromancy is divination by means of water. Results are based on the color, ebb and flow of the water, or by ripples produced when pebbles are dropped in a pool. The Jesuit M.A Del Rio (1551–1608) described several methods other of hydromancy. The first method described depicts a ring hanging by a string that is dipped into a vessel of water which was shaken. A judgment or prediction is made by the number of times which the ring strikes the sides of the vessel. Other times three pebbles were thrown into standing water and observations were made from the circles formed when the objects struck or agitated the water.

Others interpreted the colors of the water and figures appearing in it. This branch of the divination proved so important that it was given a separate name - the divination of fountains, whose waters were frequently visited. In the 2nd century AD Pausanias described the fountain near Epidaurus into which loaves were thrown by worshippers hoping to receive an oracle from the goddess. Accepted loaves sank in the water, which meant good fortune, like tossing a coin into a well.

In other cases mysterious words were pronounced over a glass of water then observations were made of its spontaneous ebullience, or the feelings it evoked. Another method was to let a drop of oil fall into a vessel of water providing a mirror through which things became visible. Del Rio called this the Modus Fessanus.

Clemens Alexandrinus said German women saw events predicted by the watching the whirls and courses of rivers. To skeptics it seems a stretch to think hydromancy was anything but subjective, unless of course the river bed was dry and this somehow that suggested a drought.

Tortures and Torments

The lower nature of humanity created gruesome ways to divine information which had no valid ties to occult philosophies. Trial by ordeal and Haruspex were dispicable practices employing legalized torture and murder.

Haruspex was the study of the entrails of sacrificed chickens or sheep as they were dying. It was heavily associated with the Etruscans and Romans during the Bronze Age. Anthropomancers looked at the organs of dying men, women and young females who had been sacrificed.

Ordeals of fire and water were joined by trials by ingestion of poison, calibar bean, hemlock; or by snake bite, which is seen even in the U.S. today. The simplest form of Persian ordeals required the accused to take an oath and then drink a potion of sulphur.

Trial by ordeal was an ancient judicial practice in medieval Eurasia by which the guilt or innocence of the accused was determined by torment with dangerous, crippling or fatal consequences. The accused suffered this painful humiliation prior to prison, or execution. These "trials" date back to the tablets of Ur-Nammu and the Code of Hannurabi.

Like trial by combat trial by ordeal was considered a legal practice. The test was one of life, or death and the proof of innocence was survival. In rare cases the accused was considered innocent if they escaped injury or if their injuries healed within 3 days.

God might help the innocent by performing a miracle on their behalf. Trials by ordeal became rarer over the Late Middle Ages and thankfully were discontinued in the 16th century.

The earliest mention of the ordeal of the cauldron was in the year 510. Trial by cauldron was an ancient custom used against both freedmen and slaves in cases of theft, false witness and contempt of court. The accused was required to plunge his right hand into a boiling cauldron and pull out a ring. As Frankish influence spread throughout Europe this inhumane ordeal spread to neighboring societies. An alternative form of the ordeal required that an accused remove a stone from a pot of wrist deep, boiling water, oil, or lead. This was pretty hard to achieve with fingers half burned off. If a person was charged with three accusations, the pot was filled up to the elbow. Generally the skinless wound didn't heal within three days and the poor soul was exiled, imprisoned or executed.

Often the ordeal would take place publicly in a church. Attendees would seek to purify themselves by praying for God to reveal the truth. This horrible practice remained part of the Catholic church until the 1100's. An early example of the test was described by Gregory of Tours in the late 6th century. A Catholic saint bested a follower of the Bishop Arius who opposed the adoption of the Trinity concept during the Councils of Nycaea. Gregory said that it took the woman about an hour to grab the stone because the waters were bubbling so ferociously, but he was pleased to record that the Arian's skin boiled off up to the elbow.

Ordeal of fire – in England it was typically required that the accused walk a certain distance, usually 9 feet (2.7 metres) over red-hot ploughshares, or while holding a red-hot iron.

In Ancient Iran, people accused of cheating in contracts or lying might be asked to prove their innocence. Two examples of such ordeals included having to pass through fire or having molten metal poured on the chest. There were about 30 kinds of fiery tests. If the accused survived he was innocent; perhaps protected by Mithra and other gods.

The ordeal of cold water was part of the Code of Ur-Nammu from Mesopotamia, written in the Sumerian language 2100–2050 BC.; and also the Code of Hammurabi, a Babylonian civil law code enacted by the 6th Babylonian king Hammurabi, about 1754 BC. The latter consists of 282 laws, with punishments being adjusted for social status.

A custom of ancient Germanic tribes was to throw newborn children into the Rhine. It was thought if the child was a bastard it would drown but if legitimate it would swim.

The custom of "swimming witches" was a trial by water where floaters cast from the waters were considered witches. Sinkers were normal. In one such tale from 1792 in Stanningfield, Suffolk, an old woman let herself be swum before the community to clear her name. All other attempts to clear her name having failed. Her husband and brother held the rope at her swimming to ensure that she was not mistreated. Fortunately she sank, but was nearly dead when they dragged her out.

A man who was accused of sorcery was bound with hands and feet together and then submerged three times. He was held down in a stream with a long pole. Survival meant acquittal. Louie the Pious of France abolished this horrible practice in 829, though it reappeared in 1338 when a man accused of poaching was to be submerged in a barrel three times. If he floated afterwards he was innocent.

Gregory of Tours complained that cruel pagans cast Quirinus, bishop of the church of Sissek, into a river with a millstone tied to his neck. He floated on the surface by a divine miracle because he was not burdened with crime. https://en.wikipedia.org/wiki/Trial_by_ordeal#Ordeal_of_fire

Some of this evil treatment was due to the stupidity of civil laws. It is difficult to imagine that any of these unspeakable crimes were perpetrated in the name of God. How much nicer was the earliest Chinese community during the time of the San Huang Trio. Order was built on a trust which emphasized communication and cooperation.

Esotericism, though secret was basically the search for hidden divine knowledge, and about where we stand in the Cosmos.

Summary of Esoteric Practices

The paired thoughts of the sacred and the mundane, began, and culminated in the quest for the unity of science and religion, as given to humanity by Enoch/Hermes and every Great Prophet since.

The only evil was brought to bear by a judicial lunatic fringe, who twisted the concept of divining information into torment as mentioned above; or accidentally contacting negative energies during séances or Ouija activities. Also magical activities which were twisted to summon dark entities. These do not appear to have much of a relation to mainstream Occult Philosophy, which seems more of a utopian idealism.

A strain of Christian belief in Hermeticism and kabbalah go back at least to Renaissance times. However most Christian authorities regard all occult practice and study as heretical, from Gnosticism to late Renaissance mysticism in Europe. Some view the occult as being supernatural or paranormal. It seems to vie with their conception of what is holy. So they deem it to be the work of an opposing, malevolent entity. This kind of "black and white" thinking is reminiscent of the Creation versus Evolution debate. Why not both? God can handle it. He encompasses all.

Some occult practices such as alchemy and astrology were the forerunners of modern scientific practices. The idea of secret religions, service based organizations and clubs, are thriving today in the United States in the form of lodges, charitable organizations, sororities and fraternities, to mention a few.

But there will come a time when human unity is so strong, that the need for secrecy, initiation, and ritual will vanish altogether.

"Whensoever holy souls, drawing on the powers of heaven, shall arise with such qualities of the spirit, and march in unison, rank on rank, every one of those souls will be even as one thousand, and the surging waves of that mighty ocean will be even as the battalions of the Concourse on high. What a blessing that will be -- when all shall come together, even as once separate torrents, rivers and streams, running brooks and single drops, when collected together in one place will form a mighty sea. And to such a degree will the inherent unity of all prevail, that the traditions, rules, customs and distinctions in the fanciful life of these populations will be effaced and vanish away like isolated drops, once the great sea of oneness doth leap and surge and roll." (Abdu'l-Baha, Selections from the Writings of Abdu'l-Baha, p. 260)

Enochian Education

There is so much more to the story of Enoch including His Apothegms, founding of the Essenes, The vision of Osiris, and His Books, including the Book of Giants; which follow in the next pages.

Enoch would probably be horrified by how some of His concepts have been twisted to confuse or harm. Luckily He left us with more peaceful guidance. Some of His wise sayings are remembered as **Apothegms**, such as the following:

"Happy is he who looks at his own deeds and appoints them as pleaders to his Lord."

"None can show better gratitude for Allah's favors than he who shares them with others."

"Do not envy people for what they have, as they will only enjoy it for a short while."

"He who indulges in excess will not benefit from it."

"The real joy of life is to have wisdom." http://islamickids.tripod.com/id108.htm

Surely these Apothegms and those of other Manifestations who came to pre-literate societies, were tailored into rhymes and stories like "Mother Goose" and the Fables of Aesop. Humanity has cherished them and taught them to their children throughout the millennia.

As if this wasn't enough, Enoch is also touted as the founder of the ancient Order of **Essenes**. Josephus Flavius and Philo of Alexandria were ancient scholars who were contemporaries of the 1st century Essenes. Josephus, born at Jerusalem in 37 A.D., was the greatest historian of the Jews in that period. Philo was the greatest Jewish philosopher of the time. Both men had personal knowledge of the ancient Essenes. Both make clear that fact that Essene origin is incredibly ancient.

"Josephus declares that the Essenes have existed 'from time immemorial' and 'countless generations'. Philo agrees, calling the Essenes 'the most ancient of all the initiates' with a "teaching perpetuated through an immense space of ages."

Josephus and Philo – as well as several other ancient writers including Pliny the Elder – are in consensus ... in regard to the origin of the Essenes: Their origin is lost in pre-history with certain ancient legends linking them with Enoch..." (Brother Day D.D. see Jesus the Christ)

OSIRIS AND HERMES

The vision of Hermes gives us information regarding death and salvation and even the possible destruction of a soul, as described by Osiris, the Lord of Light.
From Edouard Schure in "The Great Initiates" (Pp. 129-168)

One day Hermes fell asleep after having reflected upon the origin of things. A heavy torpor took hold of his body but as the latter became numb, his spirit ascended into space. Then it seemed to him that an immense being, without definite form, called him by name. 'Who are you?' asked Hermes, startled.

'I am Osiris, Sovereign Intelligence, and I can unveil everything. What do you wish?'

'To look at the source of beings, O divine Osiris, to know God!'

'You will be satisfied.'

"Immediately Hermes was flooded with a blissful light. Upon its diaphanous waves the captivating forms of all beings passed. But suddenly the terrifying shadows of sinuous shapes descended upon him. Hermes was plunged into a humid chaos filled with smoke and dismal moaning. Then a voice arose from the abyss. It was the cry of light. Suddenly a faint fire burst forth from the humid depths and reached the ethereal heights. Hermes arose with it, and found himself once again in space. In the abyss the chaos became ordered; the choirs of the stars stretched out over his head, and the voice of the light filled infinity.

'Did you understand what you saw?' Osiris asked Hermes in his dream, suspended between earth and heaven.

'No,' replied Hermes

'Well then you will know. You have just seen what is for all time. The light you first saw is divine intelligence, which contains everything, including the archetypes of all beings. The gloom into which you were plunged is the material world where men of earth live. But the fire which you saw flame forth from the depths, is the Divine Word, God is the Father, the Word is the Son, their union is Life.'

'What wondrous sense has opened within me?' asked Hermes, 'I no longer see with the eyes of the body, but those of the spirit. How is this?'

'Child of dust,' said Osiris, 'it is because the Word is within you! What in you hears, sees, acts,– is the Word itself, the sacred fire, the Creative Word.'

'Since that is so,' said Hermes, 'let me see the life of the worlds, the way of the souls, whence man comes and whither he returns.'

'Let it be as you desire.'

Hermes again became heavier than a stone and fell through space like an aerolite. Finally, he saw himself at the top of a mountain, It was night; earth was dark and bare; his limbs seemed heavy as iron.

'*Lift up your eyes and behold!*' *said Osiris' voice.*

Then Hermes saw an amazing sight. Infinite space and the starry heaven enveloped him in seven luminous spheres. In a single glance Hermes saw the seven heavens above him like seven transparent, concentric globes, whose sidereal center he occupied. The last had the Milky Way as an enclosure. In each sphere a planet with a Genius of different form, sign and light revolved. While the awestruck Hermes viewed their scattered efflorescence and their majestic movements, the voice said to him:

'*Look, listen, and understand. You see the seven spheres of all life. Through them the fall of souls takes place, and also their ascension. The seven Genii are the seven rays of Word-Light. Each of them governs a sphere of the Spirit, a sphere of the life of souls. The one nearest you is the Genius of the Moon with disquieting smile and wearing a silver sickle. He presides at births and deaths. He disengages souls from bodies and draws them into his ray. –Over him, pale Mercury shows descending or ascending souls the way with his staff, which contains knowledge.—Higher still, bright Venus holds the mirror of Love where souls alternately forget and recognize each other. Above her the Genius of the Sun raises the Triumphal torch of everlasting Beauty. –Yet higher, Mars brandishes the sword of Justice. –Sitting on his throne over the azure sphere, Jupiter holds the scepter of supreme power, which is Divine Intelligence. –At the boundary of the world, under the signs of the zodiac, Saturn bears the globe of Universal Wisdom*'

'*I see* ', *exclaimed Hermes*, '*the seven regions which make up the visible and invisible world. I see the seven rays of the Word-Light, of the only God, Who penetrates and governs them by these rays…* '*Can souls die?* ', *asked Hermes.*

'*Yes,*' *answered the voice of Osiris. 'Many perish in the fatal descent. The soul is the daughter of heaven and its journey is a test. If in its wild love of matter, it loses the memory of its origin, the divine spark which was in it and which would have become brighter than a star, returns to the ethereal region, a lifeless atom, and the soul disintegrates in the whirlpool of crude elements.*'

At these words of Osiris, Hermes trembled, for a roaring storm enveloped him in a black cloud. The seven spheres disappeared beneath thick vapors. He saw human specters uttering strange cries, carried away and torn to pieces by phantoms of monsters and animals, amidst groans and endless blasphemies.

'*This,*' *said Osiris, 'is the fate of irremediably base and wicked souls. Their torture ends only with their destruction, which is the loss of all consciousness. But see, the vapors disperse; the seven spheres reappear beneath the firmament! Look this way! Do you see that host of souls trying to climb back into the lunar region? Some are pushed down to earth like flocks of birds in the blast of the storm. With a great stirring of wings, others reach the higher sphere which draws them into its revolving. Once they have arrived, they recover the vision of divine things. But now they are not content with reflecting the latter in a dream of*

"Aegypt1987027 hg" by H. Grobe - Own work. Licensed under CC BY 3.0 via Wikimedia Commons - https://commons.wikimedia.org/wiki/File:Aegypt1987027_hg.jpg#/media/File:Aegypt1987027_hg.jpg

powerless bliss. They become infused with the lucidity of conscience lighted by grief and with the strength of will acquired in battle. They become luminous, for they possess the divine in themselves and reflect it in their acts. Therefore, strengthen your soul, O Hermes, and quiet your clouded mind by watching these distant flights of souls mount to the seven spheres and scatter like hosts of sparks! For you too can follow them; it is sufficient to will it, in order to lift oneself. See how they gather into divine choirs, each under its chosen Genius! The most beautiful live in the Solar region, while the most powerful rise as far as Saturn. Some even rise to the Father, themselves becoming powers among Power. For there where everything ends, everything eternally begins, and the seven spheres intone in unison, "Wisdom! Love! Justice! Beauty! Splendor! Knowledge! Immortality!' "

THE BOOK OF ENOCH AND THE BOOK OF GIANTS

Perhaps no discussion on Enoch would be complete without mentioning the Book of Enoch attributed to Him. There are five sections to the Book: Other Watchers (angels); final Judgement; Parables of Enoch; Dream visions (like that of Osiris); and the Epistle of Enoch.

This author has tried to make sense of the Aramaic and Ethiopian translations of the Book of Enoch. One seemed nonsensical and the other was so fractured and poorly translated into English, that it had no spiritual character and was nearly impossible to read. One of the most coherent fragments, below, gives the reader an idea of the sketchiness of the material.

4Q531 Frag. 1 3[. . . I am a] giant, and by the mighty strength of my arm and my own great strength 4[. . . any]one mortal, and I have made war against them; but I am not [. . .] able to stand against them, for my opponents 6[. . .] reside in [Heav]en, and they dwell in the holy places. And not 7[. . . they] are stronger than I. 8[. . .] of the wild beast has come, and the wild man they call [me].

It does appear to describe a giant form of Primitive human "the wild man they call [me]." There is mention of Giants (Nephilim) and possible cross breeding, (perhaps between types of humans) in Genesis 6.

These beings for the most part perished in the flood along with many modern humans. The flood likely wiped out a lot of residual Primitive diversity.

We can appreciate the efforts of the unknown editor in painting a picture.

"Many of the legends about Enoch were collected already in ancient times in several long anthologies. The most important such anthology, and the oldest, is known simply as "The Book of Enoch," comprising over one hundred chapters. It still survives in its entirety (although only in the Ethiopic language) and forms an important source for the thought of Judaism in the last few centuries B.C.E.

Significantly, the remnants of several almost complete copies of 'The Book of Enoch' in Aramaic were found among the Dead Sea Scrolls, and it is clear that whoever collected the scrolls considered it a vitally important text. All but one of the five major components of the Ethiopic anthology have turned up among the scrolls. But even more intriguing is the fact that additional, previously unknown or little-known texts about Enoch were discovered at Qumran. The most important of these is 'The Book of Giants.'

Enoch lived before the Flood, during a time when the world, in ancient imagination, was very different. Human beings lived much longer, for one thing; Enoch's son Methuselah, for instance,

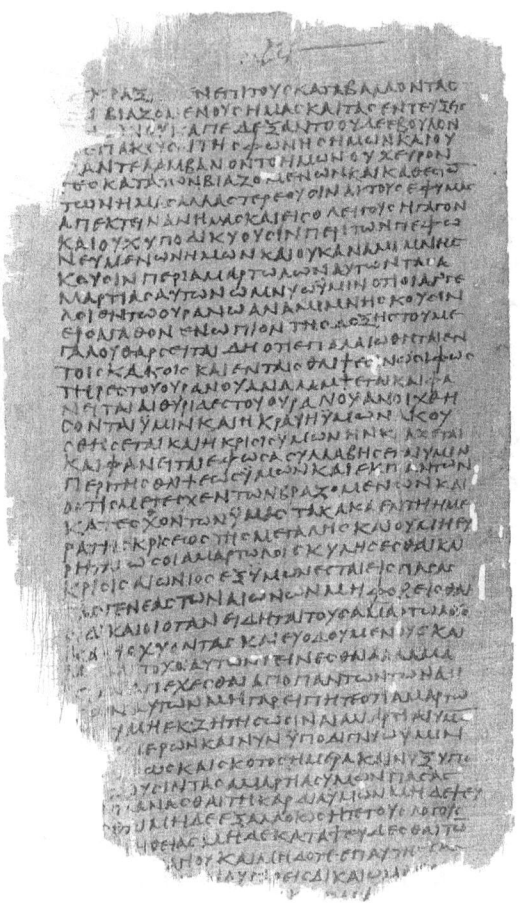

Book of Giants fragment [Public domain], via Wikimedia Commons

attained the age of 969 years. Another difference was that angels and humans interacted freely – so freely, in fact, that some of the angels begot children with human females. This fact is neutrally reported in Genesis (6:1-4), but other stories view this episode as a source of the corruption that made the punishing flood necessary. According to The Book of Enoch, the mingling of angel and human was actually the idea of Shemihazah, the leader of the evil angels, who lured 200 others to cohabit with women. The offspring of these unnatural unions were giants 450 feet high. The wicked angels and the giants began to oppress the human population and to teach them to do evil. For this reason God determined to imprison the "angels" until the final judgment and to destroy the earth with a flood. Enoch's efforts to intercede with heaven for the fallen angels were unsuccessful (1 Enoch 6-16).

Enoch elaborates on the exploits of the giants, especially the two children of Shemihazah, Ohya and Hahya. Most of the content of the present fragments concerns the giants' ominous dreams and Enoch's efforts to interpret them and to intercede with God on the giants' behalf.

Since no complete manuscript exists of "Giants," its exact contents and their order remain a matter of guesswork. Most of the content of the present fragments concerns the giants' ominous dreams and Enoch's efforts to interpret them and to intercede with God on the giants' behalf." – Chad Jones in Ocean (Other Apocrypha, The Book of Giants, in The Book of Enoch)

Gilgamesh was a giant...! (See Noah)

All we know from **Genesis** is that Enoch lived 365 years and walked with God. Then, He was not!

This is because He left and went to Egypt, where He was known to be a Supreme Manifestation, a Scribe who put together a coherent system of writing, and an Educator. He was cherished by the Greeks as Hermes, as Thoth to the Egyptians, and as Idris to Mohammad and Baha'u'llah.

Libraries of Egypt were filled with His philosophies and scientific contributions. He is the source of apocryphal texts, and His followers may also have included the Order of the Essenes.

RAM OR RAMA

"O Agni, Holy Fire! Purifying fire! You who sleep in the wood, and ascend in shining flames on the altar, you are the heart of sacrifice, the fearless wings of prayer, the divine spark hidden in everything, and the glorious soul of the sun!"
– Vedic hymn attributable to Rama

Ram's story covers a lot of time and even more geographic territory. He unfurled His gentle teachings throughout Central Europe, down the length of India, and all the way to Ceylon, long before the Indo-European languages broke apart.

In the Persian scriptures He is referred to as Yima, and sometimes Jamshid. Ram's renewal of monotheistic Faith became the source of **Proto-Indo-Iranian religions.** This primal chord of Faith later split into: Indian (Krishna); Iranian (Zoroaster) and; ancient Celtic threads, which spread across southern Eurasia, India and west to the Emerald Isles. All three religions share common language and concepts. including a universal force "rta" in Sanskrit, and "asha" in Avestan.

There will be more time spent on Ram, whose tale is long, detailed and free flowing, than some of the others. It is followed by a piece on Aesculapius and Abaris, who are arguably side stories of the Ram's healing abilities.

This chapter draws very heavily on Edouard Schure's inspired tome, *The Great Initiates*, chapters on Rama pages 35-71 selectively, because it is so good! Quotes, unless otherwise noted, are his. It would be good to remember that Schure was influenced by Antoine Fabre d'Olivet 1767-1825, before him. So some quotes have traces of ethnocentrism. Back then humans were divided into colored races. This is an outdated thought and not one condoned by this author. Besides, **the early Aryans, as it turns out were brown skinned!** White toned skin was a later development around 12,000 years ago.

The Eden of Ram

"Dense forest still covered the land from the Atlantic Ocean to the Arctic Seas, in Western, Central, and Southern Asia as well as Europe and Siberia. In the vast reaches of land now called Iran and Iraq, around and north of the Caspian and Black Seas, through the Ukraine and parts of Mongolia; and stretching through the steppe east and north to the Altai Mountains in southern Siberia. Green coasts, …dreamy rivers and somber lakes mist shrouded mountains, uncultivated plains of buffalo, and deer. Some would refer to these people as Hyperboreans (giants from the far north – beyond the north wind). They lived

as loosely aligned, nomadic warrior tribes. They generally had blonde or red hair and beards, with blue or green eyes. They loved the wild horses that shook their manes in the wind, and finally tamed the thundering herds.

"People of light skin and hair, came from the far northern boreal forests with stone tipped arrows and spears. They were accompanied by dogs and reindeer. Lead by brave men and clairvoyant women, they worshiped the sun and sacred fire. They fashioned flint knives, hatchets, bow and arrow, and slings, with which they killed wolf, bear, aurochs, and panther. Clan and tribe existed. A leader might have been buried with his weapons and horse. A practice carried on by a variety of later groups."

We do not have much actual information of Ram's material culture, so here is a glimpse of their descendants, the Scythians, who had a reputation as warriors and were known to be skilled in sneak attacks. It is said they used barbed and poisoned arrows of several types, and enjoyed a nomadic life centered on horses – they were "fed from horse-blood" according to Herodotus a fifth century Greek historian and ethnographer.

He described them in detail: "their costume consisted of padded and quilted leather trousers tucked into boots, and belted or open tunics. They rode with no stirrups or saddles, just saddle-cloths." Some women wore conical hats, as spiritual antennas, that resembled the topper of a Halloween witch. Some men resembled Tolkien dwarves, with long wild hair and beards, and donning floppy caps.

Herodotus also reported that Scythians used hemp, both to weave their clothing and to cleanse themselves in its smoke. It was also used to induce trance and divination by their soothsayers. Various groups of Scyths were supplanted by Celts, Sarmatians, and later Germanic Barbarians, as well as the Indo-Aryan peoples of India.

The Histories (Herodotus), is considered as the founding work of history in Western literature. Written from the 450s to the 420s BC." It serves as a record of the ancient traditions, politics, and geography of Western Asia, Greece, and North Africa. Cultural information can also be inferred from studying the Takla Makan mummies.

Desert Mummies

Mummified remains from 3800 years ago suggest that descendants of Ram's folk were quite tall 6-7 feet, or more. Aryan burials, desiccated in the Takla Makan desert of the Tarim Basin include a tall red-haired "Cherchen man" who wore a red twill tunic and tartan leggings. A small 1-year-old baby whose brown hair protruded from under a red and blue felt cap had two stones positioned over its eyes.

"The mummies share many typical Caucasoid body features (elongated bodies, angular faces, recessed eyes), and many of them have their hair physically intact, ranging in color from blond to red, to deep brown, and generally long, curly and braided... Their costumes and especially textiles may indicate a common origin with Indo-European Neolithic clothing.

The first thing you notice about Cherchen Woman (referred to as 'red-headed beauty') with red tattoos on her face and red yarn drawn through her earlobes is that her chin strap failed to hold her jaw shut. When a mummy's mouth is open like this it is called a mummy gape... She and the others were all painted with a yellow substance that is believed to help preserve them. Like the Cherchen Man, she has multiple tattoos on her face, and red yarn through her ear lobes. She is over six feet tall, has braided hair and took lots of clothes with her to the grave. She and the other mummies that were found with her are on display at the Museum in Urumchi where she is displayed in her long red dress and deerskin boots. The mummy of this three month old baby found with them has little blue stones covering her eyes and tiny wisps of red wool in her nostrils. All bundled up in a red garment with black striping on the sleeves with a blue cap, she had with her a cow horn cup and a sheep udder nursing bottle. Clothing indicates they were all part of the same household buried approximately 1000 B.C. Cherchen Man was around fifty years old and 6 feet 6 inches tall. He had ten hats with him. One hat looks Roman, another like a Merlin's conical magician hat, a Robin Hood cap, and a Monica Lewinski beret. They would all go well with his purple-red-brown, two piece suit; his long braided hair and would be complimented by the red strand of wool looped through both of his ear lobes. According to Dr. Barber, "Passing from the face, one's eye jumps between the violently colored leggings and the purple-red-brown two-piece suit that covers most of the man's body. Originally the man wore soft white deerskin boots to above his knees–the left one is still there, but the right one has been torn away; revealing horizontal stripes of gaudy red, yellow, and blue...

There are signs of mistreatment in one mummy, a female perhaps a sacrificial victim from another tribe. For whatever reason, she was treated horribly! Her eyes were gouged out, her arms are missing beneath the elbow joints, and the pelvis, legs and feet are missing."

"China's Mystery Mummies" (http://library.thinkquest.org/J003409/china.htm)

The so-called "Witches" of Subeshi wore 2-foot-long black felt conical hats with a flat brim. Also found at Subeshi was a man who had an operation on his neck. The incision was sewn with sutures made of horsehair. "Tarim Mummies" http://en.wikipedia.org/wiki/Tarim_mummies

Schure tells us something about the spiritual state of Ram's folk.

"But how was religion born? It has been said that it arose out of the fear of primitive man, face to face with nature. But fear has nothing in common with reverence and love. It does not unite fact and idea, visible and invisible, man and God. As long as man did nothing but tremble before nature, he was not yet man. He became man when he seized the link which connected him with the past and future, with something superior and beneficent, and when he worshiped that mysterious unknown. But how did he worship for the first time?

From the most remote times, visionary women prophesied under trees. Each tribe had its great prophetess, like the Volüspá of the Scandinavians. These women, at first nobly inspired, became ambitious and cruel. The good prophetesses changed into evil magicians. At first, they were doers of only good, but as the age deteriorated, they became corrupted and power hungry abusing their gifts, they eventually demanded human sacrifices.

At first brave warriors, who scoffed at death came forth to sacrificial altar voluntarily.

Left to the mercy of ambition and individual passion, inspiration degenerates into superstition, courage into ferocity, the sublime ideal of sacrifice, into an instrument of tyranny and sinister and cruel exploitation. They instituted human sacrifices, and the blood flowed continuously over the dolmens, to the sinister chants of the priests and the approving shouts of the ferocious onlookers.

A young priest named "Ram," rebelled against the bloody cult. He had travelled through parts Europe, Asia and later the 'southern countries' (including Egypt). "Fascinated by his personal knowledge and this modesty, the dark skinned southerners shared with him their secret knowledge. When He returned to the northern country, he was appalled at the increase in human blood sacrifices born of superstition and ambition. He saw in it the ruin of His race.

Then came a calamitous plague, a terrible disease brought back from the southern men fell on the people and Ram saw it as a punishment for the sacrilegious blood cult. The

entire body became covered with black spots and the breath became foul. Swollen limbs eaten by ulcers became deformed, and the sick person died in excruciating pain. The breath of the living and the smell of the dead spread the disease widely.

The stupefied northerners fell and died by the thousands in their forests, abandoned even by the birds of prey. Deeply sorrowful, Ram vainly looked for a means of salvation."

First Dream

"He was in the habit of meditation under an oak tree in a glade...One evening he fell asleep at the foot of the tree. In his sleep it seemed to him that a loud voice was calling him by name, and he thought he awakened. Then he saw before him a man of majestic height, clothed like himself in a white robe... He carried a rod, around which a snake was coiled. The astonished Ram was about to ask the stranger what it meant, but the latter, taking him by the hand, made him stand up and showed a beautiful branch of mistletoe on the very tree at the foot of which he had been resting. 'O Ram!' he said, 'There is the remedy you seek.' Then he took from his breast a little gold pruning knife, a golden sickle, (perhaps like Yima's golden dagger) *cut the branch and gave it to him. He murmured a few words about the way to prepare the mistletoe, and disappeared.*

Ram awakened fully, feeling very deeply comforted. An inner voice told him that he had found salvation. He prepared the mistletoe (of the oak tree, preserved by the Celts of Europe) *according to the instructions of the divine friend with the golden sickle. Then he made a sick man drink this brew in fermented liquor, and the patient was cured. The marvelous healings He brought about made Ram famous. He was summoned everywhere for healing work. His disciples travelled all over... with branches of mistletoe, and were considered divine messengers of their master....From this time on, the mistletoe became a sacred plant.*

Ram perpetuated its fame by instituting the holiday of Noel, or Day of the New Salvation, which he placed at the beginning of the year, calling it the Night Mother of the universe, or of the great renewal. As for the mysterious Being Ram had seen in a dream and who had shown him the mistletoe, in the esoteric tradition of the light skinned men of Europe, he is called Aesc-hely-hopa, which means 'hope for salvation is in the forests.; The Greeks called him Aesculapius, the genius of medicine who holds the magic rod in the form of a caduceus.

This news [of healing] *spread to the ocean, hailed as a joyful event by some, as an outrageous sacrilege by others. Their power threatened, the priestesses began to scream curses and hurl death sentences against him.*

At that time, each Eurasian tribe had its rallying sign in the form of an animal which symbolized its chosen qualities. Some chiefs nailed cranes, eagles, or vultures to the framework of their wooden houses; others, the heads of wild boars or buffalo. This is the origin of the coat of arms. But the chosen emblem of his people was the bull, which they called Thor, the sign of brute force and violence.

"Ram loved by some, hated by others, created a new symbol for his following. He took the figure of the ram, a courageous, peaceful leader of the flock"

The symbol of the ram or lamb was also applied to Enoch, and later, to Jesus the Christ.

The people of the north divided into two camps. Ram's banner fluttered peacefully. The enemies, who feared a great change was imminent flew the banner of the bull, threatening opposition. A fearful war was imminent.

"Nevertheless, Ram 'the inspired one of peace', had broader plans. He wanted to cure his people of a moral wound more disastrous than the plague... Ram worried, He meditated. If war were let loose, would this not intensify the evil? ....and utterly destroy His people. In sleep, an answer came."

Second Dream

"The stormy heaven was filled with dark clouds which swept over the mountains and moved above the bending trees of the forest. Standing on a rock, a wild-haired woman was about to strike a fine warrior who was tied before her. 'In the name of the ancestors, Stop!' shouted Ram, throwing himself upon the woman, The Druidess threatening her adversary, gave Ram a look as piercing as the blade of a knife. But the thunder rolled in the thick clouds, and amidst a flash of lightening a dazzling figure appeared. The forest paled before it. The Druidess fell as if thunderstruck, and the bonds of the captive having been broken, looked at the shining giant with a gesture of defiance... Ram did not tremble, for in the features of the apparition he recognized the divine being who had already spoken to him beneath the oak tree. This time he appeared more beautiful, for his entire body shone with light.

And Ram saw that he was in an open temple with broad columns. In the place of the sacrificial stone, an altar was raised. Nearby stood the warrior, whose eyes still feared death. The woman lying on the flagstones appeared to be dead. And now the heavenly genius carried a torch in his right hand; in his left hand was a cup. He smiled benevolently, saying, 'Ram, I am pleased with you. Do you see this torch? It is the sacred fire of the divine Spirit. Do you see this cup? It is the cup of Life and Love. Give the torch to the man, the cup to the woman. Ram did as his genius (His Lord) commanded him. Hardly was the torch in the man's hand and the cup in the woman's that the fire lighted of itself on the altar, and both shone transfigured in the light, like the divine husband and wife. At the same time the temple grew large; its columns mounted to heaven; its vault became the firmament. Then, carried by his dream, Ram saw himself borne to the top of a mountain under the starry sky. Standing near him, his genius explained the meaning of the constellations, and in the flaming signs of the zodiac.

Wonderful spirit, who are you?' Ram asked the genius. And he genius replied,' I am called Deva Nahusha, divine Intelligence, you will spread my light over the earth, and I shall always come at your call. Now, be on your way. Go!' And with his hand, the genius pointed toward the East."

An eviction of sorts, similar to Adam?

"In this dream as in a flash of lightning, Ram saw his mission and the great destiny of his [people]. From that moment he no longer hesitated. Instead of igniting the spark of war among the peoples of Europe, he decided to take the best of his (people, like Yima) into Asia.

The human sacrifices would be abolished forever...(replaced) in each home, by husband and wife joined in a single prayer, in a hymn of adoration."

They would stand near the altar, a visible symbol of the celestial fire, which would unite family, clan tribe and all peoples—a centered symbol of God on earth.

But first they must gather those who would make the journey, away from battle, to the east.

"Lighted fires, kept burning for several months on the mountains, the signal for the mass migration of all who wished to follow the Ram. Mostly, they were young, people yearning

for adventure. The tremendous migration, directed by that great shepherd of peoples, moved slowly in the direction of central Asia. They left carvings of huge ram's heads in the rocks of the Caucasus Mountains, on the way. Ram proved himself worthy of his great mission. He smoothed out difficulties, read thoughts, predicted the future, healed the sick, calmed the rebels, set courage aflame...Ram ...conceived a social law as an expression of divine law. [He] made friends with the Turanians, who inhabited upper Asia, then down through Iran, founded the city of Ver, which Zoroaster later called an admirable city.

He used magic spells against the priests of decadent cults, who kept enormous snakes and pterodactyls, rare survivors, which were worshiped like gods, and which terrified the masses. They made these snakes eat the flesh of captives."

There were recorded fights between black and white magic, especially in the passage through India, which was a series of separate and oppositional kingdoms. Ram's white, magic of course, was due to supreme power, humility and unconditional love!

"Sometimes Rama appeared unexpectedly in these temples with torches, driving out, frightening and subduing both serpents and priests. Sometimes he appeared in the midst of his enemies, exposed and defenseless among those who sought his death, departing again without anyone having dared touch him. When those who had allowed him to escape were questioned, they answered that upon meeting his gaze they were petrified, or that, while he was speaking, a mountain of brass (perhaps the blazing light of the "Farr") was placed between them and him, and they could not see him."

Following Deva Nahusha's bidding, he went east as far as He could go.

"Finally, as a consummation of his work...the epic tradition of India attributed to Rama, the conquest of Ceylon and the black magician Ravana, on whom the white magician showered down fire, they built a bridge over the sea by means of an army of monkeys, closely resembling some primitive tribe of bimanous savages."

Bimanous means having two hands distinct in form and function from the feet like all human groups. This infers that Hanuman did not look much like the other humans.

A second version is that a courageous but ill-favored man with a "monkey-like" face built a boat, and bravely ferried Rama across the water. Before the early seafaring exploits of the Denisovans the idea that anyone had seafaring abilities in those ancient times – was a real stretch! The next cultures known to build and sail ships were the Phoenicians and the Romans thousands of years later. Again, this reference to the noble **Hanuman** very clearly seems to indicate **an ancestral human form**.

One Last Dream

"He saw himself once more in the forests of his youth. He was young again, wearing the linen robe. The moon shining, it was the holy night, the Night-Mother, when people await the rebirth of the sun and the New Year. Rama was walking under the oak trees, listening to the voices of the forest.

A beautiful woman came to him. She was wearing a magnificent crown. Her hair was the color of gold, her skin the whiteness of snow, and her eyes had the deep luster of the sky after a storm. She said to him, I was the savage Druidess; through you I have become the radiant wife. And now my name is Sita. I am the woman glorified by you. I am the white race; I am your wife. O, my master and my king, is it not for my sake that you crossed rivers, charmed peoples and deposed kings? This is the reward. Take this crown in your hand, put it on your head and

rule the world with me.' She knelt humbly and submissively, offering him the crown of the earth. Its precious stones radiated a thousand lights, the rapture of love smiled into the woman's eyes and the soul of the great Rama, shepherd of the peoples, was touched. But above the forests Deva Nahusha...appeared and said to him, 'If you place that crown upon your head, you will see me no longer... Choose! Either listen to her or follow me.' Sita, still kneeling, looked at her master, her eyes overflowing with love, pleadingly awaiting his answer. ..He looked deep into Sita's eyes, placed his liberating hand on the woman's forehead, blessed her, and said 'Farewell! You are free. Do not forget me!' immediately the woman disappeared like a lunar phantom. Rama became old again. The dream showed him the fulfillment of his mission. Rama assembled the kings and representatives of the people, saying to them, 'I do not desire the supreme power you offer me. Keep your crowns and observe My law. My task is finished. I am retiring to the mountains of Airyana-Vaeia. From there I shall watch over you. Guard the sacred fire! The symbol of the divine unity of all things. If it should happen to die out, (and you fail to worship the One Creator) I shall reappear among you as a judge and terrible avenger!

Ram's crowning work, the pre-eminently civilizing instrument created by him, was the new role he gave to woman. Until that time, man had considered woman either as a wretched slave whom he overburdened and brutally mistreated, or as the turbulent priestess of the oak tree and rock, from whom he sought protection and who ruled him, in spite of himself – a fascinating, dreadful sorceress whose oracles he feared and before whom his superstitious heart trembled.

Human sacrifice was woman's revenge when she sank the knife into the fierce male tyrant's heart. Outlawing this horrible cult and reestablishing woman in man's estimation in her divine function as wife and mother, Ram made her the priestess of the hearth, the guardian of the sacred fire, the equal of her husband, the one who joined with him in prayer." (Quotations above, from *The Great Initiates* by Schure, Pp. 52-62)

This practice of families worshipping in the home was used widely through the ages and is used by many people today, as an alternative to churches.

The Hadith is a collection stories about or attributed to Mohammad, though they are not part of the sacred revealed verses of the actual Qu'ran, which is filled with chapters about the Prophets similar to the Bible.

In the Hadith a tale recalls that after leaving Eden, Adam and Eve were separated. They searched for each other, and finally reconciled at the Plain of 'Arafat, which means recognition. This is similar to the resolution of women's betrayal, and reinstatement with a new role, in the Ram story.

"The Leader of the people, the most blessed monarch" – Zoroaster is praising His predecessor, Ram.

An Epic Journey

Ram's name was changed to Rama as His people pushed into India, still following the commandment to head "East." Rama was a gifted leader. It is said He caused streams to burst forth in the desert, and put a second epidemic away with a plant called "homa" (in Greek it was "amomon," and in Egypt "persea"), from which He extracted a healing essence. Homa, a Sanskrit word for "offerings," was not only a major healing medicine, but it also became a sacrificial offering. *"This plant became sacred among His followers, replacing the mistletoe of the oak tree, preserved by the Celts of Europe."* – Great Initiates Edouard Schure 1961

Seasonal Festivals

When Ram settled in greater Iran, at the gates of the Himalayas, He ordained four festivals to be held during the equinoxes and solstices. These holy day celebrations remained throughout ancient Pagan tradition and still survive in some form in most Faiths to this day. We owe him the 12-month year and the signs of the zodiac. Rama's astrology came far earlier than the knowledge of the universe brought by such Manifestations as Enoch/Hermes of Abraham. That is why the earlier work of the Upanishads and other ancient wisdom are so beautifully amazing!

During the spring **"Naw Ruz" or Oestra (Easter)** is a regeneration of the earth and the Ancient Faith. Complete with signs of birth and new growth like eggs, chicks, bunnies and grass. It is still celebrated around the earth. This time is also dedicated to the love of husband and wife. May Day celebrations are an extension of this thought.

The **summer or harvest** belonged to the children who offered the fruit of their labor to the parents.

During the **autumn harvest** the parents were honored and they gave fruit to the children as a sign of rejoicing." (Perhaps the beginning of "trick or treat"?) Harvest was a time of celebration and thanksgiving for God's plentiful bounty.

Some celebrate Halloween, the Day of the Dead, All Souls (Saints) Day, or All Hallowed Eve in autumn, but Ram had intended it to be part of the sacred Noel of winter. Schure tell us:

"And Noel, dedicated to new-born children, the fruits of love conceived in spring and a festival dedicated to the souls of the dead, to the ancestors. A point of connection between the visible and the invisible, this religious observance was both a farewell to souls in flight, and a mystical greeting to newborn children. On this holy night, the ancients assembled in the sanctuaries of Airyana-Vaeia as they had formerly in the forests. With fires and chants they celebrated the renewal of the earthly and solar year, the germination of nature in the heart of winter the trembling of life before the abyss of death. They sang of the universal kiss of heaven given to earth, and the triumphant birth of the new sun from the great night-Mother. Thus, Ram linked the human life, with the cycle of the seasons and with the movements of the stars." – Schure

Noel, or Yule–lights in the winter forest. Who among us doesn't love winter celebrations, with glowy lights, trees, fires, snow and smiles (at least in pictures)? The winter equinox, known as the holy Night Mother, still feels sacred. Perhaps it was a very good time to celebrate the birth of Jesus the Christ, after all!

Ram was born into a herding tribe. But like the other "Firsts," he furthered agriculture by showing men how to till and sow seed in the soil. He initiated a class system for a peaceful, expanding society: priest, warrior, artisan and farmer/laborer. These blended into harmonious groups necessary for a growing society.

He revealed a code of laws and required people to elect their leaders and judges. He forbade slavery, murder, and of course human sacrifice! His people were known by neighbors as the cult of regenerating fire, which would bring about mankind's happiness. For a while idol worship was at bay, and the people worshipped only one bountiful Great Spirit.

Ram was the great Healer! Curing both spiritual and physical plagues. He wielded the Healing staff, the Caduceus used to signify medical aid, or peace on the battlefield, much like the red cross of later times.

He abolished blood sacrifice, instead offering incense smoke, such as sandalwood or homa, on the altar. He revealed laws and a plan for a peaceful society. His sacred teachings pushed civilization forward and out of decay across much of Eurasia and India.

Rama's words came in a Proto Indo-European language, which preceded Persian, Celtic and Sanskrit, yet He **established three** great world-wide Faiths; seeding the religions of the **Ancient Pagans**, **Persians** and **Hindus**.

"**Of all religions, Thou art the Source**" – Svetesvatara Upanishad

God through His servant Rama is the source of some ancient Pagan Lore, Vedic Scriptures the Aranyakas, meaning "Forest Books"; and as Yima or Jamshid in the Persian Yasht, and the Shahnamah.

Note: There are paintings associated with Ferdowski's epic poem the Shahnama, which look very much like the paintings of gods, goddesses, and demons in Tibetan religious art, including most Thangkas.

This eye-catching wild style of painting boldly colored figures in the air on a backdrop of squiggly clouds, or figures under the earth suggests some connections going back hundreds or thousands of years between Persia and China. We know that there was a connection between Krishna and Fu-Xi, but this suggests something much earlier. Could it go back as far as the late Mesolithic or early Neolithic? I wish I knew. Ram's descendants did move east into the Takla Makan desert and Mongolia. It could make sense.

He showed us the equal blending of the spiritual and material in Yin/Yang. I have seen some describe it as Ahura Mazda, God *versus* Ahriman, Evil – but that sounds like a battle between gods, and is simply dualistic rather than a human balance.

Ram ushered in the dawn of a new age! He set a **new calendar**, and gave us the **four festivals.** He also brought us the signs of the Zodiac, the Endless Knot, advances in agricultural technology, and bade our allegiance to the Endless Divine Fire.

"Through his strength, genius and kindness, say the sacred books of the Orient, Rama became master of India, and spiritual king of the earth, priests and kings bowed down before him as heavenly benefactor. Under the sign of the ram His missionaries spread afar the Aryan (Noble) Law which proclaimed equality of the conquered, the abolition of human sacrifice and slavery, respect for the woman in the home, the worship of ancestors and the institution of the sacred fire, a visible symbol of the nameless God." – Schure

ASCLEPIUS / AESCULAPIUS / ABARIS

Across Eurasia tribes celebrated the seasonal holidays and astounding healings attributed to Ram, but some called His name either Aesculapius, Asclepius, or Abaris who was sent by Apollon. The healing herbs used in these stories are often the same, mistletoe and homa.

Below is the story of the cutting of Mistletoe with a golden sickle to use a curative, and incite lovers to bear a new generation. This is followed by a note on Homa, also a potent medicine.

The sacrifice of the bulls **was not** the original intent. The noble Pagan Faith was beginning to fade.

"During the ceremony they collected the Mistletoe on the sixth day of the moon. White robed Druids clipped the mistletoe with a small golden pruning knife or sickle; while two white bulls (reminiscent of Gayomart's moon white bull) are bound by the horns and sacrificed partially in hopes to bring fecundity to barren animals, and prosperity to all." – Schure

Homa and Early "Salvation"

Homa or Sauma (from the Iranian verb form "sav" means "to press, to crush") was used for physical and spiritual healing. So it would not be surprising to find "sav" as the root of the words salvation or savant. Homa and mistletoe saved men from physical death and spiritual decrepitude. The same situation exists in every Dispensation and age. Whenever we read about "Raising the Dead" the topic is both physical *and* spiritual.

Later ephedra or other hallucinogen was substituted, and used in cultic rituals for anesthesia, for sacrifices, visions and intoxication. Its cultic use was denounced by Zoroaster, for like many spiritual matters, the use of ephedra **became a decadent corruption** of the original intent; much like the blood of sacrificed bulls!

Abaris is sometimes depicted as a kindly bearded man holding a serpent entwined staff. To the Greeks, He was a respected god of medicine, said to have purified Knossos and Sparta, as well as other areas, from plagues. He was able to restore the dead to life.

The Norse and Greek Pagan traditions give, vague reference to the healing tale of Indo European Faith.

"Hyperborea was a theocracy ruled by three priests of the god of healing, Apollon. These gigantic kings, known as the Boreades, were sons or descendants of the north wind, Boreas. Their capital contained a circular temple dedicated to Apollon; asses were sacrificed in his honor." "Aspa" was the word for horses. In early Iran horses were very important, and were killed and buried, with great leaders.

(They) were a musical race that also celebrated Apollon's divinity with a constant festival featuring music, song and dance. The hymns were joined by the sweet song of circling white Hyperborean swans. Their most famous Prophet, Abaris was given a magic arrow by Apllon, with which he performed healings of the soul and body through incantations." – Herodotus

Reports of His deeds spread far and wide – even to other nations. Not only had He cured the sick, but brought the dead (both spiritually and physically) back to life again. Of the tattered legends that surrounded His ability to restore life, one of the more coherent is this:

"Aesculapius was once shut up in the house of Glaucus, whom he was trying to cure, and while he was standing absorbed in thought, there came a serpent which twined round the staff, and which he killed. Another serpent then came carrying in its mouth an herb with which it recalled to life the one that had been killed (Now, presumably there were two snakes entwined around the staff). Aesculapius henceforth made use of the herb with the same effect upon other men." This may have contributed to the twisted thought of necromancy, where magic could be used to bring the dead back to "life." The healer received the remedies for diseases, which usually came to him in a dream.

The snake bearing Asclepian staff is an ancient sign of healing. It has also been called the Herald's Wand of Hermes or the Caduceus. It was also used, similar to the Red Cross, to symbolize a truce, in war.

The difference between this recollection and the previous tale of Lord Rama, is that in this legend the snake grants the power of healing, not God's angel.

This Greek tale gives us an insight into the fading of an older religion separated by a great distance either through time or space. By the time the Greeks told this tale the events had passed by many thousands of years.

Nowhere is the Greek commitment to Asclepius' healing more apparent than in **The Oath of Hippocrates,** Circa 2400 years ago, which stated: *"By the Aesclepiads of Kos, I swear by Apollo the physician, and Aesculapius, and Health (Hygeia), and All-heal (Panacea), and call all the gods and goddesses to witness, that I will observe and keep this underwritten oath, to the utmost of my power and judgment. I will reverence my master who taught me the art. Equally with my parents, will I allow him things necessary for his support, and will consider his sons as brothers. I will teach them my art without reward or agreement; and I will impart all my acquirement, instructions, and whatever I know, to my master's children, as to my own; and likewise to all my pupils, who shall bind and tie themselves by a professional oath, but to none else. With regard to healing the sick, I will devise and order for them the best diet, according to my judgment and means; and I will take care that they suffer no hurt or damage.*

Nor shall any man's entreaty prevail upon me to administer poison to anyone; neither will I counsel any man to do so. Moreover, I will get no sort of medicine to any pregnant woman, with a view to destroy the child.

Further, I will comport myself and use my knowledge in a godly manner.

I will not use a knife to cut for stones, but will commit that affair to those who are trained.

Whatsoever house I may enter, my visit shall be for the convenience and advantage of the patient; and I will willingly refrain from doing any injury or wrong from falsehood, and (in an especial manner) from acts of an amorous nature, whatever may be the rank of those who it may be my

duty to cure, whether mistress or servant, bond or free.

Whatever, in the course of my practice, I may see or hear (even when not invited), whatever I may happen to obtain knowledge of, if it be not proper to repeat it, I will keep sacred and secret within my own breast.

If I faithfully observe this oath, may I thrive and prosper in my fortune and profession, and live in the estimation of posterity; or on breach thereof, may the reverse be my fate."

"1590. Apollo Entrusting Chiron with the Education of Aescalapius - etching - Washington DC, NGA" by Hendrik Goltzius Workshop - National Gallery of Art. Licensed under Public Domain via Wikimedia Commons - https://commons.wikimedia.org/wiki/File:1590._Apollo_Entrusting_Chiron_with_the_Education_of_Aescalapius_-_etching_-_Washington_DC,_NGA.jpg#/media/File:1590._Apollo_Entrusting_Chiron_with_the_Education_of_Aescalapius_-_etching_-_Washington_DC,_NGA.jpg

INDO EUROPEAN CULTURE

Twenty-some thousand years ago the ancient Indo-Europeans proudly called themselves the Aryans – or Noble Ones. They were the first Mazda Yasnis; Worshippers of God in the ancient Avestan tongue. – *The Arctic Home in the Vedas'* by B.G.Tilak, Edition 1925

Maximum glaciations during the last ice age, took place about 18,000 years ago, and this reference preceded the ice!

John G. Bennett, wrote a research paper entitled "The Hyperborean Origin of the Indo-European Culture" (Journal Systematics, Vol. I, No. 3, December 1963). He claimed the Indo-European homeland, which he considered the Hyperborea of classical antiquity, was in the far north. This Polar idea was earlier proposed by Bal Gangadhar Tilak

"The Hyperborean people lived north of the land of winter in idyllic pastures, with two crops of grain per year, but most of the area was a... wildland, featuring vast and beautiful forests. The southlands were guarded by the bitterly cold peaks of the nearly impassable Rhiphaion Mountains (Urals or Carpathians). Above them dwelt the Arimaspi, men with one eye; still further, the griffins; and beyond these, the Hyperboreans, who extended to the sea.

Directly to the south was Pterophoros, (according to Herodotus) a desolate, snow-covered land cursed by eternal winter. This was the home of Boreas, god of the north wind, whose chill breath brought winter to all the lands to the south, including Scythia, Thrace, Istria, Celtica, Italy and Greece. The peaks of the Rhiphaion mountains (Urals) were also the home of gold-guarding Griffons (eagle-lions), and its valleys were inhabited by the fierce, one-eyed, (or horse loving people depending how you see the root words) Arimaspoi tribe.

The Arimaspi were a legendary people of northern Scythia, a huge swath from Greece to Siberia, who lived in the foothills of the Riphean Mountains, variously identified with the Urals. All tales of their struggles in the Hyperborean lands near the cave of Boreas, the North Wind (Geskleithron), had their origin in a lost work by Aristeas, who reported battles between griffons and warriors in Scythian style tunics and leggings...[it] became a theme for Greek vase-painters." (Herodotus (4.13) 1996 Penguin Classics)

In Early Iranian Arimaspi combines Ariama (love) and Aspa (horses). This is similar in other Indo-European languages like Lithuanian, arimaspi can refer to the plow horse, the plowman, or a rider.

Yet, Herodotus or his source seems to have understood the Scythian word as a combination of the roots arima ("one") and spou ("eye") and to have created a mythic image to account for it. Strabo and Pliny's Natural History perpetuated the fables about the northern people who had a single eye in the center of their foreheads and engaged in stealing gold from the griffins.

Tadeusz Sulimirski (1970) claimed that the Arimaspi were a Sarmatian tribe originating in the upper valley of the River Irtysh. This river runs through Siberia, China and Kazakhstan. Its headwaters lie in the Altai Mountains on the Mongol – Chinese border. This is a beautiful steppe land of green hills and valleys, a horse lover's dream.

Dmitry Machinsky (1997) associates them with a group of three-eyed ajna figurines from the Minusinsk Depression traditionally inhabited by the Afanasievo and Okunevo cultures of southern Siberia. They were known to appreciate and breed horses. Similarity of name and location could identify them with proto Fino Ugric ancestors of the Uralic people called the Mari. But in any case, it seems more likely they were horse-loving tribes of the plains rather than Cyclopeans.

The **Afanasievo culture**, dated to 5300 years ago, is the earliest modern human habitation in southern Siberia. There in the Altai Mountains, specifically in the Minusinsk Basin and Eastern Kazakhstan. Dates as early as 4,874 years ago, are given for human remains. The deceased were buried in conic or rectangular enclosures, often face up like the burials of the Yamna, who were also believed to be Indo-European.

The Afanasievo, became the first food-producers in the area, by breeding cattle, horses, and sheep. In their settlements, metal objects and the presence of wheeled vehicles are documented. The Afanasievo are strong candidates for the earliest group of a people, later known as the Tocharians.

(http://en.wikipedia.org/wiki/Arimaspi); (http://en.wikipedia.org/wiki/Afanasevo_culture); also, Anthony, David W. (2007). *The Horse, the Wheel, and Language: How Bronze-Age Riders from the Eurasian Steppes Shaped the Modern World*. Princeton, NJ: Princeton University Press. pp. 264–265; 308. ISBN 978-0-691-05887-0.

The Greater Iranian nomads continued to roam with their herds of cattle searching for pasture and water. By now these Pagan people had forgotten Zoroaster's admonitions and had accumulated a few gods and goddesses to help with natural elements along the way. They worshipped "Asman" as the sky, "Anahita" for the waters, "Zam" for the earth, "Mah" for the moon, etc.

Mithra or Mehr, perhaps the greatest, was associated with the sun and is seen as a Mediator or protector of the created world.

They used bronze for chariots. And while some still tended herds, others began to raid those herds and became warriors, who worshiped the gods of war called daevas. Their priests (Kavs) were cunning and the practiced black magic, especially in India.

("Aryan Civilization" http://www.angelfire.com/magic2/aryasociety/1.html); ("Birth of Zoroastrianism" Http://132.246.176.35/bamji/topic.htm)

The Saga of the Aryans, written by Porus Homi Havewala and published in 1995 (second edition Vol. I, Nozer Buchia Publishers) is a semi-fictional historical novel about the origins of the Aryan people. It describes the lives of ancient Indo-Europeans, who proudly called themselves the Aryans or the Noble Ones about twenty thousand years ago.

"Volume I *(of five books)* describes vividly the Great Migration of the Aryan ancestors from their ancient homeland Airyanam Vaejo in the North Pole, due to the... glaciations that occurred in that ancient age. Drawing inspiration from the sacred Scriptures of the Aryan Zoroastrians such as the Vendidad, in which the great journey is authenticated; the book unfolds the trials and tribulations that befell the ancient ancestors, in their great journey to the South and the South-West, towards Iran, India, Greece, Russia, Germany and the other nations of Europe. The Aryans display great heroism against the bitter cold and blizzards, the wild animals and the savage barbarians. Romance blooms among the young, as they travel onwards to Iran. The Saga is interspersed with heroic verse, in the great Aryan tradition.

"After they turned south, wave after wave of Proto-Indo-Europeans left the Eurasian Steppe due to changing climate, a need for the freedom, and fresh pastures for their horses, sheep, goats and cattle. They went south and west throughout Europe and India, and east through Asia – seeding many civilizations such as: Hindu, Hittite, Persian, Greek, Russian, Roman, German, Celt and others. So, many of these people share a similar ancestral language (Proto-Indo-Iranian), religion and culture."

When the proto–Indo-European languages broke apart, many words were still recognizable. The English word "new" is "navas" in Sanskrit, "newas" in Hittite, "ne(w)os" in Greek, "novus" in Latin, "nuwe" in Tocharian, "nue" in Old Irish and "naujas" in Lithuanian.

In a second example, the English word "brother" is "bhrater" in Proto-Indo-European, "phrater" in Greek, "frater" in Latin, "bratar" in Sanskrit, "bratar" also in Celtic and Avestan. The word is "broder" or "bruder" in German languages, and so forth. Such similarities are a sign that these cultures descend from a common linguistic group. (http://indoeuro.bizland.com/project/phonetics/word31.html) Mallory, James P.; Adams, Douglas Q. (2006). "Oxford Introduction to Proto-Indo-European and the Proto-Indo-European World." London: Oxford University Press.

Tribes of early Noble Ones worshiped outside in nature rather than in buildings of any kind. They were not given to creating images of: God, or the Bearers of the Holy Spirit (Great Prophets) or even other figures, until the religion became old again, degraded and sullied with blood sacrifice and polytheism.

"Sometimes they ascended mountains clad in white robes and myrtle wreaths, to offer incense, fragrant smoke, as sacrifices to the moon, sun, and stars; as well as the winds and other elements." – Schure

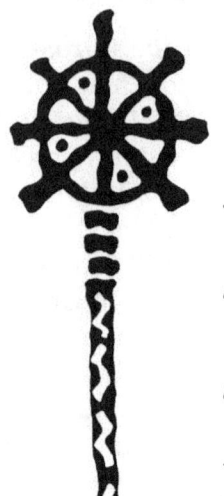

YIMA XSAETA OR JAMSHED THE SHINING ONE

The difficulty in this discussion of Yima, son of Vivanghat, is that Yima and Rama are predominantly versions of the same prophet. Much of what we learn from the Persian Creation story of Yima is the same as we find in the earliest Vedic scriptures. The main difference is that Yima's timeline is almost three thousand years longer than Rama's.

Some call Him the first man, progenitor of humans, and son of the sun. The most ancient records refers to Yima as the "first," a primordial man. In all fairness, He could have been the First Educator of a primordial form of man.

Yima, also known as the Radiant King Jamshid, could be a combination of 4 Manifestations – at least – like Adam and Fu-Xi. According to the "Shahnama" of the poet Ferdowsi, Jamshid was the fourth king of the world After Gayomart, Siamak and Hooshang. Other innovations credited to Yima are from Bronze Age times, and are more likely to be attributed to Krishna.

"His anointed name of Jamshid is taken from the root words 'Jam' or 'Yam' which means 'Bright Shining' and Shed meaning 'Radiant Sun.' He was, surrounded by a burning light; a radiant splendor though He remained humble, its radiance allowed Him to command mortals, angels and demons; banishing evil and rewarding good men with lives of plenty. His people prospered in peace, as He strove with a great dedication to keep them free from spiritual and physical disease. Evil people denied themselves this bounty, and were treated accordingly.

Yima, a shepherd before He became King Jamshed; raised the call to return to monotheism, thousands of years before Zoroaster. Jamshid was said to have had a magical seven-ringed cup filled with the elixir of immortality which allowed him to observe the universe. He had command over all the angels and demons of the world and Heaven, and was both King and divine Representative of Ahura Mazda (God).

Yima puts an end to an epidemic with a plant called homa (Greek amomon, and Egyptian persea) from which He extracted a healing essence. This plant became sacred among His followers, replacing the mistletoe of the oak tree, preserved by the Celts of Europe."
The Great Initiates Edouard Schure

The best references about a particular Manifestation are given by a succeeding Messenger, Who always acknowledges and praises His forerunners. In this case the Zend Avesta shows us Zoroaster's recognition of Yima. He is listed under "Firsts" because of the Avestan quotes in answer to Zoroaster's query.

"Zoroaster asked Ormuzd 'O Ahura Mazda, righteous Creator of the corporeal world, who was the first person to whom You taught these teachings? Who is the first man with whom you conversed?"

Then spoke God (Ahura Mazda):

Yima the splendid who watched over His subjects, O righteous Zarathushtra, I first did teach the Aryan religion to Him prior to you. Yima spoke to me, and said he would like to spread the religion among mankind by teaching others. It was then that I replied O Yima you are not created for this task by Me. You are not learned enough to increase the religion among mankind. You are not the Messenger of the religion.

Yima the righteous told me then:

O Ahura, if I am not created for the task of increasing the good religion, then I would like to advance the world, to increase it and be a righteous king and protector. I ask You this, that in my kingdom there be neither cold wind nor hot wind (neither extreme winter nor summer), there be no sickness nor death, [so] that my subjects be undying and unwanting, and gloriously happy under my reign.

I Who am Ahura Mazda, was pleased with this. I brought Yima a weapon (tool) – a Golden plough, which was dagger shaped with golden forks (the ard mentioned in Fu Xi), *to signify that His authority was divine, sanctioned by Me. He became the mightiest king the Aryans had ever known, the most righteous and most splendid...*

I told him to watch over the worlds which belong to me, and I gave him a saber of gold and a sword of victory. And Yima moved forward on the way of the sun and assembled the courageous men in the famous Airyana-Vaeja, created pure." [Zoroaster in His holy book, the Zend Avesta (Vendidad-Sade, 2nd Fargard (chapter)]

Elsewhere in the Zend:

"*Yima declined the offer of the Omniscient Creator, Ahura Mazda, to make him the vehicle of religion, and to give His Law to men. When, Yima refused, Ahura Mazda gave him a different mission: to rule over and nourish the earth, to see that the living things prosper. This Yima accepted, and Ahura Mazda presented him with a golden seal and a dagger inlaid with gold. He became king in a golden age in which need, death, disease, aging, and extremes of temperature were banished from the earth because of His virtue.*"

Overpopulation and Tragedy

When Yima's rule extended to 300 years, the Aryans had prospered so that the land became full of herds, men, dogs and birds. Sacred fires flamed in the house of every Noble family, a reminder of the Word of God flaming in the hearts of His servants. But eventually, places could no longer be found for cattle or men.

"*I made this known to Yima. And he proceeded south, towards the path of the high sun, increasing the land with his golden plough* [like Shennong] *conquering and cultivating the lands. The boundaries of the Aryan kingdom were thus extended in breadth, one third greater than before. The king stood on the mother earth, praising the country with words fit for prayer.*

He deprived the daevas, who were demonic servants of the evil Ahriman, of wealth, herds and reputation during his reign. Good men, however, lived lives of plenty, and were neither sick nor aged. Father and son walked together, each appearing no older than fifteen.

Ahura Mazda visited him once more, warning him again of overpopulation. Yima, shining with light, faced southwards, once again (towards lands freshly freed of ice).

When Yima's rule extended to 600 years, the state of abundance [overcrowding] recurred. This led to Yima proceeding again towards the south and the west, extending the boundaries of the Aryan kingdom two thirds greater than before. Thus happened the second great migration of the Aryans.

When Yima's rule extended to 900 years, abundance again led to Yima increasing the land with his golden plough, towards the south and west."

This third great migration opened up three times more land than before.

In the first 1000 years of his rule, Yima the splendid enjoined righteous order on his subjects. He controlled invisible time itself, making it so much larger in size so as to praise and spread His righteous law." (Quoted material from Bal Gangadhar Tilak 1856-1920. He was an Indian Journalist and educator, who wrote *The Arctic Home in the Vedas*, in 1903.)

Build A Vara!

The next part of the story tells of a meeting of Ahura Mazda and the Venerable Beings in Airyanem Vaeja, the first of the "perfect lands." Yima attended with a group of "the best of mortals." Here Ahura Mazda warned Him of an upcoming catastrophe: An ice age!

"*That glorious age of the Aryans did not last for ever, O Zarathushtra! It was time for the evil one's attack. I Who am Ahura Mazda spoke then to Yima Kshaeta:*

'*O splendid Yima, towards the sacred Aryan land will rush evil as a severe fatal winter; evil will rush as thick snow flakes falling in increased depth. From the three directions, will wild and ferocious animals attack, arriving from the most dreadful sites.*

O fair Yima, son of Vivanghat! Upon the material world the evil winters are about to fall, that shall bring the fierce, deadly frost; upon the material world the evil winters are about to fall, that shall make snow-flakes fall thick, even an aredvi (glacier) deep on the highest tops of mountains.

Before this winter, any snow that fell would melt and convey the water away. Now the snow will not melt but will form an ice cap. In this place, O Yima the corporeal world will be DAMAGED. Before in this seedland the grass was so soft the footprint of even a small animal could be observed. Now, there will be no footprints discernable at all on the packed sheets of hard ice that will form.

In the face of a particularly bad winter [advancing ice], Ahura Mazda advised Yima to construct a Vara [ark-like enclosure] in the form of a multi-level artificially lit cavern; two miles long and two miles wide. He must stock it with two of every animal, bird and plant, and nearly 2000 of the fittest people, and build a supply with food and water gathered the previous summer."

In a more fanciful rendition Yima creates the Vara by crushing the earth with a stamp of his foot, and kneading it into shape as a potter does clay.

He oversaw the construction of streets, shafts for light and air flow, and rooms for living, storage, worship, and special quarters for the young couples "make for them a residence... for privacy"

He brought in nearly two thousand people, and finally sealed the opening of the Vara with a golden ring.

"*So, Yima; make a mighty VARA, an enclosure as long as a riding ground, with equal four sides. Here bring the families of men and women, cattle, dogs, birds and the red flaming fire.*

Inside the Vara, make water flow in a canal, one Hathra long. Keep earth inside the Vara, to grow green vegetables as food. Make cattle pens, to house the cattle of the Aryan people. Let love blossom unfailing in the enclosure" – Tilak (Saga of the Aryans) 1925

The Site of Derinkuyu

Maybe we should have been looking underground for the"ARK"! For anyone interested, I highly recommend watching the History Channel Ancient Aliens episode "Underground Aliens." They show great film and blueprints of a huge underground excavation in Capadoccia, in Central Turkey, near a city called Derinkuyu.

The place is thought to have been built many thousands of years ago. The engineering is superb, with extensive ventilation shafts that bring air to every square foot of the 13 story construction. The supports are excellent and exhibit no signs of collapse. There is room for 20,000 men women and children. There are religious centers, store rooms, stables and even wine presses.

Site of Derinkuyu By Travel Turkey (derinkuyu Uploaded by stegop) [CC BY 2.0 (http://creativecommons.org/licenses/by/2.0)], via Wikimedia Commons

Yima was responsible for a great many inventions that made life more secure for his people. The timing for many of these, seems consistent with **Gobekli Tepe** which is also in Turkey.

He is credited with bringing or enhancing a wide range of technologies. Some of these inventions and improvements included advancements in the religion, arts, sciences and social patterns on which civilization is based.

The **weaving and dyeing** cloth made of wool, linen and silk.

The use of **chemistry** to make perfumes and wine. The invention of wine according to Persian legend, occurred when the king banished one of his wives from his kingdom. This caused her to become despondent enough to wish to take her life. She went to the king's warehouse where she found a jar that contained the remnants of spoiled grapes that were deemed undrinkable. What she thought was poison was simply the product of fermentation. After drinking it, she discovered its effects to be pleasant. When her spirits were lifted, she took her discovery to the King, who was pleased.

Yima encouraged the construction of houses with fine **brick masonry and the use of architectural plans**. Ancient Iran was a large region which included Afghanistan, Central Asia, Eastern Iran and Pakistan. It was divided into many kingdoms known as Khshathras "habitation authorities," so the reach of these innovations became widespread.

The **mining of ore** and the manufacture of **armor and weaponry,** was needed to protect the new cities. Also the **mining of jewels and precious metals.** Sounds like the beginnings of king jewelry. And he instigated the navigation of the waters of the world **in sailing ships**.

He influenced sacred clothing like the **sudreh**, a garment worn under the outer clothing, which contains a small pocket in the front to collect one's good deeds. It protects the wearer from perpetrating, or receiving evil acts. The **kushti is** a sacred Zoroastrian belt, the wearing of which is surrounded by a great deal of ritual. These are not likely to have been ritualized in the early days.

The introduction of a **solar calendar year**. Yima/Rama, also set **Naw-Ruz,** the holy day celebrated at the spring equinox. It is celebrated not only by Zoroastrians, but also Muslims and Baha'is. It is also Oestra for Pagans and is the backdrop for Christian Easter.

In all cases it is the dawning of a "New Day," a "Spiritual Springtime," represented by festivals that feature signs of birth and renewal such as flowers, grass, eggs (sometimes highly decorated, as in pysanky) and baby animals like bunnies, chicks, young fish, and other signs of springtime.

The following story seems a bit fanciful. One day Yima sat upon a jewel-studded throne and the shining beings who served Him, **raised His throne up into the air and he flew through the sky**. His subjects marveled and praised Him. Jamshid had now become the greatest monarch the world had ever known. This event occurred on the first of the month of Fravardin which was named after the Shining Beings. So they celebrated the first Naw Ruz, the "New Day."

Jamshid (as with Rama and Shennong) **divided the people into four groups**: The priests who conducted the worship of Ahura Mazda. The warriors who protected the people by the might of their arms. The farmers who grew the grain that fed the people. The artisans who produced goods for the ease and enjoyment of the people. These categories bore no stigma originally, but the idea became corrupted by humans in later years and became an oppressive Caste system.

Jamshid ruled for hundreds, well actually thousands of years. During this time human longevity increased, sicknesses were banished, and peace and prosperity reigned. He enjoined civil behavior on the people and expanded the degree of unity to include great tribes, clans, and cities. He was endowed with the royal farr, a radiant splendor that burned about him by divine favor.

But Jamshid, or more likely His followers' pride grew with power, and He (or, they) began to forget that all the blessings of His reign were due to God. The people boasted that all of the good things they had, came from Jamshid alone, not God. And they demanded that Jamshed should be accorded divine honors as if He were the Creator.

Dualism and decay had taken hold! From this time the farr departed Jamshid as did the Ancient Faith. It is as if **Rama**, when He was tested, had chosen to accept the crown from Sita, and rule over humankind.

The religion degenerated again into darkness, and the people began to murmur and rebel against Jamshid, who repented in his heart, but his glory never returned to him. Zahhak the Arabian, under the influence of Ahriman (Evil) made war upon Jamshid and it was welcomed by many of his unhappy subjects. He fled from the capital halfway across the world, but was finally trapped and brutally murdered.

After a long Golden Age, humanity again descended from the heights of civilization back into gloom. Idols were worshipped once more and humanity declined into heavy darkness, to await the coming of a new Educator.

ADAPA OR UAN

Mesopotamian myth tells us that **Adapa or Uan**, was the first of seven sages sent before the flood by Ea, the wise god of Eridu, to bring the arts of civilization to humankind. Ancient Sumerians said He unknowingly refused the gift of immortality and like Yima, was drawn to an earthly status. A counterpart, Ram, passed that test and disappeared into the mountains.

For further information, see Darmesteter's translation of the Vendidad, published in the 1898, or the American edition of Max Mueller's *Sacred Books of the East*.

MELCHIZEDEK OR MALKI TZEDEK

There are only a very few references to this holy Being. Like Jamshed, Melchizedek was known as King of Righteousness and Justice. Exactly what high station He holds is confusing.

In Hebrews 7:3 Melchizedek is referred to as a king *"Without father or mother or genealogy"* which suggests He was **born of God**, is **God's Messenger**, or actually is the *Holy Spirit*. And like the Other Manifestations, He can exhibit all three!

Rabbi Eleazar said that Melchizedek's school was one of three places where the Holy Spirit manifested itself. (B. Talmud Makkot 23b.)

"Thou art a priest for ever after the order of Melchisedec. Who in the days of his flesh, when he had offered up prayers and supplications with strong crying and tears unto him that was able to save him from death...? Though he were a Son, yet learned he obedience by the things which he suffered; And being made perfect, he became the author of eternal salvation unto all them that obey him... Called of God a high priest after the order of Melchisedec. Of whom we have many things to say, and hard to be uttered, seeing ye are dull of hearing." (King James Bible, Hebrews 5:3 to 5:11)

Melchizedek is mentioned in Genesis because He appeared to the patriarch Abraham after His victory over the four kings, who had besieged Sodom and Gomorrah and had taken his nephew Lot prisoner. (Gen. 14:18) Melchizedek blessed Abraham in the name of God Most High, Creator of heaven and earth. (Gen. 14:19.) In return, Abraham gave Melchizedek a tenth or tithe, of the spoils gained from the battle. (Gen. 14:20).

He preceded Levi, yet was referred to as the "First Priest." If Melchizedek truly is the "First Priest" he would have come from a most ancient time, preceding Abraham by many thousands of years. Some feel He was in fact the prophet Shem, son of Noah. The Rabbis taught that Melchizedek handed down Adam's robes to Abraham. (Numbers Rabbah 4:8.) (http://en.wikipedia.org/wiki/Melchisedec)

The title, "King of Salem," is suggested in the Babylonian Talmud. Salem is believed to be an ancient name for Jerusalem and Melchizedek was the priest of "El Elyon," the highest God.

The Zohar refers to Melchizedek as the king of Salem, the King Who rules with complete sovereignty! (Zohar, Bereshit, 1:86b-87a☺)

In the Book of Mormon, he is also described as the king of Salem. *"The people of the land were very wicked and Melchizedek preached repentance. The people repented and Melchizedek established peace in the land."* (Alma 13:18)

So in this world Melchizedek suffered greatly. He offered prayers, supplications and tears to the One Who could save him from death. He was called by God to be a great early Prophet. His revelatory words brought salvation to His followers, but He was treated cruelly, made to suffer like other Messengers. The fact that He returns on occasion is a sign of the undying fire of the Single Faith.

THE FIRSTS: A SUMMATION

Above all else, these tales are a stream of continuing education coming from God the Creator. They are connected by various events like: Pre-Creation, creation of the world of matter, and the creation of humanity. Many have agricultural components because as populations increased, or environments became unfriendly, there were famines and massive die-offs. The taming of animals and plant species became necessary for existence.

In Gayomart's case: A uniquely formed moon white bull, who is Gayomart's neighbor and helper, oddly becomes the progenitor of plants.

In the Torah Adam's garden is filled with plants and he is given animals to name. Stories of Shennong, Yima, and Rama also concur. The time was ripe for man to produce much of the food he ate to stave off the hunger. Wild plants and game could no longer be enough.

At the beginning "Man" starts as a spiritual or heavenly being, who is later sent to earth and given a mortal body. Adam was formed from dust, and Keyumars/Gayomart from mud, Eve from a rib, Mashya and Mashyana were created from a rhubarb plant with two main branches.

In the Torah the world was created in six days, with God resting on the seventh. On the sixth day Adam and Eve were created. According to the Zend Avesta, the Zoroastrian holy Book, the world was created in six Gahs (sounds like days, also a period of time). Gayomart (Gayo is taken from "Gaia," so "Mortal Life") was created on the sixth Gah.

Next comes the history of our education beginning with the betrayal of **spiritual knowledge (good)**, by **material distraction (evil)**. Sons of Adam and Gayomart are killed by evildoers.

There was cataclysmic destruction besides the famines and the floods. Full ice-age cycles displaced many people, and diminished the numbers of Primitive humans. Great human migrations came out of Africa. There were also great migrations from the North Pole across Europe and Asia, southward into India Ceylon, and other distant Islands.

Several different types of human beings lived, received Revelations, worshipped, combined, and clashed with one another on this planet. Thereby redefining the former concept of "human" religion. Society advanced from nuclear families, and nomadic tribes – to agrarian cities.

Prominent sacred symbols include: trees, moon, sun, rams (or lambs), bulls, snakes and dragons, and the use of a golden: ring, sword, knife, dagger, plough or sickle.

A major holy element is the mention of the Farr a Halo "bright as the sun," a radiant aura. We associate this glowing radiance with all Luminous Points, or Manifestations of God's Word, such as the Buddha, Jesus the Christ, Mohammad, the Bab and Baha'u'llah; whenever they are in the transfigured state of revelation.

From the Great Messengers people learned to prosper in an expanding society, and appreciate the arts and sciences, like chemistry, metallurgy, painting, clothing and jewelry production. Technological development overflowed with tools, weaponry, farming and fishing gear, and surprisingly city-building. We see structural and architectural miracles like aqueducts, sewers, spas; and magnificent temples, not to mention a tremendous "Vara." These innovations made life safer, easier and more enjoyable.

The Prophets praise the One who came before, and foretell the coming of Ones to come! The Avesta foretells the coming of three other Manifestations or "Returns" coming at least a thousand years apart; with the last one of them, the Saoshyant, coming at the "time of the end" when all evil is banished. It also mentions the cleansing of the earth with "molten metal" at that time.

The concept of original sin which is present in some Christian and Jewish groups does not exist in most religions. A person is responsible for their actions and choices. Humans are guided to develop virtuous qualities of their souls.

Rama resolved the issues surrounding the station of females and the "betrayal" of their spiritual purpose. Marriage, and the relationship between man and woman improved. Adam and Eve were forgiven after they repented on Earth. A Prophetic Hadith recalls that after leaving Eden, Adam and Eve were separated. They searched for each other, and were finally reunited at the Plain of 'Arafat (near Mecca) which means "recognition," their issues resolved. God had elevated woman to her state of nobility and this encouraged the respect of her children.

Three harmonious working classes and a priesthood, were laid out. The beginnings of writing, science, and magic had dawned.

Greater population size meant that plagues and disease could attack humans as their settlements became cities. A staff of Physical and Spiritual healing is wielded with either a single or a double serpent twining.

Mesopotamian myth tells us that Adapa or Uan, was the first of seven sages sent before the flood by Ea. The wise god of Eridu was sent to bring the arts of civilization to humankind.

The Ancient Faith faded and was renewed many times. Beyond the names we know are thousands we are unlikely to ever hear. What matters is that God by any name, has sent us guidance at every dark turn so that we might flourish, grow, and evolve!

POLYTHEISM: THE MATRIX IN WHICH MONOTHEISM IS BORN, FLOURISHES AND DIMS

The early Pagan Faith which though ancient and often obscured with polytheistic detours, has tried to represent the thread of human Faith throughout time. Remnants of the followers of the Ram and His Noble bands of Aryans, became the Pagans who travelled across pretty much all of Eurasia. The great migrations began around 18,000 years ago. Around 6000 years ago three branches moved out from east of the Black Sea, toward Iran, India, and Central Asia. Information regarding Pagan religions comes from several sources including, ancient scriptures, anthropological research, artifacts, and the historical accounts of Classical writers.

Around 4,000 years ago nomadic Celtic tribes who occupied the area around the Caspian Sea in southern Russia began to migrate southward into the Indus Valley and the Southeast Asian Islands, westward into Asia Minor, the Middle East, into North Africa, and at least as far west as the Takla Makan Desert and Mongolia. They also ventured eastward into the Balkans and the vastness of Europe.

A thousand years later the Celts migrated down into Greece, Italy and Spain, further west into France and Belgium, and eventually into the British Isles. And some remained in the vicinity of Poland in South Central Europe. Celtic type mummies in South America add to their mural of wanderlust.

They came with their tales of gods and goddesses. These people brought with them the ideas which formed the bedrock of the Pagan thought. By now the great Ram had faded into a "horned god."

They preserved for us Ram's ancient seasonal feasts and celebrations. This suggests that pagans were originally His followers. The marking solstices and equinoxes with the four festivals of Oestra/Easter or Naw Ruz, Harvest, Samhain or All Hallows Sabbath, and of course Noel or Yule, are still widely accepted traditions.

The collection of Pagan lore is extraordinary! It holds memories of the ancient Prophets almost like chapters of a Bible. The Prophets themselves, however, became in the fading of time, ornate aspects of god and goddess, titans and demi-gods, still recognized in some form, by Neo-Pagans or Wiccans.

Over time more of the tribes whose Pagan roots and beginnings were pure and noble began to worship various natural elements as well as Ahura Mazda (God), or maybe instead of Ahura Mazda. **Edouard Schure (The Great Initiates 1961) paints this picture:**

"Early Noble Ones (Aryans, Pagans?) worshiped outside in nature rather than in buildings of any kind. They were not given to creating images of: God, the **Great Prophets***, or other figures – until the religion became old and degraded, sullied with blood sacrifice.*

Sometimes, they ascended mountains clad in white robes and myrtle wreaths, to offer incense, fragrant smoke, as sacrifices to the moon, sun, and stars; as well as the winds and other elements..." At first, they were doers of only good, but over time, they became corrupted and power hungry abusing their gifts, they eventually demanded human sacrifices... brave warriors, who scoffed at death came forth to sacrificial altar voluntarily."

Accretions of man-made garbage including cultic rituals, taboos, intolerances, selfishness, intoxication and greed, darkened the days of past nobility.

"**Left to the mercy of ambition and individual passion, inspiration degenerates into superstition, courage into ferocity, the sublime ideal of sacrifice, into an instrument of tyranny and sinister and cruel exploitation. They instituted human sacrifices, and the blood flowed continuously over the dolmens, to the sinister chants of the priests and the approving shouts of the ferocious onlookers.**" Sounds like a precursor of the dark incantations of today's "satanists."

The term Pagan which has survived the millennia would be a good name for the entire matrix of polytheistic traditions. Many struggle to balance the dark and the light, and are caught in the grasp of blind or hopeful superstition.

Elements of polytheistic belief systems have remained. We see today, cases where praying to God alone is not enough. Instead multitudes of saints, angels, deities, or gods – or even the universe are employed to cover all our spiritual "needs." This is often a sign of deterioration or fading, found in any revelation time has passed. The potency and purity has moved on, but people have not recognized the Holy Spirit come with a new name.

Since the time of Adam and Eve, the destruction of purity in a revealed religion begins with adding things to God.

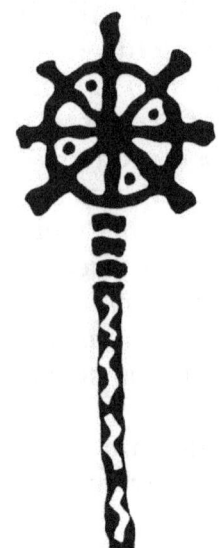

DUALISM, PANTHEISM, SYNCRETISM HENOTHEISM

First it is one other thing, sometimes the Manifestation, Himself or some other force which is worshipped with God. Next saints, angels, or elements of nature become a list. Then, figures or icons are developed, who eventually become statues that need shrines, or become etched into talismans or medals that hang from rearview mirrors.

So in this respect, there is little difference between the fade of ancient Paganism, and the rest of the world's revealed religions. Unfortunately as purity fades, people tend to be more self-centered and the ability to harm others or ignore their suffering becomes more prevalent.

Dualism

Dualism is usually simple binary opposition. Instead of one all-powerful God, there are two gods together. The Canaanite pantheon consisted of El (El Elyon) God, and Asherah (Ashteroth) – motherhood and lady of the sea. Perhaps she is the original model for the masthead on a ship. This is God wedded to maya (nature), as in the Svetesvatara Upanishad. Maya is the material realm, an illusion of who we really are – **we are souls living for a time in nature**.

Kurt Noll states that the original god of Israel was El Shaddai, God Almighty. But really El, El Elyon, Yahweh, and El Shaddai are names of the Almighty, the Most High, God. (K. L. Noll *Canaan and Israel in Antiquity: An Introduction*, Continuum, 2002, p.123

Dualism is a balance between: good and evil, dark and light, night and day, or body and soul, etc.; where each component is necessary to **complete** the other. Yet, like male and female they do not always agree. This the definition of Yin and Yang.

Often dualism is the worship of God, and His Prophet as seen in Yima's case. **Sometimes it is Monotheism and Polytheism.**

PERSPECTIVE

Wicca is a Middle English term for witch or wizard. It can be thought of as dualistic, as well as henotheistic, and syncretic. It is considered dualistic in the sense that adherents worship a Goddess and a God, usually the goddess of the moon and the horned god, likely based on Ram.

Sometimes one can still see hints of the original Prophets who inspired god-figures, and who might now be represented by icons. Both Ram (Rama) and Zoroaster are associated with healing, magic and wizardry. Zoroaster is seen as a sage and miracle worker.

Public domain – Wikipedia Commons

Wicca developed as an outgrowth of a renewed interest in witchcraft. It was founded in Great Britain in 1954 by Gerald Gardiner and Doreen Valiente who published books and passed secret written and oral teachings to initiates, as had been fashionable in early occultic societies. There are many variations and as Wicca grows and evolves, there are a number of diverse sects referred to as *traditions*. So there is some disagreement over what actually constitutes Wicca.

Generally, Wicca draws on older pagan traditions and threads of the occult such as the Hermetic Kabbalah. Some Wiccans get excited by fairies, magic and crop circles. They are knowledgeable about gods and goddesses, protective entities and spirit guardians, and cleansings or banishments. They are usually white witches or wizards in tune with nature and their own personal creativity. They are forces for good and are concerned with healing arts.

At one time Pagan worship was rejected and repressed by Christian groups who were trying to usher in their own "New Day." Perhaps they were tired of masking their holy days behind the ancient pagan festivals.

The term "Pagan" came to be used as an insult, when speaking of people whose belief in their Creator was overshadowed by the worship of many gods and goddesses. In the Christian community of southern Europe during from the third century, the term was used to describe any non-Abrahamic religions other than Christianity or Judaism.

Once Christianity and Islam began to press polytheistic worshipers, they labeled them with slurs like "Hellene" (after Greek polytheism), "Pagan," and the all-time favorite "Heathen." Unfortunately the term "Pagan" came to be used as a vile curse, a condemnation like the word "Witch." Self-righteous people sometimes used their disgust for the "old ways" as a cover for violence and murder.

Wiccans and other Neopagans practice their beliefs more or less discreetly, today. Hopefully education will bring about more tolerant behavior from people who do not understand why it is they "hate" Pagans. If one asks them why this hatred exists, "haters" may have no idea; or say it is because their parents molded their disdain, or at best, they complain that Pagans are not Christian, which is not always true.

In the nineteenth century aspects of Paganism were adopted by members of various artistic groups inspired by the "mysteries" of the ancient world. In the twentieth century, it has come to mean practitioners of Wiccan or Neopagan practices.

Contemporary Pagan movements are diverse with no single set of beliefs, practices, or shared texts. The practice became popular in the United States during the 1990s and the early 21st century. It associated with a revival of Celtic arts and tradition.

Many Wiccans follow a spirituality which they accept as being entirely modern. Others attempt to reconstruct or revive indigenous or ethnic religions found in history and folklore as accurately as possible. Though Wicca is dualistic, polytheism in all its forms: animism, pantheism, and *especially* henotheism are common features of Neopagan thought.

Mehr/Mithra/Mitra (Vedic)

It should be noted that Mithraism was also a corrupted remnant of Ram/Yima's previous Faith. As the Aryans fanned out, some strayed from the worship of one God. They began to name deities after natural phenomena. One of these was Mithra in Persian or Mitra in Sanskrit.

Zoroaster did not appreciate or recognize this dualistic "sun" path that paired another being with God. There is only One God acknowledged by Zoroaster. He had no use for "gods" sun cult icons, or bull-killing sacrifices!

It seems a sad twist on the reverence for the moon-white bull in Avestan Creation, and the bright, sacred flame of the Farr which surrounded Gayomart, Yima (Rama) and Zoroaster.

The station of Mithra was made up by wayward men pure and simple. Zoroaster taught that Faith is meant to move forward, not to stagnate, or move backward.

One can follow a trail of idyllic representations of Mithra as the sun haloed bull slayer. The cult carried down through Pagan groups to the Minoans, Moors, Egyptians, Celts, Greeks, and Romans, and even as far as the New World. Along with the cultic sacrifices, bull fights were present in many of these cultures.

Ironically, Mithra is mentioned in the prayer book Zoroastrians use today – but never by Zoroaster! The Khorda Avesta (Zoroastrian Book of Common Prayer) refers to Mithra in the Litany to the Sun.

"Homage to Mithra of Wide Cattle Pastures, Whose Word is True, who is of the Assembly, Who has a Thousand Ears, the Well-Shaped One, Who has Ten Thousand Eyes, the Exalted One, Who has Wide Knowledge, the Helpful One, Who Sleeps Not, the Ever Wakeful. We sacrifice to Mithra, The Lord of all countries, Whom Ahura Mazda created the most glorious, Of the Supernatural Yazads. So may there come to us for Aid, Both Mithra and Ahura, the Two Exalted Ones, I shall sacrifice to his mace, well aimed against the Skulls of the Daevas.

Some recent theories have claimed Mithra represents the Sun itself, but the Khorda Avesta refers to the Sun as a separate entity – as it does with the Moon with which the Sun has the *"Best of Friendships."* (http://en.wikipedia.org/wiki/Mithra)

After the time of Zoroaster the Aryan, pagan people employed Mehr priests called Karapans. They dressed in robes and long caps that flipped over a bit at the top. Unlike their original Aryan counterparts, these priests sacrificed animals and plants to fire, and they became intoxicated from haoma. The following account gives us a snapshot.

"Some could afford a karapan who was paid a little fee or kine (a word for cows). The tribal chief, could employ a full team, a feast, and large fire, with flames flying and a smoke cloud climbing. There were tender twigs or grass (baresman/barhi) spread for the gods to grace. The rites appeared graceful. Animals, one or more as the ceremonial scale and occasion warranted, were slaughtered, and their blood, flesh, and fat were offered to the gods through the burning fire. Other edibles were also put to smoke. A golden plant, called haoma/soma, was solemnly washed, pounded in a stone or metal mortar, and squeezed. The juice was filtered and mixed with consecrated water or milk. A little was poured into the fire for gods, and the rest was quaffed by the karapans. It was a mild but instant intoxicant. It lent them the pep they craved for.

Each priest had a duty to perform: kindle fire, tend it, kill and cut the animal, spread tender twigs, wash haoma, pound it, filter the juice, handle utensils, sing, recite, mumble prayers, or wait and watch other priests perform their parts. Singers performed solos and choruses. And of course, there was the touch of pep that haoma imparted to the priests and the prayerful. Above all, the ceremonies created an alliance between the chiefs and the priests, the kavis and the karapans.

The Aryans did not create idols and icons the way others did. They were not image worshippers. Their prayers did not speak of their plight in low tones of pessimism. They

"Mithra&Antiochus" by UnknownLicensed under Public Domain via Wikimedia Commons.

were upright, and they revered righteousness. They abhorred lies. They were, no doubt, superstitious, but never to the point of stooping low to worship noxious animals. Rather they killed them if they could or simply chased them away. They were a noble race, these Aryans." (http://www.spenta.edu/ceremonies.html)

Druids

"A servant of the truth, or wise man." – Anonymous

We mostly tend to remember druids as religious figures. A classic vision of a Druid is a forest priest. The word Druid, itself is rooted in trees. The word is "dru" which means oak, sometimes rowan or hazel; and "Wid," or "Vid" in Sanskrit, means "wisdom" to "know" or to "see." These words show the Proto-Aryan roots of both the Celtic and Sanskrit languages.

They venerated the tree as a symbol of unity between water earth and sky. They were said to demonstrate reverence for specific types of trees like the oak and rowan. This recalls our very ancient beginnings; when trees were an acknowledged source of sustenance, a protection from predators, and even the symbolic boundary with the Divine.

Druids believed in the eternal nature of the Soul and saw living spirit in all forms of creation. God wedded with Maya. Rituals were performed to honor nature and to build a bond between God, and the souls of men and the earth. Like many shamans Druids were skilled with herbalism and holistic remedies." (http://www.ehow.com/about_5402033_history-druids.html)

Very little is known about the ancient druids in literature. They were somewhat secretive, mystical and left no written accounts of themselves. We are left with later descriptions by Greek, Roman, and medieval Irish writers, and there are very few Druidic images. They have been called sorcerers, healers, seers, and professionals. Pliny the Elder, a Roman historian mentions that the Gauls have a lot of respect for the Druids, which were their magicians. The earliest known written reference to the druids dates to 2200 years ago.

In the second century AD, a **druid** was seen as a member of the educated professional class, among Celts during the Iron Age. The druidic class included law speakers, poets, and medical practitioners. Greek and British texts describe them as clergy like characters and masters of healing, science and spirituality. Today druids are seen more romantically as seers of the forest and wise philosophers, than professional businessmen dwelling in the forest.

Various disturbing themes emerged in a number of the Greco-Roman accounts. Druids performed animal and even human sacrifices. They came to believe in a form of reincarnation. This certainly might make murder more palatable to killers who could just tell their slaughtered prey to, "Do better next time!" Pythagorean ideas of 2550 years ago, such as cycling through incarnations until perfection was achieved, were popular at the time.

Druids disappeared in literature after the Roman conquest, for 400 years. There was a Celtic revival in the 17th and 18th centuries, which generated fraternal orders of Neo-Druids and Neo – Pagans based on Ancient Druidic ideas.

Yet, according to the British Museum "modern notions about druids have no connection to druids of the Iron Age. There are misconceptions, recent inventions, and adaptations," as can also be found in Neo – Pagan groups.

Modern mankind was seen as still evolving, and unfolding in its awareness of itself during Ram's time. Early Druids were inspired descendants of Lord Ram, and may have started out as healers who assisted Him.

Pliny says that they believed that the mistletoe of the oak placed in milk was an antidote for all poisons and stimulated fertility in animals. Druids also told of the ritual to collect the mistletoe from the oak trees with a small gold or silver sickle. Ram was given this golden sickle and the healing tonic by an angel – like being to cure those sickened by a plague.

It is thought that Britain was originally occupied by hunter gatherers returning after the Ice Age when the country was still connected to the continent. This would possibly be the time frame for Ram, but as yet there are no artifacts to suggest religious thought. Iron Age sites with evidence of other religious practices, also contain no artifacts or images which point to their use by the ancient Druids. This does not rule them out of the picture, because they carried very little religious gear...maybe a little sickle and some mistletoe.

Druidic thought might well have infused the culture of the people who once inhabited Doggerland, which existed from 10,000, to 6,000 years ago. Its ruins once bridged the gap between the United Kingdom and mainland Europe.

Remnants of Druidic traditions might be found among Celtic peoples in Scotland (Alba), Brittany (Breizh), Wales or Cymru, Ireland (Eire), Cornwall (Kernow), and the Isle of Man (Mannin).

In the Welsh Triads or "Traditional Chronicles" Hu Gadarn, or Hu the Mighty, a descendant of the patriarch Abraham, led a party of settlers from Asia Minor to the British Isles. There he established a religious practice among the Celts. He is referred to by some as the first king to teach people to plow. (Hmm.) (http://en.wikipedia.org/wiki/Hu_Gadarn)

Their purposes changed with the times. Although they had been professionals of high status and were valued by Iron Age Celts like the Gauls of the Alps, there were skeptics who accused them of being wicked bloodthirsty sorcerers opposed to Christ.

"ADruid" by Aylett Sammes - Scan. Licensed under Public Domain via Wikimedia Commons

PANTHEISM AND PANENTHEISM

Oh, and speaking of "the universe" ... Pantheism is the belief that the universe (or nature, as the totality of everything) is identical with divinity. Or that **everything** composes an all-encompassing, God. The **Universe** is defined as all of time and space and its contents. Pantheists do not believe in a distinct personal or anthropomorphic God. http://en.wikipedia.org/wiki/Pantheism

Hinduism, although it encompasses Pantheism and Panentheism, is monistic. Monism finds that one single Creative Essence surrounds and penetrates all things.

Panentheism holds that the being of God includes and penetrates all the Universe; but unlike pantheism the universe is not identical with God. When people call on the Universe, it is not the same as calling on *the Creator* – of the universe. God is not composed of creation no matter how broad the scope. A Creator needs no help from creation. What does a house know about the guy or gal who built it?

There is one absolute, eternal and infinite essence. All things, including human beings, are not independent substances, but only modes or manifestations of the Absolute, which encompasses and pervades all of the Universe. Since the late 1990's mention of the "Universe" has become more common in Europe and the United States.

SYNCRETISM

"I swear by Apollo the physician, and Aesulapius, and Health (Hygeia), and All-heal (Panacea), and call all the gods and goddesses to witness..." **(Hippocrates)**

Syncretism is the result of joining two or more distinct cultures. This might happen when a people were conquered, or a new neighboring community arose. It is an amalgamation, or reconciliation of a variety of aspects of religious cultures and beliefs, similar to what one might find today in the Unitarians.

The Sikh Faith

"The best of all Religions is the yearning for the Divine and purity of deeds."

The temple has a warm, welcoming atmosphere and the people look one in the eye with acceptance. Their cheery Punjabi greeting "Sat Sri Akal" Means **God is the Ultimate Truth.**

So why is this beautiful Faith placed under Syncretism? The *intentionally* syncretic cause of the Sikh Faith was to make sense of, and discover the unity between the teachings of Sri Krishna, Mohammad and even Christ, in a cruel time when people were being offered conversion or death.

Guru Nanak said "There is no Hindu, there is no Muslim." He did not acknowledge castes. All were to be treated as equals no matter what the perks of their birth might be. Although Guru Nanak was not a Revealer of God's Word he was a delight and a balm for humanity! A quintessential wise man. So also, were the other Gurus.

By DDT Fair Trade (Own work) [CC BY-SA 3.0 (http://creativecommons.org/licenses/by-sa/3.0)], via Wikimedia Commons

He believed in a society without any distinctions based on birthright, religion or sex. He insisted that everyone present at his gatherings sit together and share a common meal seated on the ground, whether they were kings or beggars.

"I have become dust of the feet of the slaves of His slaves and I serve His servants. Thus, I have achieved true joy and honor; I live by uttering His Holy Name"
– Guru Arjan

"Asceticism doesn't lie in ascetic robes, or in a walking staff, nor in the ashes. Asceticism doesn't lie in the earring, nor in the shaven head, nor blowing a conch. Asceticism lies in remaining pure amidst impurities. Asceticism doesn't lie in mere words; He is an ascetic who treats everyone alike. Asceticism doesn't lie in visiting burial places; it lies not in wandering about, nor in bathing at places of pilgrimage. Asceticism is to remain pure amidst impurities." – Guru Nanak

On his fourth great journey in life Guru Nanak dressed in the blue garb of a Muslim pilgrim. He traveled west to visit Mecca, Medina and Baghdad. Arriving at Mecca, Guru Nanak fell asleep with his feet pointing towards the holy Kaaba. When the watchman on his night rounds noticed this he kicked the Guru, saying **"How dare you turn your feet towards the house of God."** At this Guru Nanak woke up and said: **"Good man, I am weary after a long journey. Kindly turn my feet in the direction where God is not."**

In all there was a covenant with Ten Gurus in succession beginning with the holy Guru Nanak (1469-1539) and ending with the Sikh Holy Book. It is a compilation of Sikh wisdom known as the Sri Guru Granth Sahib Ji, which is read almost constantly, with occasional breaks for the playing of instruments. Sikhs must believe in the following:

- Equality: All humans are equal before God. All creatures have God's spirits and must be properly respected.
- Personal right: Every person has a right to life, but this right is restricted.
- Actions count: Salvation is obtained by one's actions, including good deeds and remembrance of God.
- Living a family life: We must live as a family unit to provide for and nurture children.
- Sharing: We are encouraged, to share and give to charity 10 percent of one's net earnings.
- Accept God's will: Develop your personality so that you recognize happy events and miserable events as one. The training received by moving through the events is the same. It is our reactions that matter.
- The four fruits of life: Truth, contentment, contemplation and Naam, (the name of God).

Unacceptable behavior:
- Non-logical behavior: Superstitions and rituals are not meaningful to Sikhs (pilgrimages, fasting, bathing in rivers, circumcision, worship of graves, idols or pictures, and compulsory wearing of the veil for women, are not acceptable.
- Material obsession: Accumulation of materials has no meaning in Sikhism. Wealth such as gold, portfolio, stocks, commodities, and properties will all be left here on Earth when you depart. Do not get attached to them.
- Sacrifice of creatures: or "suti": This includes widows throwing themselves in the funeral pyre of their husbands. Also lamb and calf slaughter to celebrate holy occasions, etc. are forbidden.
- Non-family oriented living: A Sikh is not allowed to live as a recluse, beggar, yogi, monk, nun, or celibate.
- Worthless talk: Bragging, gossip, lying, etc. are not permitted.
- Intoxication: Alcohol, drugs, tobacco, and consumption of other intoxicants is not permitted.

- Priestly class: Sikhs do not have to depend on a priest for performing any religious functions. They are not supposed to favor a class or caste system, where the priestly class reigns highest. Everyone is equal. From Sikhi Wiki encyclopedia

    http://www.sikhiwiki.org/index.php/Sikhism

"Humility is my mace; becoming the dust of everybody's feet is my sword. No evil doer can dare withstand these weapons." – Guru Nanak

HENOTHEISM

Henotheism, is a special offshoot of syncretism and a very predominant form of Polytheism. Literally, "one God," henotheism is defined as the belief in and worship of a single God, while accepting the existence or possible existence of other deities.

It can also be a belief in multiple gods in conjunction with a Supreme Deity. A merger of gathered affiliations, either physically, or through the ages. A fading of a monotheistic Faith. It starts as God, above the other gods, at least until the concept of a Supreme Being recedes into a pantheon.

As far as one can see, this is extremely common, and happens within every monotheistic faith as it fades.

India is a great example of a tradition which has adopted pieces of every religion which has passed its borders. The Hindu Faith finds a place for nearly everything; from Brahman to rats and monkeys. It boasts an array of gods, collected over time, by an inclusive society that believed in a variety of distinct gods, and were very definitely syncretic, in view.

Another example was the people and the places of Egypt who were not ready to listen to the monotheism posed by Ahkenaten He likely had studied both the works of Hermes and heard the teachings of Moses, who was his contemporary.

Almost immediately, people were openly henotheistic, placing the single God, Aten with more "acceptable" gods. Rather quickly they forgot Aten altogether.

An early inscription likens the Aten to the sun as compared to stars, God above the other gods. Later official language avoids calling the Aten a god at all.

The early Aryans, Pagans, Egyptians, Hindu's, Norse, Greeks and Romans have all wandered down this path, naming many gods, with the Supreme.

Maximus Tyrius (2nd century A.D.) stated: "there is one god, the king and father of all things, and many gods, sons of god, ruling together with him." (Encyclopædia Britannica, 11th edition, Maximus Tryius.)

The beautiful Upanishads are meditations on man's link to the universe and its Creator. They are not about liturgies and rituals. They are beautiful sacred teachings that described humanity as having been created, with virtue and everlasting life.

In one passage,

"A youth asks a learned man, how many gods there are. The teacher says three hundred and three. 'Yes,' responded the youth, 'but how many are there really?' The learned man narrowed the number to thirty-three. 'Yes,' responded the youth, 'but how many are there really?' Finally the learned man said, 'One.' "

Henotheism was coined by Friedrich Wilhelm Joseph von Schelling (1775–1854), to describe the early stages of "monotheism." Max Muller (1823–1900) elaborated with various subtypes of henotheism designed to describe differing forms of the idea. The Rigveda was the basis for Muller's study of henotheism. He felt this was a polytheistic tradition, striving towards a formulation of the One Divinity, or ekam.

One subtype, "monolatrism," refers to recognition of the existence of many gods, but with the *consistent worship* of only one deity. The believer worships one god alone without denying that others may worship different gods with equal validity.

Another variant is "kathenotheism," worshipping "one god at a time" in a sequence. This is like the returns of the Holy Spirit are sequential. Here Muller referenced the Vedas; where he explained each deity; such as Brahman, Vishnu, and Shiva, is treated as supreme, in its turn.

This is quite understandable, yet is the opposite of the theme of this paper, which sees the addition of gods to God as more of an unraveling process than a building process. I once took a final exam in Invertebrate Paleontology. A table full of clam fossils was to be sequenced in their order of evolution. I was very careful and took a bit of time. As you guessed, I'm sure. They were all correctly sequenced, but in reverse order. Knowing only what is, makes knowing where it started, more difficult.

Monism: The worship of a single reality, a source distinct from all living things – is basically, a definition of what many call "God" by whatever name. A prime example of the monistic aspects of the late Rigveda is the Nasadiya Sukta, a Creation hymn: **"That One breathed by itself without breath, other than it there has been nothing."** Beautiful!

Ishwar Chandra Sharma describes it as **"Absolute Reality, beyond all contradictions of existence and non-existence, light and darkness, and of time, space and cause."** There are other examples:

"Monotheism was pervasive in the educated circles in Late Antiquity" and **"all divinities were interpreted as aspects, particles or epithets of one supreme God.** Jupiter or Zeus was considered the supreme, all-powerful and all-knowing, king and father of the Olympian gods.

Plotinus taught that *above* **the gods of traditional belief was "The One,"** and polytheist grammarian Maximus of Madauros even stated that **"only a madman would deny the existence of the supreme God."** (Maijastina Kahlos, *Debate and Dialogue: Christian and Pagan Cultures C. 360-430*, Ashgate Publishing, 2007, p. 70; p.145; p.160)

Baal was a title meaning 'Lord' in the Northwest Semitic languages spoken in the Levant more than six thousand years ago. It came to be associated with the storm and fertility god "Hadad," or "Adad" as seen in Atrahasis' tale. Over time, the Hebrews associated the cultic term "Yahweh" with Hadad, and finally decried that he was a false God, a distraction, naming him Beelzebub. Possibly meaning the "Lord of the Flies" – a devil.

Or, it might be Ba'al – Zebub "of the heavenly abode" or "Master of the House." Big, big difference! Either way, that ship has passed.

PERSPECTIVE

Please review snapshots of two cultures who employ henotheistic beliefs. First will come a snippet from the Norse Eddas; which lays out a belief in Odin and many gods, aspects of nature, animals, and perhaps Primitive as well as Modern human heroes.

The second is from the Yazidi People, who today are struggling to survive terrorist persecution and genocide. They hang on to a most impressive number of fragments that were once good and pure, but now lead to bloodshed.

These examples paint evocative pictures of henotheism.

Norse Eddas and Sagas

The Eddas are a primary source for our knowledge of ancient Norse pagan beliefs. Granted, Eddas and Sagas are basically bits of history recalled in prose, and poetry. They have decentralized divinity into various heroes and gods much like other Pagan groups at the time, and they did not mind harming others. There was a lot of jockeying for space in the north lands. Some peoples used social politics, and some carved their turf out with big swords.

This translation of the Poetic Eddas by Henry Adams Bellows is highly readable.
http://www.sacred-texts.com/neu/poe/poe02.htm

pg. xxi "A convenient date to remember is that of the sea-fight of Hafrsfjord, 872, when Harald the Fair-Haired broke the power of the independent Norwegian nobles, and made himself overlord of nearly all the country. Many of the defeated nobles fled overseas, where inviting refuges had been found for them by earlier wanderers and plunder-seeking raiders. This was the time of the inroads of the dreaded Northmen in France, and in 885 Hrolf Gangr (Rollo) laid siege to Paris itself. Many Norwegians went to Ireland, where their compatriots had already built Dublin, and where they remained in control of most of the island till Brian Boru shattered their power at the battle of Clontarf in 1014.

Of all the migrations, however, the most important were those migrating to Iceland. Here grew up an active civilization, fostered by absolute independence and by remoteness from the wars which wracked Norway, and brought them constantly in contact with the culture of the South.

Christianity, introduced throughout the Norse world about the year 1000, brought with it the stability of learning, and the Icelanders became not only the makers but also the students and recorders of history. The years between 875 and 1100 period of oral literature. Most of the military and political leaders were also poets, and they composed a mass of lyric poetry concerning the authorship of which we know a good deal, and much of which has been preserved. Narrative (p. xxii) prose also flourished, for the Icelander had a passion for story-telling and story-hearing. After 1100 came the day of the writers. These sagamen collected the material that for generations had passed from mouth to mouth, and gave it permanent form in writing. The greatest bulk of what we now have of Old Norse literature,– and the published part of it makes

[Public domain], via Wikimedia Commons
Title page of a manuscript of the Prose Edda

a formidable library,– originated thus in the earlier period before the introduction of writing, and was put into final shape by the scholars, most of them Icelanders, of the hundred years following 1150.

The mass of literature thus collected and written down...maybe roughly divided into four groups. The greatest in volume is made up of the sagas: narratives mainly in prose, ranging all the way from authentic history of the Norwegian kings and the early Icelandic settlements to fairy-tales. Embodied in the sagas is found the material composing the second group: the skaldic poetry, a vast collection of songs of praise, triumph, love, lamentation, and so on, almost uniformly characterized

p. xxiii "Most of the poems of the Poetic Edda have unquestionably reached us in rather bad shape. During the long period of oral transmission they suffered all sorts of interpolations, omissions and changes, and some of them, as they now stand, are a bewildering hodge-podge of little related fragments. Under such circumstances, it is clear that the establishment of a satisfactory text is a matter of the utmost difficulty.

The poems are great tragic literature, with vivid descriptions of the emotional states of the protagonists, Gods and heroes alike. Women play a prominent role in the Eddic age, and many of them are delineated as skilled warriors. Great wanderings of the Scandinavian peoples, and particularly the Norwegians.

The impact of these sagas from a sparsely inhabited rocky island in the middle of the Atlantic on world culture is wide-ranging. Wagner's operas are largely based on incidents from the Edda, via the Niebelungenlied. J.R.R. Tolkien also plundered the Eddas for atmosphere, plot material and the names of many characters in the Hobbit, and the Lord of the Rings." – John Bruno Hare

(The Poetic Edda, by Henry Adams Bellows, [1936], at sacred-texts.com); (http://www.sacred-texts.com/neu/poe/poe02.htm

Here are excerpts of three, with commentary. Readers may wish to check out the website for further info:

Baldr's Draumar (Dreams)

p. 196 2. Then Othin rose, | the enchanter old,
And the saddle he laid | on Sleipnir's back;
Thence rode he down | to Niflhel deep,
And the hound he met | that came from hell.
3. Bloody he was | on his breast before,
At the father of magic | he howled from afar;
Forward rode Othin, | the earth resounded
Till the house so high | of Hel he reached.
4. Then Othin rode | to the eastern door,
There, he knew well, | was the wise-woman's grave;
Magic he spoke | and mighty charms,
Till spell-bound she rose, | and in death she spoke:
[2. Sleipnir: Othin's eight-legged horse, the son of Loki and the stallion Svathilfari; cf. Lokasenna, 23, and Grimnismol, 44, and notes. Niflhel: the murky ("nifl") dwelling of Hel, goddess of the dead. The hound: Garm; cf. Voluspo, 44.
3. Father of magic: Othin appears constantly as the god of magic. Hel: offspring of Loki and

the giantess Angrbotha, as were the wolf Fenrir and Mithgarthsorm. She ruled the world of the unhappy dead, either those who had led evil lives or, according to another tradition, those who had not died in battle... [The] wise-woman belongs apparently to the race of the giants, she would be unwilling to answer a god's questions. Heaven: the word used includes all the upper worlds, in contrast to hell.]

Hamthesmol

*17. From their sheaths they drew | their shining swords,
Their blades, to the giantess | joy to give;
By a third they lessened | the might that was theirs,
The fighter young | to earth they felled.
18. Their cloaks they shook, | their swords they sheathed,
The high-born men | wrapped their mantles close.
19. On their road they fared | and an ill way found,
And their sister's son | on a tree they saw,
On the wind-cold wolf-tree | west of the hall,
And cranes'-bait crawled; | none would care to linger.
20. In the hall was din, | the men drank deep,
And the horses' hoofs | could no one hear,
Till the warrior hardy | sounded his horn.
[17. The manuscript does not indicate line 1 as beginning a stanza. The giantess: presumably the reference is to Hel, goddess of the dead, but the phrase is doubtful.
19. Ill way: very likely the road leading through the gate of Jormunrek's town at which Svanhild was trampled to death. Sister's son: "stepson," for the reference is certainly to Randver, son of Jormunrek, hanged by his father on Bikki's advice (cf. Guthrunarhvot, introductory note). Wolf-tree: the gallows, the wolf being symbolical of outlaws. Cranes'-bait: presumably either snakes or worms, but the passage is doubtful.]*

Reginsmol

P.358 *Sigurth went to Hjalprek's stud and chose for himself a horse, who thereafter was called Grani. At that time Regin, the son of Hreithmar, he was more ingenious than all other men, and a dwarf in stature; he was wise, fierce and skilled in magic. Regin undertook Sigurth's bringing up and teaching, and loved him much. He told Sigurth of his forefathers, and also of this: that once Othin and Hönir and Loki had come to Andvari's waterfall, and in the fall were many fish.*

Andvari was a dwarf, who had dwelt long in the waterfall in the shape of a pike, and there he got his food. "Otr was the name of a brother of ours," said. Regin, "who often went into the fall in the shape of an otter; he had caught a salmon, and sat on the high bank eating it with his eyes shut. Loki threw a stone at him and killed him; the gods thought they had good luck, and stripped the skin off the otter.

That same evening they sought a night's lodging in Hreithmar's house, and showed their booty. Then we seized them, and told them, as ransom for their lives, to fill the otter skin with gold, and completely cover it outside as well with red gold. Then they sent Loki to get the gold;

he went to Ron and got her net, and went then to Andvari's fall and cast the net in front of the pike, and the pike leaped into the net." Then Loki said:
1. "What is the fish | that runs in the flood,
And itself from ill cannot save?
If thy head thou wouldst | from hell redeem,
Find me the water's flame."
Andvari spake:
2. "Andvari am I, | and Oin my father,
In many a fall have I fared;
An evil Norn | in olden days
Doomed me In waters to dwell."
Loki spake:
3. "Andvari, say, | if thou seekest still
To live in the land of men,
What payment is set | for the sons of men
Who war with lying words?"

[Regin is there the name of the dragon (here Regin's brother, Fafnir). names a Regin among the dwarfs, and the name may have assisted in making Regin a dwarf here. Othin, Hönir and Loki: these same three gods appear in company in Voluspo, 17-18. Andvari's fall: according to Snorri, was in the world of the dark elves, while the one when Loki killed the otter was not; here, With his eyes shut: according to Snorri, Otr ate with his eyes shut because he was so greedy that he could not bear to see the food before him diminishing. Ron: wife of the sea-god Ægir, who draws down, drowning men with her net; cf. Helgakvitha Hjorvarthssonar, 18 and note. Snorri says that Loki caught the pike with his hands.

1. Snorri quotes this stanza. Water's game: gold, so called because Ægir, the sea-god, was wont to light his hall with gold.]

People stray from the worship of one God, to seek extra assistance from animals, human icons, statues, sainted beings, angel, ancestors, gods, etc. This is not necessarily bad, unless one forgets to acknowledge the Single Creator above all else. Without a single, guiding force, virtues decay, and one of the side effects is that people, thinking only of themselves, feel freer to ignore or hurt one another.

The Yazidi

Yazidi are a Kurdish-speaking ethnoreligious community, which until recently was based primarily in the Nineveh Province of Northern Iraq.

Yazidi would probably say they practice a monotheistic faith, but there is a lot of evidence they left that path long ago. They are most definitely syncretic. They have bound together a huge accumulation of religious history, by selecting a mass of religious information from literally a dozen Faiths and religious traditions. Yazidi people present a really good example of Paganism.

There is God, but also Melek Tause, one of the Seven Angels whom they adore as icons at the holy shrines, along with Sheik Adi. But there are quite a few other elements:

1) Ancient nature-worship and reincarnation. Around 2550 years ago, Pythagoras and his followers were important for their contributions to both religion and science. His reli-

gious teachings were based on the doctrine of metempsychosis, which teaches that the soul never dies and is destined to a cycle of rebirths until it is able to free itself from the cycle through the purity of its life. Yazidis refer to reincarnation as a change of garment.

The Yazidi soul can attain purity through continual reincarnation within the faith. It can also be halted by banishment from the Yazidi community. This is the worst possible fate since the soul's spiritual progress ends, and return to the faith is impossible.

2) There are wisps from the ancient Persians. They share the image of a rock crystal sphere surrounding the earth, as in the Persian Creation. Also, the word Yezidi– worshippers of the Seven Angels "Yazatas," may relate to pre-Zoroastrian religion, where the word Yazdani means people who worship the "worthy," including the seven Bright Beings, the Amesha Spentas. The Mazda Yasnis, are the worshippers of Ahura Mazda, the Avestan name for God.

The purity of the four elements Earth, Air, Fire and Water are protected by a number of taboos. One must not spit on earth, water or fire. Spitting or pouring hot water on the ground may harm or offend spirits or souls who happen to be hit by the discarded liquid. There are also taboos concerning the disposal of bodily waste, hair and menstrual blood. Other purity taboos include: holy men refraining from certain gas causing vegetables. Purity is focal to many ancient people, like some Persians, Essenes, and Jains. Yazidis don't wear blue colors. I don't know how this relates. For many early tribes, the blue color is sacred.

3) Mithraism. Yazidis slay bulls at annual festivals. And their dead are buried in conical tombs soon after death, with crossed hands. This burial style was used prior to 3500 years ago. It is often associated with Aryan descendants, who practiced Mithraism.

4) Hebrew elements remain. Children are baptized at birth and circumcision is common, not required. Like the Essenes or early Jews, they strongly avoid too much contact with outside groups. They are isolated from outsiders to keep their lineage pure. Their concern with religious purity, and a reluctance to mix with others encourages living only in Yazidi communities, and practicing endogamous marriage.

They have a caste system of murids, sheikhs, and pirs, who marry within their own groups. Deviations could lead to abandonment, excommunication and death. Aside from the brutal exogamy taboos, too much contact of with any non-Yazidis is considered polluting. Military service is avoided because they might have to live among Muslims, and share personal items like cups or razors with outsiders.

5) Yazidis wash iconic figures of Melek Taus, and parade peacock images from village to village.

6) In more recent developments: they regard Jesus Christ as an Angel in human form, perhaps a return of one of the Seven. And it would seem that their beliefs have been influenced by a local Sufi order who live in the Yezidi mountains, because they now recognize Mohammed as a Prophet.

Most recently they recognized Sheik 'Adi as a return of Melek Taus.

There is such a build-up, one might be tempted to cite Christ on patches and wineskins. Matthew 16-17

"But no one puts a patch of unshrunk cloth on an old garment; for the patch pulls away from the garment, and a worse tear results. "Nor do people put new wine into old wineskins; otherwise the wineskins burst, and the wine pours out and the wineskins are ruined; but they put new wine into fresh wineskins, and both are preserved."

Melek Taus and the Seven

The concept of Melek Taus is the most misunderstood part of the Yazidi religion. This is one of the reasons why their community has suffered historical persecutions.

Yazidis believe that the world was created by God in his own illumination– and that's about where monotheism ends. God entrusted the world to seven Angels, "the Seven Mysteries" led by the Peacock Angel Tawûsê Melek or in English Melek Taus. The seven angels are formed by the light of God and Yazidis believe these angels are occasionally reincarnated in human form.

This fits with the Mesopotamian concept that there were seven pre-flood Manifestations of God. Also the Seven Amesha Spentas figure prominently in the Persian Yasht, a collection of hymns, called the Yasnas. One of these deals with the Seven Bright Angels, the "Amesha Spentas."

The Yazidis' reputation of being "devil worshipers" is connected to the other name of Melek Taus "Shaytan," who proudly refused to violate monotheism by worshipping Adam and Eve at God's express command. In the Judeo-Christian Bible, Satan is considered a fallen Angel, who parted from God's will and became the symbol of Evil. Muslims and Sufi's believe that the Angel Iblis, their name for (Shaytan), became the leader of the evil Jinn. His refusal to submit, caused him to fall out of Grace with God.

God ordered Melek Taus, who had filled the earth with flora and fauna, not to bow to other beings. Then God created the other archangels and ordered them to bring him dust from the earth and build the body of Adam. God gave life to Adam from his own breath and instructed all archangels to bow to him. The archangels obeyed except for Melek Taus. In answer to God's query as to why, Melek Taus replied, "How can I submit to another being! I am from your illumination, Adam is made of dust."

Melek Taus was then thrown into Hell, or hellish prison, until his tears of remorse quenched the hell fires. He descended and saw the suffering and pain of the world then he cried. His tears lasted thousands of years extinguishing the fires of hell. Like Adam, He eventually became reconciled with God, Who praised him and made him the leader of all angels and his deputy on the earth. He now serves, as an intermediary between God and humanity.

Note: The jinnī, or genie are creatures mentioned frequently in the Qu'ran. Sura (chapter) 72 is The "Sura of Jinn." But there is also mention of them in other Islamic, and pre-Islamic Arabic texts. The Quran says that the jinn are made of a smokeless scorching fire but are also physical in nature. They are able to interact in a tactile manner with people and objects, and likewise be acted upon. The jinn, along with humans and angels are creations of God. Like human beings, the jinn can be good, evil, or neutrally benevolent and hence have free will like humans. Shaytan jinn are comparable to non-human entities, including demons in other faiths.

Yazidis feel that the order to bow to Adam was merely a test for Melek Taus. God could have commanded him submit to Adam, but gave him the choice as a test. Yazidis revere Melek Taus for his choice to refusing to submit to God by bowing to Adam. Satan for many people today actually does in fact represent the CHOICE between Good and Evil.

Yazidis believe Melek Taus is not a source of evil *or* wickedness. They consider him to be the leader of the Archangels not a fallen angel. If there is evil in the world, it does not come from a fallen angel or from the fires of hell. The Yazidi don't have a Satan figure and they do not believe in the concept of Hell.

They believe that good and evil exists both in the mind and spirit of human beings. It depends on the humans themselves, as to which they choose. Melek Taus was given the same choice between good and evil by God and Yazidis believe He chose the good. They further believe that **the source of evil is in the heart and spirit of humans themselves**, not in Melek Taus. The evil in this world is completely man-made.

All people have good and evil inside of them, and choices are made free of external temptation. Maybe not such good news for suicide bombers and others who don't take personal responsibility for their actions.

Besides Melek Taus, there are other active forces in their religion. One is Sheik Adi who believed that the spirit of Melek Taus was the same as his own, perhaps as a reincarnation. He said, "I was present when Adam was living in Paradise and also when Nemrud threw Abraham into the fire. I was present when God said to me: 'You are the ruler and Lord on the Earth.' God, the compassionate, gave me seven earths and throne of the heaven." Sheik 'Adi ibn Musafir, died in 1162, and his tomb is a focal point of Yazidi pilgrimage.

The Kitêba Cilwe is the Book of Revelation or "Book of Illumination." It is believed to contain the words of Tawûsê Melek. It states that He allocates responsibilities, blessings and misfortunes as he sees fit. Humans should not question him. A second book the Mishefa Res or Black Book bears some resemblance to Judeo–Christian Genesis.

Apparently, manuscripts of both books published in 1911 and 1913 were written by non-Yazidis, but the material in them is said to be consistent with authentic Yazidi traditions.

Adam and Eve

The Black Book's tale of human Creation gives Yazidis a distinctive ancestry, separating them from other races. Before the roles of the sexes were determined Adam and Eve quarreled about which of them provided the creative element in the begetting of children. Each stored their seed in a jar which was then sealed. When Eve's was opened it was full of insects and other unpleasant creatures, but inside Adam's jar was a beautiful boy child. This lovely child, known as son of Jar (Shehid bin Jer) grew up to marry a houri (exceptionally pure and beautiful woman), and they became the ancestors of the Yazidis. Therefore, the Yazidi are regarded as descending from Adam alone, while other humans are descendants of both Adam and Eve.

The Black Book, from Devil Worship; *The Sacred Books and Traditions of the Yezidiz* by Isya Joseph (1919); (http://en.wikipedia.org/wiki/Yazidi_Black_Book)

They carry their beliefs with them, in the form oral tradition wherever they go. Arkon Daraul, wrote in Secret Societies Yesterday and Today (1961) about a Yazidi-influenced group in the London suburbs called the "Order of the Peacock Angel."

The core texts of the religion that exist today are the hymns known as Qewals. They are full of cryptic allusions that need to be accompanied by explanations of their content. They have been orally transmitted during most of Yazidi history, but are now being collected with the assent of the community, which effectively transforms Yazidism into scriptural religion, and that may improve their lot with some of their enemies.

Prayers: Yazidis pray facing the sun at sunrise and at sunset; at noon they face Lalish. Prayer should be accompanied by certain gestures, including kissing the rounded neck of their sacred shirt (reminiscent of Jewish prayer shawls). The prayers must not be performed in the presence of outsiders.

Calendar: According to the Yazidi Melek Taus came to earth 6,762 years ago. He returns annually on the first Wednesday of Hebrew Nisan (April), their New Year's Day. Wednesdays in general are holy and Saturday is their day of rest. There is a three-day fast in December.

Festivals: The Yazidi New Year falls in spring, on the first Wednesday of April. Women lament in the cemeteries accompanied by the music of clerics, "Qewals." The festival is celebrated with the joyous Sama, a social time of listening to the music of drum and oboe, communal dancing, and meals. A highlight is the decorating of eggs.

A shrine in the Tawaf village is the site of a festival held in the spring to honor its patron. The festivities include secular music, and Sama.

Another important festival is the "circulation of the peacock" where clerics and other religious dignitaries visit villages, bringing the sacred image of a brass peacock symbolizing Melek Taus. Taxes are collected at these gatherings from the pious, sermons are preached and holy water distributed.

The greatest festival of the year is the "Feast of the Assembly" a seven-day occasion held at the holiest Yazidi shrine, the tomb of Sheikh Adi ibn Musafir in Lalish, near Mosul, Iraq. The buildings contain not only many shrines dedicated to the Angels, but feature a number of other sites with symbols significant to other faiths. There are even a dog and a serpent among their icons.

The focal point is the belief in an annual gathering of the Seven Angels in the holy place at this time. During the celebration Yazidi bathe in the river, wash figures of Melek Tause, and light hundreds of lamps in the tombs of Sheikh Adi and other saints. Rituals practiced include the sacrifice of a bull or ox at the shrine of Sheikh Shams. This is one reason they have been connected to Mithraism.

The sacrifice of the ox is meant to declare the arrival of fall and to ask for precipitation during winter in order to bring back life to the Earth in the spring. The ox is also the symbol of Tashrīn, a Jewish month associated with a new year's celebration.

This annual "Feast of the Seven Days" draws a large crowd of pilgrims. It is a time for social contact and reminder of Yezidi identity. This includes Sama which means "listening" and perhaps meditation rituals, which can include: singing, playing musical instruments, dancing, recitation of poetry and prayers, wearing ethnic clothing. If possible, Yazidis make at least one pilgrimage to Lalish during their lifetime.

Persecution

Most recently the Yazidi were in the news for the persecution and genocide they suffered at the hands of the terrorists calling themselves the Islamic Republic. In August 2014 President Barak Obama authorized humanitarian air drops of food and water onto Iraq's Mount Sinjar; and targeted strikes against the terrorists in support of the beleaguered religious minority.

The strikes also protected American military personnel during airdrops of meals and water to aid thousands of individuals from religious minorities who were trapped on the mountaintop. Subsequently the British Air Force assisted the relief effort, and Australian Prime Minister Tony Abbott pledged humanitarian support.

European nations resolved to help arm the Peshmerga fighters who defended the Yazidi, with more advanced weaponry. The Peshmerga are Syrian Kurdish fighters who battled terrorist militants on behalf of the refugees. They carved out an escape route for tens of thousands who were trapped on a mountaintop.

An extremely old temple sits on the highest peak of the Sinjar mountains in northern Iraq. The Chermera or "40 Men" temple, was possibly named in relation to a burial of forty men on this site. The Yazidis may have fled up the backbone of the Sinjar Mountains, which actually appear, from above, to be an articulated spine that fell onto the sand.

The Peshmerga rescued several thousand Yazidis via a humanitarian corridor. A worker in the effort to help them cross the Tigris into Syria described the conditions on Mount Sinjar as "a genocide." Hundreds, even a thousand corpses were strewn along the way. They were caught between the prospect of death by dehydration, and murder. The U.N. estimated around 50,000 Yazidis fled to the mountain. Kurdish officials said at least 45,000 had crossed through the safe passage, leaving thousands stranded behind.

Reports coming from Sinjar stated that sick or elderly Yazidi who could not make the trek were being executed by ISIL. Yazidi parliamentarian Haji Ghandour told reporters that "In our history, we have suffered 72 massacres."

Treatment of Yazidis was also very harsh under the Ottoman Turks who massacred, and almost wiped them out completely in the 1800's. The slaughter at Sinjar is, yet another massacre for Yazidis. They are persecuted as "devil worshippers" which is not only deeply offensive to the Yazidis themselves, but quite simply wrong. Non-Yazidis have associated Melek Taus with Shaytan or Satan, but Yazidis find that offensive and do not actually mention that name.

Unfortunately, Persecution Goes Both Ways

In 2007, an incidence in an "honor killing" made world headlines. It is not clear from the video whether the young woman was ambushed on the way home, or if the mob of hundreds, maybe even thousands, stormed her home and dragged her into the street. The girl was taken to a town square and stripped to symbolize that she had dishonored her family and religion. The incident was filmed on mobile phones and widely distributed throughout the internet.

She was stripped to her underwear from the waist down. Some of the crowd tried to keep her lower body covered with what looks like another jacket.

The stoning lasted approximately 30 minutes. She can be seen in the video attempting to sit up and calling for help. The crowd taunts her and repeatedly throws large chunks of rock or concrete on her head. After her death, her body was tied behind a car and dragged through the streets, then buried with the remains of a dog. As a final insult her body was *"exhumed and sent to the Medico-Legal Institute in Mosul so that tests could be performed to see whether she had died a virgin."*

In a protest against the stoning hundreds of Kurdish residents called for an end to honor killings. It is believed the murder sparked several reprisal attacks against Yazidis. Almost 800 people, including several Assyrian Christians were killed.

(Iraq: 'Honor Killing' of teenage girl condemned as abhorrent (May 2, 2007). Amnesty. org.uk. Retrieved May 7, 2007. *"Honour Killing" Sparks Fears of New Iraqi Conflict* Institute for War & Peace Reporting (retrieved 21 May 2007)

Sadly, on May 2012 five members of another Yazidi family living in Detmold, Germany, were convicted for having murdered their sister for an "honor killing." They were sentenced to terms ranging from five-and-a-half years to life in prison. The victim had fallen in love with a German journeyman baker and ran away from her family violating the exogamy taboo. In November 2011, her siblings abducted her and a brother killed her with two shots to the head.

Yazidi intentions may be pure, but the outcomes of rigid dogma needs to be purified. Practices of dualism, syncretism and idol worship are an undeniable part of their heritage. They have tried to remain true to the threads of religion, but spirituality has instead become man-made philosophy, and culture.

IDOL WORSHIP

Idol worship arose in every single revealed religion as polytheism gained the ascendancy. This is part of the cause, of the arrival of the next Manifestation's visit.

A slight twist on seeing God in all things can produce idolatry. Most everyone agrees that trees are sacred. But imagine if instead of praying to the Creator who made this tree and is in this tree and is the source of its beautiful fruit, a person makes an offering to the tree itself so it will bear fruit. Or worse, they worship the god of the tree as an idol or amulet. Most distant of all, the person prays to a random fertility deity so the tree will bear fruit.

At this point we begin to worship a multitude of things rather than God. This thinking represents a huge materialistic departure from the original spiritual simplicity. It marks the beginning of the degeneration of spirituality and leads to the need for a regeneration of "The Word."

People of Noah

"For many generations Noah's people had been worshipping statues that they called gods. They believed that these gods would bring them (blessings), **protect them from evil, and provide for all their needs. They gave their idols names according to the power they thought these gods possessed."** – Ibn Jarir al Tabari

They worshipped the statues as their personal idols and gave them traits which they felt had some meaning to them. They had forgotten the Creator, a loving parent who was trying to guide them along an evolving spiritual journey, by demanding the constant development and honing of Virtues; they became immoral.

God would send new Great Beings periodically, like Noah to try to correct the inevitable deviations which would crop up. At times, after heartbreaking results, it would become necessary to punish people for their irremediably cruel and evil deeds.

People of Abraham and Moses

Abraham was a young man who lived among people that refused to worship One God, even though their ancestors had followed Brahman, as taught by Lord Krishna. Even the name Abram or Abraham testifies to this.

But now, "*They prayed to idols they brought with them from India. Once He asked His father, Terah 'Do you take these idols for gods? If you do, then you and your people are wrong.*' This did not sit well, because the priests of the area were wealthy, powerful and they demanded respect.

'*Our fathers worshipped them*' Terah responded.

'*You and your fathers clearly have been wrong.*'

'*When he said to his father and his people: What are these images, to which you are so devoted?' They replied: 'We found our fathers worshipping them.' He said: 'Then you as well as your fathers have indeed, been in manifest error.'*" (http://www.islam101.com/history/people/prophets/ibrahim.htm)

Terah's people pitched Abraham into a fire and tried to burn Him, rather than listen. God cooled the flames, and Abraham wisely moved on to find His people elsewhere. Babylonian ears were closed.

Very similar to the beloved people of Moses, who returned to Idol worship. They fashioned a golden bull calf as soon as He was out of sight. In truth, it happens in every age.

How Did We Come to Worship Idols?

Here are a few interesting descriptions of how it happened. This is a wonderful explanation by Ibn Jarir Al-Tabari:

"*There were righteous people who lived in the period between Adam and Noah and who had followers who held them as models. After their death, their friends who used to emulate them said: 'If we make statues of them, it will be more pleasing to us in our worship, and will remind us of them.'*

These statues were originally given the names of good people who had lived among them. After their deaths, the statues were erected to keep their memories alive. As time passed, however, people began to **worship these statues**. Later generations did not even know why they had been erected. They only knew their parents had prayed to them. That is how idol worshipping developed.

Since they had no understanding of Allah the Almighty Who would punish them for their evil deeds, they became cruel and immoral.

Ibn Abbas explained: "*Following upon the death of those righteous men, Satan inspired their people to erect statues in the places where they used to sit. They did this, but these statues were not worshiped until the coming generations deviated from the right way of life. Then they worshipped them as their idols.*"

Ibn Abi Hatim related this story: "*Waddan was a righteous man who was loved by his people. When he died, they withdrew to his grave in the land of Babylonia and were overwhelmed by sadness. When Iblis* (the Devil) *saw their sorrow caused by his death, he disguised himself in the form of a man saying: 'I have seen your sorrow because of this man's death; can I make a statue like him, which could be put in your meeting place to make you remember him?' They said: 'Yes.'*

So he made the statue and they put it in their meeting place in order to be reminded of him. When Iblis saw their interest in remembering him, he said: 'Can I build a statue of him in the home of each one of you so that he would be in everyone's house and you could remember him?'

They agreed. Their children learned about and saw what they were doing. They also learned about their remembrance of him instead of Allah. So the first to be worshipped instead of Allah was Waddan, the idol which they named thus."

Every idol from those earlier times, was a person mentioned and worshipped by a certain group of people. At first they made pictures in the sand; as the ages passed, they made these pictures into statues, so that their forms could be fully recognized. Later they were worshipped *instead* of Allah.

Therefore, a fading of belief in One God resulting in polytheism,

"... [It] results in the loss of freedom, the destruction of the mind, and the absence of a noble target in life. People lose sight of the fact that Allah alone is the Creator." (Imam Ibn Katheer Rahim'u'llah www.islaam.org.uk)

Saints

On the matter of distractions to worshipping only God, for some today it is saints, clerics, or other intercessors who became the recipients of prayer. "Saints preserve us!" was a statement often heard among Catholics of my youth. It would seem innocent enough, but consider the tale below.

Travelers told the Prophet Muhammad about the church called "Maria" which they had seen in the land of Abyssinia. They described its beauty, and the pictures therein. He said: **"Those are the people who build places of worship on the grave of every dead man who was righteous, and then make therein those pictures. Those are the worst of creation unto Allah."**

GREAT DISAPPOINTMENTS: JUSTICE AND MERCY TWO EDGES OF THE SWORD

One of the things new Revelations have in common, is rejection by the masses of a new Messenger. When people are complacent, comfortable, or even too rigid; they are likely to reject the new embodiment of the Luminous Point. Often with tragic results. The Prophet is mocked, beaten, tortured and usually murdered. Blood is spilled because of overwhelming political or clerical greed and fear of displacement.

It takes great courage to change one's Faith and dive into the unfamiliar, and often cruel fate of being a believer in a new Revelation. Often it means the sacrifice of all a would-be follower has, perhaps his family, even his life.

Too often humankind took this disrespect to great extremes and harmed, or killed these Great Beings, while refusing to listen to a single word.

They must not have known much about the process of evolution, because they did nothing to advance the growth of human civilization and became spiritual **"dead ends."** And like so many dead branches **they were pruned away to make way for new growth elsewhere**.

"The prophetic manifestations in history have been the thunderbolts and lightning of Truth... In the depth of their caves or in kings' palaces, they were truly the sentinels of God on Earth lit from the sun of divine Truth. Never do they blunder in regard to moral truths, the true mission of Israel, or the ultimate triumph of justice among men. They preached contempt for cults, the abolition of bloody sacrifices, purification of the soul and charity. They validate the ultimate victory of monotheism, its liberating and peacemaking role for all people..." – (Edouard Schurre – Great Initiates page 420)

Phrases like "Vengeful God" or "Jealous God," are neither meaningful nor true. One loving

Great Disappointments: Justice and Mercy Two Edges of the Sword

Creator brought the Universe and our planet into being so that humankind would grow, develop, and commune with its Creator.

Just as with physical evolution, societies who are psychopathically cruel and neglectful of other people and the One Who created them; sometimes lead nowhere and are not selected to continue.

"...O Muhammad; the people of Noah and the dwellers of Ar Rass, and Thamud and Ad; and Pharaoh, and the bretheren of Lot, and the dwellers of the Wood, and the people of Tubba (Sheba), every one of them denied their Messengers so My threat took effect."
– (Qu'ran 50:12-14)

Out of love and hopeful for redemption, God sent a number of these degenerated communities a Great Visitor. Each Being was marvelous and dedicated to the single Creator. Several, whose names are lost to us, sacrificed everything they had and were to correct the deviant greed and cruelty of the people to whom they were sent. They were rejected, assaulted and even killed for their efforts.

We tend to know little about these societies and places, because – well, they're gone... In fact the only reason we know about some of them is that they are mentioned by other Great Beings.

Baha'u'llah and Mohammad, in particular, make mention of several of these. They, and the places they lived, have been obliterated. They were buried under water, debris, sand and rubble. We otherwise would know very little if anything about them.

Noah and Lot are the most well remembered, but they are the tip of the iceberg. Below, are a few accounts of what befell those Great Servants and the people who rejected and abused them, lest no one remember them at all. This attempt to recall their long-suffering patience and their clear messages is a humble tribute to their ordeals.

THE STORY OF NOAH (NUH)

Circa 9,400-7,600 years ago, a stone age Noah walked with God and established His Covenant. He set dietary laws like eating no blood in the meat. And blood for blood as punishment. His people would not improve – no matter what happened and they were destroyed, as predicted. And later because of great sorrow, God promised no more deluges would wipe away humanity, and as a sign, He sent us the rainbow covenant to remember what had occurred.

Allah in His Mercy sent His messenger Noah to guide his people. Noah was an excellent speaker and a very patient man. He pointed out to his people the mysteries of life and the wonders of the universe. He pointed out how the night is regularly followed by the day and that the balance between these opposites was designed by Allah the Almighty for our good. The night gives coolness and rest while the day gives warmth and awakens activity. The sun encourages growth, keeping all plants and animals alive, while the moon and stars assist in the reckoning of time, direction and seasons. He pointed out that the ownership of the heavens and the earth belongs only to the Divine Creator.

(Imam Ibn Kathir Ad-Dimashqi, eBook: Stories of the Prophets); also (http://www.a2youth.com/ebooks/stories_of_the_prophets/the_story_of_noah_nuh/)

"Among the Prophets was Noah. For nine hundred and fifty years He prayerfully exhorted His people and summoned them to the haven of security and peace. None, however, heeded His call. Each day they inflicted on His blessed person such pain and suffering that no one believed He could survive. How frequently they denied Him, how malevolently they hinted their suspicion against Him....He several times promised victory to His companions and fixed the hour thereof. But when the hour struck, the divine promise was not fulfilled. This caused a few among the small number of His followers to turn away from Him..." Baha'u'llah (Book of Certitude)

Worshipping anything other than God is a tragedy that results not only in the loss of freedom; but it also has a serious destructive effect on the mind which was created with the knowledge that God is its Creator, and all the rest of us are worshippers. Therefore, disbelief in One Great Spirit becomes atheism or polytheism. This results in the loss of freedom, the destruction of the certain mental processes and often the absence of a noble target in life.

Noah's Epic Struggle

The people had been misled by materialism long enough. Time had come for this deceit to stop. Noah told them of God's glorification of man. He had created them and provided sustenance, and the blessings of a mind. He told them that idol worshipping was a suffocating injustice to the mind, and described the terrible punishment that would be meted to them if they continued deceiving themselves with idols and mistreating the poor and helpless among them.

Noah and His very few believers were the only ones not caught in the whirlpool of man's destruction caused by worshipping these icons. Most people listened to him in silence. His words were a shock to their stagnating minds. First they accused Noah of being an ordinary human. The disbelievers said:

"We see you, but a man like ourselves, nor do we see any who follow you, but the meanest among us, and they followed you without thinking. We do not see in you any merit above us, in fact, we think you are a liar." Quran (Ch11:25-27)

Noah, however, had never claimed otherwise. He asserted that indeed, he was only a human being; God had sent a human messenger because the earth was inhabited by humans. If it had been inhabited by angels Allah would have sent an angelic messenger.

"Indeed We sent Noah to his people" – Quran

"I have come to you as a plain Warner that you worship none but Allah, surely, I fear for you the torment of a painful Day."

Noah's people became divided into two groups after the warning. His words touched the hearts of the weak, the poor, and the miserable. However the rulers, the wealthy, and the powerful, showed cold disdain, believing they would be better off if things stayed as they were.

The conflict intensified. The disbelievers said "Listen Noah, if you want us to believe in you, dismiss your believers. They are meek and poor, while we are elite and rich; no faith can include us both." Noah's response was gentle. He explained that he could not dismiss the believers as they were not His guests, but God's.

There were many years, even decades, of pleading and exhortations on Noah's part *"O my people! There is no error in me, but I am a Messenger from the Lord of the Alamin (Creation)! I convey unto you the Messages of my Lord and give sincere advice to you. And I know from Allah what you know not." (CH7:61-62)*

Nothing seemed to work and the disrespect became worse, while His followers dwindled. God said to Noah that no other believers would be found. Noah prayed, *"O my Lord! Verily, I have called my people night and day… but all my calling added nothing but to their flight from the truth…they thrust their fingers into their ears and covered themselves up with their garments…and magnified themselves in pride."*

Noah was viciously taunted and mocked as he built the boat. He loaded the few who believed and most of his family, plus animals, feed, even insects.

God (Allah) told Noah not to grieve for the spiritually dead any longer. Noah responded "My Lord! Leave not one of the disbelievers on the earth. If you leave them, they will mislead your servants and they will beget none but wicked disbelievers." Allah accepted Noah's prayer. The case was closed. God added "…address Me not on behalf of those who did wrong; they are surely to be drowned."

And when water gushed out of his oven, which was the agreed upon sign, He left burdened with sorrow. His wife and one son remained behind.

"At last from the depth of His being He cried aloud: 'Lord! Leave not upon the land a single dweller from among the unbelievers." Baha'u'llah (Book of Certitude)

"Allah Almighty revealed: Noah's people, when they denied the Messenger We drowned them, and We made them as a sign for mankind. We have prepared a painful torment for

"Noah's Ark on Mount Ararat by Simon de Myle" by Simon de Myle (fl. 1570) - Sotheby's Paris, 23 Juni 2011 Lot 30. Licensed under Public Domain via Wikimedia Commons - https://commons.wikimedia.org/wiki/File:Noah%27s_Ark_on_Mount_Ararat_by_Simon_de_Myle.jpg#/media/File:Noah%27s_Ark_on_Mount_Ararat_by_Simon_de_Myle.jpg

the Zalimeen (polytheists and wrongdoers). Also Ad and Thamud and the dwellers of Ar Rass and many generations in between. For each of them We brought utter ruin (because of their disbelief and evil deeds)." – Mohammad; Qu'ran 25:37-39)

Water arose from cracks in the earth...rain poured from the sky for 40 days and nights, in quantities never seen before on earth. Hour after hour the water rose. The seas and waves invaded the land. The interior of the earth moved in a strange way (perhaps tectonic), and the ocean floors lifted suddenly flooding and submerging the dry land. After the waters subsided the ship landed on Mt. Judi according to the Quran, Ararat in the Torah.

http://www.angelfire.com/on/ummiby1/nuh.html

"Whenever I bring clouds over the earth and the rainbow appears in the clouds I will remember My covenant...Never again will the waters become a flood to destroy all life." Genesis 9:14-15

At His deathbed Noah admonished His sons to worship Allah alone, and in humility. Noah was followed in Prophecy by Shem. Excerpts from Genesis 11:10-26:

Shem (was) an hundred years old, and begat Arphaxad two years after the flood ...

Arphaxad begat Salah ...Salah begat Eber ...; Eber begat Peleg ...; Peleg begat Reu ...; Reu begat Serug ...; Serug begat Nahor ...; Nahor begat Terah ...; Terah begat Abram

It is noticeable that lifespans of Noah's descendants drop dramatically, into the realm of 29 to 35 years old. Terah was the oldest, at 70. Times must have become very difficult.

There really is no significant information about the immediate aftermath of the Flood, provided from Biblical texts, as would likely be the case since there were not many left to tell Noah's story. Only the Prophets can know it because they are intimately aware of one another. So it is to Mohammad, the Bab, and Baha'u'llah we must look to for information about Noah, Hud and several others.

But first there are other tales of the Flood from other peoples.

ATRAHASIS AND GILGAMESH

At first you may wonder what the connection is between Enoch and these stories of the flood, but they are all born out of the times of Enoch, and are integrally connected to His story.

Mesopotamian legends like those of Atrahasis (Babylon) and Gilgamesh (Sumerian) were recorded on clay cuneiform tablets, after an enormously long oral tradition. They recall antediluvian incidents and though the names may seem unfamiliar they are again, accretions of information spanning the cataclysms of the beginnings of remembered time, all the way to the great flood.

The tales are complicated by names of gods and goddesses, confusing because the original meaning is unavailable or forgotten. Still, excerpts from both tales, though fragmentary, add to our knowledge base of these early times.

Climactic conditions contributed to the noted die offs in these tales. Also during this time there were subsequent rises and recessions in the ocean levels, which would certainly affect many area inhabitants. Dora Jane Hamblin based on Zarins (1983) suggests the overall climate of greater Mesopotamia during the last 32,000 years went from glacial, to wet, to arid then back to moist.

There were famines due to droughts, but at other times there was enough rain to sustain domestication, and propagation of crops and herds.

From 17,000 to about 8,000 years ago, rainfall diminished drastically. This would be the time in the legends when the earth "withheld her bounties" and the people starved, died or moved away. In Atrahasis' story Enki-du eventually sends fish up the rivers to stave off complete starvation.

When the rains and fertility returned, so did Paleolithic nomads who had moved away during droughts. They were not welcomed by other agricultural groups (perhaps early Ubaids), and were chased away upon their return. They might also have been rejected for bringing diseases back from the southern places where they had sought refuge. And so it was, that one era ends, with the onset of a new one.

Atrahasis

Atrahasis like Yima lived in three shifts. Each in this case lasts 1200 years, totaling over 3600 years. The super long life of Atrahasis unmistakably parallels those of Lords Adam, Yima, Gayomart, Ram, Fu-Xi and others.

The Akkadian Epic tale of Atrahasis, thought by some to be the oldest account of the Great Flood story, begins in layers that precede the Creation of mankind. Before the flood, Atrahasis whose name means "The Wise" like Yima and Rama, was sent to earth.

Some people think He may have been the Stone Age king of Shuruppak, a bustling city-state built along the Euphrates River. This king was also known as Ziusudra in a Sumerian version of the Epic. Shuruppak ("the Healing Place") was at one time a capital city, and an area of commerce including the lower Tigris and Euphrates Rivers. It would make sense the city was "Enoch" mentioned before. What would not make sense would be that Atrahasis was just an earthly king.

Tragic Times

The people of Atrahasis grew (like Yima's story) to the point of overpopulation and noisiness. When they became as noisy as a bellowing bull, they were struck by a plague similar to Rama's folk. After Atrahasis prayed for relief **Enki told Him to have the people stop praying to their personal gods and pray the Almighty God, specifically, to have the plague healed.**

"Now there was one, Atrahasis, whose ear was open to his god Enki and he spoke to his lord. How long will the gods make us suffer? Will they make us suffer illness forever?"

Enki responded with a "me," an edict, a universal decree of divine authority:

"Enki (God) made his voice heard and spoke to his servant:

Call the elders, the senior men! Start an uprising in your own house,

Let the elders proclaim... Let them make a loud noise in the land:

Do not revere your gods, Do not pray to your goddesses...But search out the door of Namatara. Bring a baked loaf into his presence."

Dalley Pg 10 of 11 in her *Myths from Mesopotamia: Creation, the Flood, Gilgamesh, and Others (Oxford World's Classics)* by, Stephanie Dalley (Paperback – Feb 15, 2009) Pp. 25-26: – Dalley, Stephanie, ed. And trans. New York: Oxford UP, 1991

Through prayer, people had survived the initial plague, but the noise came back. The gods ceased to perform their duties, and all of nature's bounty disappeared. There came a horrible drought and gruesome famine during the second 1200 years.

Here follows an excerpt about that terrible time, an utterly horrible famine:

"When the second year arrived, they had depleted the storehouse. The people's looks were changed by starvation. When the fourth year arrived their upstanding bearing bowed, their well-set shoulders slouched, and the people went out in public hunched over. When the fifth year arrived, a daughter would eye her mother coming in; a mother would not even open her door for her daughter... When the sixth year arrived they served up a daughter for a meal, served up a son for food." Perhaps these are the conditions in which Mashya and Mashyana; of the Gayomart story, ate their first children. Or, the "days" of hunger for Adam and Eve.

A bleak, prolonged famine ravaged the people. It finally ended as mentioned before, when Enki (God) sent large quantities of fish into the rivers.

Children had been a source of joy and a fulfillment of love during the ancient conditions of Marriage and childbirth. A wife and her husband chose each other, in gardens and waysides, when the girl (had a) bosom and a beard was seen on a young man's cheek.

"The Mami (midwife) shall rejoice in the house of the woman who gives birth, and when she gives birth to the baby, the mother of the baby shall sever herself." – Dalley

After the tragedies which offset overpopulation, plans to curtail future overpopulation events included infertility, barrenness in women and unsuccessful births. This likely included abortion and infanticide. Children had become unaffordable.

The third 1200 years is ended by yet another warning from Enki of a horrible flood: "Dismantle the house, build a boat...Roof it like the Apsu so the sun cannot see inside it! Make upper decks and lower decks, the tackle must be very strong, the bitumen (pitch or tar) strong..."

Note 1: Apsu was a name given the sources of lakes, springs, rivers, covered wells, and other sources of fresh water, drawn from the abzu (aquifer).

In the city of Eridu, Enki's Sumerian temple was known as the "house of the cosmic waters," and was located at the edge of a swamp. Other cosmic waters were found in tanks of holy water in Babylonian and Assyrian temple courtyards; and more recently in Islamic washing pools for ablutions, or Christian baptismal and holy water fonts.

Note 2: Adad (below), was a Mesopotamian god; who was associated with: a bull, benevolent rains, and powerful destructive storms and floods.

Atrahasis built the boat and filled it with every type of animal, and His family. Adad began to thunder. Sick with impending doom, Atrahasis vomited bile because of His breaking heart. He sealed the door, as directed with bitumen.

"Like a wild ass screaming, the winds howled the darkness was total, there was no sun..." (Dalley cited above, p.35)

Gilgamesh

Gigamesh (He who found life) was a giant. He was a descendant of a larger human form like H. heidelbergensis or Denisova.

"Thus the name of one of the giants is Gilgamesh, the Babylonian hero and subject of a great epic written in the third millennium B.C.E." (Other Apocrypha, *The Book of Giants* – Enoch)

The Epic of Gilgamesh is known from a series of eleven clay tablets in cuneiform. In the first tablets God sent a **wild man** named Enkidu to stop Gilgamesh from oppressing the people of Uruk. Let's see; a giant, a wild man, and the people of Uruk – sounds like three types of human forms.

Similar to the story of Atrahasis, the last tablets refers to a great flood. The story is told *to* Gilgamesh by **Utanapishtim**, a survivor of the ordeal. Utanapishtim is said to be the son of **Ubara-Tutu (Enoch)**, who was the last antediluvian king of Shuruppak in Sumeria until the flood swept over. Excavations in Iraq have revealed evidence of flooding at Shuruppak. Erech now lies on the bed of the Euphrates River.

Gilgamesh sat on the throne of Erech (Uruk) on the Euphrates (above Eridu and Ur). Lamech, father of Noah, might have been the earthly king in Sumer until the flood. In Genesis, Noah is also a king of Shuruppak. Shuruppak encompassed the region of the lower Tigris and Euphrates Rivers and the upper region of the Persian Gulf, from the Arabian Desert to the Zagros Mountains. It was known, at one time as part of Chaldea. Utanapishtim recovered from the flood, and shares with us his knowledge. "He saw what was secret and revealed what was hidden...He brought back tidings from before the flood" This passage does suggest that Utanapishtim is a Manifestation of God, who is recounting the past from the collective memory of the Holy Spirit. It might also suggest that Utanapishtim is either Atrahasis, or of His lineage.

Gilgamesh described vast tracts of cedar forests in what is today southern Iraq. Forests which were cut down and destroyed, as cities and civilization moved north to Babylonia and Assyria. Deforestation has ever been a huge factor in the rise and fall of these civilizations. (Perlin 1991) Enoch mentioned that His father cut down forests to build cities, including one named after Him.

Fragments of a Sumerian tablet about Nibru the planet beyond Pluto, also mention Gigamesh's death. In various pieces it is mentioned that "He who climbed mountains...he has lain down never to arise again," "on the couch of sighs" but most interesting are hints that he was beaten, held captive behind a bolted door; trapped like a gazelle!

MANU

A **Hindu** story involved Lord Vishnu in his fish avatar. Manu was thought to be the author of the first Code of Laws for the Indo-Europeans (Ram).

God ordered the virtuous king to construct a huge boat with animal and plant specimens of all forms, to escape a Great Deluge. Finally when the water receded, the great boat was found atop high mountains.

By English: thesandiegomuseumofartcollection (Flickr) [Public domain], via Wikimedia Commons

DEUCALION

In a Greek version Deucalion is warned of the flood. He builds an ark and stuffs it with creatures. Deucalion also sends a pigeon to search for land, and the bird returns with an olive branch. When he completes the voyage he gives thanks, and takes advice from the gods on how to repopulate the Earth.

In a more colorful version, Zeus was angered by the extreme pride of the "Pelasgians," the indigenous inhabitants of the Aegean Sea region, so he decided to punish them.

Lycaon was the king of Arcadia, which was a part of the Peloponnese peninsula. It was an unspoiled, harmonious wilderness, thought to be the home of Pan. To punish Zeus for his oppression, Lycaon offered a blood sacrifice. Arcas, a son of Zeus, was placed upon the burning altar. Zeus was appalled by this savage offering. Lycaon then said to Zeus "If you think that you are so clever, make your son whole and un-harmed." Zeus was enraged. He made Arcas whole, then directed his anger toward Lycaon, turning him into the first werewolf. Then Zeus unleashed a deluge so that the rivers ran in torrents and the sea flooded the coastal plain. The flood engulfed the foothills with spray and washed everything clean. Deucalion, with the aid of his father Prometheus, was saved from this deluge. (https://en.wikipedia.org/wiki/Arcas)

What Do We Think We Know About The Flood?

When was the Flood? How did it happen? Though there have been several great floods in the last 10,000 years, perhaps the flood of 7,600 years ago may be the one we most remember as a people. Thanks to the traditions of the Hebrews, Babylonians, Sumerians, Aryans and tribal people everywhere we have remnants of tales marking this time.

Several hypotheses have been offered as possible explanations for the catastrophic flooding events. Greeks believed that Earth had been covered by water on several occasions, citing the seashells and fish fossils found on mountain tops as evidence of this history.

Sea levels rose dramatically in the millennia following the last ice age 18,000 years ago. Global sea levels raised 120 meters and reached current levels about 8,000 years ago.

The floor of the Gulf had been a huge low-lying fertile region of Mesopotamia, extending the area later known as Shuruppak. This oasis area was inhabited by humans for at least 100,000 years. The geography of Mesopotamia was considerably changed after sea waters rose to fill the Persian Gulf. A sudden increase in settlements above the current shoreline around began 7,500 years ago, suggests the oasis basin had flooded before then.

"Matsya Avatar, ca 1870" by Anonymous - V& A Museum [1]. Licensed under Public Domain via Commons - https://commons.wikimedia.org/wiki/File:Matsya_Avatar_ca_1870

Another possible factor is that a meteor crashed into the Indian Ocean around 5,000 years ago, creating the 30-kilometre (19 mi) undersea "Burckle Crater." It generated a giant tsunami that flooded coastal areas. If not this tsunami, another would certainly help explain the covering of the earth with vast quantities of water that took a while to subside.

In the Mediterranean Sea, a large tsunami hit Crete when Thera erupted 3600 years ago. Although this tsunami had a local rather than a region-wide effect. Other eruptions flooded Mediterranean history, if not the entire Middle East.

The Black Sea deluge hypothesis suggests a catastrophic deluge occurred when waters poured from the Mediterranean into the Black Sea; by means of a breached sill in the Bosporus Strait. About 7500-8500 years ago. The Black Sea then changed from freshwater to salt-water, in what was clearly a "great flood." This event might be tied to a tectonic uplift.

About 7500 years ago as glaciers and ice caps melted sea levels rose dramatically. They overflowed the narrow Bosporus Strait, which was then a river. The salty water was said to hit the Black sea with 200 times the force of Niagara Falls. Each day the Black Sea rose about six inches. Famed Explorer, Robert Ballard found remnants of a flooded settlement 95 meters beneath the modern day sea level, off the north coast of Turkey, which shows great tragedy and displacement.

Such a massive flood may have played a role in the migration of people away from the region, possibly helping to spread the Indo-European languages throughout India and Europe.

In 1997, William Ryan and Walter Pitman published evidence that a massive flooding of the Black Sea occurred about 5600 BC through the strait. But **before** that date, glacial meltwater had turned the Black and Caspian Seas into vast freshwater lakes which drained into the Aegean Sea.

As glaciers retreated, some of the rivers emptying into the Black Sea declined in volume and changed course, to drain into the North Sea. The levels of the lakes dropped through evaporation, while climate changes caused overall sea level to rise. The rising Mediterranean finally spilled over a rocky sill at the Bosporus. The event flooded 155,000 km² (60,000 sq. mi) of land and significantly expanded the Black Sea shoreline to the north and west. According to the researchers, "40 km³ (10 cu mi) of water poured through each day, two hundred times the flow of the Niagara Falls…The Bosporus flume roared and surged at full spate for at least three hundred days."

While it is agreed that event occurred, there is debate over its suddenness, dating and magnitude. Over the last 30,000 years, water has intermittently flowed back and forth between the Black Sea and the Aegean Sea in relatively small amounts. (https://en.wikipedia.org/wiki/Flood_myth)

Robert Ballard, a National Geographic Society explorer, used an underwater camera to explore a former river valley beneath the Black Sea. He found ancient ruins characteristic of other Stone Age structures dated 7500 years ago, including a collapsed structure with preserved wooden beams that had been worked by a hand chisel. He found two other stone tools with holes drilled through them, which may have been used as net weights, or dowel straighteners. (http://archives.cnn.com/200/NATURE/09/13greatflood.finds.ap/)

All these pieces and guesses point roughly to 7600 years ago. But there are other possibilities.

Summary of Flood Stories

The tales of Noah, Atrahasis Gilgamesh, Manu, and Deucalion discuss multiple gods, and idols. You can see that there is some leaning toward one God. The Hindu story points to an avatar of Vishnu. For Atrahasis "Enki" or "Ea" (Akkadian); for Utanapishtim "Enlil," a Mesopotamian God so powerful the other gods can't even look at Him. He is represented by a helmet or hat with horns. Enlil was known as the inventor of the mattock, an agricultural digging tool similar to a pick, or hoe. He helped with the growing of plants, which suggests he may have been one of the "Firsts" associated with agriculture like Adam or Shennong.

The construction of the ark takes a lot of space in the narratives, with varying details on materials and measurements. Utanapishtim's ark width and length are equal. Atrahasis was warned to roof it completely keeping the sun out. Both accounts mention information for applying bitumen tar or pitch to increase resistance to flood waters. Noah's story contains the most detailed description, including the number of floors, overall size and shape, and the placement of sky lights. In the tale of Yima there is a great subterranean Vara with sky lights cut into the earth, instead.

Deucalion, Utanapishtim and Atrahasis, release ravens and doves, like Noah, though numbers of each vary slightly.

It seems plausible that the flood stories around the world differ for a number of reasons. They are expressions given at various times, by a variety of people. The full physical cause of the flooding is still shrouded in mystery, but science is contributing explanations.

The stories of Atrahasis, and Utanapishtim of the Gilgamesh Epic, are a conglomerate of events and individuals, very much like the stories of Fo-Xi, Yima, Adam and Gayomart. They are verbal renditions of a long religious history stuffed in a sausage skin, much like the "Begats" of the Torah or Old Testament, or a weave of Pagan traditions.

Truer versions usually come from those people, to whom the Manifestation directly appeared. But information that far back is a misty tangle because most of the people in the area were erased. The very best way to sort it out is through the words of an ensuing Manifestation, since for all intents and purposes; He was there.

It is partly for this reason that **the Prophet Mohammad warns that there is error recorded in the stories salvaged from the past. Baha'u'llah, also warns us to deal with the glory and magnitude of the Present Day and not get too caught up in the tales of the past.**

HUD/HEBER/EBER

In the Bible, Hud is referred to as Eber or Heber the son of Shelah, grandson of Arphaxad, who was the great grandson Shem.

"And after Noah the light of the countenance of Hud shone forth above the horizon of creation. For well-nigh seven hundred years, according to the sayings of men, He exhorted the people to turn their faces and draw nearer unto the Ridvan [garden] of the divine presence. What showers of afflictions rained upon Him, until at last His adjurations bore the fruit of increased rebelliousness, and His assiduous endeavors resulted in the willful blindness of His people?" – Baha'u'llah (Book of Certitude)

Legend has it that Eber refused to help with the building of the Tower of Babel so his language was not confused. He and his family alone, retained the original human language called lingua humana in Latin. After this the language was called Ibrite, Eberite or Hebrew, after Eber, also known as Heber.

Hud, Arabic for Eber, was a noble man, who was firm yet tolerant. He is said to have lived six generations before Abraham. He spoke around 6500 years ago if the flood date given above is valid.

Hud came to the 'Ad, a proud people who lived in the windswept hills of south Yemen and Oman. This land of curved sand hills lies at the end of the Arabian Peninsula. But it was not always a place of sand. In Hud/Eber's time it had been lush with agriculture.

Hud strongly condemned idol worship and exhorted people to trade their many gods for the One Universal God. He said they ought to be thankful for the many bounties and blessings, which Their Creator had showered upon them.

Yet they worshipped several main deities and idols, for protection, health and healing, as well as others for various personal purposes. The people knew about God and did not mind including Him with their other idols. But they were not interested in worshipping Him alone and above all others. When Hud warned His people they commented that His words were "a customary device of the ancients." They were confident nothing would happen to them. Their many blessings and good fortune kept them arrogant, and resistant towards God and His Messengers

Note: The word eber signifies "the region beyond" or the country beyond the Euphrates. At times when the word eber appears in literature, it just means "somewhere out there." Sometimes it means, within a ship's reach of Cyprus," or "the country beyond the Euphrates." In this case, it may refer to the Southern Arabian Peninsula — well beyond the usual reach of Mesopotamia.

The 'Ad: People of the Towers

"(The 'Ad) built a landmark on every high place and get ... for themselves fine buildings in the hope of living therein (forever)." – (Qu'ran, Sura Ash-Shuara)

They were gifted with thriving agriculture, and were well known architects. They built many lofty square columns and towers in a unique and beautiful style. It is rumored that some of them were decorated with gold or silver.

Besides serving as middlemen in the spice trade route which passed by there, the 'Ad produced and marketed aromatic frankincense from rare trees. At the time, frankincense was at least as valuable as gold.

These tall and handsome people of the Arabian Peninsula were also blessed with bountiful irrigated farms, and clever craftsmen. They were powerful and inclined to treat less fortunate people with disrespect and injustice. They had built large towered fortresses for protection in the unlikely case of trouble, however, no one dared to cross their corrupt rulers.

"My people, what is the benefit of these stones that you carve with your own hands and worship? In reality it is an insult to the intellect. There is only One Deity worthy of worship and that is Allah. Worship of Him and Him alone, is compulsory on you. He created you, He provides for you and He is the One who will cause you to die. He gave you wonderful physiques and blessed you in many ways. So believe in Him and do not be blind to His favors, or the same fate that destroyed Noah's people will overtake you." – (Qu'ran, Surih of Hud)

The 'Ad, totally unwilling to worship One God, scorned Hud and His message. They refused to humble themselves and accept that which had been sent to them. Hud pointed to their immorality, tyranny, and their ill-treatment of the less fortunate. They exploited all who traveled through their lands.

He only asked that they allow the light of truth to touch their hearts and minds. He wanted them to acknowledge that God had sent rain and many other bounties to them. Yet the people were obstinate, and they still felt themselves to be invincible.

Hud patiently explained that God demands a Judgement after death. People must account for the times when evil overpowers the good in each person's life as such crimes will not go unpunished. Justice, in the end, will prevail. Humans must account for their deeds, thoughts and words; and be rewarded or punished for them. The 'Ad listened but did not believe Him. Nor did they believe in life after death or a judgmental meeting with their Creator. They thought Hud was only a man who had invented this "lie."

"He is no more than a human being like you, he eats of that which you eat, and drinks of what you drink."

The rulers asked "Is it not strange that Allah chooses one of us to reveal His message to?" Hud replied "What is strange in that? God wants to guide you to the right way of life, so He sent me to warn you. Noah's flood and His story are not far away from you, so do not forget what happened. All the disbelievers were destroyed, no matter how strong they were." Again the rulers asked "Who is going to destroy us, Hud?" "God," replied Hud.

"We will be saved by our gods." The rulers asserted. Hud made it clear that the gods they worshipped would be the reason for their destruction. That it was God alone, who had the power to save or harm anyone. The people became more stubborn, expressing clearly that they thought Hud was a lunatic, whom their gods had seized with madness.

"I put my trust in God, my Lord and your Lord! There is not a moving creature but He has grasp of its forelock... My Lord will make another people succeed you, and you will not harm Him." (Qu'ran, CH11:54-57)

Still most people rejected Hud. They asked Him if he was looking to become a ruler, or wanted some kind of payment. He tried to explain that any kind of payment He may have coming to Him would come from God alone.

"I am free from the sin of ascribing to Him, other gods as partners! So scheme your worst against me, all of you, and give no respite. Fear Allah Who has bestowed on you freely cattle and sons, and gardens and springs. Truly I fear for you the Penalty of a Great Day."

A strong warning came when the area suffered a three year drought. The people asked Hud, **"What is this drought?"** He answered **"Allah is angry with you. If you believe in Him, He will accept you and the rain will fall and you will become stronger than you are."** They mocked Him and were sarcastic in their unbelief.

"I have conveyed the Message with which I was sent to you. If ye turn away My Lord will make another people to succeed you, and you will not harm Him in the least. For my Lord hath care and watch over all things."

The drought increased, and the formerly fruitful trees turned yellow and the plants died. Then came a day when the sky was full of clouds. The people were sure it was rain come in the nick of time to give relief from the drought. The weather surprised them. It went from burning dry and hot, to stinging cold. The wind blasted everything: trees, people and buildings.

The 'Ad, who had been great descendants of Noah, were erased by a horrible cyclonic sandstorm. The wind increased day and night. The huge cloud became a terrible sandstorm and it advanced on them for eight days and seven nights, leaving only devastation. The entire region was reduced to ruins and its wicked people were swallowed up by the sands of the desert. A huge wall of sand removed them from sight as if they had never existed.

Only Hud and those who followed their precious Prophet, remained unharmed. They had migrated to Hadramaut and lived there in peace, worshipping Allah, their Lord.

"Such were the 'Ad people they rejected the Signs of their Lord and Cherisher" and disobeyed His Messengers, They chose to follow the commands of every powerful, obstinate transgressor, and on the Day of Judgment. "Ah! Behold! Removed (from sight) they were the 'Ad, the people of Hud! "

"So when Our decree issued. We saved Hud and those who believed with Him, by (special) Grace from Ourselves We saved them from a severe penalty." – As related by Mohammad (Surah Hud: 50-60)

"And the 'Ad, they were destroyed by a furious Wind, exceedingly violent. He made it rage against them seven nights and eight days in succession: so that thou couldst see the (whole) people lying prostrate in its (path), as they had been roots of hollow palm-trees tumbled down!" – Mohammad (Surat al-Haaqqa)

As with Noah, we see a time and a people not ready to return to the Cause of God and advance civilization. They were unwilling to change their own ways and advance the path of humanity. And they were replaced.

Ubar or Iram, the former city of the 'Ad, has recently been excavated from beneath 12 meters of sand!

"Seest thou not how thy Lord dealt with the 'Ad people? Of the city of Iram, with lofty pillars the like of which were not produced in all the land." – Mohammad (Sura al Fajr: 6-8) (www.angelfire.com/on/ummiby1/hud)

Rediscovery of Iram, Known by the Bedouin as Ubar

Ptolemy made a map 1800 years ago that labeled a region of the Arabian Peninsula with the name "Iobaritae" meaning that it belonged to the Ubarites. Later legends referred to the fabulous wealth of the lost city and used the region name of "Ubar." T. E. Lawrence (of Arabia) named it the "Atlantis of the Sands."

In the early 1980's a group of researchers interested in the history of Iram used NASA remote sensing satellites, ground penetrating radar, Landsat program data, and images taken from the Space Shuttle Challenger, as well as SPOT data, to identify old camel trails. They studied the data and the old maps noting points where they converged.

These trails and roads were used as frankincense trade routes around 4800-1900 years ago. One area in the Dhofar province of Oman was identified as a possible outpost of the lost civilization. A team including adventurer Tanulph Fiennes, archaeologist Juris Zarins, filmmaker Nicholas Clapp, and a lawyer, George Hedges, scouted the area on several trips.

Clapp found the tracks, which the Bedouins had shown to an English researcher named Thomas, before he died. He also studied ancient manuscripts and maps which showed an old city and the trails that led to it.

Before excavation Ubar could only be seen from space because it was now covered with 36 feet of sand! Right from the beginning it was understood that this belonged to the 'Ad, because prominent towers lay among the structures of the ruins. Though the area is now desert dunes it was once mist-covered fertile land; with forests, and wild game. The people built dams, and cleverly designed irrigation canals, which supported extensive cultivation.

Nearby a 16th century fort was excavated. It proved to be a much older settlement, in which artifacts were found that had been traded from near and far. The fort was built on top of a limestone cavern which would have served as a water source. This makes it an important stop on the trade route to Iram.

This excavation and four others were conducted to trace the historical presence of the 'Ad. Truly a region distant from people living in Mesopotamia and the Middle East.

Below are a few literary references to the descendants of these people.

The 'Ad who left with Hud and moved to South Yemen were known as the Hadramites. **"Hadrami" or "Ad-i-Iram-i"** means the 'Ad from Iram. They founded a new civilization, which is not mentioned in the usual historical records. The Hadromites, the Sabaeans, and the Qatabaeans flourished for a very long time, but in 240 AD they disappeared totally, after a long decline.

The Hadoram in Gen 10:27, might be the inhabitants of the villages near Wadi Hadramawt, referred to locally as the Hadharem or 'the people of Hadramawt.' They are the Adramites named by Ptolemy and Pliny. http://www.jewishencyclepedia.com/view.jsp?artid=17&letter=E)

"In the olden days – Hadhramout's importance came mainly from supplying the incense trade, which made it prosperous and strong. The Hadharem, as the people of Hadhramout are called, love traveling and adventures. Historically, few Arabs have traveled as extensively as Hadhramys have, and fewer have left their marks in other parts of the World, as the people of Hadhramout have done." (http://knol.google.com/k/barsawad/hadhramout-or-hadhramaut-or-hadhramawt/4ly0o3x1bmwm/1#)

It would seem that the promise of fortune Hud offered the 'Ad was realized by His few followers. The Greeks defined the Hadramites as the richest race in the world due to agriculture of frankincense, one of the most valuable plants of that time. These people must have inherited the architectural superiority of the 'Ad. Their city was reportedly a marvel. The palace was magnificent. Shabwah featured interesting columns which were both elaborate and round. Other sites feature square columns.

"It is said that they have built many columns covered in gold or made of silver. Spaces between these columns are remarkable to behold" – Photius 132 B.C. ("Iram" http://en.wikipedia.org/wiki/Iram_of_the_Pillars)

The Hadramite capital city Shabwah was situated at the west of the Hadramaut Valley. It is said to house the tomb of the Prophet, Hud. However there is also a mosque covered cave in north Jordan, which is said to be Hud's burial place.

Sheba/Tubba

Unfortunately, Hud's children struggled not only with the stubborn princes of Babylon, but also with Sheba (Bible) or Tubba (Qu'ran). The people of Sheba were sometimes called the people of Tubba' because Tubba' was used as the title for Sheba's kings. The Qur'an mentions that the people of Tubba, were destroyed by God.

In "Genesis" 10:25 *"And unto Eber were born two sons: the name of one was Peleg; for in his days was the earth divided; and his brother's name was Joktan."*

Peleg or Phaleg in English means "brook" or "little river." He is known as an ancestor of the Israelites. – Genesis 10-11 (http://en.wikipedia.org/wiki/Peleg)

Joktan means "small" or "smallness." He is an ancestor of the southern Arab tribes. Genesis 10: 25-30; Genesis 11:18-26) The name Sheba (Saba) is listed in the Table of Nations as a son of Joktan or Yoktan (Hebrew), in the Torah.

In Pseudo-Philo's account (ca. 70 A.D.), three princes command all persons to bake bricks for the Tower of Babel. However, twelve, including several of Joktan's own sons, as well as Abraham and Lot, refused the orders.

Joktan smuggled them out of Shinar, and into the mountains, to the annoyance of the other two princes. The traditional history of the Ethiopian Orthodox, or Coptic Church, maintains that Joktan's sons would take no part in the tower building, so they were allowed to preserve the original Ge-ez language, which their descendants the Agazyan, carried across the Red Sea into Ethiopia. There they mixed with the Cushtic and Agaw tribes to form the Habesha. (http://en.wikipedia.org/wiki/Joktan)

Sheba or Saba, was mentioned in both Hebrew and Qur'anic traditions. It was the ancient Semitic civilization of Yemen, between 1200 BC until 275 AD. Its capital was Marib. Its lands stretched as far as Aqaba, with small colonies protecting their trade routes. The people were known as Sabaeans. (Not the same people as Abraham's Sabians.) Here are a few references to these people who were extinguished.

In northern **Ethiopia** archaeologists found an ancient temple dedicated to the Sabaean god El-Maqah. The biblical Queen of Sheba, named Makeda in Ethiopian tradition, and Bilqīs in Arabic tradition lived there.

In the Kitab al-Magall, A hidden book of St. Clement the Apostle, it says "Nimrod died in the days of Reu, son of Peleg. In his days a king reigned over the town of Saba and annexed to his kingdom the cities of Ophir and Havilah, his name was Pharaoh... and after the death of Pharaoh, Queens reigned over Saba until the time of Solomon, son of David."

In the Qur'an, Sheba is mentioned by name at 27:22 in a section that speaks of the visit of the Queen of Sheba to King Solomon, son of David. (Qur'an 27:20-44) Muslim scholars, including Ibn Kathir, related that the People of Tubba' **were Arabs from South Arabia**.

The Jewish-Roman historian Josephus describes a place called Saba as a walled royal city of Ethiopia, which Cambysis afterwards named Meroe. It was protected by segments of the Nile and two other rivers. According to Josephus, it was the conquering of Saba that brought great fame to a young Egyptian Prince, simultaneously exposing his personal background as a slave child, **named Hosarsiph, who later became Moses**. (http://en.wikipedia.org/wiki/Sheba)

wikipedia commons http://www.queenofsheba.info/files/articles.html

SALIH/SALEH: THE RIGHTEOUS ONE

"And after Him [Hud] there appeared from the Ridvan of the Eternal, the Invisible; the holy person of Salih, Who again summoned the people to the river of everlasting life. For over a hundred years He admonished them to hold fast unto the commandments of God and eschew that which is forbidden. His admonitions, however, yielded no fruit, and His pleading proved to no avail. Several times He retired and lived in seclusion. All this, although that eternal Beauty was summoning the people to no other than the city of God." Baha'ullah (Book of Certitude)

The people of Thamud lived in the Northwest corner of Arabia, between Medina and Syria. They built palaces and castles in the open rocky land located on the trade route from southern Arabia to Syria. They were blessed with gardens fed by springs, which brought forth date palms and other fruit trees. They carved Nabatean style stone dwellings, similar to those in Petra. But also out of stone, they carved idols.

The Thamud were related to, and successors of the 'Ad. They took pride in fertile farms and outstanding architecture. With the advantages of a lavish material civilization they too became arrogant idolaters, and became lax in virtue. They did not feel beholden to a Supreme Creator and were not moved to develop virtuous or caring behavior. Rather they cheated and mistreated the people who passed through their lands. Their good qualities continued to decline and they became materialistic tyrants. So a Messenger worthy of all trust known as Salih meaning "Righteous" came to them nine generations after Noah, and three before Abraham Roughly 4600 years ago.

Salih was so righteous that His community already relied heavily on Him. In fact, He might have been chosen as their king if he had followed their ways (Similar to Ram and Yima). But He had been chosen by God for a higher mission, which was to preach against the selfishness of the fortunate, and to condemn the practice of idolatry. The wealthy and wicked saw no need to worship one God, since the idols of their parents seemed to be doing quite nicely.

Stone idols might have been enough for their parents, but these were the people chosen to advance civilization once again, and they flatly refused. They chastised and rebuked Salih, whom they had once adored. The poor and needy of the community became His only believers. This caused the others to mock His efforts even more.

Salih asked that the rich stop oppressing the poor, and adopt a more virtuous behavior. A few more people accepted His words. Not surprisingly, most of them refused to heed His warning, and instead began to harass Him to cause a miracle as proof of the Power of

God. Salih kept telling them to look around and remember the numerous miracles God had already bestowed upon them. He reminded His people of the countless castles and palaces they had built, and of their rich farm fields, and technical superiority. He also reminded them of the fate of the 'Ad, and how they were destroyed for their similar, unrepentant sins.

"*Produce a camel from the rocks,*" they shouted. Still, He exhorted them to worship One God, and be thankful to the One from whom all blessings flow. There was still time to turn from idolatry to monotheism. Even a few of His believers turned away, because most people wanted proof that God was all powerful.

The She-Camel

Salih performed a visible miracle as a last resort. In answer to their request. He beseeched God, Who brought forth a beautiful she-camel as a gift for the sustenance and to the astonishment of the community, and a sign of His divine grace. A large beautiful pregnant camel appeared to step out of the rock, itself.

"*Let this camel be a sign for you that Allah alone exists. Let no harm come to her, leave her to graze Allah's earth, and let her come and have a baby. Do no harm her or you will be seized with a horrible punishment.*" (Qu'ran)

At first the people were amazed and stunned, but eventually they hurt Salih by their words and deeds. Salih warned the people to protect and cherish the camel as their gift from God's benevolence. But the miracle failed miserably.

From the beginning, the camel was at great risk. After a time the people of Thamud complained that the she drank too much water. They turned their hatred for Saleh on her, even though He warned...

"*O my people! This she camel of Allah is a sign to you. Leave her to feed of Allah's earth, and touch her not with evil lest a near torment will seize you.*" —Qu'ran (Ch11:64)

For a while they suffered the camel to graze and drink freely even though they hated her. She had caused more people to believe in one God. The people were now divided and quarreling with each other.

Most still felt that the camel drank too much water and gave too much milk. They said they needed more water for their cattle. So they plotted its death. Two women were promised as prizes to young men if the men would kill the camel. They happily set about the task. One man, Masra'i shot an arrow into her leg. She tried to get away, but couldn't move well, so another man, Qadar hacked at another leg with his sword. When she fell to the ground, he pierced her with the blade. The killers were treated like heroes, celebrated and cheered with songs and poetry composed for their deed. People mocked Salih, who begged them to reconsider their crime and repent.

"*Oh My people! I did indeed convey to you the message for which I was sent by My Lord: I gave you good counsel, but ye love not good counsels!*" – Salih (as recorded by Mohammad) Qur'an 7:79

"*Enjoy life for three more days then the punishment will descend on you.*"

"***Why wait three days? Let the punishment come as quickly as possible.***" They jeered. Salih begged them to ask Allah for pardon. He told them they were being tested. The nine evil chiefs and their sons refused to reform and plotted to attack Saleh and His household at night.

They would use the cloak of darkness so they could swear that they never saw the destruction of His home and family. But three days after the warning, before they had a chance to act on their vicious plan, thunderbolts filled the air, followed by earthquakes (perhaps tectonic) so severe that they destroyed the entire tribe and its homeland along with all living creatures in it.

There was one terrific cry which had hardly ended when the disbelievers were struck dead, all at the same time. Their strong bodies, exquisite buildings, or rock-hewn idols could protect them.

"So the earthquake took people unaware, and they lay prostrate in their homes in the morning." Quran 27:45-53

The people who believed in Saleh's message were saved because they had already left that place.

Later, when Mohammad passed the stricken area, some of His people filled their water skins at a well and started to cook. He warned them to dump out that water and give the dough to the camels rather than eat it. He let them refill the skins only from the well where the she-camel drank. Only He could know this after thousands of years that the spring was still there in the rubble. (http://en.wikipedia.org/wiki/Saleh)

With residual physical reminders as blatant as this, it is hard to believe anybody would still doubt the power of a Single Creator. But wait...

Other Tragic Attempts

"And we did give to Moses the Book, and place with him his brother Aaron as a minister; and we said, 'Go ye to the people who say our signs are lies, for we will destroy them with utter destruction.' And the people of Noah, when they said the apostles were liars, we drowned them, and we made them a sign for men; and we prepared for the unjust a grievous woe. And 'Ad and Thamud and the people of ar Rass, and many generations between them. For each one have we struck out parables, and each one have we ruined with utter ruin." (The Qur'an (E.H. Palmer), Sura 25 – The Discrimination)

Below are references to other failed attempts to move humanity forward and advance civilization which were found in the Qu'ran, the Baha'i writings, and the Old Testament. These include: the people of Ar Rass, Antioch, the sad story of the people of Sodom, Gomorrah and other Cities of the Plain, and the story of Sho'aib.

The Dwellers of Ar Rass (Persia)

"A Zoroastrian wrote 'Abdu'l-Bahá to ask why Zoroaster was not mentioned by Muhammad; the Master referred him to Qur'án 25:40 and 50:12, 'those who dwelt at Rass,' explaining that Rass is the Araxes River, and the reference is to Zoroaster and Others." (Marzieh Gail, Six Lessons on Islam, p. 13)

Of the Rass Abu Bakr Muhammad Ibn Al Hassan recounts "reportedly a village derived from their ancestors the Thamud, had a great well sufficing them and their land. They also had a just and good-hearted king. When he died, they were much grieved for him. After four days Satan took his form and said "I was not dead, but I kept absent from you to see your reaction."

He commanded them to set up a curtain between him and them and told them that he would never *really* die. A great number of people believed him. They were fascinated, and worshipped him.

Allah sent them a Great Prophet called Huzlah-Ibn-Safwan (Zoroaster) who told them they had only been worshipping Satan, who, Wizard of Oz-like, was addressing them from behind the curtain. He forbade them to worship the fake, and to worship only Allah – no partner with Him. Out of spite they killed their Prophet. They denied Him and then killed Him and threw His body into a well. Therefore Allah destroyed them, and their homes.

The circumstances of Zoroaster's death are unknown. Many claim that he was assassinated while at prayer, murdered by Turanians at the storming of Balkh in present day Afghanistan. This version is found in a Persian epic poem called the Shahnameh, written around 1000 CE, or about 1500 years after Zoroaster's death. (http://altreligion.about.com/od/holidaysfestivalsevents/p/zarathust-no-diso.htm)

The Yasin People of Antioch

This account is about the dwellers of a town said to be Antioch, or Antakya in southern Turkey, near Syria. Humans had occupied the area for at least 8,000 years. It is a dry land with cave pocked hills and beautiful brick arches. The most recent version of Antioch, founded 2,300 years ago became very important to Christianity.

"There came two Messengers, to them, but they ridiculed and chided them both. So Allah (God) reinforced them with a third and together they said: 'Verily! We have been sent to you as Messengers.' The townspeople said 'You are only human beings like ourselves and the Most Beneficent God has revealed nothing, you are only telling lies.,' the Messengers said 'Our Lord knows that we have been sent as Messengers to you, our duty is only to convey plainly the Message.'" Qu'ran

The people responded **"For us we see an evil omen from you, if you cease not we will surely stone you and a painful torment will touch you from us."** The last of the Messengers responded: "Your evil omens be with you! So you call it an evil omen because you are admonished? Nay, but you are a people ...transgressing... by committing all kinds of great sins, and by disobeying Allah."

The Messengers were threatened with stoning and torture, but God sent a sign.

"And there came running from the farthest part of the town, a man who shouted 'O my people! Obey the Messengers! Obey those who ask no wages of you for themselves; they are rightly guided. Why shouldn't I worship Allah alone, He Who created me and to Whom I shall be returned? Shall I take besides Him gods? If Allah intends me any harm, the intercession of your idols will be of no use whatsoever; nor can they save me... Verily! I have believed in you, Lord, so listen to me!'"

As the disbelievers killed him, they jeered 'Enter Paradise! The victim said 'Would that my people knew my Lord Allah has forgiven me and made me of the honored ones!'"

"We sent not against his people a host from heaven nor do We send such a thing. It was but one shout and lo! They all were silent (dead, destroyed) Alas for mankind! There never came a Messenger to them, but they used to mock at Him. Do they not see how many generations We have destroyed before them?" – (Qu'ran 36:13-31)

Very similar is this, to the story of Lot in the Bible.

Sodom and Gomorrah; and Three Other "Cities of the Plain"

Lot, nephew of Abraham, was warned of the doom of Sodom, Gomorrah and three other "Cities of the Plain" Zeboim, Admah and Bela by two Angels, whom the men of these towns would not listen to, but wanted to rape.

Abraham begged the Angels who came to Him to spare the cities if fifty righteous people could be found there. The angels agreed but not even ten righteous people could be found.

Lot fled in the night with his family and the guardian Angels, though Lot's wife, like Noah's, was lost in the process. The five towns were destroyed, utterly, by fire and a hail of brimstone (sulphur balls). The ashes and sulphur formed a hard crust that completely covered everything.

Abraham migrated from the land of Ur into the land of Canaan at the command of God. "The Everlasting appeared to Him and said: 'I am the Almighty God; walk before me and be thou perfect...I will establish My covenant between Me, and Thee and Thy seed, for an everlasting covenant...'" and so He led His people to the west. "They fled the shameless festivals of Babylon; they averted their heads as they passed by the orgies of Moab, the horrors of the cult of Baal." – Schure

After the destruction of Sodom and Gomorrah, Abraham paid homage to Melchizedek, the Priest of Elohim the Most High God, possessor of heaven and earth (Genesis 14:18,19)

Uncovering Sites of Destruction

The remains of the huge Canaanite cities of Sodom and Zoar, and parts of Admah, now stand out as whiter shapes in the surrounding tan desert, Ron Wyatt and friends, have found their ruins west of the Dead Sea. They produced a very convincing video about the ruins of Sodom and Gomorrah which were destroyed by ash and sulfur, fire and brimstone. You may wish to see the Youtube video, posted on October 18, 2007.

According to Wyatt Gomorrah was a metropolis which may have housed up to a million people. There are melted shapes of undefined structures within the city walls. One shape in Gomorrah may have been a sphinx marking a corner of the city, but there are also *"frozen shapes of buildings which still stand out with forms reminiscent of towers and ziggurats. The ruins are coated with dense friable layers of calcium sulfate, a byproduct of limestone burned for a long time with sulphur."*

Grey layers are ashy and the white layers are

By Michel Wolgemut, Wilhelm Pleydenwurff (Text: Hartmann Schedel) (Own work (scan from original book)) [Public domain], via Wikimedia Commons

fairly hard. Balls of sulphur sit within the grey ash. Alternating white layers include pure calcium sulfate, and calcium carbonate with silicates, which indicate limestone was used in the construction of these cities.

The brimstone is sulphur, which appears to be a pressed powder tested at 98% extremely pure elemental sulphur with small amounts of magnesium. It burns very easily when lit by a match and remains burning for an unusually long stinky time. There are no trace elements in the samples. These are results one would expect to find only in an extremely hot furnace. Geothermal sulphur by comparison is only 40% pure. The burned sulfur at Gomorrah is white, rather than the more typical yellow, which is found near geothermal vents.

The ruins of Admah discovered to the north of the Dead Sea also smell of sulphur, even though there is no volcanic activity in the area, but brimstone and charcoal are present in the ash. These cities are high above the Dead Sea so the white color is not due to an accumulation of salt." (Ron Wyatt "Solomon's Pillars" – Youtube)

SHO'AIB/SHUAYB

One of the most recent accounts is that of the Midianites. Allah (God the Almighty) revealed the story of Sho'aib whose name means "Who Shows the Right Path" through the voice of Mohammad. He is said to have lived four generations after Abraham, and is hopefully the last of the Great Prophets to have revealed God's Word to a spiritually dead people. He ministered in the area of Arabia and ancient Palestine without success.

The Qu'ran states that Sho'aib was appointed by God to be a Great Prophet who delivered God's clear message around 2600 years ago, to the Midian (Syrian) Arabs who lived in the country east of Mount Sinai toward the sea, and to the "people of the wood."

This is actually consistent with the time accepted for the Dispensation of Gautama Buddha. It would have been a long 2,668 mile journey from Nepal to Syria, and might have taken around 5 months. But there was a well-travelled trade route that had existed since the time of Harappa around 6,000 years ago.

Early people referred to Sho'aib as **"the eloquent preacher amongst the Prophets."**

The Midianites were settled in towns booming with commerce. Some were nomadic shepherds who traveled in small bands with their goats, sheep and camels in the dry season. They moved into larger groups during lambing, in the wet season. They lived in goat hair tents and ate goat meat and dairy products, along with a bread which they baked in hot charcoals and sand. The site of Midian may have extended from the eastern shores of the Sinai Peninsula to the deserts bordering the Gulf of Aqabah, Edom and Moab. It is near Mt. Horeb (Sinai) in the land where Moses fled to Jethro, and expiation.

Sho'aib proclaimed the Faith of the One God and warned the idolatrous people, who were cruel cheats and liars in their business transactions, to end their fraudulent ways. Like so many others before them, they showed no gratitude at all for their many bounties.

They cheated and lied to their customers. They shorted buyers on products, embellished the quality of their goods and minimized their defects. Hmmmm... sound familiar? Anyone?

They were a greedy people who did not believe that Allah existed. Even if He did, it would not affect them. They greatly preferred to worship their precious gods, including, perhaps Baal-peor and Ashteroth, as the Queen of Heaven.

Carved gods asked little of them, but adoration. They did not try to change their culture, discipline, or threaten them. Sho'aib called the Midianites to the path of One God and forbade them to worship false, self-satisfied gods. He was said to have presented many miracles, but as in the past they eventually amounted to nothing.

Sho'aib, however remained steadfast in service to God, reminding everyone of the punishments that had befallen the heedless populations before them. Warning that their ignorance would lead to their destruction. He gave historical examples of earlier prophets, including Noah, Hud, Salih and Lot. All of those people were destroyed by God for deviating from the spiritual evolutionary path meant for the advancement of humankind.

He told His people to stop being dishonest in their daily activities and strove to change their hearts for a painstakingly long period of time. Still the majority of them refused to listen to Him and rejected the Message. They taunted Sho'aib and told Him that, were it not for His prestigious family (if somehow this does refer to Buddha, He was a Royal Prince), He would surely have been stoned to death. The Prophet asked disdainfully if they feared his tribe more than their Lord. "Is my family of more consideration with you than God?" Still the Midianites refused to believe, and they were destroyed by a mighty earthquake.

"O my people! Worship Allah, you have no other (God) *but Him. Verily! A clear proof from your Lord has come unto you... wrong not men... And sit not on every road, threatening and hindering from the Path of Allah, those who believe in Him... Remember when you were but few, He multiplied you. And if there is a party of you who believes that which I have been sent, and a party who does not believe... be patient until Allah judges between us... He is the best of Judges."* (Qu'ran, see below)

"...I am a trustworthy Messenger to you. So fear Allah, keep your duty to Him, and obey Me. No reward do I ask of you for it. Give full measure, and cause no loss to others. And weigh with true and straight balance. Defraud not people... nor do evil, making corruption and mischief in the land. Hear Him Who created you and the generations of the men of old."

The leaders of the arrogant disbelievers among his people said; *'If you follow Sho'aib, it is you who will be the losers!'*

They set about driving the Prophet and His few followers from the area. It was clear they would not leave the religion of many gods. They seized the believers' property and belongings, and chased them away.

"O my people! I have indeed conveyed my Lord's Messages unto you and I have given you good advice." (Qu'ran 7:85-93)

They said: *"You are only one of those bewitched! You are but a human being like us and verily, we think that you are one of the liars! So cause a piece of heaven to fall on us, if you are of the truthful!"*

The Messenger turned to His Lord for help, and His plea was answered. Allah sent down on them scorching heat and the towns suffered terribly. On seeing a cloud gathering in the sky, they rejoiced, thinking it would bring cool, refreshing rain to drench their plentiful, but parched fields. They rushed outside expecting raindrops.

Instead the cloud burst, hurling thunderbolts and fire. They heard a roaring sound from above which caused the earth under their feet to tremble. There was an overshadowing gloom, perhaps accompanying a shower of ashes, cinders, and sulphur from a nearby volcanic eruption. Thus a day of terror drove them into their homes. And in the night they perished in this state of horror, as the earthquake tremors finished them.

"But, they belied Him, so the torment of the day of shadow (a gloomy cloud) seized them, indeed that was the torment of a Great Day... And verily! Your Lord, He is indeed the All Mighty, the Most Merciful." (Qu'ran sh. 26:176-191)

And the people of the wood? Perhaps they were nomads who visited the Midianites. Or dwellers of jungle and mountain in the northern regions of the Himalayas.

SUMMARY OF DISAPPOINTING TIMES

These early Manifestations of God's Word, were sent to cruel and wicked communities which were heedless of God's guidance, pleas, and warnings. Instead, the foolish people threatened and punished their precious Messengers. After years of hopelessness Allah, or God, (depending on the language) asked His Servants if they still lived; to leave their communities with the few who had listened and believed in God's power. Those who were mean, cruel, and not spiritually inclined, were subsequently destroyed in hopes that the next group would accept their Prophet, and the Renewal would succeed.

The following examples show that other ancient people became willing servants of, or returned to, the Cause of One Loving God. These people moved humanity forward in huge strides and treated each other with greater respect and dignity. At least in the beginning, but each Dispensation has become corrupted by man's influence, over time.

RESOUNDING SUCCESSES

Even though people still have a difficult time recognizing and acknowledging the coming of the Promised Return, there are enough believers to change the course of Civilization, which is why they are called successes.

Migrations to India

Prior to the time of Krishna migrants came in waves from the steppes of central Russia. They came through Afghanistan and over the Kyber Pass, fighting, blending, and marrying the local inhabitants. Some migrated south along the western coast of the Indian continent, and some went down the eastern coast to an area called Kalinga. A few went to the southern Isle of Lanka. But the Dravidians of south India were quite impervious to newcomers. – based on Schure

At first the people were nomadic herders that followed their grazing cattle. Eventually, however, they established small villages. Instead of a central ruler each village had its own leader or chief, who was usually a skilled warrior called a Raja. They became farmers of the fertile Indus River Valley and raised cattle, horses, sheep, water buffaloes and goats. They also kept dogs.

Sometime around 8000 years ago a nomadic herding people settled in villages in the Mountainous region west of the Indus River. There they grew barley and wheat, which they harvested using sickles with flint blades. They lived in small houses built with adobe bricks.

A thousand years later, their climate changed, bringing more rainfall, so they were able to grow more food. They also grew in population. They traded farm goods for products such as beads and shells, with distant areas in central Asia and areas west of the Kyber Pass, and they began to use bronze and other metals around 6000 years ago.

By 4600 years ago a Bronze Age civilization as grand as that in Mesopotamia and Egypt had arisen on the Indus plain seventy or more cities had been built, some of them upon buried, older towns. There were cities from the foothills of the Himalayas to Malwan in the south.

Two of these cities were Mohenjo-Daro on the Indus River, 250 miles north of the Arabian Sea, and Harappa, 350 miles to the north on the Ravi River. These cities had populations of around 40,000 each.

The long term Harappan civilization featured advanced cities rather than early settlements. Structures were built on a grid system and they had bathrooms and indoor plumbing. The city of Mohenjo Daro had several public wells, the streets were paved, and included a drainage system. There were craftsmen who produced pottery, high quality tools, cotton clothing, and jewelry.

Each city had streets lined with shops and featured a market place. Some houses were spacious and had large enclosed yards. Each house was connected to a covered drainage system that was more sanitary than other commercial centers. Mohenjo-Daro even had a building with an underground furnace and dressing rooms, suggesting they bathed in heated pools, as in modern Hindu temples.

The inhabitants of Mohenjo-Daro and Harappa shared a sophisticated system of weights and measures, used an arithmetic with decimals, and they had a crude written language that was partly phonetic and partly ideographic. The Indus script from around 5000 years ago, found in north-western India, and what is now Pakistan, has not yet been deciphered. It is unclear whether it should be considered actual writing, or a set of "signs" as used by other Bronze Age "writing" systems.

"They spun and wove cotton, mass produced pottery with fine geometric designs, and made figurines sensitively depicting attitudes." They farmed wheat, rice, mustard and sesame seeds, dates and cotton. Tamed animals included: dogs, cats, camels, sheep, pigs, goats, water buffaloes, elephants and chickens; and they buried valuable objects with their dead.

The Harappans built protective walls to guard against flood waters and invaders. Yet their civilization ended 3700 years ago. "Their departure may have been facilitated by climactic conditions, which vacillated between too much and too little water. (*"Civilization in the Indus Valley"* http://www.fsmitha.com/h1/ch05.htm)

Aryans roamed the Indus River Valley after the Harappan civilization collapsed. Some may have come from central Asia near the Black and Caspian Seas. Others may have crossed over into India along the 28 mile Khyber Pass, which is a narrow passage along the borders of present day Pakistan and Afghanistan. They were highly skilled warriors with advanced weaponry and chariots, and may have been at least partially responsible for the sudden collapse of the Harappan civilization. It is said they had to remove and carry their precious chariot wheels to make the trip over the mountains.

These folks used a Proto-Indo-European language related to all modern European languages except Basque, Finnish, and Hungarian. From it Sanskrit was derived. Around the time writing spread to the Hebrews, it came to the Aryans in India.

Quite a few tribes had begun to worship idols as suggested by their clay figurines. And the coming of a new Revelation was imminent.

Rishis had protected the sacred oral scriptures known as the Vedas and the Upanishads for ages, until they could be written. There are four Vedas. The Rig Veda consisted of ten books of hymns or chants. The Yajur Veda focused more on ritualistic procedures. The Sama Veda was concerned with the Creator of the Universe. The fourth, the Atharva Veda was a collection of healing information. It contains prayers, and healing rituals for curing disease and evils. It gives information on protection from enemies and sorcerer's charms for love, health, prosperity, influence, and long life.

Some Vedic references suggest that evil is the work of demons that might take a human form, or that of some other creature; which could be removed by the prayers and rituals of "priests." This is in stark contrast to human beings causing much of their own suffering, as proposed, by Gautama Buddha.

The beautiful Upanishads are meditations on man's link to the universe and its Creator. They are not about liturgies and rituals. They are beautiful sacred teachings that described humanity as having been created with virtue and everlasting life.

"A youth asks a learned man, how many gods there are. The teacher says three hundred and three. 'Yes,' responded the youth, 'but how many are there really?' The learned man narrowed the number to thirty-three. 'Yes,' responded the youth, 'but how many are there really?' Finally the learned man said, 'One.' "

Another teaches that "...everything is unified but there is a world of the senses, which is illusion, and there is a world of the spirit. One must turn from the illusion of the material life, to the world of realization.

God is a mystery...He existed before all else. He was alone. He divided male and female and brought creation into being."

"There is one reality, the impersonal God, called Brahman. All things and Beings are an expression of Brahman. Vishnu (Holy Spirit Messenger) has appeared on earth in nine forms and will come a tenth time to bring the world to an end."

These are but a few of the repeated themes found in the Upanishads Breath of the Eternal translated from Sanskrit by Swami Prabhavananda and Frederick Manchester: Mentor Religious Classics: New American Library, New York and Toronto; 1957

KRISHNA

The Vedas focused on Brahman, the One Supreme God. Long after the time of Rama, and the ancient Vedas and Upanishads made their way to earth there was another great Prophet, the "Radiant One" the blessed, Sri Krishna.

Krishna was born three generations before Abraham, probably sometime between 5400 and 4,800 years ago (Birth date given according to Hindu calendar 4805 years ago).

Like Mary, mother of Jesus of Nazareth, Lord Krishna's mother was forewarned of a virgin birth. She was told to flee from her brother's palace because he would not take kindly to being replaced by a King of all men. Krishna grew up on the mountainsides as a herder of cattle. He then became a hunter of great renown and after He was anointed, He became the kind, charismatic teacher of all mankind thanks to one great pupil, one apostle. His name is Arjuna. The tale of Arjuna and what he learned on the plains of Kurukshetra is the ballad of the Bagavad Gita, the Song of God.

"Thou carriest within thee a sublime Friend whom thou knowest not. For Brahman (God) dwells in the inner part of every man, but few know how to find Him. The man who sacrifices his desires and his works to the Being from whom the principles of everything stem, and by whom the Universe was formed, through this sacrifice attains perfection. For one who finds his happiness and joy within himself, and also his wisdom within himself is one with God. And, mark well, the soul which has found God is freed from rebirth and death, from old age and pain, and drinks the water of Immortality." –Bagavad Gita.

According to selections from Schure's story of Krishna, Pg 65-122:

"From the conquest of India by the Aryans emerged one of the most glorious civilizations the earth has ever known. The Ganges and its tributaries saw great empires and vast capitals arise, like Ayodha, Hastinapur and Indrapechta. The epic accounts of the Mahabharata and the Purana include the oldest historical traditions of India speak of royal opulence, heroic grandeur and the chivalrous spirit of those times. Women are portrayed as delicate, noble and exalted wives like the passionate Sita and the gentle Damayanti."

Solar and Lunar Kings

"The oldest traditions speak of a solar dynasty and a lunar dynasty. The solar cult favored the masculine attributes of godliness. They worshipped the God of the universe. The solar kings cherished all that was pure in the Vedic tradition, including the science of the sacred fire and of prayer, the esoteric conception of the supreme God, a respect for woman, ancestor worship, elected and patriarchal royalty.

The lunar cult attributed the feminine sex to divinity, under whose sign the religions of the Aryan cycle have always worshipped nature, even blind, unconscious nature in its violent, terrible manifestations. At times this cult leaned toward idolatry and black magic, preferred polygamy and tyranny, supported by the passions of the masses.

The battle between the Pandavas or the sons of the sun and the Kuravas, sons of the moon, is the theme of the great Hindu epic, the Mahabharata. It contains a summary of the history of Aryan India before Krishna.

The great battle abounds in spirited combats and strange, endless adventures, but In the middle of this gigantic epic the Kuravas, lunar kings become the conquerors. The Pandavas, noble children of the sun, guardians of the pure rites are dethroned and banished. As exiles they hide in the forests, seeking refuge among the anchorites (religious people who have gone into seclusion for spiritual purpose), wearing clothing made of bark, and leaning on hermits' sticks."

The Hermit Sages

"From time immemorial these ascetics dwelt in retreats in the depth of the forests, beside rivers, or in the mountains near sacred lakes. They were sometimes found alone, sometimes assembled into brotherhoods, but they were always united in a single spirit.

One recognizes in them the spiritual kings, the real masters of India. Heirs of the ancient wise men, the Rishis, they alone held the secret interpretation of the Vedas. In them lived the spirit of asceticism, hidden knowledge and transcendent powers. In order to obtain this wisdom they endured everything in the form of hunger cold, burning sun, even the terror of the jungle. With their voice, their gaze, they summon or drive away serpents, and calm lions and tigers. Happy is one who obtains their blessing, for he will have the Devas (here referring to angelic beings, as compared to Zoroaster's disdain for what His people later called "devas," a multiplicity of gods.) Woe to one who abuses or kills them..."

At the beginning of the Kali-Yuga Age, nearly 5000 years ago, the thirst for gold and power invaded the world. Sages say "Agni the celestial fire (like the Farr) which forms the glorious body of the Devas and purifies the souls of men, had spread its ethereal effulgence's over the earth. But the burning, breath of Kali, goddess of desire and death, who comes out of the abysses of the earth like a fiery exhalation, then passed over all hearts.

Justice had reigned with the noble sons of Pandu, solar kings who obeyed the voices of the wise men. As victors they pardoned the conquered and treated them as equals. But since the children of the sun had been exterminated or driven from their thrones, and their few descendants were hiding among the anchorites, injustice, ambition and hatred had gained the upper hand. Changeable and deceitful the lunar kings engaged in a ceaseless war among themselves. Nevertheless, one had succeeded in overcoming all the others by means of terror and unusual powers."

Kansa and Kalayeni

"In northern India, on the banks of a wide river, the proud and powerful city of Madura flourished. It had twelve pagodas, ten palaces and one hundred gates flanked with towers. Multi-colored banners floated over its high walls, resembling winged serpents. Kansa reigned there with a crafty mind and an insatiable soul. All the lunar kings payed him hom-

age, but Kansa wanted to conquer all of India. So he allied himself with Kalayeni, a snake magician of the Vyndhia Mountains. He was a powerful king of the Yavanas, men with yellow faces; and had dedicated himself to the arts of black magic. He was a follower of the goddess Kali. Kalayeni was called the friend of the, nocturnal demons and the king of serpents because he used them to frighten his people and his enemies.

At the far end of a dense forest was the goddess Kali's temple, carved in a mountain. It was a great dark cave of unknown depth: the entrance was guarded by giants with animal heads, carved in the rock. There they led those who wished to pay homage to Kalayeni, in order to obtain from him some secret power. He would appear at the entrance of the temple in the midst of a host of monstrous snakes that entwined themselves around his body and rose up at the command of his scepter. He forced his servants to kneel before these serpents whose heads, twisted into knots and hung over his own head. At the same time he muttered a mysterious formula. It was said that those who performed this rite and worshipped those serpents obtained tremendous gifts and everything they desired. But perhaps unwittingly, they fell irrevocably under Kalayeni's power. From then on whether they were living far or near, they remained his slaves. If they tried to disobey him or escape, they thought they saw the terrible magician, surrounded by his reptiles, arise before them; they saw themselves encompassed by the serpents' hissing heads, and were paralyzed by their spell-binding eyes."

Kansa asked Kalayeni for support, which was granted as long as Kansa married his daughter, the beautiful Nysumba. *"If I may have a son from you,"* Kansa told Nysumba,*"I shall make him my heir. Then I shall be master of the earth; I shall no longer fear anyone."* But it turned out that Nysumba was barren.

During a massive ceremony to beseech fertility for the queen's womb, the Devas were invoked and in front of a great fire, all the people put in their wishes for her fertility. When *"Queen Nysumba approached and threw in a handful of perfumes into the fire with a gesture of challenge, she uttered a magic formula in an unknown language. The smoke thickened, the flames swirled, and frightened priests cried out. 'O Queen, those are not the Devas, but the Rakshasas (night demons) who passed over the fire! Your womb will remain sterile!'*

Kansa approached the fire and asked the priests, which of his other wives would bear the master of the whole world.

At this moment Devaki, the king's virgin sister came near the fire. She was a pure and unpretentious woman, who had spent her childhood spinning and weaving, living as in a dream. He body was on earth, but her soul seemed forever in heaven. Devaki knelt humbly begging the Devas to give her brother and beautiful Nysumba a son. The priest looked at the fire and then at the virgin. Suddenly he cried out in complete amazement, 'O king of Madura, none of your sons will be master of the world! He will be born in the womb of your sister who is kneeling here!' Great were Kansa's dismay and Nysumba's anger at these words. When the queen was alone with the king, she said 'Devaki must die at Once!'"

'How', asked Kansa, could I cause my sister to die? If the Devas are protecting her, their vengeance would fall upon me!' Nysumba threatened seductively to leave Kansa. He was burning with desire. 'Very well,' he said, 'Devaki will die, but do not leave me.'"

Devaki

"But that same night in a dream the purohita (priest from the fire sacrifice) saw king Kansa drawing his sword against his sister. Immediately he went to Devaki, told her that mortal danger threatened her, and ordered her to flee to the anchorites without delay. Devaki, directed by the priest of the fire, disguised herself as a penitent and left Kansa's palace, and the proud city of Madura.

The king questioned the guards of the city who claimed that the gates had remained closed all night. But in their sleep, they had visions that the dark wall of the fortress broke under a ray of light, and a woman followed the ray and left the city. Kansa realized an invincible power was protecting Devaki and he began to hate her with a mortal hatred.

Devaki dressed in bark strip clothing which hid her beauty and she entered the vast solitudes of the giant forest. She staggered, exhausted from fatigue and hunger, but as soon as she felt the shade of the awesome forest, tasted the fruit of a mango tree and inhaled the freshness of a stream, she took on new life, like a blossoming flower. First she passed beneath tremendous arches formed by massive tree trunks, whose branches planted themselves in the soil again (like vine maples), multiplying their arcades infinitely. For a long time she walked, sheltered from the sun, as in a dark pagoda without an exit. The buzzing of the bees, the cry of the amorous peacocks, the songs of a thousand birds, drew her still further on.

And still larger became the trees, the forest denser and more entangled. The trunks crowded close beside each other and they were covered with foliage, which served for cupolas and pylons. Sometimes Devaki walked through corridors of greenery which the sun flooded with light, and where tree trunks lay overturned by the storm. Sometimes she paused beneath arbors of mango trees and Asoka's, from which cascaded garlands of lianas and a profusion of flowers. Deer and panthers leaped in the thickets; and buffalo snapped branches. Bands of monkeys passed, shrieking through the trees. Toward evening, above a thicket of bamboo she saw the motionless head of a wise elephant. He looked at the virgin with an intelligent, protective air, raising his trunk as if to greet her. Then the forest became light, and Devaki saw a landscape of deep peace and celestial, paradisiacal charm.

A pond strewn with lotus and water lilies spread out before her; its heart of blue opened into the great forest, like another sky. Bashful storks dreamed motionless upon its banks, and two gazelles were drinking from its waters. On the other side, in the shelter of the palms stood the hermitage of the anchorites. A soft pink light bathed the lake, the forest and the dwelling of the holy Rishis. Against the horizon the white summits of Mount Meru rose above the ocean of forests. The breath of an invisible river gave life to the plants *while the softened thunder of a distant waterfall was wafted on the breeze like a caress or a melody.*

At the edge of the pond Devaki saw a boat. Standing near it, a man of mature age, an anchorite, seemed to be waiting. Silently he gestured to the virgin to get into the boat, and he took up the oars. As the little boat moved forward, stroking the water lilies, Devaki saw a female swan swimming over the pond. In a bold flight a male swan came through the air and began to describe lace circles around her. Then he descended upon the water near his companion, shaking his snow white plumage. At this spectacle, Devaki trembled greatly without knowing why. The boat reached the opposite shore, and the lotus-eyed woman found herself before Vasichta, leader of the anchorites, sitting on a gazelle's skin, clothed in the hide of a black antelope. He had the venerable appearance of a god rather than a man. For sixty years he had eaten only wild fruit. His hair and beard were as white as the summit of the Himavat (Himalayas), his skin was transparent, and the gaze of his dim eyes was turned inward in meditation. Upon seeing Devaki, he arose and greeted her.

'Devaki, sister of the famous Kansa, you are welcome in our midst. Guided by Mahadeva (Great God), the supreme master, you have left the world of sorrows for that of happiness. For here you are near the holy Rishis, masters of their senses, content with their destiny and seeking the path to heaven. We have waited long for you, as the night waits for the dawn. For we are the eyes of the Devas fixed on the world. We live in the densest of forests. Men do not see us, but we see men and we observe their actions. The dark age of desire, blood and crime is raging over the world. We have chosen you for the task of deliverance, and the Devas have chosen you through us, for it is in the womb of woman that the ray of divine splendor must take on human form.'

Old Vasichta ordered the Rishis leaving the retreat for evening prayer to bow down to the ground before Devaki. They bowed low as Vasichta continued, 'This one will be the mother of all of us, for from her will be born the spirit which is to regenerate us.' Then, turning to her, he said, 'Go, my child. The rishis will lead you to a neighboring lake where the penitent sisters live. You will dwell among them, and the mysteries will be fulfilled.'

Devaki went to the retreat surrounded by lions. There she was to live with the devout women who feed tame gazelles and devote themselves to ablutions and prayers. Devaki took part in their sacrifices. These Penitents had been commanded to dress her in exquisite scented fabrics like a queen and to let her wander alone in the open forest. And the forest, filled with perfumes, voices and mysteries attracted the young woman. Sometimes she met processions of old anchorites returning from the river. Upon seeing her they knelt before her and then continued on their way. One day near a stream covered with pink lotus, she noticed a young anchorite in prayer. He stood up at her approach, cast a long, sad look at her and walked away in silence. And the serious faces of the old men, the image of the two swans and the look of the young anchorite haunted the virgin in her dreams.

Near the stream was a tree of unknown age, with wide branches, which the holy Rishis called "the tree of life." Devaki liked to sit in its shade. Often when she fell asleep there, she was visited by strange visions. Voices sang behind the foliage, 'Glory, glory, glory be to you Devaki!'

Were these the anchorites or Devas, who sang like this? Sometimes it seemed that a distant power or a mysterious presence, had suspended over her, and forced her to sleep.

Then she fell into a deep sweet, inexplicable slumber, out of which she awakened bewildered and disturbed. She turned around as if to look for someone, but she never saw anyone. But several times she found roses strewn on her bed of leaves, and a crown of lotus in her hands.

One day Devaki fell into a deeper ecstasy. She heard heavenly music like an ocean of harps and divine voices. Suddenly the sky opened into depths of light. Thousands of magnificent beings were looking at her and in the brightness of a flashing ray of light, the sun of suns, Mahadeva, appeared to her in human form. Then having been overshadowed by the Spirit of the worlds, she lost consciousness, and oblivious of earth, in a boundless felicity, she conceived the holy child.

When seven moons had described their magic circles around the sacred forest, the chief of the anchorites summoned Devaki. 'The will of the Devas has been fulfilled,' he said. 'You have conceived in purity of heart and divine love. Virgin and mother, we greet you. A son will be born of you, who will be the savior of the world. But your brother Kansa is looking for you to kill you, along with the tender fruit you carry in your womb. The brothers will lead you to the shepherds who live at the foot of Mount Meru, beneath scented cedars, in the pure air of the Himavat. There you will bring into the world your divine child, and you shall call him Krishna, the holy one. But see that he knows nothing of his origin and yours; never speak to him about it. Go without fear, for we are watching over you.'"

Young Krishna

"At the foot of Mount Meru stretched a fertile valley, green with pastures and surrounded by vast forests of cedar trees, where the pure air of Himavat sighed gently. In this high valley lived a tribe of herdsmen over which the patriarch Nanda, friend of the anchorites ruled. Here Devaki found refuge from the persecutions of the tyrant of Madura, and here in Nanda's home, she brought her son, Krishna, into the world. Except Nanda, no one knew who the stranger was, nor where this son came from.

The shepherds called him "The Radiant One" because his presence alone, his smile and his big eyes had a way of spreading joy. Animals, children, women, men, everyone loved him and he seemed to love everyone, smiling at his mother, playing with the lambs and the young children of his own age, or speaking with the old men. The child was fearless, full of daring and he performed astonishing feats. Sometimes he was found in the woods lying on the moss wrestling with young panthers and holding their mouths open, without their daring to bite him.

Above all things and all beings, Krishna adored his young mother, so beautiful and so radiant, who spoke to him of the heaven of the Devas, of heroic battles and of the wonderful things she had learned from the anchorites. And the shepherds who led their flocks beneath the cedars of Mount Meru would say, 'Who is this mother, and who is this son? Although she is dressed like our women, she looks like a queen. The amazing child was raised with ours, yet he does not look like them. Is he a genius? Is he a god? Whoever he is, he will bring us happiness.'"

Devaki's Departure

"When Krishna was fifteen years old, his mother Devaki was summoned by the leader of the anchorites. One day she disappeared without saying goodbye to her son. When he saw her no longer, Krishna went to look for the patriarch, Nanda and asked him, 'Where is my mother?' Nanda answered, bowing his head, 'My child, do not question me. You mother has gone on a long journey. She has returned to the country from which she came, and I do not know when she will return.'

Krishna said nothing at all, but he lapsed into such a deep reverie that all the children kept away from him as if gripped by a superstitious fear. Krishna deserted his friends, left their games, and lost in his reflections, went alone to Mount Meru. He wandered for several weeks. One morning he came to a high, wooded peak where his view reached over the chain of the Himavat Mountains. Suddenly near him, he saw an old man in the white robe of an anchorite, standing under the giant cedars in the morning light. He seemed one hundred years old. His snow-white beard and his bare head shone with majesty.

The lively child and the centenarian gazed at each other for a long time. The eyes of the old man rested benignly upon Krishna, but Krishna was so startled at seeing him that he remained silent in admiration. Although Krishna saw him for the first time, it seemed as if he knew this aged man.

'Whom do you seek?' the old man asked at last.

'My mother.'

'She is no longer here.'

'Where shall I find her?'

'With Him who never changes.'

'But how shall I find Him?'

'Seek.'

'And shall I see you again?'

'Yes, when the daughter of the serpent incites the son of the bull to crime, then you will see me again in a purple light. Then you will kill the bull, and will crush the head of the serpent, son of Mahadeva (God), know that you and I are but one in Him. Seek, always seek.'

The old man extended his hand in a gesture of benediction, then he turned and took a few steps under the high cedars in the direction of the Himavat. Suddenly it seemed to Krishna that the old Man's form became transparent and disappeared with a luminous vibration on the shimmering glow of the fine needled branches.

When Krishna came down from Mount Meru, he appeared to be transformed. A new energy emanated from His being He gathered his companions together and told them. 'Let us fight the bulls and snakes; let us defend the good and subdue the wicked!' With bow in hand and sword at his side, Krishna and his companions, sons of the shepherds, now transformed into warriors, began to beat the forests, fighting the wild beasts. In the depths of the woods one could hear the roaring of hyenas, jackals and tigers, and the young men's cries of triumph over the defeated animals. Krishna killed and tamed lions; he made war on kings and freed oppressed peoples. But sadness remained in the depths of his heart, which had but one deep, mysterious desire; he longed to find his mother and to see the strange, august old man again. He asked himself, 'Did he not promise me that I would see him again when I crushed the head of the snake? Did he not tell me that I would find my mother again with Him who never changes?' But it was useless for him to fight, conquer, and kill. He had not seen the majestic old man or his own glorious mother."

Krishna and Kalayeni's Snake

"One day he heard people speak about Kalayeni, King of the serpents, and he asked to fight with his most terrible serpent in the presence of the black magician. It was said that this creature, trained by Kalayeni, had already eaten hundreds of men, and that its glance could paralyze the most courageous with fear. Krishna saw a long, greenish-blue reptile come from the depths of Kali's dark temple, at Kalayeni's call. The serpent slowly raised its thick body, distended its red crest, and its piercing eyes lit up in its monstrous head, which was covered with shiny scales, 'This serpent, said Kalayeni, knows many things. It is a powerful demon. It will tell the secrets, only to the one who kills it, but it kills those who fail.

It has seen you; it is looking at you; you are in its power. All that is left for you to do is worship it, or die in a senseless struggle.' Krishna was indignant at these words, for he felt that his heart was like the tip of a lightning bolt. He looked at the snake, and then threw himself upon it, seizing it beneath the head. Man and serpent rolled on the steps of the temple. But before the serpent could encircle him in its coils, Krishna cut off its head with his sword.

Disentangling himself from the still writhing body, the young conqueror triumphantly raised the head of the serpent in his left hand, and it was still alive. 'Why did you kill me, son of Mahadeva? Do you think you will find truth by killing the living? Foolish one, you will only find it in dying yourself. Death is in life, life is in death. Beware the daughter of the serpent and spilt blood. Be careful! Be careful!' With these words, the serpent died. Krishna let the head fall and went away, filled with horror. But Kalayeni said, 'I have no power over this man; Kali alone can subdue him with a spell.'

The autumn moon showed its shining orb above the cedar forests and the night air was perfumed with the scent of wild lilies in which the bees had hummed all day long. Sitting beneath a large cedar tree at the edge of a meadow, weary of the vain battles of earth, Krishna dreamed of heavenly combats and the boundless heaven itself. The more he thought of his glorious mother and the august old man, the more his childish exploits seemed despicable and celestial things came to life within him."

Gopis

"A consoling charm, a divine recollection flooded his entire being. Then a hymn of thankfulness to Mahadeva arose from his heart and overflowed from his lips in a sweet divine melody. Attracted by this wonderful song, the daughters and wives of the herdsmen, known as Gopis left their houses. Some came nearer, calling, Krishna! Krishna! Then very ashamed, they ran away. Gradually becoming bolder, the women surrounded Krishna in groups like timid, curious gazelles, charmed by his melodies. But, lost in his dream of God, He did not see them. More and more enchanted by his song, the Gopis began to grow impatient at not being noticed. Nichdali, Nanda's daughter, with eyes closed, had fallen into a kind of ecstasy. But Sarasvati, her sister, bolder than she, quietly moved near Devaki's son, pressed against his side and said in a soft voice, 'O Krishna, don't you see that we are listening to you, that we can no longer sleep in our homes? Your melodies have cast a spell upon us. O adorable hero, we are captivated by your voice, and can no longer do without you!' 'O keep singing!' a young girl said. 'Teach us to sing! Teach us dancing,' said a woman.

And Krishna, coming out of his dream, looked favorably upon the Gopis. He spoke kind words to them and, taking their hands, made them sit on the grass near the

huge cedars, in the bright moonlight. Then he told them what he had seen within himself. He told them the story of the heroes, and the exploits of the divine Rama. The women and young girls listened captivated. These tales lasted until dawn. When pink Aurora arose behind Mount Meru and the Kikilas began to chirp beneath the cedars, the Gopis furtively returned to their homes. But the next night, as soon as the crescent moon appeared, they returned more eagerly than ever. Seeing that they were enchanted by his narratives, Krishna taught them to sing and to portray in gestures the sublime actions of the Heros and God. To some he gave vines with strings which vibrate like soul, to others resounding cymbals like the hearts of warriors, to others drums which imitate thunder. Others he inspired with thoughts, to extend their arms, and move about in a divine dream, the sacred dancers portrayed the majesty of and emotions, and the glory which Krishna saw within himself, come to life again in these happy transfigured women.

One morning the Gopis had scattered. The sound of their musical instruments and their singing, laughing voices had faded in the distance. Krishna who had remained alone under the huge cedar tree saw Sarasvati and Nichdali, Nanda's daughters, coming toward him, Both girls were afraid of feeling the emptiness when he would leave them, and in their own way, wished to be his wives. But he could not marry them both. Instead there became an eternal bond between the three. While he spoke to them about everlasting love, it seemed to the girls that he increased in height. Suddenly they were afraid of him and returned home sobbing.

Krishna took the road to Mount Meru alone. The following night, the Gopis met for their games, but they waited for their teacher in vain. He had disappeared, leaving them only an essence, a perfume from his being; the sacred songs and dances."

After a month of ablutions and prayers on the banks of the Ganges, having purified himself in the light of the sun and in the thought of Mahadeva, Krishna returned to his native country, among the herders of Mount Meru."

Vasichta the Old One

"...King Kansa began to persecute and hunt the anchorites like wild beasts, when he learned that his sister Devaki had lived among them. Their leader, old Vasichta, though one hundred years of age, set out to speak to the king of Madura. The guards saw with amazement a blind old man led by a gazelle which he kept on a leash, appear at the gates of the palace. Out of respect for the Rishi, they allowed him to pass.

Vasichta approached the throne where Kansa was sitting beside Nysumba, and said, 'Kansa! King of Madura! Woe to you, daughter of the serpent, who breathes hate into him!

The day of your punishment is near. Devaki's son lives! He will come, covered with armor of impenetrable scales, and will drive you from your throne in shame. Now tremble and live in fear; that is the punishment the Daevas allot you!'

The warriors, guards, and servants knelt before the holy centenarian as he departed, led by his gazelle, no one daring to touch him. But from that day, Kansa and Nysumba dreamed of secret ways to bring about the death of the leader of the anchorites.

Devaki was dead and no one except Vasichta knew that Krishna was her son. Nevertheless, the news of that latter's feats had reached the king's ears. Kansa needed a strong man to protect him. 'The one who killed Kalayeni's great serpent will not be afraid of the anchorite.' Accordingly, Kansa called the patriarch, Nanda and said, 'Send me the young hero, Krishna, so I may make him the driver of my chariot and as my first counselor.' Nanda informed Krishna of the king's command and Krishna went in hopes that he could learn more about the whereabouts of His mother.

Kansa was pleased with Krishna's strength, skill and intelligence and entrusted him with the care of his kingdom. "But Nysumba, upon seeing the hero of Mount Meru, trembled throughout her whole body with an impure desire, and her cunning mind shaped a secret plan, inspired by a criminal thought. Unknown to the king she had the driver of the chariot summoned to her apartments. As a magician, she possessed the art of instantly becoming young again by means of potent filters. Devaki's son found the ebony-breasted Nysumba lying almost naked on a bed of velvet, draped in gold bracelets, a jeweled crown and perfumes. She said, 'I alone know who you are. The Devas have made you master of men; I alone can make you master of the world. Are you willing?' (Like Sita's offer in Rama)

'If it is Mahadeva who is speaking through you,' Krishna said, looking grave, 'you will tell me where my mother is, and where I shall find the tall old man who spoke to me beneath the cedars of Mount Meru.'

'Your mother?' asked Nysumba with a smile of disdain. 'It certainly is not I who will tell you; as for that old man, I do not know him. Foolish one, you continue to dream and do not see the earthly treasures I am offering you! There are Kings who wear crowns who are not kings. There are sons of shepherds who bear royalty on their foreheads and who do not know their strength. You are young; you are handsome. Hearts belong to you. Kill the king in his sleep, and I shall place the crown upon your head, and you will be master of the world. For I love you, and you were pre-destined for me. I so wish, and I so command!'

As she spoke, the queen raised herself, domineering, fascinating, and terrible as a beautiful snake. Sitting upright oh her couch, she cast a flame of such dark fire into Krishna's limpid eyes that he trembled. Hell appeared in those glances. He saw the abyss of the temple of Kali, goddess of desire and death, where snakes writhed in an everlasting agony. Then suddenly Krishna's eyes seemed like two swords. They pierced the queen through and through, and the hero of Mount Meru cried out, 'I am faithful to the king who chose me as protector! As for you, know that you will die!'

Nysumba gave a piercing scream and rolled over on her couch, biting the velvet covering. All her artificial youth had faded; she had become old and wrinkled once again. Krishna went away, leaving her to her anger.

Tortured night and day by the anchorite's words, the king of Madura said to the driver of his chariot, 'Since the enemy has set foot in my palace I no longer sleep in peace. An infernal magician named Vasichta, who lives in a dense forest came and left his curse on me. Since that time I no longer breathe; the old man has poisoned my days. But with you who fear nothing, I do not fear him. Come with me to the accursed forest! A spy who knows all the paths will lead us to him. As soon as you see him, run to him and strike him without allowing him to say a word to you, or look at you. When he is mortally wounded, ask him where the son of my sister Devaki is, and what his name is. The peace of my kingdom hangs on this mystery.'

'Calm yourself,' Krishna said, 'I was not afraid of Kalayeni nor of Kali's serpent. Who can make me tremble now? However powerful this man may be, I shall find out what he is hiding from you!'"

The Hunt

Disguised as hunters, the king and his driver rode in as swift chariot, drawn by spirited horses. The spy who had explored the forest followed them.

"*It was the beginning of the rainy season. The rivers were rising, growing plants covered the roads, and the white line of storks was seen on the tops of the clouds. When the men neared the sacred wood the horizon darkened, the sun hid itself; the air was filled with a copper colored mist. From the stormy sky, clouds hung over the wild foliage of the forest.*

'Why,' Krishna asked the king, 'has heaven suddenly darkened and the forest become so black?'

'Well do I know,' said the King, 'It is Vasichta the evil recluse, who is darkening the sky and arming the accursed forest against me. Krishna, are you afraid?'

'Let the sky change its face and the earth its color! I am not afraid!'

'Then, forward!'

Krishna lashed the horses with his whip and the chariot dove beneath the thick shade of the baobabs. It moved forward for a time at an amazing speed. But the forest became still wilder and more frightening. Lightning flashed, thunder roared.

'Never,' said Krishna, 'have I seen the sky so dark and the trees twisting in this way. Your magician is powerful!'

'Krishna, slayer of serpents, hero of Mount Meru, are you afraid?'

'Let the earth quake and the sky crumble! I am not afraid!'

'Then keep going!'

"Again the daring driver whipped the horses and the chariot continued on its way. Now the storm became so dreadful that the giant trees bent and the quaking forest roared like the howling of a thousand demons. Lightning struck near the travelers; a shattered baobab blocked the way; the horses stopped and the earth trembled.

'Your enemy must be a god', said Krishna, 'since Indra (god of Rain, thunder and war) himself is protecting him.'

'We are approaching the goal!' Cried the king's spy, 'Look at that path of green! At the end of it is a wretched hut. It is there that Vasichta, the great lives, feeding birds, feared by wild animals and protected by a gazelle. But not for a kingdom shall I take one step more!'

At these words, the king of Madura became white. 'He's there? Really? Behind those trees?' Clinging to Krishna, he whispered in a low voice, while his whole body trembled, 'Vasichta! Vasichta, who is plotting my death, is there! He sees me from his secret retreat... His eye is following me! Save me from him!'

Yes, by Mahadeva!' said Krishna, getting out of the chariot, 'I want to see the one who causes you to tremble like this!'

For a year the aged Vasichta quietly had awaited death in his hut, hidden in the thickest part of the sacred forest. Before the death of his body, he was freed from his fleshly prison. His eyes were blind, but he saw with his soul. His skin hardly felt heat and cold, but his spirit lived in a perfect unity with the Sovern Spirit. Praying and meditating without ceasing, he saw things of this world only in the light of Brahman. A faithful disciple brought him grains of rice, on which he lived. The gazelle who ate from his hand warned him of the approach of wild beasts. Then he drove the latter away by whispering a mantra and by extending his bamboo staff with its seven nodes. As for men, whoever they were, by means of his gaze he saw them when they were still several miles away.

Krishna, walking along the dark path, suddenly found himself before Vasichta. The leader of the anchorites with legs crossed, was sitting on a mat, leaning against the post of his hut in a deep calm. From the eyes of the blind man came the inner glimmer of the seer. As soon as Krishna saw him, he recognized him. The majestic old man! He felt a sensation of joy; reverence entered his soul. Forgetting the king, his chariot and his kingdom, he knelt on one knee before the saint and adored him.

Vasichta seemed to see him. His body, leaning against the post, sat up with a slight trembling; he extended both arms to bless his guest and his lips murmured the sacred syllable, AUM.

Meanwhile, Kansa, hearing no outcry and not seeing his driver return, slipped furtively along the path and stood petrified with astonishment upon seeing Krishna kneeling before the holy anchorite. The latter turned his blind eyes toward Kansa. Raising his staff, he said, 'O king of Madura, you are coming to kill me! Greetings! For you will free me from the pain of this body. You wish to know where is the son of your sister Devaki, who is to dethrone you. Here he kneels before me and before Mahadeva; he is Krishna, your own charioteer! How foolish and cursed you are, since your most fearful enemy is this very one here! You have brought him to me, so that I can tell him that he is the chosen one. Tremble! You are lost, for your infernal soul will indeed be the prey of demons!'

Stupefied, Kansa listened. He did not dare look the old man in the face. Pale with rage, seeing Krishna still kneeling, he took his bow and arching it with all his might, discharged an arrow at Devaki's son. But his arm trembled; the arrow swerved and sank deep into Vasichta's chest. With his arms extended in the form of a cross, Vasichta appeared as though waiting for the arrow in a kind of ecstasy.

A cry was heard, a terrible cry.—It was not from the heart of the old man, but from Krishna's. He had heard the arrow hum past his ear, and then he had seen it sink into the saint's flesh and it seemed to Krishna that it had sunk into his own heart, so closely had his soul become identified with the Rishi's at that moment. With that sharp arrow all the pain of the world pierced Krishna's soul, tearing it to its core.

Nevertheless, Vasichta, with the arrow in his chest and without changing position, was still moving his lips. He murmured, 'Son of Mahadeva, why do you cry out? Killing is vain! The arrow cannot reach the soul and the victim is the conqueror of the assassin. Be victorious, Krishna, destiny is being fulfilled! I am returning to Him Who never changes. May Brahman receive my soul! But you, His elect, savior of the world, stand up! Krishna! Krishna!'

And Krishna stood up, his hand on his sword; he wanted to strike the king, but Kansa had fled.

Then a flash rent the dark sky and Krishna fell to earth, thunderstruck, paralyzed by a blinding light. While his body remained inert, his soul, united with that of the old man through power and sympathy, ascended into space. Earth, with its rivers, seas and continents disappeared like a black ball, and both souls arose to the seventh heaven of the Devas, to the Father of Beings, to the Sun of suns, to Mahadeva, the Divine Intelligence. They were plunged into an ocean of light, which opened before them. In the center of the sphere Krishna saw Devaki, his radiant mother, his glorified mother, who with an ineffable smile stretched forth her arms and drew him to her breast. Thousands of Devas came to bathe in the radiance of the Virgin Mother, as in a fountain of light. And Krishna felt permeated with love from Devaki. Then from the heart of his shining mother, his being radiated throughout all the heavens. He felt that he was the son, the divine soul of all beings, the Word of Life, the Creative Word, superior to universal life, nevertheless he pervaded it through the essence of grief through the fire of prayer and the happiness of a divine sacrifice.

When Krishna came to himself, thunder still rolled in the sky, the forest was dark and torrents of rain were falling upon the hut. A gazelle was licking the bloodstained body of the slain ascetic. The majestic old man was but a corpse. Krishna arose as if revived. An abyss separated him from the world and its vain appearance. He had lived the great truth; he understood his mission. As for Kansa, filled with terror he was fleeing through the storm in his chariot, and his horses galloped as if flogged by a thousand demons.

Krishna was greeted by the anchorites as the anticipated, the predestined successor to Vasichta. They performed the funeral ceremony for the holy man in the sacred forest, and Devaki's son received the staff with seven nodes as a sign of command. After having performed the sacrifice of fire in the presence of the three eldest anchorites who knew the three Vedas by heart, Krishna withdrew to Mount Meru to think upon His teaching and the way of salvation for all men."

The Great Teacher

"His meditation and austerities lasted seven years. At the end of that time he felt that he had subdued his earthly nature through his divine nature, and that he had become sufficiently identified with the son of Mahadeva to merit the name, the son of God. Then only did he call to him the anchorites, young and old, in order to reveal his teachings to them. They found Krishna purified and matured; the hero had changed into the saint; he had not lost his lion's strength, but he had gained the gentleness of the dove. Among those who hastened to Krishna, the first to come to him was Arjuna, a descendant of the solar kings, one of the Pandavas dethroned by the Kuravas, or lunar kings. Young Arjuna was full of fire, but was easily discouraged and inclined to doubt. He became deeply attached to Krishna.

Seated under the cedars of Mount Meru, facing the Himavat, Krishna began to speak to his students about truths inaccessible to men who live in slavery to the senses. He taught them the doctrine of the immortal soul, its rebirths and its mystic union with God. The body covering the soul is a finite thing, but the soul which inhabits the body is invisible, imponderable, incorruptible and eternal.

When a body is dissolved, when Satwa (wisdom) has the upper hand, the soul flies to the regions of those pure beings who have knowledge of the Most High. When the body experiences this dissolution while Raja (passion) rules, the soul comes again to live among those who have become attracted to the things of the earth. Likewise, if the body is destroyed when Tama (ignorance) predominates, the soul, overshadowed by matter is again attracted by irrational beings.'

Not only do good, but be good. Let the motive be in the deed, not in the reward.

Renounce the fruit of your works, but let each of your acts be like an offering to the Supreme Being.

If in the heavens the splendor of a thousand suns glittered at the same time,' said Krishna, 'this would hardly resemble the splendor of the only All-Powerful.' While he thus spoke of Mahadeva, such light streamed from Krishna's eyes that his students could not bear its brightness, and knelt at his feet. Arjuna's hair stood up on his head, and bowing deeply, he said, 'Master, you words frighten us and we cannot bear the sight of the Great Being you portray before us.' (Farr in a revelatory state)

Krishna continued, 'Listen to what He tells you through me. Although by my nature I am not subject to birth or death, and although I am the master of all creatures, since I command my being, I become visible through my own power.

Every time virtue wanes in the world and evil and injustice are victorious, I become manifest, and thus I appear from age to age for the salvation of the righteous, the destruction of the evil in men, and the re-establishment of Virtue'

Speaking thus, Krishna looked upon his students with tenderness and kindness. Arjuna cried out 'Lord! You are our Master, you are the son of Mahadeva! I see him in your kindness, in your ineffable charm, even more than in your terrible brightness!

Neither penitence nor alms-giving, nor the Vedas, nor sacrifice are worth a single one of your glances. You are truth! Lead us to the fight, to the battle, to death! Wherever it is, we will follow you!'

Smiling and enraptured, the students pressed closer to Krishna, saying, 'Why didn't we recognize it sooner? Mahadeva is speaking through you!' Krishna answered, 'Your eyes were not open. I have given you the great secret. Tell it only to those who can understand it. You are my chosen ones. You see the purpose; the crowd sees only the end of the road. And now let us preach to the people the way of salvation!'

Another evening, on a riverbank, on the outskirts of a city, the crowd gathered around him, what he preached was charity towards one's neighbor. 'The evils with which we torment our neighbor, follow us, just as our shadow follows our body.

Works, which have love for one's fellow man as a basis are those which must be pursued by the righteous, for they are those which will weigh most on the heavenly scale.

If you go only among the good, your example will be useless; do not be afraid to live among the wicked in order to lead them back to the good! The virtuous man is similar to the huge banyan tree whose beneficent shade gives freshness of life to the plants surrounding it!

Man's knowledge is but vanity; all his good actions are illusion when he does not know how to relate them to God. One who is humble in heart and spirit is beloved of God; he does not need anything else. Infinity and space alone can understand infinity; only God can understand God.'

The shepherds of Mount Meru were amazed at what the boy they knew had become. The two daughters of Nanda still loved Krishna, but the older daughter had married, then been sold to another man, whom she had left out of contempt. Then one day, desolate in heart, heavy with remorse and displeasure, she returned and went to find her sister, Nichdali. 'My poor sister! I forgive you, but my brother will not. Krishna alone can save you!' A flame shone in Sarasvati's lifeless eyes. 'Krishna!' she exclaimed. What has he become?'

'A saint, a great prophet. He preaches on the banks of the Ganges.'

'Let us find him!' cried Sarasvati. And the two sisters set out, the one stained with passion, the other perfumed with innocence. Yet both were consumed by the same love.

Krishna was seated at a feast in the home of a famous leader when the two women asked to be presented to the prophet. They were allowed to enter because of their penitents' dress. Sarasvati and Nichdali knelt at Krishna's feet. Sarasvati cried out, shedding a flood of tears, 'Since you left us, I have spent my life in wrongdoing and in sin; but if you will, Krishna, you can save me!'

Nichdali added 'O Krishna, when I saw you before, I knew I would love you forever; now that I find you again in all your glory I know that you are the son of Mahadeva!' And both of them kissed his feet.

The Rajas said 'Holy Rishi, why do you allow these common women to insult you with their foolish words?'

Krishna answered, 'Let them pour out their hearts. They are worth more than you, for this one has faith, and that one, love.'

From that day on, Sarasvati and Nichdali became closely attached to Krishna and followed Him with His disciples. Inspired by him, they taught other women."

Krishna Visits the King

"Kansa still reigned in Madura. Like a dry leaf he trembled for his life, and often, in spite of his guards, he would turn around suddenly, expecting to see the young hero, terrible and radiant, standing at his door.

Nysumba tossed on her couch and dreamed of her lost powers. When she learned that Krishna, now a prophet, was preaching on the banks of the Ganges, she persuaded the king to send a troop of soldiers to bring him back captive. When Krishna saw the soldiers he smiled and said,' I know who you are and why you come. I am ready to follow you to your king, but first, let me tell you about the King of Heaven who is mine!' When he was finished, the soldiers presented their arms to Krishna. 'We shall not take you as a prisoner to our king, but we shall follow you.'

When he learned of this Kansa was very frightened, but Nysumba convinced him to send the finest soldiers in the kingdom! They had promised not to listen, but when they saw the radiance of Krishna's countenance, the majesty of his carriage and the respect the crowd showed him, they could not help hearing Him.

The Kshatriyas (warriors) were filled with joy and surprise, for they felt relieved of a tremendous burden. 'Truly you are a great magician, for we had sworn to lead you to the king in chains, but it is impossible for us to do this since you have freed us from ours.'

They returned to Kansa and said to him, 'We cannot bring this man to you! He is a great Prophet and you have nothing to fear from him.'

The king, seeing that all was useless, had his guard increased and iron chains put on all the gates of his palace. Nevertheless, one day he heard a great noise in the city and shouts of joy and triumph. The guards came and exclaimed, 'It is Krishna entering Madura! The people are forcing the gates; He is breaking the iron chains!' Kansa wanted to flee, but the guards themselves compelled him to remain on his throne.

Followed by His students and a great number of anchorites, Krishna was making his entry into Madura. The city was decked with flags and in the midst of a turbulent host of people who resembled a sea disturbed by the wind, Krishna came showered by garlands and flowers. Everyone acclaimed him. The Brahmans grouped under the sacred banana *trees before the temples in order to greet Devaki's son, the conqueror of the serpent, the hero of Mount Meru, but above all, the prophet of Vishnu (God). Followed by a brilliant procession Krishna appeared before the king and queen.*

'You have reigned only with violence and evil. And you deserve a thousand deaths because you killed the holy elder, Vasichta. Nevertheless, you will not die yet. I want to prove to the world that it is not in killing that one triumphs over one's conquered enemies, but in forgiving them!'

'Evil magician,' said Kansa, 'you have stolen my crown and my kingdom! Kill me!'

'You speak like a madman,' said Krishna, 'for if you died in your present state of irrationality, hardness and crime, you would be lost irrevocably in the other life. If, on the other hand, you begin to understand your folly and repent in this one, your punishment will be less in the other, and through the intercession of pure spirits, one day Mahadeva will save you.'

Nysumba whispered words of vengeance to her husband. Krishna looked severely at her, but with great pity. 'O wretched one, always your poison! Corrupter, black magician, you have nothing in your heart, but the venom of serpents! – And now you shall go with the king to a place of penitence to expiate your crimes under the supervision of the Brahmans.'

Afterwards, with the consent of the noblemen and the people of the kingdom, Krishna consecrated Arjuna, his disciple as king of Madura. He gave supreme authority to the Brahmans."

Essence of the Bagavad Gita

"When the lunar kings heard that a solar king had again ascended the throne of Madura and that through him the Brahmans were to become masters of India, they formed a powerful league in order to overthrow him. Arjuna gathered around him all the solar kings from the temple of Dvarka, Krishna observed and guided them. The two armies formed themselves face to face, and the decisive battle was imminent."

In the Mahabharata the 18 day war occurred when Krishna was 89. And this was 36 years before the Kali Yuga began so the war began in 4895 BC) According to the Laws of Manu, one of the earliest known texts describing the yugas, the length is 4800 years + 3600 years + 2400 years + 1200 years for a total of 12,000 years for one arc, or 24,000 years to complete the cycle (one precession of the equinox). There is no mention of a year of the demigods or any years longer than the solar, which is consistent with description in The Holy Science. However, the one debatable interpretation from the Shrimad Bhagavatam states the following: "The duration of the Satya millennium equals 4,800 years of the demigods; the duration of the Dvāpara millennium equals 2,400 years; and that of the Kali millennium is 1,200 years of the demigods... As aforementioned, one year of the demigods is equal to 360 years of the human beings. The duration of the Satya-yuga is therefore 4,800 x 360, or 1,728,000 years. The duration of the Tretā-yuga is 3,600 x 360, or 1,296,000 years. The duration of the Dvāpara-yuga is 2,400 x 360, or 864,000 years. And the last, the Kali-yuga, is 1,200 x 360, or 432,000 years in total." (Shrimad Bhāgavatam 3.11.19) [2]. These 4 yugas follow a timeline ratio of (4:3:2:1)." – (http://en.wikipedia.org/wiki/Yuga)

One morning at daybreak, Krishna appeared to Arjuna, who said. 'Without you I cannot do it. Look at these two great armies, these multitudes who are about to kill each other!' Sun glinted off the leader's gilded mail and thousands of cavalrymen, horses and elephants awaited the battle signal. The leader of the enemy army, the oldest of the Kuravas (lunar kings), blew his great shell, whose sound resembled the roaring of a lion. At once on the vast battle-

field was heard the neighing of horses, the confused noise of arms, drums and trumpets. There was a great uproar. Arjuna had only to mount his chariot, drawn by white horses, and to blow his sea shell of celestial blue, in order to give the battle signal to the sons of the sun. But the king was overcome by pity and discouragement. 'Upon seeing this multitude about to attack each other, I feel my limbs weaken, my mouth is parched, my body trembles, my hair stands on end, my skin burns, and my head swims. I see evil signs! No good can come from this massacre! What shall we do with kingdoms, pleasures and even with life?

Those very men for whom we want kingdoms, pleasures and joys are standing there ready to fight each other, forgetting their lives and their possessions. Teachers, fathers, sons, grandfathers, uncles, grandsons, relatives are going to slaughter one another. I do not wish to kill them in order to reign over this earth! What pleasure can I find in killing my enemies?'

'O Arjuna! There is no good, nor evil—only Brahman. You weep over those for whom one should not mourn. Wise men weep, neither for the living nor for the dead. Thou and I and those leaders of men have always existed, and we shall never cease to exist in the future. Truth lives through everything, and is above destruction. No one can destroy the indestructible. All these bodies will not last, and you know it. You cannot kill them, for I already have!

The incarnate soul is everlasting, indestructible and infinite. You must fight, descendant of Bharat... The soul does not kill, neither is it killed. It is not born; it does not die and cannot lose this being which it always had... The soul passes through everything unharmed. Therefore you should worry neither about death nor about life, O Arjuna!' Arjuna leaped into his chariot and gave the battle signal. Then Krishna said farewell to his followers and left the battlefield, for he was certain of the victory."

Ending

Krishna knew that far from doing penance, Kansa had taken refuge with his father-in-law, Kalayeni, king of the serpents. "*Kansa's hatred, constantly aroused by Nysumba, caused them to send spies, seeking the appropriate moment to strike him. But Krishna felt that his mission was ended and only required the supreme seal of sacrifice in order for it to be fulfilled. Therefore, he stopped evading and paralyzing his enemy with his will and he knew the long awaited blow would strike him in the darkness. But the son of Devaki wished to die far from men, in the solitude of Himavat where he would feel nearer to his radiant mother, and the sublime old man and the sun of Mahadeva.*

Only Sarasvati and Nichdali read his plan, in their Teacher's eyes, by means of the deviation that exists in woman and in love. Sarasvati threw herself at his feet, kissed them passionately and cried, 'Master, do not leave us!'

Nichdali looked at him and said quietly, 'I know where you are going. Since we love you, let us follow you!' Krishna said, 'In my heaven, love can be refused nothing. Come!'

After a long journey the Prophet and the holy women reached the huts grouped about the tall, bare cedar, on a snow-capped rocky mountain. On one side, arose the immense domes of the Himavat; on the other, in the depths were a maze of lower mountains; in the distance stretched the plain of India, lost in a dreamlike golden mist. In this retreat lived several penitents, dressed in dark clothing, their hair uncut and twisted in a knot, their beards long, bodies dirty and dusty, their limbs withered by the wind and the hot sun. Some were little more than dried skin on a dry skeleton. Sarasvati cried, 'Earth is far away, and heaven is silent. Lord why have you brought us to this spot, forsaken by God and men?'

'Pray,' replied Krishna, 'if you want earth to come near and heaven to speak to you.'

'With you, heaven is always present,' said Nichdali, 'but why does heaven wish to leave us?'

'It is necessary,' answered Krishna, 'that the son of Mahadeva die, pierced by an arrow, in order that the world may believe his word.'

'Explain this mystery to us!'

'You will undertake it after my death. Let us pray.'

For seven days they engaged in prayer and ablutions. Often Krishna's face became transfigured and was shining. On the seventh day toward sunset, the two women saw archers coming. Krishna did not cease praying.

The archers came and looked at the women and the penitents. They were rough soldiers with yellow and black skins. Seeing the ecstatic form, they were speechless. At first they tried to draw him out, by throwing stones, but nothing could shake him. He remained kneeling in prayer.

Then the soldiers seized him and tied him to the trunk of the old cedar. When the first arrow pierced him, Krishna cried out, 'Vasichta, the sons of the sun are victorious!' With the second arrow, he said, 'My radiant mother, let those who love me enter with me into your glory!' At the third he simply said 'Mahadeva!', and gave up his spirit.

Krishna's body was burned by his followers in the holy city of Dvarka. Sarasvati and Nichdali threw themselves into the fire so they could join their teacher. The crowd thought they saw Mahadeva arise out of the flames in a body of light.

For the Brahmans, absolute masters of Hindu society, sole guardians of its traditions, often remolded and transformed the story in the course of ages. But they faithfully preserved all the basic elements, and if their sacred teaching has changed with the centuries, its core has never been touched."

Such is the legend of Krishna, reconstructed in its organic whole and placed in historical perspective, by Edouard Schure, who was visited by this Great Lord. (The Great Initiates Pp.75-126)

As with the coming of any piece of God's Faith there is a beginning, a zenith, a decline, an end, and a renewal. This is the truer meaning of "the end of the world" and the "dawning of a new age." Abraham (From Brahman) picks through the cinders of His father's religion and shakes its very core, as He renews the eternal Faith of God.

ABRAHAM /AVRAM/ABRAM

Abraham came from the lineage of Noah through Shem. He was born about 4000 years ago in the city of Ur, along the lower Euphrates River in Mesopotamia. His father, Terah was a follower of the now decadent Brahmanic Faith of Sri Krishna. Terah and his people were worshippers of idols.

This is not surprising as each Manifestation of God's Word is born from the preceding spiritual tradition, and through Him comes the new revelation and a regeneration of the same ancient Faith. Each of these Bearers of the Holy Spirit lovingly confirms and praises the Message of the One Who came before Him. He usually also makes mention of the One who will follow, and a Great One, Who will arise at the time of the end, to begin the new cycle or age. There is never a disagreement among them, just among the people who claim to be their followers.

Abraham is the acknowledged father of all of the existing revealed religions, such as Judaism, Christianity, Islam and the Babi and Baha'i Faiths. Perhaps He should have even been placed in the next section if He had followers around the world. In truth all of the Messengers of God are related, before and after Abraham by lineage, and by the Unity of the Holy Spirit which they bear.

The following story can be found in several religious traditions and in many places, most notably the Qu'ran. This site is quite useful: Islam 101 – Prophet Ibrahim (Peace be upon Him) http://www.islam101.com/history/people/prophets/ibrahim.htm

A Fiery Youth

When Abraham was young, He lived among people who refused to worship One God. *"They prayed to idols they brought with them from India. Once He asked His father, Terah 'Do you take these idols for gods? If you do, then you and your people are wrong.' This did not sit well, because the priests of the area were wealthy, powerful and they demanded respect.*

'Our fathers worshipped them' Terah responded. 'You and your fathers clearly have been wrong,' said Abraham.

When he said to his father and his people: 'What are these images, to which you are so devoted?' They replied: 'We found our fathers worshipping them.' He said: 'Then you as well as your fathers, have indeed, been in manifest error.' They said: 'Is it really the truth that you have brought for us, or are you jesting?' He replied: 'Nay, your Lord is the Lord of the heavens and the earth; He brought them into existence and I am of those who bear witness to this, and by Allah, I will certainly plan against your idols after you have gone away and turned your backs.' " Qu'ran (21: 53-58)

True to His word, when the people were gone one day He broke all their idols and images to pieces, except for the very biggest one, which was thought to speak and listen. When the villagers returned, they were very angry, and remembering His admonitions about idolatry, they sought out Abraham. When they found Him, they asked *'Did you do this to our gods?'* He answered, *'No, it was the biggest one of them, who did it. Why don't you ask him, he can tell you; if it is really true that he can speak properly?'* Some of them felt ashamed and said *'You know they cannot speak.'* He said *'Do you worship things that can neither be of any good to you nor do you any harm?'*

The people, angrier than ever, pitched Him into a fire to burn, but God cooled the flames, and He escaped permanent harm. Disgusted, He left Nemrud and the rest of the idolaters, and by the grace of God, fled to another country where He raised up a great nation.

The Pagan followers of the Mithraic Faith derived from followers of the distant Pre-Flood Prophets, were by now idol worshippers, forgetful of their One loving Creator. So these people rejected Abraham and His blessed teachings because they were afraid of losing their idols and powerful priesthood. They also did not like the thought of treating the miserable, and the poor with justice and kindliness.

A Shocking Realization

As a young man Abraham thought the stars, moon and sun could be signs of God, but later he realized that they were only creations, and that He too was guilty of idol worship like the other people. Realizing that there was only One Creator who made all of the beautiful things such as stars, moon and the sun He proclaimed that He would no longer worship any god but the Master of the worlds. He shared this with the people.

The sun, moon and stars could not give them anything to eat. God made the earth so people can live on it. Therefore people should turn away from false gods, worship and serve the One God alone, and always choose the good over the evil.

(Allah) speaketh the Truth: follow the religion of Abraham, the sane in faith; he was not of the Pagans" (Quran 3:95).

"Verily, my Lord hath guided me to a way that is straight, – a religion of right, – the path (trod) by Abraham the true in Faith, and he (certainly) joined not gods with Allah" (-God in the Quran 6:161).

Later in life, Abraham was told by an angel to sacrifice Isaac, His only son at the time. He knew if it was God's will he must do it, but first He asked His son. The son was good and pious, and he consoled his father. "Dear father, he said calmly, if Allah has ordered it, then you must obey, so sacrifice me. Do not fear: With the help of God, I shall be brave." As Abraham sorrowfully prepared to kill His son, he heard a voice "You have shown your good intentions. This is sufficient. You have already fulfilled God's will." They were so relieved and thankful! They slaughtered a ram instead, as they were bidden.

Abraham's other son; Ishmael later built the Ka'ba in Mecca toward which Muslims all over the world turn to pray.

Sabians

In case you wondered about the followers of Abraham, you might look to the Sabians of Middle Eastern tradition. They were a monotheistic Abrahamic group mentioned three times as people of the Book in the Quran; similar to the Jews, the Muslims, and the Christians. Their further identity is still a matter of discussion, and complex investigation by scholars, who look at three differing peoples with similar names.

According to Muslim authors, Sabians followed the fourth book of Abrahamic tradition, the Zaboor, which was given to the Prophet David of Israel according to the Qur'an.

The "Zaboor" is identified by many modern scholars as the book of Psalms in the Old Testament. Sabians practiced initiation through submersion in water, intended to harken to the flooding of the world during the deluge of Noah which temporarily cleansed man's sinful nature from the face of the earth.

Ablution before prayers, is practiced by people of all the living Faiths, including that of Abraham. This was also a rite of Mehr religion, which is still being practiced by Sabians in Iraq.

Sabians like the Essenes, lived in Iraq and they washed themselves with water, had long hair, and wore white robes. They followed a monotheistic faith, acknowledging the Zaboor and the teachings of the other Great Prophets.

Their beliefs resembled those of Jews and Christians, yet they were neither. In their view, the Great Prophets provided the Word of God. There was no one specific route to salvation.

They believed that the universe had a Creator and Sustainer, wise and above any resemblance to created beings, but many of them, or most of them, (i.e. the Sabians of Harran) said: we are unable to reach Him without intermediaries, so we have to approach Him through the mediation of spiritual, pure, and holy Beings, who are above place and time. (http://en.wikipedia.org/wiki/Sabians)

It seems certain that Sabians were wise enough to acknowledge Bearers of God's Word which came both before and after the Great Patriarch. The fast of Ramadan was practiced by the Sabians, including the Harranians before it was observed by today by followers of Mohammad.

Interestingly, Harranian Sabians, again like the Essenes acknowledged Hermes (Enoch) as a Prophet and the Corpus Hermeticum, a dialog between Hermes and His disciples, as their sacred text. Validation of Hermes as a prophet comes from his identification as Idris, who is also known as Enoch in the Qur'an (19.57 and 21.85).

Harran came to be a center of intellectual and religious activity, which evolved into a philosophic tradition based on Hermes Trismegistus.

Whatever the relationship was between Abraham and the Sabians is less important than the notion that Abraham renewed the very ancient Faith, which some might call Mehr, (Mitra) "Light," or Mithraism, by recalling the original purity of its light, bright shining as the sun.

Muhammad and his companions were often considered to have been Sabians, because they shared the Sabian phrase *"La ilaha ila Allāh." "There is no God but Allah."*

So even the faintest threads of Faith continue to connect us to only one God.

ROOTS OF ONE PLANETARY FAITH

Moses: Zoroaster: Buddha: Christ: Mohammad

From the time of Moses, the direction of religion was to evolve from a personal, family, then tribal unity; to the state of "Israel" a place for all believers in the Single God; and even forward through the unity of states into nations, and nations into a World Faith.

First a look at Moses, Zoroaster, Buddha, Christ and Mohammad. Then a brief look at the dawn of a new Age, with words revealed by The Bab, and Baha'u'llah, the first two Prophet founders of a New Day, meant to last 500,000 years.

Isaiah 66:18 "...it shall come to pass that I will gather all nations and all tongues; and they shall come, and shall behold my glory."

With the more recent Revelations spreading around the entire planet, we see a definite change in the scope of Religion. Many of us beg allegiance to one of these Manifestations of God's Holy Word. You know where you can find information on these newer, Great Prophets. And it is not my wish to recount all of that information here. But here are a few interesting thoughts about each of them anyway...

HOSARSIPH/MOSES

By the 3200 years ago, the state of the religious world was bleak. The Lights of Abraham, Isaac, Ishmail and Jacob were fading and some of their followers became drawn to the adoration of stone and wood idols and the frightful worship of Moloch. The Bright Light of India was dimming and Asia as a whole was sinking into materialism. The rulers of Assyria proclaimed themselves lords of the four kingdoms.

"They crushed peoples, deported them in hordes, conscripted them and pitted them against one another. Neither the rights of men, human respect, nor religious principle, were cherished, only personal, unbridled desire..." – Edouard Schure (Quotes and some of the historical material in this section, unless otherwise noted, are from the Great Initiates Pp 169-220)

It was dark, stormy, and definitely time for another renewal! The Holy Spirit came once again to earth, to refresh and re-organize the Ancient Faith into a broader base of believers. Hosarsiph, son of Imran was an Egyptian priest of Osirus. He has been hypothesized by some to be an Egyptian initiate and priest of Osiris, who later took the name of Moses. Rabbis calculated a lifespan of 120 years for Moses, from 3391–3271. Others like Irish Archbishop James Ussher 3625 to 3656.

According to Schure:

"Hosarsiph was of short stature. He had a humble and thoughtful look, a forehead like that of a ram and piercing black eyes, with the gaze of an eagle and a disturbing intensity...He often stammered while speaking, as if groping for words...He appeared shy, but suddenly, like a sharp thunderbolt, a terrible idea would burst forth in a single word, leaving behind it a trail of light...Already between his eyebrows the fatal crease of men predestined to difficult tasks began to form, and upon his forehead hovered a threatening cloud.

He was extremely bright and his mother, a princess, hoped he would one day take the seat of the Pharaohs. When she called him to wish him well on his long ordeal of entering the priesthood, she reminded him he might one day rule.

And with a broad gesture she pointed to the obelisks, temples, Memphis and the entire horizon.

A smile of disdain passed over Hosarsiph face, which usually was a smooth mask of bronze.

'Then,' said he, 'you wish me to rule these people who worship gods with heads of jackals, ibis and hyenas? In a few centuries what will remain of all these idols?'

'Then you scorn the religion of our fathers and the science of our priests?'

'On the contrary! I am striving for them, but the pyramid is motionless; it must start to walk. I shall not be a Pharaoh...' His heart belonged to the desert.

'I do not know you! In the name of Osiris, who are you then? What are you going to do?'

'Do I myself know? Osiris alone knows; he will tell me perhaps. But give me your blessing, O my mother so that Isis (in the form of Divine Intelligence) may protect me and the land of Egypt be kind to me!'

One day Hosarsiph with three other priests of Osiris had borne the golden ark which preceded the priest in great ceremonies. This ark contained the ten most secret books of the temple, dealing with magic and Theurgy (magic ritual).

Returning to the sanctuary the priest Membra said to Hosarsiph *'You are of royal blood. Your strength and knowledge are beyond your age. What do you wish?'*

'Nothing but this.' And Hosarsiph placed his hand on the holy ark...

'Then you want to become a pontiff of Ammon Ra and prophet of Egypt?'

'No! Only to know what is in these books!'

'How can you know since no one but a priest can know them?'

'Osiris speaks as he wishes, when he wishes, to whom he wishes. What is enclosed in this ark is but the dead letter. If the living Spirit wishes to speak to me, he will speak to me!"

'To hear the Spirit, what do you intend to do?'

'Wait and obey.'

Because of the Pharaoh's fear and suspicion about Hosarsiph's agenda for His throne, the young priest was sent as a scribe to inspect the tasks of the Hebrews who lived in the valley of Goshen. The Hebrews did not easily submit to the disagreeable tasks they were given, and were at times resistant. While Hosarsiph was there, an Egyptian guard beat a Hebrew mercilessly with heavy blows.

Hosarsiph sympathized with these unmanageable stiff-necked people whose elders, faithful to the Abrahamic tradition, worshipped the One God; who revered their leaders, but kicked back beneath the yoke and protested against injustice. The guard was so cruel, beating the man to death, that Hosarsiph reacted and killed the guard with his own weapon." (Pg 183)

Priests of Osiris, who committed murders were severely judged and this priest did not have favor with the Pharaoh, so he chose voluntary exile. Some part of him realizing that this was his destiny.

Jethro and Salvation

Schure again tells us p.183:

"Beyond the Red Sea and the Sinai Peninsula, in the land of Madian, was a temple which was not under the control of the Egyptian priesthood. This region extended like a green band between the Elamitic Gulf and the desert of Arabia. In the distance, beyond the arm of the sea, one could see the somber mass of Sinai, with its bare peaks. This isolated country, hemmed in between the desert and the Red Sea, protected by a volcanic mass, was sheltered from invasions. The temple there was dedicated to Osiris, but the Almighty God named Elohim (Allah), was also worshipped. For this sanctuary of Ethiopian origin served as a religious center for Arabs, Semites and men of the black race who were seeking initiation. Thus for centuries Sinai and Horeb had been the mystical center of a monotheistic cult. The bare, wild grandeur of the mountain rising up in isolation between Egypt and Arabia awakened the idea of a single God.

Many Semites went there on pilgrimages to worship Elohim. There they would remain for several days, fasting and praying in the caves and passages carved in the sides of Sinai. Before this, they would go to purify themselves and to receive instruction in the temple of Madian. Here Hosarsiph took refuge.

The high Priest of Madian or the Raguel (the watchman of God), of the temple was a black skinned man named Jethro, who was a great sage. He had long studied the treasury of the sciences stored in his memory and in the stone libraries of the temple. He was protector and spiritual father of the wandering, unconquered peoples of the desert. Libyans, Arabs, nomadic Semites, eternal wanderers, forever the same with their dim seeking after the one God, represented something changeless in the midst of ephemeral cults and crumbling civilizations. In them one felt as if in the presence of the Everlasting; one found in them the memorials of bygone ages, the great silence of Elohim. Jethro was the spiritual father of these unconquered people, these wanderers these free men. He knew their souls, he had a foreboding of their destiny. When Hosarsiph asked for shelter in the name of Osirus-Elohim, he was received with open arms."

Schure 185:

"Hosarsiph wanted first of all to submit himself to the expiations the law of the initiates imposed upon murderers. When a priest of Osiris had committed even an unpremeditated murder, he was supposed to lose the benefit of his anticipated resurrection 'in the light of Osiris,' a privilege he had obtained through the tests of initiation, and which placed him far above the masses. In order to expiate his crime and to find his inner light once again, he had to submit himself to further cruel tests and once more to expose himself to death. After a long fast and with the aid of certain potions the atoning one was plunged into a deep sleep; then he was placed in a cave beneath the temple. He remained there for days, sometimes for weeks. During this time he was to undertake a journey to the other world, into Erebus or the region of Amentis, where float the souls of the dead who are not yet detached from the terrestrial atmosphere. There he had to search for his victim, to undergo the latter's anguish, obtain his pardon and help him to find his way to the light. Only then was he considered to have expiated the murder; only then was his astral body washed of the black stains which the poisoned breath and the curses of his victim had soiled. But from this real or imaginary journey, the guilty one very well might not return, and often when the priests went to awaken the expiator from his sleep, they found nothing but a corpse.

Hosarsiph did not hesitate to undergo this test, and others as well...With complete abnegation he offered his being in a holocaust to Osiris, asking for the strength (If he returned to the earthly light) to reveal the Law of Justice.

When Hosarsiph emerged from the dreadful sleep in the crypt of the temple of Madian, he felt himself a transformed man. His past was as though detached from him; Egypt had ceased to be his homeland, and the immensity of the desert with its wandering nomads stretched before him as a new field of action. He looked at the mountain of Elohim on the horizon and for the first time, like a vision of a storm in the clouds of Sinai, the idea of his mission passed before his eyes: From these moving tribes he was to mold a fighting people who would represent the law of the Supreme God amidst the idolatry of cults and the anarchy of nations... On that day he took the name Moses, which means the Saved One."

Genesis

While living alongside Jethro, Moses read and studied with great care two books on cosmogony mentioned in Genesis: **The Wars of Jehovah** and **The Generations of Adam**. It was necessary to gird His loins well for the work he was considering. Before Him, other Manifestations like Rama, Krishna, and Hermes, had re-created and purified the Religion of the people they came to.

More than a renewal – Moses created a people for the everlasting religion. As a foundation for such a courageous undertaking, He wrote the *Sepher Bereshith*, the *Book of Beginnings*. This Book became the basis for Genesis. Schure call this book *"...a concentrated synthesis of the science of the past and a framework for the science of the future, a key to the Mysteries, a torch of the initiates, a rallying-point for the entire nation."*

But there was a problem. Moses wrote, as He was taught, in a three part text used by the Egyptian priesthood. It had three levels of meaning. One was superficial and the other two were accessible only to the initiated, and even then, keys were needed to open their esoteric meanings. So they were pretty much unintelligible to common folk.

Moses wrote Genesis in Egyptian hieroglyphs with **three meanings**. Two language keys, and oral explanations were passed along to His successors. *"Certainly in (Moses') thought, Genesis radiated a different light, it embraced worlds which were much more vast than the naive conception of the tiny earth which appears in the Greek translation of the Septuagint, or in St. Jerome's Latin translation...*

Israel gravitates around Moses as surely, as inevitably as the earth turns around the sun. But once this is established, it is something else to know what the basic ideas of Genesis were, what Moses wanted to will to posterity in this secret testament of the Sepher Bereshith...He entrusted the keys and the oral explanation to His successors."

Schure explains: *"In Solomon's time, Genesis was transliterated into Phoenician characters; when after the Babylonian Captivity, Esdras edited it in Chaldaic-Aramaic characters, the Jewish priesthood could make but very imperfect use of these keys. At last, when the Greek translators of the Bible appeared, they had no more than a vague idea of the esoteric meaning of the texts. Despite his serious intentions and his great mind, when St. Jerome prepared his Latin translation from the Hebrew text, he could not fathom the basic meaning...Therefore when we read Genesis in our translations we have only the elementary, inferior, meaning."*

So any who would scrutinize these scriptures, are missing the comparative and superlative meaning of the ancient text, and the profound meaning of Genesis escapes them... *"The sacred language that is missing is one, in which every vowel and each consonant has a universal meaning in harmony with the acoustic value of the letter and the state of consciousness of the man who produced it."* For further information of the validity of Moses and his work, please refer to The Great Initiates, Schure Pg. 188.

Suffice it to say that Genesis has taken a lot of criticism for its simplistic description of the origin and development of Creation. It was meant to be far more rich and explicit. "Many well-meaning Bible readers would be dumbstruck by the vast dimensions and depth of the original material." For further esoteric discussion please see Schure Pp.192-200.

"Go to the Mountain of God, to Horeb!"

Moses climbed steep rocky Mt. Horeb, which was desolate, dangerous and even forbidding. "A dark mass of granite stands so bare beneath the splendor of the sun that one would think it had been furrowed by lightning and carved by thunder. 'This is the summit of Sinai, the Throne of Elohim,' say the children of the desert. Facing it is a lower mountain, the rocks of Serbal, also steep and wild. In its sides are copper mines and caverns. Between the two mountains is a dark valley, a chaos of rocks which the Arabs call Horeb, the Ereb of Semitic legend. This valley of desolation is gloomy indeed when night falls upon it along with the shadow of Sinai. It is even gloomier when the mountain is crowned with a mantle of clouds, from which sinister flashes of light dart forth. Then a terrible wind blows down the narrow valley. It is said that here Elohim overthrows those who try to fight Him, casting them into the abyss where torrents of rain pour. The Midianites say that here wander the evil ghosts of giants, the Refaim, tumbling the rocks upon those who try to climb the sacred cliffs. Popular tradition still has it that sometimes, in the flashing fire, the God of Sinai appears in the form of a Medusa head with eagle's wings. Woe to those who see His face! To see Him is to die!

This is what the nomads related in the evening, while sitting in their tents, when the camels and women were asleep. In reality only the boldest of Jethro's initiates climbed to the cavern of Serval and spent several days there in fasting and prayer. It was a place dedicated from time immemorial to supernatural visions, to Elohim, or to luminous spirits. No priest, no hunter would have consented to lead a pilgrim there.

Fearlessly Moses had climbed up past the ravine of Horeb. Courageously he had crossed the valley of death with its chaos of rocks. Like every human effort, initiation has its phases of humility and pride. In climbing the mountain Moses had reached the summit of pride, for he was approaching the summit of human power. Already he felt himself at one with the Supreme Being. The burning red sun hung low over the volcanic massive form of Sinai and purple shadows were lying in the valleys below, when Moses found himself before a cavern (near the top of the volcanic peak).

At sunset, Moses stood where few seekers of vision dared come. Thin brush guarded the entrance the cavern.

He prepared to enter, but suddenly He was blinded by a light which enveloped him. It seemed to him that the sun burned about him, that the granite mountains had changed into a sea of flames.

At the entrance to the grotto a blinding light shone upon him. An angel with drawn sword blocked his way. Thunderstruck, Moses fell prone upon the ground. All his pride had been broken. The angel's gaze had pierced him with its light. Then, with that deep sense of things which is awakened in the visionary state, he understood that the Being was about to impose serious tasks upon him. He would have liked to escape his mission and creep into the earth like a miserable worm.

But a voice said, 'Moses! Moses!' And he answered: 'Here am I.'
'Come no closer: take off your shoes. For the place where you are standing is holy ground!'
Moses hid his face in his hands. He was afraid to look at the angel again, to face his gaze.
And the angel said to him, 'You who seek Elohim, why do you tremble before me?'
'Who are you?'
'A ray of Elohim, a solar angel, a messenger of the One Who is and Who will be.'
'What do you command?'
'You shall say to the children of Israel: The Everlasting, the God of your fathers, the God of Abraham, the God of Isaac, the God of Jacob sent me to you, to lead you out of the land of slavery.'

'Who am I,' asked Moses, 'that I should lead the Children of Israel out of Egypt?'

'Go,' said the angel, 'for I shall be with you. I shall put the fire of Elohim in your heart, and His word upon your lips. For forty years you have been calling upon Him. Here I seize you in his name! Your voice has reached Him. You belong to me forever!'

And Moses cried out boldly, 'Show me Elohim, that I may see His living fire!'

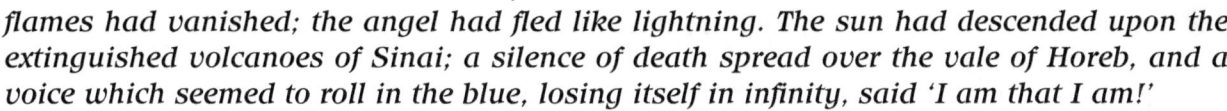

He raised his head. But the sea of flames had vanished; the angel had fled like lightning. The sun had descended upon the extinguished volcanoes of Sinai; a silence of death spread over the vale of Horeb, and a voice which seemed to roll in the blue, losing itself in infinity, said 'I am that I am!'

"Moses came out of this vision as though dumbfounded. He thought for a moment that his body had been consumed by the fire of ether. But his spirit was stronger. When he went down to Jethro's temple again, He was ready for his task. His living idea walked before him like the angel, armed with the sword of fire." (Schure Pp.200-203)

"The Blessed Beauty is the One promised by the sacred books of the past, the revelation of the Source of light that shone upon Mount Sinai, Whose fire glowed in the midst of the Burning Bush. We are one and all, servants of Their threshold, and stand each as a lowly keeper at Their door." 'Abdu'l-Baha (Regarding Baha'u'llah's relation to the Burning Bush)

By God's decree Moses delivered and protected His followers from the destruction of the Idol worshipers of Egypt, by the means of plagues (Blood, Boils, Darkness, Death of the First Born, Flies, Frogs, Hail and Fire, Lice, Locusts, and Pestilence); followed in the end, by a cleansing of water.

His study of magic and theurgic ritual must have been an assistance as He wielded the staff as a sign of God's insistence, that the Pharaoh release his grip.

Time and again God had warned the Pharaoh and those whom he represented, to give up their ways and recognize, to remember, the bounties given them by a loving Creator, Who was the Source of their being and copious bounties, and to move humanity forward with that knowledge. They must refrain from worshipping a man who literally built palaces on the backs of the people. He begged them to stay clear of idolatry.

"Moses' plan was one of the most extraordinary and courageous that man has ever conceived. He was to tear a people from the yoke of a nation as powerful as Egypt, to take it to the conquest of a country occupied by hostile and better-armed inhabitants, to lead it for ten, twenty, forty years in the desert, to consume it with thirst, to weaken it with hunger, to torment it like a blood-horse under the arrows of the Hittites and Amalekites, ready to cut it to pieces, to isolate it with its Tabernacle of the Lord in the midst of these idolatrous nations, to impose monotheism upon it with a rod of fire and to instill in a nation such a fear and veneration of this one God, partly by means of the powerful magical Ark and its sacred contents....Such was the amazing work of Moses!" –Schure 204

The firm patience Moses exhibited with the whining rebellions of His people, as they wandered, is heartbreaking. In the end, even though the unity of God's religion was in a sense secure, Moses knew the people would betray Israel, and another Great Being would have to pick up the pieces of the Great Religion, later.

"Moses was not a patriot, but a civilizer of peoples, having before him the destinies of all humanity. Israel was but a means for him –universal religion was his goal, and far above and beyond the nomads of the time, His thought went out to future ages. From the departure of Egypt until Moses' death, the history of Israel was but one long struggle between the Prophet and His people." – Schure 208

But Moses' justice didn't come until Jethro, his old mentor begged him to bring laws to guide His people so that he wouldn't waste himself, by personally trying to settle every little dispute.

Moses' executive power was an outgrowth of judicial power, which was under control of His successors like Jethro, and Joshua and Samuel. After Saul the kings usurped the task of judgement, and things went downhill from there. And so it remains to this day.

Many, people including some Jews and Christians, have no idea of the immensity of Moses' station as a unifying Prophet, God's Word and will, incarnate.

"Beware lest thy sovereignty withhold thee from Him Who is the Supreme Sovereign. He, verily, is come with His Kingdom, and all the atoms cry aloud: 'Lo! The Lord is come in His great majesty!' He Who is the Father is come, and the Son, in the holy vale, crieth out: 'Here am I, here am I, O Lord, My God!', whilst Sinai circleth round the House, and the Burning Bush calleth aloud: 'The All-Bounteous is come mounted upon the clouds! Blessed is he that draweth nigh unto Him, and woe betide them that are far away.'"

(Baha'u'llah, The Summons of the Lord of Hosts, p. 83)

As an added blessing, Moses foretold the existence of several Great Prophets who would succeed Him. He refers to them all, including Himself in the past tense. The others are His familiar Companions, especially the one with the fiery sword, who He first met in the form of the Solar Angel on Mt. Horeb; the beloved "Glory of God," whom many feel is Baha'u'llah.

"Now this is the blessing with which Moses the man of God blessed the children of Israel before His death.

"And He said: 'The Lord came from Sinai (Moses), **and dawned on them from Seir** (Christ); **He shone forth from Mount Paran** (Mohammad), **and He came with ten thousands of saints** (the daring followers of the Bab, who died preparing the world for the imminent coming of the Promised One of all ages); **from His right hand came a fiery law for them** (the justice of Baha'u'llah)." –Moses (Deuteronomy chapter 33, verses 1&2)

Akhenaten

There appears to be a definite connection between the monotheism of Akhenaten and Moses. Some even feel Akhenaten *was* Moses, but they of course had separate destinies, and burial places. Moses at the foot of Mt. Nebo in the Moab Valley, and Akhenaten near Amarna, Egypt.

Akhenaten or Ikhnaton, was known before the fifth year of his reign as **Amenhotep IV.** The Greeks called him Amenophis IV. These names mean "Amun is satisfied." He was an Eighteenth Dynasty Pharaoh who ruled for 17 years and died perhaps 3,334 years ago, very much at the time of Moses.

"Pharaoh Akhenaten." Licensed under CC BY-SA 1.0 via Wikimedia Commons - https://commons.wikimedia.org/wiki/File:Pharaoh_Akhenaten.jpg#/media/File:Pharaoh_Akhenaten.jpg

Within a hundred years of Hosarsiph departing Amenhotep III dies. He and is succeeded by his second son, Amenhotep IV. But he is not really trusted as a leader so he trains for a few years before taking his new name. Amenhotep IV changes his name to Akhenaten – "he who is beneficial to the Aten" – and he shuts down the polytheistic, religious capital at Thebes.

Akhenaten built a new monotheistic capital 180 miles north at Amarna. There he served as high priest to the Aten with his beautiful wife Nefertiti. (http://www.allaboutarchaeology.org/moses-the-exodus-and-akhenaten-faq.htm)

His bold attempts to turn his subjects away from the state pantheon of gods and turn Egypt to the worship of a single God known as the Aten – represented by a disk of the sun, met with mixed feelings.

The people of Egypt were not ready to listen to one God, alone. Very soon they were openly henotheistic. At first, giving the Aten a status above mere gods, as is the case where belief in one God deteriorates over time, similar to Brahman's followers, who eventually had a temple and celebration for just about anything under the sun.

An early inscription likens the Aten to the sun as compared to stars, and later official language avoids calling the Aten a god at all. Besides Egypt and India, the Greeks, Romans and others have wandered down this trail.

In the end monotheism was rejected. After Akhenaten's death, polytheism was gradually restored. Soon, rulers without clear rights of succession from the Eighteenth Dynasty founded a new dynasty. They discredited Akhenaten and his immediate successors, referring to Akhenaten himself as "the enemy" or "that criminal."

Today Akhenaten is famed for his son, Tutankhamun, and the majestic beauty of his wife, Nefertiti. We also admire his love of style, and the high quality of the pictorial arts he encouraged. **But his most impressive achievement was his dedication to changing the hearts and heads of the Egyptians from fancying idols, to the worship of a single, enigmatic God.**

ZOROASTER/ ZARATHUSHTRA/ ZARDOSHT

Zoroaster was said to be the son of a priest, in a pastoral tribe. His father Pourushaspa of the Spitama clan raised cattle and was famous for his horses. His mother was known for her enlightened ideas. She was informed in her pregnancy, of the profound affect her son would have on the fate of the world, by an Angel. As a boy, Zoroaster was very intelligent, and penetratingly observant. He cared deeply for others and strove to find the truth of all religions.

He became a man of great mystery. It is said Zoroaster was born in Azerbaijan in Northeastern Iran or Southwest Afghanistan. His family might have lived near the bank of the Oxus River at one time, now called Amu Darya, which runs from the Pamir Mountains, almost to the Aral Sea. Waters flow into the river from parts of today's Afghanistan, Uzbekistan, Turkmenistan and Tajikistan. The Amu Darya was once the border between the land of Greater Iran and Turan.

The Pamir mountain range in Central Asia lies at the junction of the Himalayas with Tian Shan, Karakoram, Kunlun, and Hindu Kush mountain ranges. They are among the world's highest and most rugged mountains. They are known as the "Roof of the World."

The Bundahisn or "Creation," which draws from the history of the Zend, says the Dhraja (Darya) River in Eran Wej was His birthplace, and the home of His father. There is another reference in the text that the district of Arran on the river Aras (Araxes) close by the northwestern frontier of the Medes, was once His home.

There is no consensus among scholars about the period of His life. Suggestions for the time of his birth range from 6000 years ago to 3200 to 2600 years ago. Some place the date of Zoroaster to 47 years after Abraham. The range of dates is stunning. The sketchy details might be a result of information lost from the time of His murder; or perhaps it is due to difficulty making sense of some Avestan translations. Neither the exact location nor birth date, is important to His Message.

Zoroaster's Fravashi, the "everlasting prototype" of His station as a Great Prophet was visibly enhanced by the farr or aura which was created when He dwelt in Heaven as a Being filled with the Holy Spirit. He dwelt in the realm of the Transcendent Beings, and like every one of God's Manifestations before, became clothed in human flesh, and descended to earth; perhaps we can just say, for practicality, about 3,200-3,500 years ago.

Zoroaster was born into a Bronze Age culture, rife with a polytheistic religion which included animal sacrifice and the ritual use of intoxicants. This religion was quite similar to faded forms of Hinduism in the Indus Valley.

The name Zoroaster is a Greek translation of Zarathustra. He is also known as Zaratosht in Middle Persian and Gujarati, an Indo-Aryan language spoken by Mahatma Gandhi. What exactly the name refers to is again debated, but it probably has something to do with "Golden Camel" as his father was famous for the quality of his horses and camels.

Born into the Spitama clan, he worked as a priest. He was a family man, with a wife, three sons and three daughters.

His birth and early life are little documented except for what is recorded in the Gathas, a central piece of the Zend Avesta, which also contains hymns thought to be composed by Zoroaster himself!

It is said that Angels appeared in the house and praised the unborn child. At birth, the infant Zoroaster smiled broadly rather than crying, and His face was shining with a divine glow. Legend has it that He glowed so brightly that the villagers were frightened and tried to destroy him. Luckily, all attempts, including **fire** and **stampeding animals**, failed.

As a young boy, Zoroaster spent much time wandering through forests, mountains, rivers and lakes, as do many other Embodiments of the Holy Spirit. He dove to the depth of things to find their cause and meaning. He was naturally curious and rarely satisfied with the answers people gave. He meditated constantly on Ahura Mazda (God) as a friendly and loving Fashioner and Changer, and Desroyer of creation.

Zoroaster rejected the religion of the Bronze Age Iranians with their many gods and oppressive class structure. The Karvis and Karapans (princes and priests) controlled the ordinary people. He also was opposed animal sacrifices and the use of the hallucinogenic Haoma plant (possibly a species of ephedra) in rituals.

At the age of nine He had a meeting with the head priests of the region, but neither side seemed to satisfy the other. Some of the questions He posed left the head priest deep in fretful thought. Legend has it that this high priest was so agitated, in fact, he actually died on his way home, from a heart attack. This did not increase Young Zoroaster's popularity.

At the age of fifteen Zoroaster put on the "kushti" a sacred string belt or sash symbolic of His passage into manhood. He wandered in partial solitude, searching for further answers to questions about God and His creation.

"When the Earth-Soul cried out for a Saviour, Zarathushtra was born to redeem the ancient Aryan faith. The glorious birth of the Prophet in Iran is vividly described, followed by the many miraculous events in his early childhood."

The Saga of the Aryans, Vol. 2 by the Parsi writer Porus Homi Havewala and published in 1995 (First Edition), 2000 (Second Edition) and in 2011 (Third Edition)

Zoroaster's ideas did not take off quickly. When He was twenty-some years old Zoroaster left home for about a decade to find a people more open to new ideas. Cast out of His original home, He was left to wander with a few friends and animals, as noted in Yasna 46.

He left for different countries, with His family and few followers, said to be a small group of twenty three people. Every land they visited had the same results, either because the priests and rulers had warned everyone against Him, or the people were totally ignorant of His Monotheistic concepts and were unwilling to change.

Very little is known of the unrecorded decades, except that during this period Zoroastrianism spread to Western Iran. By the time of the founding of the Archaemenian Empire,

Zoroastrianism was already a well-established religion. (http://www.bbc.co.uk/religion/religions/zoroastrian/history/zoroaster_1.shtml)

Anguish

"To what land shall I flee? Where bend my steps? I have no favour from the village to which I would belong; or from the wicked rulers of the country. How then, O Lord, shall I serve Thee?" –Zoroaster

His plea is somewhat reminiscent of the Fire Tablet, where Baha'u'llah laments to God.

"...I have been forsaken in a foreign land: Where are the emblems of Thy faithfulness, O Trust of the worlds?...The agonies of death have laid hold on all men: Where is the surging of Thine ocean of eternal life, O Life of the worlds?...The whisperings of Satan have been breathed to every creature: Where is the meteor of Thy fire, O Light of the worlds?..."

In the case of Baha'ullah, we have God's response, and expect that Zoroaster's plea, was answered similarly.

"O Supreme Pen, We have heard Thy most sweet call in the eternal realm: Give Thou ear unto what the Tongue of Grandeur uttereth, O Wronged One of the worlds! Were it not for the cold, how would the heat of Thy words prevail, O Expounder of the worlds? Were it not for calamity, how would the sun of Thy patience shine, O Light of the worlds? Lament not because of the wicked. Thou wert created to bear and endure, O Patience of the worlds...We have made abasement the garment of glory, and affliction the adornment of Thy temple, O Pride of the worlds..." (Baha'u'llah – from the "Fire Tablet")

When He was around the age of thirty, Zoroaster went out just before dawn to draw water from the river. *"Vohu Mana, the archangel of "Good Mind" or "Good Thought"; an aspect and emissary of God appeared, and opened a portal to the Divine Light of Ahura Mazda (God). The Angel transported Him in spiritual form to the Great Spirit. Vohu Mana told him there was but one true God, Ahura Mazda, and that Zoroaster was to become His Prophet.*

In the splendor of the dawn, Zoroaster became transfigured with illumination." -Schure

He perceived the relationship between Ahura Mazda, and the "Amesha Spentas" meaning Bounteous Spirits, Beneficent Immortals. They are the Embodiments of Holy Spirit "Spenta Mainyu"; and are Bearers of the Ahura Mazda's (God's) Word to earth.

Zoroaster understood the station of the Angels and the rest of Creation. He knew the Archangels of several key Virtues. Vohu Mana, translates as "Good Purpose" or "Good Mind"; a moral state of mind that enables one to accomplish his duties. It is one of the "divine sparks" such as Justice (Dominion), Truth, Devotion, Wholeness, and Immortality (Immersion into Ahura Mazda). These Angels (or Genii) are much like the Beings mentioned by Rama, Hermes and Moses, and Others. They are also central figures in the Yazidi religion.

He mostly lived and preached in the Inner Asian Steppes, receiving Revelation from Ahura Mazda, and aided the angelic divine sparks known as the Amesha Spentas.

His transfiguration was followed by other visions in which each of the Archangels of Ahura Mazda appeared and revealed further truths. Zoroaster continued to commune with God thereafter, and His dialogues are composed into 17 hymns or songs, called the Gathas.

After His illumination Zoroaster sought to share His revelation. Nobody in His family believed Him for 10 years or more after His anointing. He may have wandered to other lands seeking followers. (See Viracocha, next). Zoroaster's first believer in His homeland was a cousin, Maedyoimaha, and then His own wife Hvova, later His children, one by one chose His teachings. Then two relatives, Frashaoshtra and Jamasp believed, and they continued to be among Zoroaster's most steadfast disciples until the end.

After returning from His travels, Zoroaster found "recognition" in the country of King Vishtaspa, in Bactria. Reportedly, when Zoroaster was 42 he cured the ailing dark stallion of King Vishtaspa (Hystaspes to the Greeks), who ruled parts of modern day eastern Iran.

The king's conversion was crucial in the spread of Zoroastrianism, because his family also believed. Upon accepting Zoroaster' holy revelation King Vishtaspa, Queen Hutaosa, and their children transformed completely. Their princes gave up their rights to the throne and became zealous missionaries. His son Darius the Great, became a strong exponent of the Faith. Rock inscriptions from the time of Cyrus and Darius mention Ahura Mazda. Cyrus showed great tolerance by allowing the conquered Babylonians to practice their own religion, rather than trying to convert them by force. This is a reflection of the gentle way of Zoroaster.

The Faith of Zoroaster spread far and wide within His lifetime. He had redeemed the ancient Aryan Faith, which trailed back all the way to Gayomart – in the realm of Pre-Creation. He stood for peace and denied man-made deities. He urged humanity to progress and prosper on this good earth and look forward to a blissful life beyond. *Superiority belongs only to the virtuous, who know God. They will love people and care for animals, plants, water, air and minerals, so that all creation feels refreshed, happy and full of love because of their presence.*

The kings of ancient Iran became proud to call themselves Aryans (Noble Ones). Society of the time featured the husbandman; a good man who looked after the cattle and tilled the soil in peace and neighborliness. He was upright and had a burning regard for truth. It was his duty to keep away from those who worshipped many inconsequential and imaginary gods "daevas', and resist them with force if necessary.

Zoroaster preached a renewed Faith, denying the polytheism, which had once more blemished the Religion. His message shattered myths and reestablished pure beliefs, by challenging rites and rituals of sacrifice, born of superstition and ignorance. He argued with countless priests and rulers who supported worthless dogmas, and had once again chosen witless gods rather than the One, the Single God.

By this time the people had mixed Lord Yima with Mithra the sun, and the dedicated Angelic Spirits, and a host of other gods and spirits, who though not harmful in themselves, should not be joined with God. Even the idea of worshipping a Prophet had become a distraction which kept mankind from worshipping the One Spirit. Zoroaster often referred to idolatry as the Druj or "Lie" which became an evil seduction from worshipping Ahura Mazda, the single Creator.

"No longer shall the evil teacher – Druj that he is! – destroy the second life, the speech of his tongue misleading (people) to the evil life."

"As the sheep, on which the wolf is pouncing, tremble at the odour of the wolf, so these Drujes tremble at the perfume of the blessed one."

(The Zend-Avesta, Avesta Fragments)

It was inevitable that many priests and rulers became His enemies. So He met with great opposition in the streets, and was likely murdered in a state of prayer. Zoroaster died in His late 70s after a long, difficult service to humankind.

The circumstances of Zoroaster's death are uncertain. Many claim that he was assassinated while at prayer, murdered by Turanians at the storming of Balkh in present day Afghanistan. This version is found in a Persian epic poem called the Shahnameh, written about 1500 years after Zoroaster's death. (See People of Ar Rass, listed under "Great Disappointments.")

Abu Bakr Muhammad Ibn Al-Hassan, a companion of Mohamad, said: *"The dwellers of Ar-Rass [which means "an old well"] had a well sufficing them and their land. [Zoroaster] forbade them to worship [the curtained form], and commanded them to worship only Allah and no partner with Him. In spite of that, they killed their Prophet and threw his body into a well. Therefore, Allah destroyed them and their homes."* (http://altreligion.about.com/od/holidaysfestivalsevents/p/zarathust-no-diso.htm)

Such ill-treatment is the fate of the most beloved of all Beings.

Goeffrey Ashe, *The Ancient Wisdom* 1977, Macmillan; Mary Boyce, *Zoroastrians, Their religious beliefs and practices*, London 1979, pg. 17, Copyright 1998-2006, The Circle of Ancient Iranian Studies. http://www.iranistics.com/organisation/circle-ancient-iranian-studies

The Zend Avesta

At first the Aryans did not have a written language. They memorized and chanted the verses, teachings, poems, and hymns. Eventually, a written system for their language was developed, which came to be known as Avestan, an Indo-European language very similar to Sanskrit, and Latin, as well as the ancestral dialect of Pashto common to South-Central Asia. Many modern day Eurasian languages have roots in these languages, as mentioned in the Chapter on Indo European culture.

By BMHC (Own work) [CC BY-SA 4.0 (http://creativecommons.org/licenses/by-sa/4.0)], via Wikimedia Commons

The Holy Book of the Iranian Aryans in the Avestan Language contains historical data, praises to God, revelation, daily and seasonal ritual, and prayer. The Gathas, are the history of the Faith, and Zoroaster's teachings.

Most ancient are the Yasht, a recounting of the history prior to Zoroaster's day. The language is similar to that of the melodic Indian Vedas (reflecting the days of Rama/Yima). Here one can find material which springs from the earliest times.

These recollections had been brought forth in purity from the mouths of many inspired sages, who like the Rishis of Hinduism carried Yima/Rama's treasured scripture through many generations. Unfortunately, only remnants of this early part of the Avesta remain. They are recorded in a very ancient poetic form traced back through Norse parallels in early Indo-European times.

The ancient homeland was destroyed because white feathers began to fall from the sky and covered the earth. It became necessary for the people and their animals to move southward, in advance of increasing ice and glaciation. (see Indo European culture)

Later, they employed Mehr priests called Karapans who may have worn gowns and long caps (not hoods) similar to those of the wicked Ku Klux Klan. These priests sacrificed animals and plants to fire, and became far too intoxicated from haoma.

"In a simple home, the family gathered around the hearth morning and evening, and once or twice more. The parent, male or female, led the prayers. The deities, especially the favorite ones, were praised, a portion of the family's food was offered. Since the fire was the only vis-

ible deity, rising brightly upward, they considered it to represent all the gods and goddesses. It devoured what was offered and sent up a column of burnt offerings to the deities on high.

There were tender twigs or grass (baresman/barhi) spread for the gods to grace. The rites appeared graceful. Animals, one or more as the ceremonial scale and occasion warranted, were slaughtered, and their blood, flesh, and fat was offered to the gods through the burning fire. Other edibles were also put to smoke. A golden plant, called haoma/soma, was solemnly washed, pounded in a stone or mental mortar, and squeezed. The juice was filtered and mixed with consecrated water or milk. A little was poured into the fire for gods, and the rest was quaffed by the karapans. It was a mild but instant intoxicant. It lent them the pep they craved for.

A better family had a better ceremony. It could afford a professional priest, a karapan. There was more mumbling for all, more food for the gods, still more for the priest, plus a little fee..." In the case of a chief, *"Each priest had a duty to perform: kindle fire, tend it, kill and cut the animal, spread tender twigs, wash haoma, pound it, filter the juice, handle utensils, sing recite, mumble prayers, or wait and watch other priests perform their parts. Singers performed solos and choruses. And, of course, there was the touch of pep that haoma imparted to the priests and the prayerful. Above all, the ceremonies created an alliance between the chiefs and the priests.*

The Aryans fancied their gods (as humans), just like many other peoples, but they did not create idols and icons the way others did. They were not image worshippers." (http://www.spenta.edu/ceremonies.html)

This contrasts strongly with the teachings found in the ancient Vedas and Upanishads, carried down through the ages by the sanctified memories of gifted priests, who reduce the number of existing gods from well over three thousand (3306) to only ONE. So it seems there is always a need to return to monotheism with the aid of a newer Revelation.

Zoroaster believed in one creator God, only that One was worthy of worship. Furthermore, some of the deities of the old religion, the daevas (devas in Sanskrit), appeared to delight in war and strife. Zoroaster said that these were evil spirits and were workers of Angra Mainyu, God's adversary. Many ordinary people did not like Zoroaster's downgrading of the Daevas to daevas – evil spirits.

The local religious authorities opposed His ideas. They felt their own faiths, power, and particularly their rituals, were threatened. Zoroaster spoke against ritualized ceremony as empty repetition. When Zoroaster was thirty years old, he had a divine vision of God and the Amesha Spentas during a purification. This vision radically transformed His view of the world, and he tried to teach this view to others.

Zoroaster's personal teachings are presented in the Gathas, 17 hymns of inspired, passionate utterances, directed to God; written in the older Gathic Avestan.

The Yasna (liturgical Book), the Vispered (lesser liturgy), the Vendidad, which gives a priestly code of ritual purification, and finally, the Khorda a prayer book; came later and were influenced by the thoughts of men. These were written in the younger Avestan language under the Sasanians and recorded in Middle Persian or "Pahlavi." Much of the Vidivat is concerned with purity and ritual, which may or may not have come from Zoroaster.

It is the ancient law against evil, composed of Fargad "chapters" which contain guidance. Two examples are: 1) At death, people are placed in a dakhma "tower of silence" where the body can be eaten by birds or beasts, similar to the practice of some of the Plains Tribes of North America; or it may be buried in a stone casket lined with lead, so as not to contaminate, earth, water or fire. 2) Children at age 7 receive a sacred white cotton shirt, a "sudreh" which they wear the rest of their lives. At 15 years of age the boys receive a "Kushti" or woolen sash signifying manhood. Others guidance includes a strong aversion to extramarital sex, prostitution and homosexuality. Another warns against the ill-treatment of dogs, who are praised as God's glorious creation, created as the guardian of the household and farm. Superstitious folk had mistreated dogs and cats as vermin. ("Birth of Zoroastrianism" Http://132.246.176.35/bamji/topic.htm)

Zoroaster's Teachings and Laws

Zoroaster spoke of four developmental stages of Creation. The first stage is solely spiritual existence, during which time God designed a physical universe. During the second stage, the material universe was created. It was shortly thereafter that a negative force began to challenge Ahura Mazda. There was a battle in the third stage for the souls of the many inhabitants who now occupied the land. In the final stage God will send down a succession of saviors who will eventually defeat the negative opponents and bring salvation to all spiritual beings in the universe. The world is moving towards the end of that fourth stage. Some will say it has recently arrived!

The concept of reincarnation is foreign to Zoroastrian teachings. In fact, none of the Manifestations discuss it. Sometimes the prophecy of their "Return" is considered validation of the man-made concept of reincarnation, as presented by Pythagoras and others.

Zoroastrian virtues are many. They include: truthfulness, trustworthiness, cleanliness, chastity, justice, compassion, charity, education, service, and care of the soil and natural elements. Worship consists mainly of prayers requesting assistance to live righteous lives. Believers may offer sandalwood or other sacred herb to be burned in the sacred fire during prayers to Ahura Mazda.

A family gathered around the hearth in the morning, during the day and in the evening. One parent male or female led the prayers. A portion of the family's food was offered to the fire.

Zoroastrian prayers usually begin with the phrase "Glory be to God" (Kshnotra Ahurai Mazdao). Prayers continue to thank Him for the sun, which gives its heat and light, the air we breathe, the water, animals, plants, flowers and other things we humans need, or things that bring us happiness. Even as they arise from bed, Zoroastrians pray to do good deeds and make the world a better place, not only for themselves but for everyone around them.

Their traditional worship sites are fire temples in which the sacred flame burns eternally in a consecrated chamber. It is a symbol of divine purity where sandalwood is offered. Zoroastrians sometimes apply the cold ashes of the altar to their foreheads and wear them as a sign of humility.

The Sash, or Kushti is made of 72 threads as a symbol of the 72 chapters of the Yasna texts. Zoroastrians are urged to live active, productive honest and charitable lives. The dead are placed in the towers of silence where the flesh is eaten by birds, so the bodies will not pollute the earth, or water.

Ahura Mazda said, *"He who performs charity knowingly and discriminately is like me, I who am Ahura Mazda. And he who performs charity ignorantly and without understanding and indiscriminately is like Ahriman ... Whatever charitable men give, I give them twofold in return, and I store it up."*

As taught by all of the Manifestations, the Creator is formless, birthless and deathless. Zoroastrians refrained from making images of any sort, and do not worship idols.

"Ahura (God) is everywhere at once. He is all-knowing. He knows what we are thinking and doing at this very moment. When Ahura Mazda first created humanity, He gave the following order: "Be diligent to save your souls; I shall then provide for your bodily matters. For it is impossible to save your souls, without you.

There is a remedy for everything but death, a hope for everything but wickedness, and everything will lapse except righteousness." – Zoroaster

God created humans to be born in a sinless state and each person has complete freedom of will to choose good or evil and shape his own destiny. People are deluded if they strive after material things.

It is said that after we humans die our urvan (soul) returns to its Fravashi or Enlightened One, perhaps to recount our thoughts, actions and deeds during a period of four days.

"Angra Mainyu (Evil/ material attachment) is best fought by joy; despondency is a symptom of his victory." – Zoroaster

Although Zoroaster preached in plain words to ordinary people His teachings were handed down orally from generation to generation and were adorned with subtleties, richness and complexity. As with the Rishis in India, priestly seers sought to express in lofty words their grasp of the divine.

He brought laws and knowledge of the universe. He taught us that God regulates the universe through "Asha," the law of precision. At the physical level Asha represents the laws in the universe. Psychologically Asha is the powerful force of truth. While at the spiritual level Asha is the fusion of order and truth leading us to the path of righteousness. This causes us to do the right thing at the right time. Unlike other species, we can choose between right and wrong in thought, action and speech.

"Asha" is Zoroaster's "way," much as the Tao, or Christ's "I am the Way, the Truth and the Life." It is a spiritual path to truth, righteousness, world-order, and eternal law. Truthfulness is a supreme virtue. This concept is validated by other Faiths.

"Truthfulness is the foundation of all human virtues. Without truthfulness, progress and success, in all the worlds of God, are impossible for any soul. When this holy attribute is established in man, all the divine qualities will also be acquired."
–Baha'u'llah (By Shoghi Effendi, *The Advent of Divine Justice*, p. 26)

Zoroaster asserts that the righteous person earns an everlasting reward, namely integrity and immortality. He who opts for the "lie" (material, evil) is condemned by his own conscience, as well as by the judgment of God, to a misery akin to Christian hell. After judgment is passed by Ahura Mazda, the good enter the kingdom of everlasting joy and light, and the bad are consigned to the regions of horror and darkness.

This motivation for good works and good behavior in this world is similar to St. Paul's **"Be not deceived; God is not mocked: for whatsoever a man soweth, that shall he also reap."** -Galatians 6:7 King James Bible (Cambridge Ed.)

"A thousand people cannot convince one by words to the extent that one person can convince a thousand by action" – Zoroaster

The End of the World

In the very ancient time Gayomart had no disease, illness, hunger or thirst. The dog, cow, bull, horse, and birds existed in their natural world. Evil was introduced, which one day will be purged **when the world will be bathed with the purification of fire**.

Zoroaster told of three saviors to follow Him culminating with the Saoshyant. He revealed pertinent information for the day in which he lived, and forewarned us of a future reckoning. Sadly, if a person lives in falsehood in this world, there is no remedy for them, once they pass, until "the time of the end" when the Saoshyant appears.

In a final combat, the forces of evil will be put to flight and destroyed. The universe will be restored to a purified state. Men and other creatures will be made immortal and join in the praises of Ahura Mazda.

The chalice of immortality will be offered to those who have fought against Ahriman (Evil), and a new creation will be established. In old German mythology Paradise itself will be established on the earth in the Kingdom of God. The English word "paradise stems from the Avestan "Pairi Daize." The word "garden" may stem from the Avestan "Garod-man" House of Songs – the ancient name for heaven used by the Aryans.

Before the end of the world, there will be three saviors who will come at intervals of one thousand years. They will appear after Zoroaster, every thousand years during the remainder of the era. These spiritual successors will bear the Holy Spirit again to the earth, in order to renew the changeless Faith of God and help humanity progress. These saviors will culminate in Saoshyant, who will prepare the way for the resurrection of the dead.

"At the end of the age Ahura Mazda will wipe out all trace of evil. The souls from hell will be brought up and purified and will join the souls of the righteous, and the world will enter a new cycle of perfection. In the final judgement, all sinners will be punished, and then forgiven; and humanity will be made immortal and free from hunger, thirst, poverty, old age, disease and death. The world will be made perfect once again."

I often wonder if the current gestures of asking forgiveness and mercy for unsettled spirits, and through the process of cleansing unhappy or negative souls as demonstrated by heroic people, especially psychics and mediums, is part of this transitional process.

The last in the succession, the Saoshyant, meaning "World Savior" also Shah Han Shah "King of Kings" would appear 3000 years after Zoroaster. The final battle between the forces of good and evil will take place, resulting in the eradication of evil. The resurrection of the dead will cause them to rise to a more spiritually attracted state. – Edouard Schure

When the final or Whole World Savior comes, **the world will be purged by fire; by molten metal** and evil will once and for all be vanquished. But when will that time be? According to the Torah, Abraham was born 3815; so it is likely Zoroaster was born over 3000 years ago. The Saoshyant is due!

"O Jamasp, when lamps shall be lit without candles, When carriages shall be driven without horses, When men shall fly like the birds, then know, O Jamasp, that the time has arrived" – Zoroaster to His faithful disciple, Jamasp.

A great prayer, the Ahunavar ends with the words Kshrethamchai Ahurai Ayim, *"The kingdom of God will come."*

"O Zarathushtra! I have created no one better than you in the world...You are my chosen one, and I have made this world apparent on account of You. And all these people and monarchs whom I have created have always maintained the hope that I should create you in their days, so that they should accept the religion, and their souls should attain to the supreme heaven." – Zend Avesta

Summary

Zoroaster was sent by God to reaffirm the ancient monotheistic Faith of God promulgated by Gayomart, Siamak, Hooshang and Yima, and many other Prophets and Mediators before and after Him. He did not convert people He simply purified the Faith. He pried it from its manmade imperfections, such as the polytheistic gods or daevas which had been personifications of attributes and vices the people felt were important for one reason or another.

Zoroaster forbade all sacrifices to Ahriman and the daevas, who He then degenerated to hostile deities. He also forbade the Mehr or Mithraic sacrifice of cattle, and the consumption of intoxicating beverages that led to orgiastic excess.

However Zoroaster retained the ancient ritual of fire. The sap of sacred plants like sandalwood was to replace blood as an offering.

Zoroaster taught that men attained virtue by good thoughts and conduct rather than by sacrifice. **All of a man's good works are actually entered into the book of life as credits, and bad works as debits.** He admonished us to **"Choose the better over the bad."**

Background information provided by: *Early History of the Indo-European Languages*, by Thomas V Gamkrelidze and V.V. Ivanov Scientific American March 1990; Bal Gangadhar Tilak In 1903, *The Arctic Home in the Vedas*; Ninian Smart, *The Religious Experience of Mankind*; Prentice Hall, 1969; Dr. Meredith Sprunger: An Introduction to Zoroastrianism 1982

THE WANDERINGS OF ZOROASTER: A THEORY: THE "WEEPING GOD" VIRACOCHA

So to what other countries might gentle Zoroaster have travelled during the 10 or so years when no one back home believed His new revelation? There have been the usual suggestions of India and China without much support. Curiously, there is another place in the world where a Messenger of God appeared for a few brief but profound few years.

Viracocha/Quetzalcoatl arrived in South America from the east and left from the west coast of Peru, during that same vague period of time that was Zoroaster's time, roughly 3800 years to 3200 years ago. But first let's weave a backdrop for this arrival.

Many crossings were made to the Americas. It became a tremendous meeting ground, going back, apparently, to the Denisovans, who likely preceded other human groups in some South Sea Islands and perhaps the Americas. We know they left DNA all the way down to Australia, and for such world travelers, it was possible for them to reach South America.

These people managed skills that weren't apparent anywhere else for thousands of years! Though we know little about them other than their maritime skills were adequate.

Much, much later, after Viracocha's time there were other substantial immigrations. From Europe: Basques, Andalusians, Croats, Greeks, Norsemen, Celts, French, Italians and Portuguese. Chinese and Korean from Asia. Beyond that, many tribes of people circulated throughout the Americas. So it is not surprising that the people of South America have a variety of skin tones.

That being said: there was a vague time around 3800-3200 years ago when a small group of Phoenician ships arrived in the Yucatan, then in South America, with a Messenger of God on board!

After traversing rivers to the mountains, they arrived near today's border between Peru and Bolivia, by Lake Titicaca. The people they first met, might possibly have been part of the Norte Chico or Caral (Sacred City)-Supe (valley) civilization. This was a complex society that included as many as 30 major population centers in what is now the north-central coast of Peru. It flourished between 5,000 and 3800 years ago.

Norte Chico civilization was known for its monumental architecture, including large earthwork, platform mounds, fortress walls, and sunken circular plazas. They produced

Quetzalcoatl, as depicted in the Codex Magliabechiano (16th century). "Quetzalcoatl magliabechiano" by Unknown - http://www.crystalinks.com/ quetzalcoatl.html. Licensed under Public Domain via Wikimedia Commons

woven goods, but no pottery and little other evident art. These were fishermen who relied on marine harvest, rather than agriculture. In comparison to the degree of their material development, their religion was seemingly unremarkable. (civilizations.http://en.wikipedia.org/wiki/Norte_Chico_civilization)

Moving forward, at Tiahuanaco near the Bolivian side of Lake Titicaca there are stone engravings representing this Messenger of God's Word. He was known as Viracocha (sea foam), or as the "Weeping God." It is said that He wept grievously because He was sad to leave His cherished followers and return to a distant destination.

At the Gate of the sun, winged condor-headed and human-headed figures kneel toward the large, central weeping figure, as if in adoration. Each one holds before him a staff or scepter, which is reported in detail by Ephraim G. Squire in 1877, *Incidents of Travel and Exploration in the Land of the Incas*, and many other sources. The Weeping God is also found on Huari vessels and other pottery forms.

At Ollantaytambo, a small village of southern Peru, there is a representation of Viracocha as 'The Creator of Civilization' named Wiracochan or Tunupa. The village is part of a chain of small villages along the Urubamba Valley. Later it became known as the sacred Valley of the Incas. Facing the ancient ruins of Ollantaytambo, in the rock face of Cerro Pinkuylluna is the 140 meter high figure of Wiracochan.

The face of Viracocha at Ollantaytambo can be captured as noted by Fernando and Edgar Elorrieta Salazar, below.

The angry-looking formation of his face is made up of indentations that form the eyes and mouth, a protruding carved rock denotes the nose. Inca ruins built on top of the face are considered to represent a crown on his head. Artists' impressions of the rock face also include a heavy beard and a large sack upon his shoulders. *"Wiracochan, the pilgrim preacher of knowledge, the master knower of time, is described as a person with superhuman power, a tall man, with short hair, dressed like a priest or an astronomer with tunic and a bonnet with four pointed corners."* Descriptions of the hat vary from image to image, but the presence of one, seems significant. (Fernando E. Elorrieta Salazar & Edgar Elorrieta Salazar (2005) *Cusco and the Sacred Valley of the Incas*, pages 83-91 ISBN 978-603-45-0911-5) (http://en.wikipedia.org/wiki/Viracocha)r

Viracocha (pronounced Wiracocha) is known by many names. Legends about this holy Being are carried down among the Aztecs as Quetzalcoatl the "Feathered or Plumed Serpent" and "Nine Wind." And among the Chavin He was known as Huemac "He of the Strong Hands."

The Yucatec Mayans called Him "Kukulcan" and later "Gucamatz," which also means "Feathered or Plumed Serpent." Kukulcan brought the Maya their laws and also their script. "He was worshiped like a god by the people. To the Chibchas he was Bochia, the White Mantle of Light. To those of Peru he was Hyustus, and to this day they will tell you that he was fair, and had blue eyes." – Peter Honore, *In Quest of the White God*

But here we will refer to Him as Viracocha "Sea Foam" as He was known in Bolivia and Peru.

Viracocha was a gentle Messenger, yet powerfully charismatic, like Christ. People came from as far as North America and even from the tip of Tierra del Fuego to see and to serve Him.

Also like Christ, He was tempted by Evil. In this case by the wizard Tezcatlipoca the god of night and material things. Viracocha is the center of Mesoamerican religion and His ascension to Heaven is represented by the Morning Star.

As previously stated He was light skinned and bearded. His comrades also had the lighter skin, reddish-blonde hair, red beard, and the blue or green eyes common to Indo-European descendants. The bearded men with Him were known as "angelic warriors of Viracocha." The next white men to enter these lands would not be as kind.

The color of skin is unimportant. People make too much of it. It is only helpful as a marker to trace travels and timelines in this case. By no means is the supremacy of any people tolerated or propagated here.

When *"Cortes arrived he wore both a hat and robe, and landed almost in the same spot where it was said the White God had bid his people farewell," promising to come again. But with Cortes, came white men who were mercenaries and adventurers. They were not interested in this civilization, and the spiritual nature of its people, who did not understand the Spanish lust for gold and material treasures."* (– Pierre Honore, In *Quest of the White God: Mysterious Heritage of South American Civilization*, 1975.)

Viracocha did not allow human sacrifice, but sadly as the memories of the faithful faded, human sacrifice, once again prevailed. Even worse, such sacrificial offerings were dedicated to this non-violent Being!

He trained healers with unusual knowledge, curanderos who treated body, mind and soul. Herbs were used in the gentle arts of healing. Curanderos or Kallawayas were found in the northwest area of the sacred Lake Titicaca and elsewhere.

The Kallawayas of today are descended from the ancient healers who travelled up and down the Andes, bringing with them powers, which are nowadays attributed to the mountain soul or "Achachila," of one of the snowcapped peaks of the Andes, such as the sacred Akamani, instead of God directly.

The Kallawayas were among the first to use penicillin, streptomycin and quinine. They used more than 200 plants and natural products to aid in healing. For example, the mysterious Coca leaf has been used as a natural medicine for thousands of years. Known for its vitamins and minerals and a unique effect on hunger control. It is also used to treat ailments of the skin.

According to Metaphysical laws, there are two main sources of power on earth. Male and female represent the two antagonistic forces or dichotomy of life. Good and bad, night and day, light and dark, or body and soul also form a complete circle of nature, much like the concept of Yin and Yang, or the Solar and Lunar aspects of Hinduism. To this day the Sun and Moon are ubiquitous symbols in the Americas.

Pyramids are dedicated to the Prophet as well as to His principles of Light and Darkness represented by the sun and the moon. At Teotihuacan those who built the pyramids of the Sun and Moon also carved snake heads surrounded by feathers on their temples. Other temples were dedicated directly to Quetzalcoatl or Viracocha, or another of His names.

Two things come to mind when seeing the term Plumed Serpent. First is the thought of the composition of man. He has an earthly body confined to the earth like the serpent; but his soul has the wings to rise like a bird if properly trained. Secondly, it is possible that the prow of the vessels in which He rode featured a dragon or horse motif, similar to the one adopted by the Vikings. The horse with flying mane could easily be perceived as a striking serpent, if you had no idea what a horse was.

After a visit of a few brief years, it was necessary for the people of the ships to leave with their precious Educator. Viracocha wept to leave such a wonderful place and its courageous people. There are standing stones on the western shore of Peru looking out to sea where He left. Like all Prophets, He promised to return one day.

Thor Heyerdahl claimed in Kon-Tiki (1950) that the Incans told of a sun-god named Con-Tici Viracocha who was the supreme head of the mythical fair-skinned people in Peru. He said the original name for Viracocha was Kon-Tiki or Illa-Tiki, which means Sun-Tiki or Fire-Tiki. Perhaps like Zoroaster, He was the Son of the Undying Fire. This legendary Prophet lived among white and brown skinned people, who built enormous ruins on the shores of Lake Titicaca.

The term Illa is reminiscent of the Abrahamic Sabian and Moslem phrase *"La ilaha ila Allāh" or "There is no God but Allah."* Perhaps Illa-Tiki meant something similar.

"The legend continues with the mysterious bearded white men being attacked by a chief named Cari, who came from the Coquimbo Valley." A battle was fought on an island in the lake, and the lighter skinned folk were massacred. Kon-Tiki and his closest companions escaped. Eventually they arrived on the Pacific coast. "Kon-Tiki and his companions were last seen, according to the legend, as they disappeared westward, out to sea.

It is far easier to sail west than east, and that is how the Pacific Islands were discovered by Europeans… Indeed, both Polynesia and Melanesia were first discovered by Spaniards who followed the current from Peru on the advice of Inca mariners. Even Micronesia, with the Palau's and other islands just off the coast of Asia, was first discovered from South America… For two centuries all the caravels left Mexico and Peru to cross the tropical belt of the Pacific westward to the coast of Asia." – Heyerdahl

So we know it could be possible the Messenger made it back to Asia – to Greater Iran, which took up a lot of Asia at that time.

When the Spaniards came to Peru in 1533, the Incas told them that the colossal monuments which stood deserted over the landscape had been erected by a race of white gods who lived there prior to the time the Incas became rulers.

They described these white gods as wise, peaceful instructors who had originally come from the north in the "morning of time" and taught the Incas' primitive forefathers architecture, as well as manners and customs. They were unlike other Native Americans in that they had light skins and long beards, and were taller than the Incas. They said that the "white gods" had then left as suddenly as they had come, fleeing westward across the Pacific.

In Peru the Quechua Indians speak of a migrating seafaring hero named Kukulcan, the "Plumed" or "Feathered" Serpent. Tonaca was a name given to Viracocha as He left for the Pacific, toward Oceania.

He was a gentle soul who, tied together the continents of America a long time ago, with one Faith. His fellow voyagers, perhaps Phoenicians, brought with them a love for agriculture and tremendous architectural experience. Since they had helped to build Mediterranean area temples and tombs.

The Phoenicians

It seems the only seafarers of that time capable of making a successful protracted journey to unknown lands were the Phoenicians, or less likely the Egyptians. They had sailed papyrus boats as early as 4750 years ago, in search of trade goods such as spices, drugs, valuable metals and precious stones.

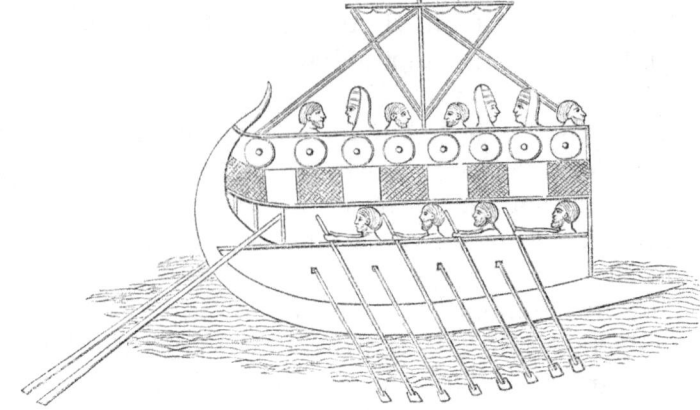

By Ernst Wallis et al (own scan) [Public domain or Public domain], via Wikimedia Commons

Phoenician merchants traveled the Mediterranean Sea, the Atlantic Ocean and the African Coast for financial opportunities at least 2700 years back.

Phoenicia lay on the eastern coast of the Mediterranean in the area of modern day Lebanon Syria and Tunisia. Their greatest cities were Tyre and Sidon. Phoenicians excelled as traders, acquiring goods and raw materials, then reselling them around the Mediterranean. Their ships were able to cover great distances and they eventually passed beyond the borders of the Straits of Gibraltar (Pillars of Hercules) toward the Atlantic coasts of Africa and Europe. They wisely brought with them animals and seed. When their food stores ran low they could reside in some distant location for a couple of years to replenish their stocks and then continue their journey.

Due to their curiosity and courage as well as good planning they provided a wealth of information to the world about geography and culture. The result of ever-advancing trade routes was fostered by rulers who wished to increase their sphere of influence.

The Egyptian Pharaoh Necho commissioned Phoenicians to sail around the continent of Africa 2700 years ago, as recorded by Herodotus 300 years later. It is reported that they made the trip around Africa two, possible three times to pick up trade goods including; fine cloth, spices, perfumes and oils, precious metals and unfortunate captives to sell as slaves.

They also trafficked in drugs like cocaine and tobacco from the Americas, which were traded to Egypt and consequently were found in royal mummies, to such an extent that excavated mummies were at one time ground up into "medicinal" powders used especially by ailing Europeans.

A sunken Phoenician ship wreck was discovered at a depth of 3,000 feet in the Mediterranean Sea, which dates back 2500 years, making it one of the oldest deep sea wrecks to date. It contained hundreds of clay pots, amphora's containing remnants of olive oil, honey and wine.

Two hundred similar large amphoras were found in Guanabara Bay off the coast of Rio de Janeiro, Brazil. Below are excerpts from a New York Times article (http://www.nytimes.com/1985/06/25/science/underwater-exploring-is-banned-in-brazil.html)

"A DISPUTE between the Brazilian Navy and an American marine archeologist has led Brazil to bar the diver from entering the country and to place a ban on all underwater exploration. Robert Marx, a Florida author and treasure hunter, asserts that the Brazilian Navy dumped a thick layer of silt on the remains of a Roman vessel

that he discovered inside Rio de Janeiro's (Guanabara) Bay. The reason he gave for the Navy's action was that proof of a Roman presence would require Brazil to rewrite its recorded history, which has the Portuguese navigator Pedro Alvares Cabral discovering the country in 1500.

Then a Brazilian diver brought up two complete jars with twin handles, tapering at the bottom, the kind that ancient Mediterranean peoples widely used for storage and are known as amphoras. Brazilian experts disagree over the age of the jars, which have been turned over to the Navy who stored them in a warehouse.

Mr. Marx, who has long sought to prove that other sailors reached the Americas well before Columbus, obtained permission to explore the site in late 1982. Diving at a depth of about 90 feet, he found the parts of perhaps 200 broken amphoras and several complete ones, he said in an earlier telephone interview."

Elizabeth Will, a specialist in ancient Roman amphoras at the University of Massachusetts at Amherst, said the jars are very similar to the ones produced at Kouass, a center for amphora-making on the Atlantic coast of Morocco.

"Marx became convinced that, below the potsherds, they had found the remains of a wooden wreck. A Roman vessel, he argued, had been blown off its course and reached Brazil." In January 1983, Marx returned to begin salvaging the wooden wreck. *"The Navy people I worked with told me the site had been covered up, to keep it from being plundered."*

They said the incident was too controversial, and asked him to leave. One last dive confirmed that the spot was now covered by a large mound. *"Government officials told him 'Brazilians don't care about the past. And they don't want to replace Cabral as the discoverer.' "*

So it seems a path to "New World" using Phoenician (or Roman) vessels is documented. Now let's look at the great city of Tiahuanaco.

Tiahuanaco (Tiwanaku)

The ruins nestle 12,500 feet up a mountainside. They once contained a pyramid 700 feet by 500 feet and 50 feet high. On top was a temple 440 feet long with 14 foot columns reaching to the roof. Some believe this great city was founded only 1800 years ago. The date is clouded. There are those who believe work began here nearly 3,600 years ago. But it is clear that Tiahuanaco, was already old prior to the time the Incas took over the area.

The structures were eventually destroyed by the people of the area, who looted stones from the buildings to build houses in a nearby village. Looting of building material is common everywhere. Recycling. It happened to European castles and gave them that ruined look. It is also why many of the ghost towns of the American West disappeared, entirely. Later some of the blocks from Tiahuanaco were used to form a railroad access.

There is no denying that the bearded strangers who planned and built Tiahuanaco were impressive architects. Their leader was the kindly and charismatic Viracocha, who gave laws by which men should live. He spoke lovingly to the people and urged them to treat each other with kindliness so they might become more united.

The people of Tiahuanaco settled on the Bolivian side of Lake Titicaca along the Tiahuanaco River almost nine and a half miles from the lake. They became a self-sustaining society. Urban centers, a bustling city, and walled courts were exquisitely constructed of well fitted, precision carved stones which might have housed up to 50-60,000 people. There was a drainage moat that restricted traffic to the areas frequented by royalty, then led to canals found throughout the city. All runoff was dumped into the Tiahuanaco River. The entire Tiahuanacan population is estimated to have been around 365,000 people. About 250,000 of whom were engaged in farming, herding and fishing. The fields in the 32 square mile Tiahuanaco valley, alone employed 120,000 workers.

Tiahuanaco eventually evolved into a royal city of terraced platform pyramids and arches, courts and urban areas. A few remnants stand today like silent dolmens. "A magnificent attraction calculated to inspire awe. The walls of the temples, the stone monolithic statues and gateways, stand now without their gold and trappings made of textiles, and paint. It must have shimmered from afar in bright sunlight." (Kolata, Allen L., *Valley of the Spirits*, John Wiley and sons, Inc., 1996); (Richardson III, James B., People of the Andes, Smithsonian Books, Washington DC., 1994); (Mason, J. Alden, *The Ancient Civilizations of Peru*, rev. ed.1988.)

The People

When the Spaniards discovered the Inca Empire in 1533, Pedro Pizarro the chronicler wrote that, while the mass of Andes Indians were small and dark, the members of the Inca family ruling among them were tall and had whiter skins that the Spaniards themselves. He mentions in particular certain individuals in Peru who were white and had red hair.

"Pizarro asked who the white-skinned redheads were. The Inca Indians replied that they were the last descendants of the Viracocha's. The Viracocha's, they said, were a divine race of white men with beards. They were so like the Europeans that the Europeans were called Viracocha's the moment they came to the Inca Empire. It is a historical fact that this was the reason why Francisco Pizarro, with a handful of Spaniards, was able to march straight into the heart of the Inca domain and capture the Sun-King [Atahualpa] and all his enormous empire, without the vast and valiant Inca armies daring to touch a hair of their heads. The Incas thought they were the Viracocha's who had come sailing back across the Pacific. According to their principal legend, before the reign of the first Inca, the sun-god Con-Ticci Viracocha had taken leave of his kingdom in Peru and sailed off into the Pacific with his subjects.

When the Spaniards came to Lake Titicaca, up in the Andes, they found the mightiest ruins in South America– Tiahuanaco. They saw a hill reshaped by man into a stepped pyramid, classical masonry of enormous blocks, beautifully dressed and fitted together, and numerous large stone statues in human forms. They asked the Indians to tell them who had left these enormous ruins. The well-known chronicler Cieza de Leon was told in reply that these things had been made long before the Incas came to power. They were made by white and bearded men like the Spaniards themselves.

The white men finally had abandoned their statues and gone with their leader, Con-Ticci Viracocha, first up to Cusco, and then down to the Pacific. They were given the Inca name of Viracocha, of 'sea foam', because they were white of skin and vanished like foam over the sea." Excerpts from *Kon-Tiki*, 1950 by Thor Heyerdahl.

"The Inca referred to a White God who brought them their system of science, and engineering, gave them their legal codes, and helped them achieve a high level of civilization..." (Peter Honore In Quest of the White God: Mysterious Heritage of South American Civilization 1975.)

Architecture

The engineers of Tiahuanaco like the architects of the Dendera temple in ancient Egypt, and the Parthenon atop the Athenian Acropolis hill built in the time of Pericles, shared very specific kinds of building techniques, like the pouring molten metal staples into cut keystone grooves. This added additional stability to stone structures.

Phoenician builders were quite familiar with erecting royal temples and pyramids for kings on the coast of the Mediterranean and in Egypt. So they were familiar with architectural advances like sewers and drainage systems. They carried with them the skills for transporting and utilizing stone megaliths. The stone slabs weighing as much as 100 tons, were cut and brought from several miles away. The blocks were used for wall and pyramid bases. The Tiahuanacans utilized remarkable facing techniques as they built doorways, dolmens, statues and stela – all cut, dressed and fitted together without mortar and with unequalled precision! Not even the later work of the Incas compares. Remnants of other beautiful pre-Incan ruins survive at sites like Ollantaytambo and Qenqo.

"The long-ears of Tiahuanaco did not leave a mayor behind who preserved the secrets; no one who could show posterity how the trick was done. But they had paved roads, as on Easter Island. And some of the largest stone blocks must have been carried for thirty miles across Lake Titicaca itself in huge reed boats, as they were hewn from a particular kind of stone found only in the extinct volcano of Kapia on the other side of the lake.

Local Indians have shown me the assembly point near the shore where gigantic dressed blocks still lie abandoned at the floor of the volcano ready to be shipped across the great inland sea. The ruins of a wharf are still there, and the local Indians call it Taki Tiahuanaco Kama, 'The Road to Tiahuanaco.' Incidentally, the neighboring mountain they refer to as the 'Navel of the World" – Heyerdahl

Perhaps the navel was the tie to the Universal Reality, as taught by Lord Viracocha.

Agriculture and Aquaculture

The Phoenicians were also familiar with agriculture techniques such as raised bed farming, and complex canal systems which were new to the Andean area. Canals as long as 650 feet were dug 16-30 feet apart. They were inlaid with a base made of cobblestones, topped with gravel and impermeable clay which kept salt from the brackish lake from upwelling into the fields during flooding.

The canals provided fish, aquatic birds like ducks and plants for food and fertilizer. The water boundaries also served to create warmer temperatures to protect crops, like potatoes, quinoa and canihua from frost, even in temperatures below zero. Dirt from digging the canals was heaped up to form the raised beds for crops. Visually the effect might have been similar to seeing lush hanging gardens with fish ponds.

Thousands of acres were devoted to lattices of raised beds, striped with canals or pools of water surrounding Lake Titicaca, especially in the Puno marsh area on the Peruvian side.

The local farmers call them "waru waru" or "camellones." It should also be noted that raised beds and canals also laced the "plains" of the Amazon Basin, where Phoenicians probably passed on their way to Lake Titicaca, presumably looking for a way back to the western ocean and home.

The waru waru patterns in the Amazon are only visible during the dry season. These remarkable engineering features allow for a 400% increase in agricultural productivity when compared to more recent, standard farming methods.

Material gleaned for this piece was from – Richardson, James B. People of the Andes-Smithsonian Exploring the Ancient World, St. Remy Press, Montreal 1994 pg. 122-131.

For well over 1000 years Tiahuanaco directed innovative farming, and sat at the hub of a commercial network, which covered the majority of the Andes. Yet **their greatest contribution to the culture of the Altiplano was a powerful religion brought by their gentle Prophet, known as Con Tiki, or Viracocha.**

WHISPERS OF TIAHUANACO: CHACHAPOYA, PARACAS, DIAGUITAS, AND CALCHAQUI

Tiahuanacan culture spread to Eastern Bolivia, North Chile and Peru. They brought their agriculture, ceramic work and painted pottery, along with their exquisite architecture where ever they went.

The rise of farming, and the subsequent appearance of permanent human settlements allowed for overlapping civilizations in South America. Several cultures show traits which were associated with Viracocha's folk.

The **Chachapoyas** were the "Warriors of the Clouds" in the northern Andes. Though the region was inhabited for 8,000 years, the height of the Chachapoya culture was 1200 years ago. It filled the basin of the Utcubamba River, which was isolated from the coast and other areas of Peru by large rivers and surrounding mountainous terrain.

Spanish chronicler Pedro Cieza de Leon noted that, *"...among the indigenous Peruvians, the Chachapoyas were unusually fair-skinned and famously beautiful: They were most handsome of all the people that I have seen in the Indies. Their wives were so beautiful because of their gentleness...many deserved to be Incan wives and also taken to the Sun Temple. The women and their husbands always dressed in woolen clothes and in their heads they wear their two tiered turban, a llawt'u which is a sign they wear to be known, everywhere."*

Another Spanish author, Pedro Pizarro described all indigenous Peruvians as "white." Some authors have quoted Pizarro saying that the Chachapoyas were "blond."

Much of what we do know about the Chachapoya culture is based on archaeological evidence from spectacular ruins, pottery, impressive tombs and other artifacts. Their handmade ceramics and their clothing were generally colored in red. Chachapoyas painted their walls with murals depicting stages of a ritual dance, and couples holding hands.

The presence of two tomb patterns is unique. One is represented by conical or bullet-shaped wooden **sarcophagi**

Peru Sillustani Chullpas by Unukorno (Own work) [CC BY 3.0 (http://creativecommons.org/licenses/by/3.0)], via Wikimedia Commons

with flat, owl-like wooden face masks perched on top. They stand side by side in vertical rows like dolls on a shelf, in caves that were excavated into the highest cliffs.

The other tomb pattern featured groups of **mausoleums** constructed like tiny red and cream-colored houses of a neighborhood. These were situated in caves, and worked into cliffs. (http://en.wikipedia.org/wiki/Chullpa)

Sarcophagi in sites like Carajia are extraordinary! They have huge roundish robed bodies, often painted with *wing like markings* similar to those of the **Zoroastrian Faravahar** found throughout the Middle East, and in Egypt they are known as the wings of Isis. These sarcophagi are sometimes cradled by faces carved in the surrounding cave rock. You can pull up Chachapoya images online, they are amazing!

Some of the wooden masks might be bearded, the faces have strong noses, and the hat style reminds one hats typical in the Tiahuanaco or Huari culture. These tiered hats also sit atop statues on the Peruvian coast and in the highlands. The burials were wrapped in bundles of cloth. Some coverings look like burlap, but others were of beautiful red woven textile.

The **mausoleums** may be modified forms of the chullpa funeral architecture, used by the Tiahuanaco and Huari cultures.

Chullpas are above-ground mortuary monuments or tower sepulchers. They were used as **group burials** in many prehistoric and historic South American societies. Chullpas were not the only type of group burial monument used in South America: other types used are *slab-cist tombs, subterranean cist tombs and cave tombs.* These sequestered tombs are sometimes referred to as chullpas, but that term is generally reserved for the tower burials, which are visibly prominent.

The above ground burial styles go back to Tiahuanaco. The towers at Sillustani near Puno, on Lake Titicaca, show pre-Inca characteristics that were later redressed with Inca stone blocks. (http://archaeology.about.com/od/mortuarystudies/qt/Chullpa.htm)

Architecture for living Chachapoyas was characterized by circular stone rooms and circular towers, which had tall conical thatched roofs, alongside the rectangular sort. Walls were sometimes decorated with symbolic figures.

There are raised platforms constructed on the spectacular mountain slopes, which face several canyons. Almost all of the canyons are topped with precipitous cliffs that might contain tombs. Such a view provides understanding. People could gaze upon their ancestors both above them and across the valleys. The monumental fortress of Kuelap and the ruins of Cerro Olan are prime examples of this architectural style.

The Chachapoyas built **major urban centers** surrounded by great fortresses as displayed in Gran Pajaten and Kuelap. These cities might contain more than four hundred interior buildings and massive exterior stone walls that reached upwards of 60 feet in height! This may have been a defense against incursions of Huari, who covered most of the coast and highlands around 800 AD.

Kuelap is very impressive. It has been referred to as the "Machu Picchu" of the north, but it receives few visitors due to its remote location. Chachapoyan architecture thrived until the latter part of the 16th century, when the Spanish arrived in Peru.

The Chachapoyas became one of the many nations ruled by the Incan Empire. However their incorporation had not been easy, because of strong resistance to the Inca troops. The conquest took place, according to De Leon during the second half of the 15th century (1475).

According to de la Vega, the Chachapoyas anticipated an Inca incursion, and began defensive preparations at least two years ahead of the invasion.

Cieza de Leon also documented Chachapoyan resistance. They killed Inca governors, captains and soldiers. As a result, many were imprisoned and enslaved. Though the defeat of the Chachapoyas was fairly swift, smaller rebellions continued, for many years. The Incan conquerors attempted to avert these rebellions by forcing large numbers of Chachapoya people to resettle in remote locations of the empire.

"To quell the rebellion, Inca troops proceeded to Cajamarquilla at over 28,000 feet high, with the intention of destroying 'one of the principal towns of the 'Chachapoyas.' From Cajamarquilla, a delegation of women came to meet them, led by a matron who was a former concubine of Tupac Inca Yupanqui. They asked for mercy and forgiveness, which the Inca granted them." In memory of this peace agreement, the place where the negotiation took place was declared sacred and closed; so from now on 'neither men nor animals, nor even birds, if it were possible, would put their feet in it.'"

As a result of this peace treaty *"Cajamarquilla became a sophisticated center for culture, religion, and commerce. At the site, it is possible to observe the remains of temple pyramids, wide streets, ceremonial squares, cemeteries, underground grain silos, canals, and numerous other enclosures and buildings; many of unidentified use — all constructed using 'tapial',"* (plastered adobe brick). (http://en.wikipedia.org/wiki/Cajamarquilla)

The Incas, with their capital city of Cusco, dominated the Andes region from 1438 to 1533. To be clear – **Incas have often been mistakenly credited with any fine architecture or roads in the area.** They only ruled the Andes for 100 years!

They did introduce their own architectural style after conquering the Chachapoyas, such is the case with the ruins of Cochabamba. One million people were connected by a 25,000 kilometer road system. Cities were built with precise stonework, constructed over and around mountainous terrain. Terraced farms were still the basis of agriculture. (http://en.wikipedia.org/wiki/South_America#Pre-Columbian_civilizations)

Due to harsh treatment by the Inca they suffered years of pitiful subjugation. Many remaining Chachapoya actually chose to side *with* the Spaniards rather than fight them. But in the end, the Incas and the Spanish conquerors were the principal recorders of the Chachapoyan civilization. They had been devastated, but they remained a presence within general indigenous peoples in modern Peru. Chachapoyan traces were strong in several cultures.

The **Paracas** continued to improve agriculture by demonstrating an extensive knowledge of irrigation and water management between approximately 2800 and 2100 years ago. They also made significant contributions to new styles of ceramic art and textiles, including matchless woven goods. They wore highly decorative two tiered turban toppers from around

2300 years ago, and used a lot of beautiful red cloth which featured black-laced intricate designs, similar to the Chachapoyas.

They are also distinguished by trephinations, and the mummification of their dead. The Paracas Cavernas are **shaft tombs** set into the top of Cerro Colorado. Each tomb contains multiple burials. There is evidence that these tombs were reused for centuries. In some cases the heads of the deceased were removed, apparently for rituals. They were later reburied with associated ceramics, a very fine, plain ware. Some pieces had white and red slips, while others were decorated with patterns of the Paracas tradition. The textile burial wraps include many complex weaves and elaborate plaiting and knotting techniques.

The necropolis of Wari Kayan consisted of two clusters of hundreds of burials set closely together inside and around abandoned buildings on the steep north slope of the Cerro Colorado. Each burial was a conical, corn kernel shaped textile-wrapped bundle, almost reminiscent of a Hershey's kiss.

The deceased was seated facing north across the bay of Paracas. Each body was bound with cord to hold it in a seated position. It was then wrapped in many layers of intricate, ornate and finely woven textiles interspersed with grave goods. Paracas Necropolis embroideries are the finest ever produced by Andean societies and are the primary works of art by which they are known. Burials contained food, trinkets, baskets, ceramics and weaponry. Many of the mortuary bundles include textiles similar to those of the early Nazca; who as it turns out, were also masters of water management, both above and underground. Burials at Wari Kayan continued until 1750 years ago. (http://en.wikipedia.org/wiki/Paracas_culture)

"On the Pacific coast, in the desert sand of Paracas, there are large and roomy man-made burial caves in which numerous mummies have been perfectly preserved. When the colorful, still unfaded wrappings are removed, some of the mummies are found to have the thick, stiff, black hair of the present-day Indians, while other, which have been preserved under the same conditions, have red, often chestnut colored hair, silky and wavy, as found among Europeans. They have long skulls and remarkably tall bodies, and are very different from the Peruvian Indians of today. Hair experts have shown by microscopic analysis that the red hair has all the characteristics that ordinarily distinguish a Nordic hair type from that of Mongols or American Indians." (Heyerdahl p.351-352)

Diaguita people shaped one of the most durable and advanced Pre-Columbian cultures in Northwest Argentina, and the regions of Atacama and Coquimbo in Chile. They lived, like the Paracas and Nazca in a very arid climate, which required sophisticated agricultural techniques, including irrigation. They were sedentary farmers whose staple crops included corn, pumpkins and beans. They also tended herds of llama and alpaca.

Up to seventy five percent of the population was of mixed Euro-Amerind background, higher than any other region in Chile. Diaguitas were unique in that they lacked a caste system, and a desire for gold and other precious metals. They tended to live in clans, and are known for their ceramic arts. Their preferred decoration colors were white, red and black.

Many of their buildings had rounded corners, and were packed together like bricks, as found on a ridge, in the ruins of Quilmes. (*"Pueblos Diaguitas,"* Memoria chilena (in Spanish) (Bibiloteca Nacional de Chile), retrieved January 30, 2014)

When the Inca started extending their empire southwards in the 15th century, the Diaguitas fiercely resisted the invasion and they were decimated.

The **Calchaquí** were a tribe of the Diaguitas group, who are now extinct. They occupied northern Argentina. Their stonework was impressive, and their ruins show that they had reached a high degree of Bronze Age civilization. They also, strongly resisted the Spanish colonists, who arrived from Chile. Their language known as Cacan became extinct in the mid 1600's.

THE OLMECS AND MAYANS OF MESOAMERICA

Both of these cultures acknowledged contact with a Great Teacher, who came to the Yucatan on His unprecedented journey. The infancy of the Olmec culture was about 5500 years ago, compared to 4000 years ago for the Maya. The Olmecs faded about 2400 years ago, and the Maya about 2000 years ago. This would have made them both possible candidates for a visit by Phoenician ships, about 3500 years ago.

Undoubtedly the Phoenicians would have had trade goods aboard their ships. Among the offerings would be spices, cloth, precious metals, drugs and remedies, seed crops and animals for food; and one other precious commodity – slaves acquired in West Africa. These may have been traded during a landfall on the peninsula, where they may have become respected warriors and leaders represented by the colossal stone heads of the Olmecs. Given the sheer size of the heads, these portraits almost certainly represented high status members of Olmec society. There may have been other ways that Africans could have reached the Olmecs, during that time frame, but is unlikely. Either way, the heads are very real.

Four of the heads are found at La Venta, in the state of Tabasco. Seven were found at San Lorenzo, and another at Tres Zapotes, in the state of Vera Cruz. Each statue is fashioned from a single block of basalt weighing up to 20 tons. All heads feature distinct broad faces, wide cheeks, rounded jaws, full lips, and flattened noses uncannily similar in appearance to some black Africans, or arguably, Pacific Polynesians. Some researchers specifically identify the Olmec heads with the Mande, also known as Mali or Mandingo people of West Africa. It would seem to be a very good fit if you look at Mande images. West Africa is where the Phoenicians had docked at least two times in the past.

Constance Irwin and Dr. Wiercinski state in *Fair Gods and Stone Faces*, that skeletal remains of Africans have been found in Mexico. They claim that some of the Olmecs were of African descent. This is supported by skeletal evidence from two Mesoamerican sites Tlatilco and Cerro de las Mesas. Intriguingly Dr. Wiercinski, a Polish craniologist, studied over 98 skeletons uncovered from Tlatilco, and determined that no less that 13.5 percent could be directly compared to skeletons of black Africans; 25 skeletons studied at Cerro de las Mesas, revealed a 4.5 percent similarity. Other studies corroborate this theory. See African Presence in Early America, 1987 by Ivan Van Sedima, for an in-depth review of this topic.

The Olmecs on the Yucatan peninsula were early recipients of Viracocha's ministries as the ships made landfall there as one of its southward stops. It is also very possible that the ships landed on the Eastern seaboard in what is now the United States. There are tribes who

had an unexpected percentage of light skin and eyes. There were also stories of a gentle white skinned teacher, whose south coastal ministry as Deganaweda was remembered until recent times. Interestingly after the 1990's reference to Deganaweda asserted that He was a Huron.

Though the Mayans were socially isolated in jungles, "... they developed or obtained knowledge far beyond their social and architectural development; including a complex number system that read into the millions, as a result, they possessed an accurate calendar. They could predict the rising and setting of the sun, eclipses of the sun and moon, and the path of Venus. Their measured year was 365.2420 days, compared to the current 365.2422. Notably they understood the concept of zero long before anyone else in America, perhaps even a thousand years earlier. But the people who received these mathematical, astronomical and architectural miracles, did not employ their knowledge in everyday matters. For example, they had a 600 foot suspension bridge, but did not know how to build an arch." Some of the concepts were the result of contact by people who had advanced knowledge, as did the Phoenicians, as the following piece, drawn from Peter Honore (1975) further states.

"When the Spanish came to Mexico, the Aztec's script was a primitive, phonetic, hieroglyphs and this is always used as evidence against the theory of a transfer of civilization. But suppose there was a highly developed script in earlier Indian civilization which had afterwards perished? This may sound unlikely, but...the Maya did in fact have such a script, and an extremely complicated one. The Mayans themselves said it was their White God Kukulcan who brought them their script. Among the most frequent symbols in Mayan script are those for their days and months, which sound distinctly Semitic such as BenEbCabanEznabAkbal. They are indeed very like the ancient Phoenician and Greek letters, in fact some are identical. In many cases the Phoenicians and Maya have very similar characters for the same letters, and also similar meanings for the 'characters.' Thus both scripts have a common root from which they both developed. We may therefore say that the Mayan legends were right...Kukulcan...taught their people the script that he had brought with him, which was the script of the ancient Cretan, or the Phoenicians.

About 1700 B.C., Cretan Script, which was a purely pictorial script, developed and changed into simpler symbol, which was even further simplified around 1450 B.C. Three different scripts succeeding one another have been found in Crete. The Greek script traces back to 800 B.C., but the Mayan scripts seem to have been taken from the two older Cretan scripts, not from the youngest one. Thus when (they)... came to the Indian's they brought many things with them, such as different concepts...and gold was then 'kuri' in the Inca language.

It is clear that cultural influences from the Mediterranean area reached the Indian civilization VERY EARLY in history, and one of these was the Cretan (Phoenician) script. Some say the Mayan civilization started between 300 B.C., and A.D. 300, but the Cretan script had perished as far back as 1400 B.C., and the Cretan successors in the Mediterranean area no longer knew about it. Thus the Mayans of 300 B.C., must have received their components of civilization from a more ancient people who received it from the old world." – Pierre Honore, In Quest of the White God, 1975.

Mayans seemed to be isolated and peaceful. They built cities and great pyramids surrounded by public buildings, terraces, temples and markets. They became a commercial center and drew in their farming and fishing neighbors. There were apparently no wars, because there were no fortifications. The cities were not even walled in. In the end, however, the people abandoned these thriving business centers, perhaps due to changes of climate and water availability, and moved away 1200 years ago. They left as silently as did their peaceful Prophet.

SOUTH SEA CONNECTIONS:
Light Skins; Long Ears; Blonde-Red Hair and Beards

There may be two main sources for these traits in the South Pacific. One possibility is that Mediterranean folk, perhaps beginning with the voyage, which brought Viracocha to the New World, added traits to the gene pool.

Less likely is that Denisovans preceded everyone else by floating from Australia, through various South Pacific Islands, even to the Americas many thousands of years ago. So perhaps some of the red hair may have come from Denisovan descendants, but as yet no burials have been found that would indicate their arrival in South America.

Tongan Giants

However, there is significant support for the existence of giant people in the South Pacific. Penisimani Ikavuka Toutaiolepo, a well-respected man who lived on an Island that lies about midway between Easter Island and Eastern Australia, mentioned to me at breakfast one day,

"You know 66 years ago a man in my neighborhood was digging a pit to move his outhouse. When he did, he dug up a skeleton. Big skeleton! The man was my height 6'2'', and he held the leg bones up. The thighbone went up to his waist, from the ground, and the shin bone, went up to the middle of his thigh."

I asked what he did with the bones, he said, *"The man reburied them and a house may now be covering all, or part, of the gravesite."* I was curious what kind of dirt would protect these bones, and he told me, *"It was sand."* Nobody there had mentioned seeing large bones before. There was no legend. This burial must have taken place a *very long* time ago. So at least one VERY large person made it halfway to Easter Island.

Perhaps it was these excessively large people who left some of the unexplainable stone monuments, like the **Ha 'amonga 'a Maui,** a six meter-tall trilithon, consisting of three coral slabs (two pillars holding up the third, as a crosspiece).

There are also over 20 earthwork platform mounds called "langi," and a quarry containing huge rock slabs located in the east end of Tongatapu, Tonga's main island. The Langi contain "royal tombs" covered by stone vaults which have never been opened. These are surrounded by earthwork platforms that are supported by carefully placed retaining walls made of outrageously, large stone blocks. This gives a stepped pyramid effect.

A friend of ours named Viliami Fotu said that when he was a child in the 1930's, His father told him that they would hear, on certain nights when there were dark clouds and it was kind of windy, the sounds of men chanting directions, yelling and dragging huge stones. If the pulling stopped, somebody up in front of the crew would be killed, struck down by a war club to the head. Viliami also heard this drama several times during his life. The words were unintelligible, but the residual actions were undeniable.

Huge stone and earthworks are evident on other islands, as well. Some are quite ancient and unexplained.

Nan Madol, near the southern side of the Pohnpei Island, is the only ancient city ever built atop of a coral reef. Its imposing yet graceful ruins are made of stones and columns so heavy that no one has figured out how it was built. Besides the elegance of the walls and platforms, there is no carving, no art – nothing except legend – to remember the **gigantic people called the Saudeleur,** who ruled the island for more than a millennium. They were deeply religious and sometimes cruel. Modern Pohnpeians view the ruins as a sacred and scary place, where spirits own the night. (Read more: http://www.smithsonianmag.com/history/nan-madol-the-city-built-on-coral-reefs-147288758/#b3Hsb1qp2aVyfyT1.99)

Rapaiti (Little Easter Island) has pyramidal structures on its mountain tops that are very unnatural. While Heyerdahl was there a mountain was cleared rapidly, revealing a civilization that dwelt in the mountains and farmed in the valleys. The conclusion that Heyerdahl came to, was the people were **"afraid of someone,"** someone that they could see coming across the ocean; presumably this was either Kon-Ticci Viracocha's people, or more likely **giants, who some say were cannibalistic.**

Thor Heyerdahl proposed that Kon Tiki's people colonized the then-uninhabited Polynesian islands as far north as Hawaii, as far south as New Zealand, as far east as Easter Island, and as far west as Samoa and Tonga around 1500 years ago. They likely sailed from Peru to the Polynesian islands on pae-paes—large rafts built from balsa logs, complete with sails, and each with a small cottage.

From his Kon-Tiki voyage Heyerdahl knew that warm currents flowed from South America, through Polynesia. Some South American Indians had traditions of building reed boats and Easter Islanders had a similar knowledge.

"The mayor directed building of a one-person and two-person reed boat, which apparently was nigh unsinkable and rode the waves elegantly. Having arrived at this point, it was probably not too much of a stretch to lash multiple boats together to get a much larger boat. The bulrush reed they used for building these boats was the totoro, a freshwater reed found at Lake Titicaca, Peru, and which the Easter Islanders planted down in the marshy recesses of their extinct volcanoes."

So although there was recent thought the Easter Islanders were totally stranded after all the trees were gone, maybe not. Heyerdahl also cites plants as a tie between South America and the Islands.

"The most important plant on Easter Island when Roggeveen and Captain Cook came there was the sweet potato, which the Easter Islanders call kumara. This plant, is carefully transported by man, and that the same name kumara was also used by the Indians in large parts of Peru for exactly the same plant." It spread to other Islands, like Tonga, where the word for sweet potato is called kumala, since they do not use "r."

We know [South Americans] repeatedly called at the Galapagos Islands, and we know too, that large numbers of raft centerboards, with carved handgrips, are preserved in the pre-Inca graves of Paracas, where the tall, red-haired mummies are found. A centerboard can't be used without sails, and a sail can't be used without a vessel. A single centerboard in a pre-Inca grave can tell us more about the highly developed sailing technique of Old Peru than any dissertation on Inca legend... There is a striking resemblance of the Paracan mummies to Europeans, quite unlike the Indians, similar traits were found among the long-ears of Easter Island.

Evidence suggests that seagoing war canoes were as large as Viking ships, and two lashed together had brought people from Peru to Polynesia around 1100 AD, where they mingled with Tiki's people."

Moai at Rano Raraku, Easter Island by Aurbina (Own work) [Public domain], via Wikimedia Commons

The travelers built enormous stone statues carved in the image of human beings on Pitcairn, the Marquesas, and Easter Island that resembled those in Peru. They also built huge pyramids in Tahiti and Samoa with steps like those in Peru, and possibly Tonga.

All over Polynesia, Heyerdahl found indications that a peaceable race had not been able to hold the islands for long. The oral history of the people of Easter Island, at least as it was documented by Heyerdahl, is completely consistent with this theory.

He obtained a radiocarbon date of 400 AD for a charcoal fire located in the pit that was held by the people of Easter Island to have been used as an oven used by the "Long Ears."

Rapa Nui sources, reciting oral tradition identified a white race which had ruled the island in the past. Below is the gruesome result.

"Early people on Easter Island built statues as they had at home. Another, Asiatic, race then joined them, beginning the second period of Easter Island history. The long-ears liked to work, apparently in contrast to the short-eared immigrants, and built the large statues in the form currently seen. They had a regular factory production, chiseling them out of the rock, transporting them to their location, then lifting them up, and placing a huge, red rock transported from the other side of the island (sometimes via sea) and lifting it onto the head as a red hairpiece, or hat.

The work stopped suddenly however, as witnessed by the statues in various stages of production and the ones halfway transported, due to a conflict with the short-ears. The long-ears retreated to one end of the island, which had been cleared of stones for more effective cultivation. Here they dug a large ditch across the island and filled it with brush to protect against a short-eared invasion. The long-ears' chief's, short-eared wife betrayed them, however, letting short-eared warriors crawl around the ditch and when the long-ears lit their bonfire as protection against the opposing army, the short-ears pushed them into their own ditch. The "long-ears' earth oven" burned about 300 years ago, although it may have been built (perhaps long before the conflict) as early as A.D. 400. Only one long-ear was allowed to survive, and from him all the current long-ears are descended." (Heyerdahl 1958) http://en.wikipedia.org/wiki/Thor_Heyerdahl#Theory_on_Polynesian_origins)

Long Ears and Ear Spools

Heyerdahl continues, "*[Legend] says that Con-Ticci Viracocha had long-ears with him when he sailed off westward across the sea. It is said that the last thing he did before he left Peru was to stop at Xusxo (Cuzco) in the north on his way from Lake Titicaca down to the Pacific coast. In Cuzco he appointed a chief named Alcaviza and ordered that all his successors should lengthen their ears after he himself had left them. When the Spaniards reached the shores of Lake Titicaca, they heard from the Indians there too that Con-Ticci Viracocha had been chief of a long-eared people who sailed on Lake Titicaca in reed boats. They pierced their ears, put thick sheaves of totora reed in them, and called themselves ring rim, which meant 'ear.' The Indians added that it was these long-ears who helped Con-Ticci Viracocha transport and raise the colossal stone blocks weighing over a hundred tons, which lay abandoned at Tiahuanaco.*"

The Inca have legends of white long-eared rulers, backed up by mummified Caucasian bodies complete with red hair. Pedro Pizarro had also mentioned that it was especially the long-ears who were white-skinned.

The long-ears once ruled a great empire and left stone monuments. According to the Inca they frequently sailed to the Galapagos Islands. Then the legend says that before the first Incas, the sun-god Kon-Ticci Viracocha sailed off with his subjects, never to return.

The Spanish recorded that the ruling Incan families called themselves orejones or long-ears because they were allowed to have artificially lengthened earlobes, in contrast to their subjects.

By piercing their ears and inserting bars, plugs or flesh tunnels of increasing sizes, these cultures were able to stretch their ears. The Mayans of Central America and southern Mexico, and through them, the Aztecs of central Mexico also used ear gauging as a means of personal adornment and to attain social standing.

On **Easter Island** the lengthening of ears was imported. Heyerdahl explains,

"*Their first King had long-ears with him when he reached the island in a seagoing vessel, after having steered for sixty days toward the setting sun on a journey from the east.*"

Heyerdahl continues:

"*...The mayor of [the Marquesan Island, of* **Nuku-Hiva** *came from such a red-haired family... his ancestors who had made the great statues on* **Easter Island** *called themselves* **'long-ears.'** *Is it not strange that they should bother to lengthen their ears, so that they hung down to their shoulders?*" Piercing of the ears to lengthen them was a solemn ceremony.

The giant stone heads and bodies of the Taotaomonas on **Guam** should not be overlooked. There one statue called Anufat has been said to have wounds in his head (ears) with ferns stuffed in them. The people of Tiahuanaco were said to have holes in their ears through which rushes were drawn, to distinguish them from others. This feature is not uncommon on other Islands, and elsewhere. Remember that the red-haired Takla Makan mummies had red yarn drawn through holes in their ears. Similar customs existed in the Marquesas Islands, also in Borneo, and among certain tribes in Africa.

Mark Wilson, says in an article on "Tribal Practices in Ear Gauging" in *Art and Humanities*, submitted 2012-03-24, "Our knowledge of ear gauging with respect to its use *by ancient civilizations in Asia, Africa, Japan and South America; has been acquired through studying ancient relics, paintings and even mummified bodies. The oldest person known to have used ear gauging is Otzi the Iceman, discovered high in the Alps and believed to have originated from 3300 BC. Otzi had gauged ears, and also tattoos, providing proof that body decoration was common at least five thousand years ago. Ear gauging was, and still is, used by tribal elders to signify status."* Ear gauging has been seen in Thailand and Myanmar (Burma). The Ainu of Japan observed a similar custom, as did the Berawan people of Borneo, but this has now all but died out. (http://goarticles.com/article/Tribal-Practices-in-Ear-Gauging/6272489/)

Red Hair

Heyerdahl said that when the Europeans first came to the Pacific islands, they were astonished that they found some of the natives to have relatively light skins and beards. There were whole families that had pale skin, and hair varying in color from reddish to blonde. In contrast, most Polynesians had golden-brown skin, raven-black hair, and rather flat noses. Heyerdahl took Blood samples on the Marquesas from the descendants of light skinned and red haired people. Not surprisingly, they were unrelated to Polynesians, Americans (South America, especially), separate from the Malays, Melanesians, Micronesians, and other Asiatic people of the West Pacific.

Heyerdahl claimed that when Jakob Roggeveen discovered Easter Island in 1722, he noticed that many of the natives were white-skinned, and could count their ancestors, who were *"white-skinned"* right back to the time of Tiki and Hotu Matua when they first came sailing across the sea *"from a mountainous land in the east which was scorched by the sun."* The ethnographic evidence for these claims is outlined in Heyerdahl's book Aku Aku: The Secret of Easter Island.

"Where do you think the red-haired strain on Easter Island came from?" Heyerdahl's aku-aku asked. *"I only know they were living there when the first Europeans came. And the mayor is descended from such stock. Besides, all the old statues depict men with red topknots... people with red hair must have landed on the island in the past. At any rate, the aboriginal settlers must have included some redheads... There were redheads on several of the islands in the Marquesas group."*

The Marquesans have **large tattooed statues, huge stone walls, and red haired descendants**.

"It was the same with the few figures on Pitcairn and Raivavae. Easter Island, with its deep-rooted culture towered above the rest, a cornerstone in the prehistory of the East Pacific."

So where did red hair come from? Again we are probably looking at *two origins*. The first is a speculation that the large Denisovans carried the gene into the Pacific a long ago. There may be a sense of fear associated with these giants and occasional accounts of cannibalism.

Secondly, it reappeared several thousand years ago, with an influx of Indo Europeans from the Arctic region. Eventually making its way to the "New World."

Historical accounts by Greek writers mention redheaded people. "A fragment written by the poet Xenophanes described Thracians, as blue-eyed and red haired. Herodotus described the Budini people as being predominantly red haired. Dio Cassius described Boudica, Queen of the Iceni, to be tall and terrifying in appearance with a great mass of red hair flowing over her shoulders. Tacitus, a Roman historian commented on the **red hair and large limbs of the inhabitants of Caledonia, which he related to red haired Gaulish tribes from**

Germanic and Belgic tribes.

Today red hair is particularly prominent in the peoples of the British Isles.

"Scotland has the highest proportion of redheads; 13% of the population has red hair and approximately 40% carries the recessive redhead gene. Ireland has the second highest percentage; as many as 10% of the Irish population has red, auburn, or strawberry blond hair. It is thought that up to 46% of the Irish population carries the recessive redhead gene. A 1956 study of hair color amongst British army recruits also found high levels of red hair in Wales and the English Border counties. Yet, some ethnographers consider the Udmurt people of the Volga river basin to contain the most red-headed men in the world. Redheads are common among Germanic and Celtic people due to their Indo-European heritage.

Red hair frequency is significant among the Riffians 10% from Morocco and Kabyles from Algeria, 4%. Red hair is also found amongst the Ashkenazi Jewish populations. In European culture, prior to the 20th century, red hair was often seen as a stereotypical Jewish trait: during the Spanish Inquisition, all those with red hair were identified as Jewish. In Italy, red hair was associated with Italian Jews, and Judas was traditionally depicted as red-haired in Italian and Spanish art. Writers from Shakespeare to Dickens would identify Jewish characters by giving them red hair. The stereotype that red hair is Jewish remains in parts of Eastern Europe and Russia.

Red hair was also found among the ancient Tocharians, who occupied the Tarim Basin in what is now the northwestern most province of China. Caucasian Tarim mummies have been found with long flowing red hair dating to 4000 years ago.

In the United States, it is estimated that 2–6% of the population has red hair, and that number is definitely higher in spots like Tri-cities Washington, where it is said to be a whopping 12-13%. This would give the U.S. the largest population of redheads, at 6 to 18 million, compared to approximately 650,000 in Scotland and 420,000 in Ireland." – Various sources cited in https://en.wikipedia.org/wiki/Red_hair

American Native author Vine Deloria, did some serious study into legendary red-haired giants through Indigenous traditions. He mentioned the **Red Headed giants of central Nevada** quite frequently. According to Paiute oral history, the Si-Te Cah or Sai'i are a legendary tribe of red-haired **cannibalistic giants.** There were several very large skeletons removed from Lovelock Cave. Legend has it the Paiutes, tired of their cannibal neighbors, trapped them in a cave, and lit a huge fire at the entrance, which killed the giants, eventually. There are several skulls and a jawbone of the Nevada giants in the Humboldt Museum, in Winnemucca.

There is also a picture of a Paiute woman with a red haired scalp on her belt that she claimed was from a red-haired giant. There are several other references to cannibalistic giants in the Unites States. (http://www.treasurecenter.com/treasure_diary.htm)

Summation

It was said that the Prophet arrived with ships from the East. He and His companions had blonde hair, red beard, and blue eyes. He had long ears and wore a two tiered cap, perhaps red. The ships in which He rode stopped at the Yucatan Peninsula, then again, at a bay off the Brazilian coast.

From there the travelers made their way up navigable rivers to eventually reach the site which would become Tiahuanaco in Bolivia.

He left from the coast of Peru, where great stone heads, like those on Easter Island mark His passage, and await His return.

It is tantalizing to think that the silent stone structures on Tongatapu and the Marquesas, as well as Easter Island, were made in the wisps of memory by the long eared, light-skinned visitors as they picked their way through the Pacific on their way home, to build the colossal Zoroastrian Faith in Persia. Could Viracocha have been Zoroaster? Maybe, but it doesn't really matter. In the end it is only the teachings that matter. You decide.

BUDDHA

"I am not the first Buddha, nor shall I be the last. In due time another Buddha will arise in the world...He will reveal the same eternal truths which I have taught you"
–Maha-Parinibbana Suttanta

His Life

The founder of Buddhism was Siddhartha Gautama, son of a rich Kshatriya (warrior caste) ruler. His mother died shortly after his birth, and he was raised in an environment of loving care, respect and joy, by his mother's sister. His birth took place 2,565 years ago in Nepal near the city of Kapilavastu in today's Lumbini. He married at age 19 and was gifted a son he called Rahula.

His father wanted his son to become a great king. So Siddhartha lived a luxurious and sheltered life which He found boring and inadequate. He studied science, and philosophy; and enjoyed art riding, archery and fencing. He excelled in everything yet he was unhappy. His doting parents built him three seasonal palaces: hot weather, cold weather, and rainy season. They arranged dances, banquets and musical performances, all attended by lovely ladies, but He only became more depressed. He was taken for trips outside the palace. To his father's dismay, on one such trip he saw: a decrepit old man, a diseased man, a corpse and an ascetic monk. He was told that suffering, disease and death are part of human existence.

Siddhartha was amazed that all beings faced sickness and death. He was determined to find the cause of "suffering." He knew that the superficial prosperity and relative stability of a political environment could not relieve people of worry, fear, anxiety and suffering; and it could not lead them to ultimate happiness.

As a young man, Siddhartha left his wife and son Rahula, and his inheritance. Exchanging his fine clothes for those of a beggar, He began a quest of poverty, yoga, meditation and extreme asceticism.

Eventually, he realized that a life of begging for humble food, austerity, penance and pain was really no better than a life of luxury and pleasure. He said:

"If merit comes from purity of food, then deer should have the most merit."

Finally at the age of 35 he sat under a tree, determined not to leave until he attained enlightenment. ("http://www.crystalinks.com/buddha.html)

After his Transfiguration, the Buddha held sermons which attracted believers and disciples. In order to house His followers, monasteries were built in various regions. This process was repeated recently when the cherished 14th Dalai Lama fled to India with the monks and nuns of Tibet. Housing the refugees became a great concern for the Buddhist leader.

Two of Gautama's great disciples were Shariputra and Maudgalyayana. Formerly they were disciples of an agnostic. When they accepted the Buddha as their Teacher, they went back to the agnostic and brought all of his followers to the Buddha. Ananda, became the Buddha's personal servant throughout His later life. To the end and beyond, he was a devoted disciple of the Beloved.

A schism arose in the community when Buddha's own brother tried to take Shakyamuni's place. He hired killers. They became followers of the Buddha. The brother then rolled a boulder down a peak, injuring the Buddha and creating terrible karma for himself. Buddha declared that his brother's words or actions should not represent the community in any way. Very similar attempts, brought torment to Baha'u'llah and His followers, and also to the Christ.

Accounts of Gautama Buddha's life, discourses, and monastic rules were summarized after his death and memorized by his followers. Various collections of teachings attributed to him were passed down first by oral tradition, then committed to writing about 400 years later.

Reincarnation

Buddha's are "Educators." They are the Revealers of God's Word and are emanations of one Entity. One Luminous Primal Point, which returns time and again to guide humankind toward civilization and a greater maturity. Many refer to that Luminous Point as the Holy Spirit. Buddha said:

"I am not the first Buddha to come upon the Earth, nor shall I be the last. In due time another Buddha will come…" Similarly, Christ said, "I go away…and I come again"

Today some people focus on personal reincarnation, a clouded perception of the spiritual concept of birth, death and rebirth. There are many spiritual and telepathic ways to know lives besides the ones we are currently living. It is unnecessary to recycle souls through this rudimentary part of life, to share this experience. In essence, it would be like repeating kindergarten – What's the point?

"He will reveal the same eternal truths which I have taught you."

These words do not imply that Gautama will return personally, nor do they imply that human beings will return personally. Life is a process. We are continually, endlessly, progressing towards God, the source of Creation.

When a Manifestation of the Word of God, like Buddha says that He will return, He speaks of the return of the Holy Spirit enthroned in a Buddha or a Christ or any one of the Great Prophets.

We may or may not be able to recognize or remember this fact. Five hundred years before the coming of the Christ, at about the same time as the life of Gautama Buddha, a Greek sage named Empedocles said:

"However sublime a spirit may be, once buried in flesh, it temporarily loses the remembrance of its entire past; once taken into the activities of corporeal life, the development of its earthly consciousness is subjected to the laws of the world where it is incarnated. It comes under the power of the elements. The higher its origin, the greater will be its effort

to regain its dormant powers, its celestial qualities, and to become aware of its mission."
 -Edouard Schure, *The Great Initiates*, pg. 428

God: All, or Nothing?

In recent times, some believe the man-made premise that Buddha did not speak of "God" or "soul" as concepts. The difference between the concept of an "Oneness" or "Nothingness" versus a personal god, is lost on some people. The following quotes may restore our certainty.

"Buddha did not teach us to believe in personalized gods, but the journey of attaining Nirvana, eternal, blissful, and inconceivable is the yearning of the soul to re-unite with its Source. It was Brahman who encouraged Him to teach humanity. Buddha didn't wish to. He felt it was hopeless. But Brahman said there were some who would listen and retain some of the purity of His message. So with pity for those few in His heart, He began to educate mankind, once again." (Unknown)

"The religion of the future will be a cosmic religion. It should transcend personal God and avoid dogma and theology. Covering both the natural and the spiritual, it should be based on a religious sense arising from the experience of all things natural and spiritual as a meaningful unity. Buddhism answers this description." -Albert Einstein http://www.spaceandmotion.com/Albert-Einstein-Quotes.htm#Religion.Einstein

"In former days, in the time of the Buddha and Zoroaster, civilization in Asia and in the East was very much higher than in the West and ideas and thoughts of the Eastern peoples were much in advance of, and nearer to the thoughts of God than those of the West. But since that time superstitions had crept into the religion and ideals of the East, and from many differing causes the ideals and characters of the Eastern peoples had gone down lower and lower..." (Abdu'l-Baha, Abdu'l-Baha in London, p. 69)

"Blinded indeed is this world. Few are those who see the truth. Like a bird breaking out of the net, few are those who go to heaven." (Buddhist, Dhammapada – *Sayings of the Buddha 1* (translated by John Richards 1993)

"Human inability to grasp the divine essence does not lead to agnosticism, 'manifestations,' are viewed as occupying two 'stations,' or occurring in two aspects. The first 'is the station of pure abstraction and essential unity,' in which one may speak of the oneness of the messengers of God because all are manifestations of his will and exponents of his word.

This does not constitute syncretism since 'the other station is the station of distinction.... In this respect, each manifestation of God hath a distinct individuality, a definitely prescribed mission....' Thus, while the essence of all religions is one, each has specific

features that correspond to the needs of a given time and place and to the level of civilization in which a manifestation appears." – (The Encyclopedia Brittanica Book of the Year 1988, "The Baha'i Faith", p.5)

Now, it is true that there are many gods, goddesses, saints and demons cluttering current Buddhist "traditions." These entities are residue from Ancient Paganism and Shamanism. They were an integral part of the culture to which the Buddha revealed His teachings – definitely not a part of Shakyamuni's revelation. They may still be very real to some, but they should not be focal points of Buddhism. What is the purpose of an icon, really?

"He who has abandoned human bonds, and transcended those of heaven, is liberated from all bonds."

"If a person month after month for a hundred years, should sacrifice with a thousand offerings, and if but for one moment that person paid reverence to one whose soul is grounded in knowledge, better is that reverence than a hundred years of sacrifices."
(Buddhist, Dhammapada – Sayings of the Buddha 2 (tr. J. Richards))

Buddha's scriptures are divided into parts. The Tripitaka (Three Baskets of Wisdom) Buddha's parables are attractive bite sized bits of charming education. They truly are hard to resist. And they are wonderful to inspire meditation. (http://www.san.beck.org/EC9-Buddha.html)

Wisdom

Glimpses of His wisdom and guidance gleaned from throughout the book, *The Teachings of The Compassionate Buddha*, Edited by E. A. Burtt; Mentor Religious Classic, 1960, Pp. 27-122

Shakyamuni (Buddha) was sitting under a tree, when a Brahman approached Him in awe, asking if He was a god. The Tathagata (Buddha) said 'no.' The Brahmin asked if he were some kind of nature spirit, but again – 'no.' He was then asked if he was human, and denied that also. The man asked if he was not divine, nor human, then what he was. The reply was 'Buddha.'

Shakyamuni and Tathagata are attributes and names for Gautama Buddha, but they may also refer to other Manifestations of God's Word.

Another Brahmin student asked the Buddha why humans differed so much in birth, intelligence, means, and health. It was explained that beings are heirs of karma, the consequences of their actions. Evildoers may experience happiness until their deeds ripen, and the good being may experience bad things until their good deeds ripen. The pure and the impure create their own destinies: no one can purify another.

The Buddha said the two greatest wrongs were not to ask forgiveness after committing a wrong and not to forgive one who has confessed and asked for forgiveness.

A woman was grief-stricken when her only son died. Unable to find a physician who could bring him back to life, she went to the Buddha. He told her to get a handful of mustard seed, but it must be from a house where no one has ever lost a child, spouse, parent, or friend. Eventually she came to realize how common death was and put aside her selfish attachment to her child.

"This is the only Law: That all things are impermanent."

A line that sticks with me from a movie on the life of the current Dalai Lama, is **"Things change Kundun!"** His mentor was trying to prepare the young leader for the Chinese conflict over the future of the state of Tibet. As a result the Dalai Lama was able to scramble away from certain extinction, and keep the soul of the Tibetan Buddhists alive.

Buddha encouraged people to *be compassionate, and kind to all creatures, take only what has been given, be chaste, speak the truth and be worthy of trust. Live as a binder of those who are divided, an encourager, and a peacemaker.* His own compassion was unquestioned. He once bathed and treated a monk, suffering from dysentery. He had been neglected by his fellows because he was lying in his own excrement. This compassion is well modeled today by Buddhist leaders. The noble 14th Dali Lama Tenzin Gyatso said:

"If you want others to be happy, practice compassion. If you want to be happy, practice compassion." and,

"Our prime purpose in this life is to help others. And if you can't help them, at least don't hurt them."

Awaken the four qualities of loving friendship, compassion, altruistic joy, and equanimity.

Four motives for evil deeds are: partiality (prejudice), enmity, stupidity, and fear. Six channels for dissolution of wealth are: addiction to intoxicants, frequenting the streets at unseemly hours, haunting fairs, gambling, bad companions, and idleness.

We are the results of our thoughts: pure or impure. Lift up yourself, by yourself.

He advised us to be detached from the world and follow the path of virtue, for the world is like a bubble or mirage. Most of the world is blind, but wise people escape the illusion by conquering temptation.

Anyone who tries to settle a matter by violence is not just. The wise consider a matter calmly what is right and what is wrong; proceeding in a way that is nonviolent and fair.

The sooner the wish to injure disappears, the sooner all suffering will stop.

Speak true words that are useful and not harsh.

Buddha said a man was wise not to accept things blindly, but to question with reason and by experience. After thorough investigation whether the teachings are good, free from faults, praised by the noble, and when practiced, lead to the welfare and happiness of oneself and other beings, then they may be accepted and lived.

Independent investigation of Faith is the only way we can see the Truth for ourselves.

The Gospel of Buddha

He laid out the Four Noble Truths and the Noble Eightfold Path: The cause and cure of evil and suffering, for the spiritual development of humanity.

The First Noble Truth: the human condition includes suffering, because life strays from spiritual reality.

The Second Noble Truth: we cause much of our own suffering, by indulging material concerns, rather than those of pure spirit. All forms of selfishness tend to separate us from others, life and reality.

The Third Noble Truth: Suffering will cease when we overcome these misleading, and meaningless desires. People should shun attachment to the things of this world.

The Fourth Noble Truth: explains how to accomplish this through the Middle Way of the **Noble Eight – Fold Path.**

Right Knowledge: a person needs principles and values to form a wise life plan.

Right Aspirations: The heart and the head must agree to follow the plan. Avoid being tempted.

Right Speech: People should change their speech and thinking toward truth and charity.

Right Behavior: Five Precepts help us along our path. Do not kill, steal, lie, be unchaste, or drink intoxicants.

Right Livelihood: Spiritual progress is not furthered by engaging in unseemly occupations, which pull in the opposite direction. Serve in occupations that strengthen and promote life.

Right Effort: people must struggle diligently to grow toward spiritual attainment. Great stress is laid on the importance of the will in determining our spiritual destiny.

Right Mindfulness: to sustain growth. The mind is the shaper of the course of human life. **"All we are is the result of what we have thought."**

Right Contemplation: meditation is necessary to transcend worldly preoccupation with things, desires, and suffering.

"Therefore, I say, Right Understanding is of two kinds":

1. The view that alms and offerings are not useless; that there is fruit and result, both of good and bad actions; this is called the "Mundane Right Understanding," which yields worldly fruits, and can brings good results – practiced by the "Worldly"

2. But whatsoever there is of wisdom, of penetration, of right understanding, conjoined with the "Path" – the mind being turned away from the world, the holy path being pursued; this is called the "Ultra mundane Right Understanding," which is not of the world, and is practiced by the "Noble Ones."

Buddha's teachings stressed the unity of self and self-transformation.
"Work out your own salvation with diligence."
"From the unreal lead me to the real; from darkness lead me to light; from death lead me to deathlessness" – Upanishad prayer.
"In the recorded history of mankind, there have been only a few such Manifestations of God. They have appeared at intervals of about a thousand years. Krishna, Buddha, Zoroaster, Moses, Christ, Muhammad, the Báb and Bahá'u'lláh – Each has founded a religion for the people of His own age and, like a perfect mirror, has re-

flected the light of God, to them. His words are spoken with the authority of God. Each is the Lord of His age and His teachings, which become the spirit of the age, are promulgated in accordance with the capacity of the people among whom He appears. He releases to the world of humanity, spiritual energies designed to advance the human soul in its journey to God." (Adib Taherzadeh, quoting Abdu'l –Baha, The Revelation of Baha'u'llah v 1, p. 3)

Asian countries are charged with changing the plight of humanity in these days. Peoples of the East must arise in glorious humility!

"'And ye who are the people of the Orient – the Orient, which has ever been the dawning-point of lights – from whence the Sun of Reality has ever shone forth casting its effulgence upon the West – ye therefore must become the manifestations of lights. Ye must become brilliant lamps. Ye must shine as stars radiating the light of love toward all mankind. May you be the cause of love amongst the nations. Thus may the world become witness that the Orient has ever been the dawning-point of illumination, the source of love and reconciliation. Make peace with all the world. Love everybody; serve everybody. All are the servants of God. God has created all. He provideth for all. He is kind to all. Therefore must we be kind to all.'" (H.M. Balyuzi, Abdu'l-Baha – The Centre of the Covenant, p. 287)

Buddha's Pity

> The Enlightened One, because He saw mankind drowning in the Great Sea of Birth Death and Sorrow, and longed to save them,
> For this He was moved to pity.
> Because He saw the men of the world straying in false paths, and none to guide them,
> For this He was moved to pity.
> Because He saw that they lay wallowing in the mire of the Five lusts, in dissolute abandonment,
> For this He was moved to pity.
> Because He saw them still fettered to their wealth, their wives and their children, knowing not how to cast them aside, (with detachment)
> For this He was moved to pity.
> Because He saw them doing evil with hand, heart, and tongue, and many times receiving the bitter fruits of sin, yet ever yielding to their desires,
> For this He was moved to pity.
> Because He saw that they slaked the thirst of the Five Lusts as it were with brackish water,
> For this He was moved to pity.
> Because He saw that they longed for happiness, they made for themselves no karma of happiness; and though they hated pain, yet willingly made for themselves a karma of pain, and though they coveted the joys of Heaven, would not follow His commandments on earth,
> For this He was moved to pity.
> Because He saw them afraid of Birth, old age and death, yet still pursuing the works that lead to birth, old age and death,

For this He was moved to pity.
Because He saw them consumed by the fires of pain and sorrow, yet knowing not where to seek the still waters of Samadhi (Enlightened Awareness).
For this He was moved to pity.
Because He saw them living in an evil time, subjected to tyrannous kings and suffering many ills, yet heedlessly following after pleasure.
For this He was moved to pity.
Because He saw them living in a time of wars, killing and wounding one another; and knew that for the riotous hatred that had flourished in their hearts they were doomed to pay an endless retribution,
For this He was moved to pity.
Because many born at the time of His incarnation had heard Him preach the Holy Law, yet could not receive it,
For this He was moved to pity.
Because some had great riches that they could not bear to give away,
For this He was moved to pity.
Because He saw the men of the world ploughing their fields, sowing the seed, trafficking, huckstering, buying, and selling; and at the end winning nothing but bitterness,
For this He was moved to pity.

This piteous state is reconfirmed in the chilling quote of the Bab, below.
"By the righteousness of Him Who is the Absolute Truth, were the veil to be lifted, thou wouldst witness on this earthly plane all men sorely afflicted with the fire of the wrath of God, a fire fiercer and greater than the fire of hell, with the exception of those who have sought shelter beneath the shade of the tree of My love."
(The Bab, Selections from the Writings of the Bab, p. 12)
Gautama Buddha said:
"I am not the first Buddha to come upon the earth, nor shall I be the last. Previously there were many Buddha's who appeared in this world...In due time another Buddha will arise. He will be a master of angels and mortals. He will reveal to you the same Eternal Truths which I have taught you. He will proclaim a religious life, wholly perfect and pure; such as I now proclaim.' 'How shall we know him?' asked Ananda."
In the following answer, Buddha likely mentions two; the One to follow Him, and the one who will come at the time of the end; as is typical.
"The Buddha replied, 'He will be known as Maitreya which means kindness or friendliness.' …"
"He will return as the Fifth Buddha, also be known as Amita'bha (Sanskrit) endowed with boundless light, from Amita "infinite, immeasurable, and abha "ray of light, splendor, the bliss of enlightenment"

CHRIST

"I am the way the truth and the (Light or) Life, no one cometh to the Father but by me." – (John 14:6)

"Joy to the world, the Lord is come. Let earth receive her king!"
(Christmas Carole attributed to Isaac Watts 1719.)

On the position of Christianity, let it be stated without any hesitation or equivocation that its divine origin is unconditionally acknowledged, that the Sonship and Divinity of Jesus Christ are fearlessly asserted, that the divine inspiration of the Gospel is fully recognized, that the reality of the mystery of the Immaculacy of the Virgin Mary is confessed, and the primacy of Peter, the Prince of the Apostles, is upheld and defended...." -Shoghi Effendi, *The Promised Day is Come*, rev. ed. (Wilmette: Bahá'í Publishing Trust, 1980); p. 109)

"He will be great and will be called the Son of the Most High. The Lord God will give him the throne of his father David, and he will reign over the house of Jacob forever; His kingdom will never end. " – (Luke 1:32-33)

But not everybody did recognize Christ. They were blinded by their own imaginations of whom He would be, and made up their own image of what He would look like, and how he would act.

Today it is the exact same situation with some Christians and Moslems, who imagine the Promised one to be as they choose to define Him, and are blind to other Faiths.

"In one era He is called Abraham, at another time Moses, again He is called Buddha, another time Jesus, and yet another time Mohammad. All turned to the divine reality for their strength. Those who followed Moses accepted him as their mediator; those who followed Zoroaster accepted him as their mediator; but all the Israelites deny Zoroaster, and the Zoroastrians deny Moses. They fail to see in both the one light. Had the Zoroastrians comprehended the reality of Zoroaster, they would have understood Moses and Jesus. Alas! The majority of men attach themselves to the name of the mediator and lose sight of the real purport."

"Therefore did Baha'u'llah cry, 'O God, deliver us from the sea of names!'"
(Attributed to Abdu'l-Baha, Divine Philosophy, p. 32)

His Early Life

When Joseph and Mary were in Bethlehem, enrolling in the Roman census, Jesus came into this world. They left after paying tax, and fled to Egypt with the baby until the death of King

Herod, who sought to kill him. Later they returned to Nazareth. It is said that Jesus may have had four brothers James, Joseph, Simon and Judas; as well as two unnamed sisters.

"Mary was of noble birth, and related to the Essenes..." – Schure) One fact seems to stand out in the legendary story of Mary—that Jesus was a child dedicated to a prophetic mission by the wish of his mother before his birth. The same is reported concerning several heroes and prophets of the Old Testament. These sons, dedicated to God by their mothers, were called **"Nazarenes."** Schure, *The Great Initiates*, pg. 425

Early on, the child was visited by three Magi, who came seeking the predicted return of their own Prophet, Zoroaster. This is a monumental moment in religious history! Followers of one Manifestation of God recognized the arrival of the Return! All too often the picture of "welcome," by a previous faith is much more grim.

Little is known of Jesus' (also known as Yeshua) childhood in the Gospels, more is known from the Qu'ran given here. *"When Jesus was 12 years old the family traveled to Jerusalem for a Passover pilgrimage. A day after the caravan of pilgrims left; his parents realized that Jesus was not just playing with other children on the caravan—he was not there! They returned to look for him, and after a second day's journey back, found him in the temple courtyard among the teachers. (2:41-52) They were amazed by both his questions and his answers...The youth was scolded by his parents and returned with them to Nazareth."*

PERSPECTIVE

We have very little other actual information about Jesus in the Bible, before He was anointed by John the Baptist. Edouard Schure speculates that he may have taken refuge with the order of the Essenes, and become initiated in their spiritual doctrines. Since it was a very secretive order, this might explain the lack of public data. We also have a basic overview by Brother Day, D.D. below, and a snippet from Edgar Cayce.

The Essenes

Basic overview of the ancient Essenes, by Brother Day, D.D. http://www.essene.org/Ancient_Essenes.htm

*"Two ancient scholars, were contemporaries of the first century Essenes: **Josephus Flavius** and **Philo of Alexandria**. Josephus, born at Jerusalem in 37 A.D., was the greatest historian of the Jews in that period. **Philo was the greatest Jewish philosopher** of that period. Both men had personal knowledge of the ancient Essenes; both make clear that the Essenian roots are incredibly ancient.*

Josephus declares that the Essenes have existed "from time immemorial" and "countless generations." Philo agrees, calling the Essenes "the most ancient of all the initiates" with a "teaching perpetuated through an immense space of ages."

*Josephus and Philo – as well as several other ancient writers, including Pliny the Elder – are in consensus on two points in regard to the origin of the Essenes: Their origin is lost in pre-history with certain **ancient legends linking them with Enoch**..."*

Let us first consider the original founding of the Essenes by Enoch, then the later manifestation by Moses.

Enoch lived many centuries before Moses. Enoch was so in harmony with the laws of God that he was taken from Earth to an Angelic realm without having to die first! There, Enoch was given the angelic name "Metatron," and given the duty of guiding other human beings

This is a part of a scan of an historical document: Title: Schedelsche Weltchronik or Nuremberg Chronicle, Wikipedia Commons

into their angelic destiny. His main work on Earth was the founding of the Essene Church. The Essene Church is considered (by the Essenes) to be a doorway into the angelic realm, as many of the Dead Sea Scrolls make abundantly clear, see The Dead Sea Scriptures, translated by Theodore Gaster, for numerous references to the Essene belief that their order served as a doorway into the angelic realm.

The fact that Enoch was considered the "founder" or "initiator" of the Essenes can even be seen in his name; the word "Enoch" means in Hebrew: "founder," "initiator," "centralizer." A modern scholar, Edmond Bordeaux Szekely, in his excellent book, **From Enoch to the Dead Sea Scrolls**, writes: "The origin of the Essene brotherhood is said to be unknown... Some believe it comes from Enoch, and claim him to be their founder."

After the original founding of the Essenes by Enoch, many centuries passed in which the Essenes existed as a Mystery School, out of the eyes of the public.

There was a major manifestation of the Essenes by Moses at Mount Sinai.

Both the ancient scholar Philo, and a modern scholar, Rabbi Harvey Falk (in his Another Look at the Jewishness of Jesus), informs us that Moses trained thousands of disciples as Essenes. The Essenes themselves describe that event in one of their most important texts: The Essene Book of Moses. In that text, God, at Mount Sinai, gave Moses the Essene Communions on a stone tablet. It was hoped that all the Jewish people would follow the way of life described on that tablet. But when Moses descended Mount Sinai and met with the people, it was clear that the majority were not ready to follow the esoteric Essene teachings engraved on that tablet. Heavy of heart, Moses again climbed Mount Sinai and asked God for an exoteric, easier set of teachings for the masses who were not ready to receive the Essene teachings. God responded by giving the famous Ten Commandments on a second stone tablet; those commandments would be for the masses. Moses was to keep the esoteric Essene Communions for "the Children of Light," for only they could understand them. We read:

"And the Lord called unto Moses out of the mountain, saying, 'Come unto me, for I would give thee the Law for thy people, which shall be a covenant for the Children of Light.'... And God spake all these words, saying, 'I am the Law, thy God, which hath brought thee out from the depths of the bondage of darkness.... I am the invisible law, without beginning and without end.... If thou forsake me, thou shalt be visited by disasters for generation upon generation. If thou keepest my commandments, thou shalt enter the Infinite Garden where stands the Tree of Life in the midst of the Eternal Sea.'"

At that point, God then gave Moses the Essene Communions on the first tablet. Besides the Communions, that tablet included a synopsis of the main Essene teachings, including vegetarianism: "Thou shalt not take the life of any living thing." Then continues:

"And the people knew not what became of Moses, and they gathered themselves... and made a molten calf. And they worshipped unto the idol, and offered to it burnt offerings. And they ate and drank and danced before the golden calf... and they abandoned themselves to corruption and evil before the Lord."

The reference above to "burnt offerings" is a reference to "animal sacrifice." When Moses returned, he found the people offering bloody animal sacrifices to their golden idol. Although

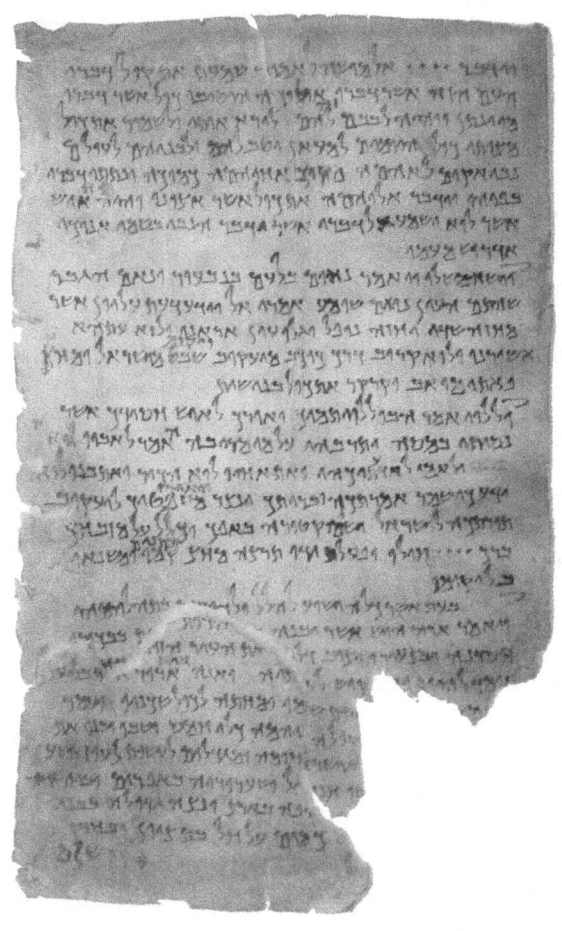

Jordan, Amman, Dead Sea Scroll 4Q175. By Berthold Werner (Own work) [GFDL (http://www.gnu.org/copyleft/fdl.html) or CC BY-SA 3.0 (http://creativecommons.org/licenses/by-sa/3.0)], via Wikimedia Commons

he knew that these people had not "the ears to hear" the esoteric Essene tablet, – they were given the exoteric Ten Commandments instead – Moses preserved the Essene teachings for the Children of Light (the Essenes became known as the "Children of Light"); we read: "And Moses hid the invisible Law within his breast, and kept it for a sign for the Children of Light."

It was at this time, according to both the ancient scholar Philo and the modern scholar Falk, that Moses trained 2,000 of the spiritual "elect" – those Jews who had remained vegetarian and refused to participate in animal sacrifice and idol worship – to be Essenes. AND FROM THIS TIME ON THE ESSENES EXISTED AS AN ESOTERIC MINORITY SECT. (Note: When modern scholars assert that the Essenes of Qumran were founded about 200 years before the time of Jesus, they are correct in regard to that one Essene group at Qumran; but the overall Essene movement is far more ancient.)

Although the Essenes began as an esoteric minority sect within Judaism, they went on to become the very first "Christians," called "Essene-Nazarenes" or "Ebionites." That happened as follows. Several hundred years before the birth of Jesus, the head priest of the Essenes, known as the "Teacher of Righteousness," had a vision: An Angel told him that a great Avatar, the Mashiakh (Christ Messiah), would come to Earth through the Essenes."Halakoth" (preparation) was practiced in a group context. In the winter issue of "The Essene Path," Rev. Michael Robinson provided related information:

"Essene prophets who were attuned to the will of the Almighty, by virtue of their Holy meditations and their lifestyle of Righteousness, prepared for generations for the arrival of the Messiah of Peace. Genealogies were consulted and candidates were chosen and raised to a holy life. Pure diet, free of the taint of death and blood, as well as training in the Essene mysteries, brought forth children of a Holy nature, from which new candidates were chosen."

In the book, Edgar Cayce's Story of Jesus, edited by Jeffrey Furst, we read: ..." the Essenes... dedicated their lives, their minds, their bodies, to a purpose, to a seeking for that which had been to them a promise of old.... Hence, there was the continued preparation and dedication of those who might be the channels through which this chosen vessel might enter – through choice– into this material realm. Thus in Carmel – where there were the chief priests and leaders of this faith – there were the maidens chosen who were dedicated to this purpose.... Among them was Mary, the beloved, the chosen one."

Again from Cayce:

"The Essenes were dedicated to their purpose and made holy Mount Carmel their headquarters. This was the original place where the school of prophets was established during Elijah's time....

"Here, the Essenes prepared themselves for several generations to open as it were a door into this realm for the Messiah.... And he became known as Jesus the Nazarene, for he was of the Essenian sect of Nazarenes in the region of Carmel."

In regard to the above references to the Essene headquarters at Mount Carmel and Jesus being affiliated with the Essenian sect of Nazarenes in the region of Carmel, there is much supporting evidence. Indeed, it is quite clear that the headquarters of the entire Essene movement was Mount Carmel in Northern Israel, not Qumran in Southern Israel, and that Jesus was primarily associated with Carmel. Equally clear is the fact that the Northern Essenes in the region of Mount Carmel were called "Nazarenes." The Essene Monastery where John the Baptist lived (and where the Dead Sea Scrolls were discovered), was in Southern Israel.

The Essenes – John the Baptist – the Temptation

From Schure's creative story, not to be confused with history, we get an idea of a spiritual community His mother at least may have associated with, selecions from chapter 40 Pp. 434 through 449.

"The Gospels have maintained an absolute silence about Jesus' deeds and travels before his meeting with John the Baptist, when, as they relate, he assumed his ministry. Immediately afterward he appears in Galilee with a teaching which has been formulated with the assurance of a prophet and the consciousness of the Messiah. But it is evident that this bold and premeditated beginning was preceded by a long development and a virtual initiation.

He could learn what he wished to know only from the Essenes. Essenes preserved in Israel the real traditions of the prophets, together with their way of living. This is apparent, not only from inner relationships between the teaching of Jesus and that of the Essenes, but also from the very silence Christ and his disciples maintained concerning this sect.

'In Jesus' time the Order of the Essenes constituted the last remnants of those brotherhoods of prophets organized by Samuel. The despotism of the masters of Palestine, along with the jealousy of an ambitious and servile priesthood had pushed them into retreat and silence. They no longer fought as did their predecessors; they were content with preserving tradition. They had two main centers: one in Egypt beside Lake Maoris, the other in Palestine at Engaddi, beside the Dead Sea.

The name 'Essenes' which they had given themselves, came from the Syrian word, Asaya, meaning physicians, in Greek, therapeutes, for their sole avowed ministry, so far as the public was concerned, was that of healing physical and moral maladies. 'They studied very carefully,' said Josephus, 'certain writings on medicine, which dealt with the secret properties of plants and minerals. Some possessed the gift of prophecy like Menahim, who had predicted to Herod that he would reign.' 'They serve God,' said Philo, 'with a great piety, not by offering Him victims, but in sanctifying their spirit. They flee from cities, and apply themselves to the arts of peace. There is not one slave among them; they are all free and work for one another.'

On these occasions (of study) the original interpretation of the sacred books of Moses and the prophets was given, but in the explanation of the texts as well as in initiation there were *three meanings and three stages. For it is found in all places of 'The soul,' as Josephus reported, "descending from the most subtle ether and drawn into the body by a certain natural charm, lives there as in a prison; freed from the bonds of the body as from a long servitude, it flies away with joy.'*

Among the Essenes, the brothers themselves lived in remote places under a community of property and in a state of celibacy, tilling the soil and sometimes educating the children of outsiders. As for the married Essenes, they constituted a sort of Third Order, affiliated with and subject to the other. Silent, gentle and serious, they were seen here and there practising the arts of peace. Weavers, carpenters, vine growers or gardeners, they never were weapons makers or merchants. Spread in little groups throughout Palestine, in Egypt, even as far as Mount Horeb, they were dedicated to most generous hospitality. Thus we shall see Jesus and his disciples travel from city to city, from province to province, always certain of finding shelter. 'The Essenes,' said Josephus, 'were of an exemplary morality; they strove to repress all passion and all emotion of anger; they were always kind, peaceful and of the highest good faith in their relations. Their word had more weight than an oath; they considered the oath superfluous in ordinary life. Rather than violate the least religious precept they bore the most cruel tortures with an admirable strength of soul and with a smile on their lips.'

Joseph's premature death left Mary's son, now a man, entirely free. His brothers could continue their father's trade and maintain the home. His mother allowed him to leave in secret for Engaddi.

He understood the abyss which separated the official Jewish doctrine from the ancient wisdom of the initiates, that is, the spirit of Evil, the spirit of egotism, hatred and negation joined with absolute political power and priestly imposture. He learned that under the seal of its symbolism, Genesis contained a Theogony and a cosmogony as far removed from its literal meaning as the deepest science from the most childish fable. He contemplated the Days of the Elohim, of eternal creation through the emanation of the elements and the formation of the worlds, the origin of souls and their return to God by progressive existences.

'... of bringing mankind together in order to lift them higher, a chosen one becomes identified with Divinity, draws It to him through strength, wisdom and love and in turn, manifests It to men. Then the Divine, through the power and the breath of the Spirit, is completely present in him; the Son of Man becomes the Son of God and His living Word. In other ages and among other peoples there had already been Sons of God, but since Moses none had been raised in Israel. The seers even said that this time he would be called the Son of Woman, of celestial Isis, of the divine Light.

These hidden things which the patriarch of the Essenes unveiled to the young Galilean on the arid shores of the Dead Sea in the solitude of Engaddi, in the Book of Enoch: 'From the beginning, the Son of Man was in the Mysteries. The Most High kept him in His presence, and manifested him to His elect . . . But the kings will be frightened and will bow their faces to earth, and fear will seize them when they shall see the Son of Woman sitting on the throne of his glory. Then the Elect will call all the forces of heaven, all the saints from on high, and the power of God. Then the Cherubim, the Seraphim, the Ophanim, all the angels of Power, all the angels of the Lord, that is, of the Elect and of the other Power, who serve on earth and above the waters, will lift up their voices.'

They met in a grotto carved inside a mountain, a vast room containing an altar and seats of stone. The leader of the Order was there with a few Elders. At times two or three Essene women, initiate prophetesses, were admitted to the mysterious ceremony. Bearing torches and palms, they greeted the new initiate, who was clothed in white linen, as 'Bridegroom and King,' whom they had foretold and whom they now saw for the first time. Then the head of the Order, ordinarily a man of one hundred years (Josephus says that the Essenes lived to a very advanced age), presented the golden chalice to him, the symbol of supreme initiation, which held the wine of the Lord's vineyard, symbol of divine inspiration. Some said that Moses had drunk from it with the Seventy. Others believed that it dated back to Abraham, who received from Melchizedek, this same initiation with the elements of bread and wine.

Now at this time John the Baptist was preaching beside the Jordan. He was not an Essene, but was a prophet of the people, a member of the strong race of Judah. Driven into the desert by a fierce piety, he had led the most ascetic life in prayers, fasts and macerations. Over his bare skin, tanned by the sun, he wore a garment of camel's skin as a sign of the penance he wished to impose upon himself and his people. In line with the Judaic idea he imagined that the Messiah would come soon as an avenger and a judge; John announced to the multitudes the imminent arrival of this Messiah; he added that it was necessary to prepare oneself by repentance of the heart. Borrowing the custom of ablutions from the Essenes, transforming it in his own way, he had conceived of baptism in the Jordan as a visible symbol, an external fulfillment of the inner purification he required.

This new ceremony, this vehement preaching before immense crowds in the desert, which bordered the waters of Jordan between the rugged mountains of Judea and Perea, gripped imaginations, drew multitudes. It recalled the glorious days of the ancient prophets; it gave the people what they did not find in the Temple: the inner appeal, and, after the terrors of repentance, a dim but mighty hope. From all parts of Palestine they came to hear the saint of the desert, who announced the Messiah. Large groups, drawn by his voice, remained camped for weeks so they could hear him each day. They did not want to go away, for they were waiting for the Messiah to appear. Many asked to take up arms under his command, to begin the holy war again.

Herod Antipas and the priests of Jerusalem were becoming troubled by this movement. Besides, the signs of the time were serious. Tiberius, seventy-four years of age, was ending his life surrounded by the debaucheries of Capri; Pontius Pilate re-doubled his violence against the Jews. In Egypt, the priests had announced that the Phoenix was about to be reborn from its own ashes.

Inwardly aware that his prophetic calling was increasing, but still groping his way, Jesus also came to the desert of Jordan, accompanied by a few Essene brothers, who already were following him as a teacher. He wanted to see the Baptist, to hear him and to submit himself to public baptism. He wanted to enter upon his tasks by way of an act of humility and reverence for the prophet who dared lift his voice against the rulers of the day and to awaken the soul of Israel from its sleep.

He saw the rude ascetic, shaggy and hairy with his visionary leonine head, standing in a wooden pulpit under a rustic tabernacle covered with branches and goatskins. Around him, among the sparse bushes of the desert, was an immense crowd, a whole encampment: tax collectors, Herod's soldiers, Samaritans, Levites from Jerusalem, Idumeans with their herds of sheep. Even Arabs had stopped there with their camels, tents and caravans at 'the voice which cried in the wilderness.' And that thundering voice rolled over the multitude: 'Repent, prepare the way of the Lord; clear his paths!' He called the Pharisees and Sadducees 'a generation of vipers.' He added that 'the axe is already at the root of the trees,' and about the Messiah, he said, 'I baptize you only with water, but he will baptize you with fire!'

Then toward sunset, Jesus saw these masses of people pressing toward a cove on the banks of the Jordan, and Herod's mercenaries and brigands bent their rough backs beneath the water which the Baptist poured over them. Jesus went nearer. John did not know Jesus; he had heard nothing of him, but he recognized the Essene by his linen robe. He saw him, lost in the crowd, descend into the water to the waist, humbly bending himself to receive the baptism. When the neophyte stood up again, the fearful eyes of the wild preacher and the gaze of the Galilean met. The man of the desert trembled under this ray of wondrous sweetness, and the words escaped him involuntarily, 'Are you the Messiah?' The mysterious Essene answered nothing, but bowing his thoughtful head and crossing his hands upon his breast, he asked the Baptist for his benediction. John knew that silence was the law of the Essene novices. Solemnly he raised his two hands; then with his companions the Nazarene disappeared among the reeds beside the river.

The Baptist watched him depart with a mixture of doubt, secret joy and profound melancholy. What were his own knowledge and his prophetic hope before the light he had seen in the eyes of the Unknown, a light which seemed to light up all his being? If this young Galilean was the Messiah, he had seen the joy of his days! But his own task was finished, his voice was about to be silent. From that day on he began to preach with a deeper and more emotional fervor on the sad theme, 'It is necessary that he grow and that I diminish.' He began to feel the lassitude and sadness of old lions who are weary with roaring and lie down in silence, awaiting death. . . ."

'Was he the Messiah? The Baptist's question also resounded in Jesus' soul. Since the unfolding of his consciousness, he had found God in himself and the certainty of the kingdom of heaven in the radiant beauty of his visions. Then human suffering had thrust into his heart its terrible cry of anguish. The Essene sages had taught him the secret of religions, the science of the Mysteries; they had shown him the spiritual decay of mankind, its expectation of a Saviour. But how could he find the strength to save mankind from the abyss? – Here the direct call of John the Baptist fell into the silence of his meditation like the lightning of Sinai. – Was he the Messiah?

Jesus could answer this question only by withdrawing into the deepest part of his being. Hence that retreat, that fast of forty days, which Matthew sums up in the form of a symbolic legend. In reality, in Jesus' life The Temptation represents that great crisis, that sovereign vision of Truth which all prophets and all religious initiates must experience before beginning their work.

Above Engaddi where the Essenes cultivated sesame and grapes, a steep path led to a grotto opening in the face of the mountain. It was entered between two Doric columns carved in the rock, similar to those of the retreat of the Apostles in the Valley of Jehosaphat. There one remained suspended over the deep abyss as though in an eagle's nest. At the end of a gorge below, one could see vineyards and human dwellings; in the distance was the Dead Sea, motionless and grey, while further away rose the desolate Mountains of Moab. The Essenes had obtained this retreat for their members who wished to submit themselves to the trial of solitude. Here were found several scrolls of the prophets, strengthening aromatics, dry figs and a little stream of water, the only food of the ascetic in meditation. Here Jesus came.

'The voice of the Lord cried to him, "Rise up, and speak!' It was a question of finding the living word, the faith which moves mountains, the strength which breaks down strongholds.

Jesus began to pray with fervor. Then, an anxiety, an increasing disturbance overcame him. He had the feeling of losing the marvelous felicity which previously had been his, and of sinking into a dark abyss. A black cloud, filled with shadows of all kinds, enveloped him. He distinguished the faces of his brothers, of his Essene teachers, of his mother. The shadows spoke to him, one after the other: 'Fool who desires the impossible! – You do not know what is in store for you! Give it up!' The invincible inner voice answered, 'I must!' Thus he fought for a series of days and nights, sometimes standing, sometimes kneeling, sometimes prostrate on the ground. And deeper became the abyss into which he descended, thicker became the cloud around him. He had the sensation of approaching something terrible and indescribable.

At last he entered the state of clear ecstasy to which he was accustomed, in which the deepest part of the consciousness awakens, enters into communication with the living Spirit of things, projecting the images of the past and future upon the diaphanous fabric of a dream. He closes his eyes; the external world disappears. The seer contemplates Truth by the light which floods his being, making of his intelligence a glowing furnace.

Thunder rolls; the foundations of the mountain tremble. A whirlwind from the depths carries the seer away to the top of the Temple of Jerusalem. Rooftops and minarets shine below him like a forest of gold and silver. Hymns arise from the Holy of Holies. Clouds of incense ascend from all the altars, whirling around Jesus' feet. People in festival robes fill the porticoes; beautiful women sing hymns of ardent devotion for him. Trumpets sound, and a hundred thousand voices cry, 'Glory to the Messiah! – To the King of Israel!' 'You will be that king if you will worship me,' says a voice from below. 'Who are you?' asks Jesus.

Again the wind carries him away through space to the summit of a mountain. At his feet are the kingdoms of earth, spread out in their golden light. 'I am the king of spirits and the prince of earth,' says the voice from below.

I know who you are,' cries Jesus. 'Your forms are innumerable; your name is Satan! Appear in your earthly form!' The form of a crowned monarch appears, sitting upon a cloud. A dim aureole surrounds his imperial head. The dark figure is outlined against a blood-red cloud; his face is pale, his gaze is like steel. He says, 'I am Caesar. Only bow, and I will give you these kingdoms.' Jesus says to him, 'Get behind me tempter! It is written, You shall worship only the Lord your God.' At once the vision fades.

Finding himself alone in the cave of Engaddi, Jesus asks, 'By what sign shall I conquer the powers of the earth?' 'By the sign of the Son of Man,' answers a voice from above. 'Show me this sign,' says Jesus ..."

A shining constellation appeared upon the horizon. It consisted of four stars in the form of a cross. The Galilean recognized the sign of the ancient initiations, familiar to Egypt and preserved by the Essenes. In the dawn of the world, the sons of Japhet had worshipped it as the sign of earthly and heavenly Fire, the sign of Life with all its joys, of Love with all its marvels. Later the Egyptian initiates had seen in it the symbol of the great Mystery, the Trinity dominated by Unity, the image of sacrifice of the Ineffable Being Who is broken in order to reveal Himself in the cosmos. Symbol of life, death and resurrection, it covered innumerable tombs and temples ... The splendid cross grew larger, coming nearer as though drawn by the heart of the seer. The four living stars flamed into suns of power and glory. 'This is the magic sign of Life and Immortality,' said the heavenly voice. 'Men once possessed it, but they lost it. Do you wish to give it back to them?' 'I do,' answered Jesus. 'Then look! This is your destiny!'

Abruptly the four stars were extinguished. Night fell. A subterranean rumbling shook the heights, and from the bottom of the Dead Sea came a dark mountain, surmounted by a black cross. A dying man was nailed upon it. A demon-ridden people swarmed over the mountain, shouting with an infernal mockery, 'If you are the Messiah, save yourself!' The seer opened *his eyes wide, then he fell backward, dripping with a cold sweat. For this crucified man was himself . . . He understood. In order to conquer, it was necessary to become identified with this frightful double, evoked by himself and placed before him like a sinister interrogation. Suspended in uncertainty as in the emptiness of infinite space, Jesus felt the tortures of the crucified one, the insults of men and the deep silence of heaven, all at the same time. 'You can accept or reject it, said the angelic voice.*

Suddenly Jesus saw near him the sick people of the pool of Siloam, and behind them came a whole host of despairing souls, murmuring with lifted hands, 'Without you we are lost! Save us, you who know how to love!' Then the Galilean slowly arose, and opening his arms with fullest love, cried out, 'Give me the cross! – And let the world be saved!'

Immediately Jesus felt a great tearing in all his limbs, and he uttered a terrible cry . . . At the same time, the black mountain crumbled, the cross was swallowed up; a soft light, a divine happiness, flooded the seer, and in the azure heights a triumphant voice was heard saying, 'Satan is no longer master! Death is conquered! Glory to the Son of Man! Glory to the Son of God!'

When Jesus awakened from this vision, nothing around him had changed. But he was no longer the same. A new and radiant consciousness had come forth in the breaking of his earthly being, which he had trodden under his feet and thrown into the abyss. He knew that he had become the Messiah by an irrevocable act of his will.

Shortly afterward he descended to the village of the Essenes. There he learned that John the Baptist had just been seized by Antipas and was imprisoned in the citadel of Makerous. Far from becoming frightened at this event, he saw in it a sign that the time was ripe, that now it was necessary for him to act. Therefore he announced to the Essenes that he was about to preach in Galilee "the Gospel of the Kingdom of Heaven." Such courage had not been seen since the time that Sakya Muni, the last Buddha, moved by tremendous pity, had preached on the banks of the Ganges. The same sublime compassion for humanity moved Jesus. But to this he added an inner light, a power of love, a greatness of faith and a strength of action which were his alone." – Edouard Schure

King David refers to the ministry of the coming King *"a priest forever according to the Order of Melchizedek."* Psalm 110:1-4

The Messiah

The Bible and Qu'ran delineate what is known of the three years of Christ's ministry on earth, and I do not wish to rewrite what is easily found. Christ had a profound impact on the bedrock of worldwide monotheism prepared by Moses. Today, His blessed followers cover the globe with His love. But it was not always so.

The Jews were submerged in the sea of ancestral imitations; they could not comprehend the truer meaning of the prophecies. All the words of the prophets were fulfilled, but because the Jews held tenaciously to hereditary interpretations, they did not understand the inner meanings of the Holy Bible; therefore, they denied Jesus Christ, as the Messiah. The purpose of the prophetic words was not the outward or literal meaning, but the inner symbolical significance. For example, it was announced that the Messiah was to come from an unknown place. This did not refer to the birthplace of the physical body of Jesus. It has reference to the reality of the Christ – that is to say, the Christ reality was to appear from the invisible realm. The divine reality of Christ is holy, and sanctified above place.

His sword was to be a sword of iron. This signified His tongue which should separate the true from the false, and by which great sword of attack He would conquer the kingdoms of hearts. He did not conquer by the physical power of an iron rod; He conquered the East and the West by the sword of His utterance. It is true that many of His followers seemed to think that a sword of steel, was condoned by their Faith.

He was seated upon the throne of David, but His sovereignty was neither a Napoleonic sovereignty nor the vanishing dominion of a Pharaoh. The Christ Kingdom was everlasting, eternal in the heaven of divine Will.

The Sinaitic Law of Moses is the foundation of the reality of Christianity. Christ promulgated it and gave it meaning and higher, spiritual expression." (Abdu'l-Baha, The Promulgation of Universal Peace, p. 199)

"The truth is that Christ fulfilled the Mosaic Law and in every way upheld Moses; but the Jews, blinded by blind imitation of what had come before, and prejudices about what the Messiah would be and do, decided He was the enemy of Moses.

Blessed are the Poor

Abdu'l-Baha also explains:

"You must be thankful to God that you are poor, for His Holiness Jesus Christ has said 'Blessed are the poor'; He never said blessed are the rich. He said too that the kingdom is for the poor and that it is easier for a camel to enter a needle's eye than for a rich man to enter God's kingdom. Therefore you must be thankful to God that although in this world you are indigent, yet the treasures of God are within your reach; and although in the material realms you are poor, yet in the kingdom of God you are precious."

"His Holiness Jesus himself was poor. He did not belong to the rich. He passed His time in the desert travelling among the poor, and lived upon the herbs of the field. He had no place to lay His head; no home. He was exposed in the open to heat, cold and frost; to inclement weather of all kinds, yet He chose this rather than riches. If riches were considered a glory the prophet Moses would have chosen them; Jesus would have been a rich man."

"…Jesus was a poor man. One night when He was out in the fields the rain began to fall. He had no place to go for shelter so He lifted His eyes toward Heaven saying 'O Father! For the birds of the air Thou hast created nests, for the sheep a fold, for the animals dens, for the fishes places of shelter; there is no place where I may lay my head; my bed consists of the cold ground, my lamps at night are the stars and my food is the grass of the field, yet who upon earth is richer than I? For the greatest blessing Thou hast not given to the rich and mighty, but unto me, for Thou hast given me the poor. To me, Thou hast granted this blessing. They are Mine. Therefore am I the richest man on earth."

"Through Him the Word of God conquered and subdued the East and West. His conquest was effected through the breaths of the Holy Spirit, which eliminated all boundaries and shone from all horizons." – (As above, p. 33)

Gospel of Christ

"In His day, according to prophecy, the wolf and the lamb were to drink from the same fountain. This was realized in Christ. The fountain referred to was the Gospel, from which the Water of Life gushes forth. The wolf and lamb are opposed and divergent races symbolized by these animals. Their meeting and association were impossible, but having become believers in Jesus Christ those who were formerly as wolves and lambs became united through the words of the Gospel."

"Consider how harmful is imitation (of mistaken belief). Interpretations handed down from fathers and ancestors, and because the Jews held fast to them, they were deprived; they denied Christ; nay, they even went so far as to crucify Him.

It is evident, then, that we must forsake all such imitations and beliefs so that we may not commit this error. We must investigate reality, lay aside selfish notions and banish hearsay from our minds. The Jews consider Christ the enemy of Moses, whereas, on the contrary, Christ promoted the Word of Moses. He spread the name of Moses throughout the Orient and Occident. He promulgated the teachings of Moses. Had it not been for Christ, you would not have heard the name of Moses; and unless the manifestation of Messiahship had appeared in Christ, we would not have received the Old Testament.

Why did they reject Him when He did appear? They denied Him absolutely, refused to believe in Him. There was no abuse and persecution which they did not heap upon Him. They reviled Him with curses, placed a crown of thorns upon His head, led Him through the streets in scorn and derision and finally crucified Him. Why did they do this? Because they did not investigate the truth or reality of Christ and were not able to recognize Him as the Messiah of God. Had they investigated sincerely for themselves, they would surely have believed in Him, respected Him and bowed before Him in reverence. They would have considered His manifestation the greatest bestowal upon mankind. They would have accepted Him as the very Savior of man; but, alas, they were veiled, they held to imitations of ancestral beliefs and hearsay and did not investigate the truth of Christ. They were submerged in the sea of superstitions and were, therefore, deprived of witnessing that glorious bounty; they were withheld from the fragrances or breaths of the Holy Spirit and suffered in themselves the greatest debasement and degradation.

Reality or truth is one, yet there are many religious beliefs, denominations, creeds and differing opinions in the world today. Why should these differences exist? Because we do not investigate and examine the

Etching by W. Hollar for a fable by Aesop. See page for author [CC BY 4.0 (http://creativecommons.org/licenses/by/4.0)], via Wikimedia Commons

fundamental unity, which is one and unchangeable. If they seek reality itself, they will agree and be united; for reality is indivisible and not multiple. It is evident, therefore, that there is nothing of greater importance to mankind than the investigation of truth." (Abdu'l-Baha, The Promulgation of Universal Peace, p. 62-63)

And when much people were gathered together, and were come to him out of every city, he spake by a parable: A sower went out to sow his seed: and as he sowed, some fell by the way side; and it was trodden down, and the fowls of the air devoured it. (Parable, King James Bible, Luke 8:4-5)

Days of Resurrection

In addition to the usual stories of Jesus Christ contained in the New Testament, the forty days of Jesus' ministry that took place after the Crucifixion is referred to briefly by Luke *"Jesus said and did many more things after the resurrection."*

Jerusalem was a powder keg of exceptional Roman brutality under Pontius Pilate, who had no qualms about killing, whether or not there was a reason. The Disciples wisely feared for their lives. They were terrified of the slow death and torture of crucifixion. Pilate was eventually dismissed from his post because of his unimaginable cruelty –by the Romans— which says a lot!

The Disciples had lost their Beloved Lord and were severely depressed as anyone can imagine. They exuded sadness and darkness. They felt their mission had failed, that hope had fled and they were utterly lost. The events of the next 40 days served to change anxious men into fearless Apostles. There are at least six references to visions of Christ after what is called the Resurrection.

Two days after his death, Jesus Christ appeared to Mary, who had returned to the tomb. She recognized Him immediately. She ran to tell the other Apostles, He was not dead. Two Disciples followed her to the empty tomb. They were frightened and returned to hiding, while Mary stayed.

Mark declared the Sabbath was now over, and Mary Magdalene and Mary wondered how they would remove the stone over the tomb. Upon their arrival, they found the stone was already gone, and they went into the tomb. This shows that, according to Mark, they expected to find a dead Jesus. Instead, they found a young man dressed in a white robe (according to Luke and John there may have been two angels) who told them:

"Don't be alarmed. You are looking for Jesus the Nazarene, who was crucified. He has risen! He is not here. See the place where they laid him. But go, tell his disciples and Peter, He is going ahead of you into Galilee. There you will see him, just as he told you' "(Mark 16:6–7 Matthew 28:9–10 and John 20:14–18.)

Six Sightings:

1. So, in the first of the encounters, Mary Magdalene saw the angels after finding the empty tomb and showed it to two other disciples. She returned to the tomb, talked with the angels, and then Jesus appeared to her, and taught her directly.

Not only did Mary Magdalene attend the crucifixion and later encouraged the disciples. She authored apocryphal (hidden) texts "They have killed but the body; the reality can never die, for it is supreme, eternal, the word of God, the son of God. Why, therefore are ye agitated?"

In Gnostic texts Jesus Christ teaches her about some of the esoteric meanings of "life" and "death" and that each individual must be responsible for their own spiritual development, and not rely on outside institutions.

These themes were not popular with the newly appointed Roman bishops at the Conference of Nicaea, where the goal was a standardized church. So this information which suggested that people could have a direct, personal path to God was not included in the New Testament.

"My hope is that each one of you may become as Mary Magdalen, who confirmed the wavering disciples in their faith – for this woman was superior to all the men of her time and her reality is ever shining from the horizon of Christ" – Attributed to Abdu'l – Baha Divine Philosophy p. 50

2. A little later He appeared to the same two disciples who Mary showed the empty tomb, on the road between Jerusalem and Emmaus. They were taking their broken hearts home and thinking of the life they had known before the impact of Christ in their lives. A stranger asked them what was wrong. They thought this man must have been hiding under a rock if he did not know about the recent horrific events. Christ had changed enough as to be unrecognizable by the men. The three took shelter at an inn, where Jesus rebuked their doubt; and confirmed the concrete enormity of the new Revelation and explained to them why the Messiah had to die.

The three men shared a meal at the Inn. Christ took some bread, blessed it and broke it. As the halves of bread fell to the table, Jesus disappeared. At that same moment the men realized the identity of their wonderful companion. They returned to Jerusalem and ran to the Upper Room to tell the other disciples what they had seen. – Luke 24:13–35.

3. Christ then appeared to the Apostles in the Upper Room where they were hiding and discussing the recent sightings. Jesus appeared at dinner to all the remaining eleven Apostles. He rebuked them for not believing the earlier reports of his resurrection and gave them instructions to go and proclaim His message to all Creation.

Those who believe are saved, but unbelievers will be condemned. He stood among them and commissioned them to evangelize and tell everyone that He was still alive, and He expected each of them to proclaim the nascent Faith without regard to physical limitation or danger.

He even told some of those present that they would suffer and die horribly for their belief. His goal was to dispel the scourge of negativity and fear that had a grip on them. **"Peace be with you."**

4. When Thomas returned to the other Disciples, now called Apostles, he was greeted in the Upper Room with eager stories of the resurrection of their beloved leader. He did not believe them. He wanted proof or evidence, so Jesus then reappeared in the Upper Room and asked Thomas to put his fingers into the wounds on his hands, and place his hand into the wound on His side. Thomas was abashed before Him, and believed that Jesus still lived.

Like Mary, Thomas has a unique perspective since he is also the recipient of directly revealed information, as a confidant of Jesus. **"Understand this and you can be like Me."** In fact the word Gnostic means knowing, a personal understanding of the Word of God. Here the Kingdom of God is not just something that is coming randomly at the end of time; it is inside and outside of the individual. It is living in the presence of God.

Thomas' Gospel shares teachings from Christ, which conclude that **"Whoever can understand the secret meaning of these words will not taste death."**

Words of personal inspiration like these threatened to weaken the control of the church, since really all one had to do was turn to God directly. And that was why they were abolished.

5. The fifth sighting of Christ took place on the shore of the Sea of Galilee, where Jesus hailed the Apostles who were fishing on a boat not far from shore. They had been at it all night with nothing to show for the effort. Christ hollered for them to throw their nets in a certain place which they did and caught 153 fish. Jesus had built a fire on the shore and had bread and fish he was preparing. He invited them over to His fire. Peter recognized Him, and the purpose of this visitation is that the believers had to bring spirituality to their daily lives, wherever they lived. They did not need to live in seclusion to teach the Faith of Christ.

6. The last listed sighting took place on the Mount of Olives where Christ invited the Apostles to join Him. He blessed them and took His leave. They had been through life and death and resurrection together, now he was ascending, yet He had told them He would always be with them and they believed.

Still the Apostles were grieved. John went to the temple and was verbally attacked for being a follower of a loser like Jesus. He went to the desert where he was asked **"Why do you weep? I am the one who is with you always."**

7. There is yet another story in 1 Corinthians 15:6 Where Paul said Christ appeared to more than 500 at one time.

Christ charged His newly promoted Apostles with a specific mission to carry the Message to the whole world. They taught for decades and many died horrible deaths, but it no longer mattered! They were on fire! They did not recant their faith, nothing could shut them up. In Acts 1:8, Jesus told the disciples, hereinafter called Apostles that they were going to bear witness unto Himself. And praise be to God—they did!

"Ye shall receive power, after the Holy Ghost is come upon you, and ye shall be witnesses unto me both in Jerusalem, and in all Judea, and in Samaria and unto the uttermost part of the earth.

Therefore, let all the house of Israel know assuredly, that God hath made that same Jesus, whom ye have crucified, both Lord and Christ! –Peter (Acts 11)

12:31 But rather seek ye the kingdom of God; and all these things shall be added unto you.

12:32 Fear not, little flock; for it is your Father's good pleasure to give you the kingdom.

12:33 Sell that ye have, and give alms; provide yourselves bags which wax not old, a treasure in the heavens that faileth not, where no thief approacheth, neither moth corrupteth.

12:34 For where your treasure is, there will your heart be also." (Luke, King James Bible)

But about a physical resurrection...was it body or Spirit? Reports of ghost sightings can also be fully lifelike apparitions, who can touch and talk. So, it is unlikely that was the only point of the Resurrection.

"Concerning the Resurrection of Christ you quote the twenty-fourth chapter of the Gospel of St. Luke, where the account stresses the reality of the appearance of Jesus to His disciples who, the Gospel states, at first took Him to be a ghost. From a Bahá'í point of view the belief that the Resurrection was the return to life of a body of flesh

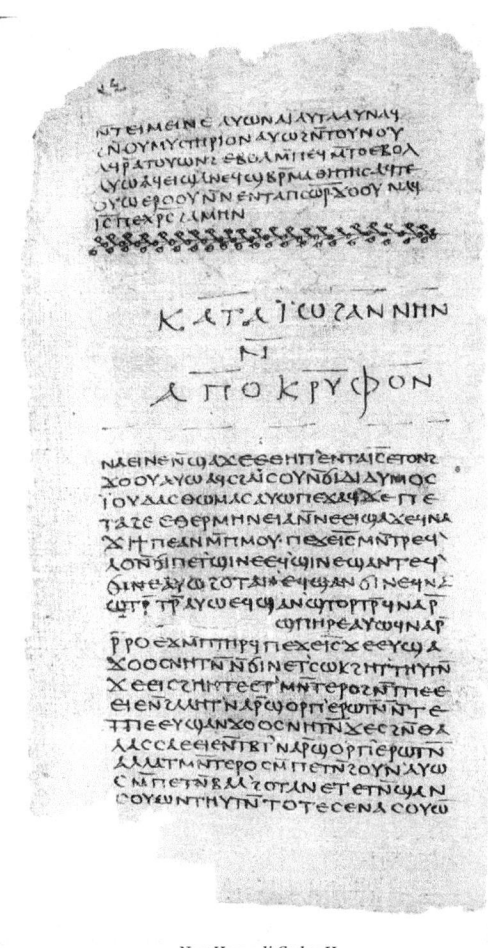

*Nag Hamadi Codex II.
[Public domain], via Wikimedia Commons*

and blood, which later rose from the earth into the sky is not reasonable, nor is it necessary to the essential truth of the disciples' experience, which is that Jesus did not cease to exist when He was crucified (as would have been the belief of many Jews of that period), but that His Spirit, released from the body, ascended to the presence of God and continued to inspire and guide His followers and preside over the destinies of His dispensation." (The Universal House of Justice, 1987 Sept 14, Resurrection of Christ)

A History of the Apocryphal and Gnostic Texts

In 1945, near a small town known as Nag Hamadi two Egyptian farmers came across a huge 6 foot tall jar in the earth they were digging for fertilizer. When the farmers got the courage to open the jar they found 13 leather bound volumes containing 52 books written in Coptic (Egyptian Christian language). They were translations of Greek originals, which were written on papyrus and dated some three hundred years after the death of Christ. These books were hidden because it became dangerous to have any other stories about early Christianity than those agreed upon during the Council of Nicaea. In fact, anyone who had possession of such material might be tortured and put to death.

The original writing of the various Nag Hamadi texts probably took place 30-50 years after the death of Christ, and copies of the originals might have been made in a monasterial library. The texts include some 114 sayings of Christ. About half of these can be found in the four Gospels of the New Testament. There are also Gospels of Mary, Philip and Thomas, among others, who received personal revelations.

The teachings of the Forty days of Resurrection, are advanced level, mystical teachings. They are secretive and personal revelations, writings and dialogues between individuals and Christ. Some include mystical poetry. Some describe how the universe was created, and how we came into existence. For further examination: Robinson, James (1988). The Nag Hammadi Library in English. ISBN 0-06-066934-9. (549 pages)

The Canonical Texts

The life of early Christians became hellish, as it so often does in the first years of a Revelation. Thousands were put to death. Then something remarkable happened in 312 AD.

Constantine, then a Roman general, had a vision of the cross made of swords, and a voice told him he would be victorious in battle, under the sign of the cross. He became

Christian for perhaps questionable reasons, but his mother reportedly took her new faith to heart! The persecutions stopped, at least until after the Councils in Nicaea (in present day Turkey) 13 years later, when outlawed, texts again put believers' lives in danger.

Constantine had a strong agenda: to unite his new empire, and there were many versions of the stories of Christ, which had developed and spread, and probably mutated. The multiplicity became a problem. In fact, Christians had actually killed each other over the versions they favored. Constantine felt the strong need to impose a unity.

So the empire would determine how the story would, or would not unfold. During the Catholic (all embracing) council of Nicaea in 325 AD, the 1800 or so bishops and their entourages, set about unifying the Christian doctrines. This format appealed to Constantine because it lent structure; which as a soldier, he appreciated. Here was a hierarchy of Bishops, priests and deacons resembling that of the Roman army with which he was very familiar.

They narrowed dozens of texts down to a canon of selected texts (canon is a Greek word for list) by using four criteria: 1) The text had to be ancient – back to the days of Jesus or His Apostles. 2) It had to be written by a recognized Apostle or a companion of the Apostles. 3) It had to be a widely recognized story, not a local legend; and 4) It could not offer some kind of heretical or "false" teaching and had to toe the line theologically, to become one of the 27 canonical texts. All other texts were to be destroyed under the strictly enforced penalty of death. They became apocryphal (hidden) and are now known as the Gnostic texts.

Because the bishops at the Council if Nicaea didn't want to deal with the esoteric and divergent thinking of the 40 days of the resurrection period, and any resulting Apocryphal texts, they came up with an **official resurrection story, a Creed**:

"For our sake He was crucified under Pontius Pilate; died and was buried, and on the third day He rose again, according to the scriptures and He ascended into heaven."

Here, there is no mention of the cherished forty day resurrection; critical to belief in Christ, by many Christians. Other Christians don't even know about it and yet they still believe. Because of this Nicene Creed many Christians do not know anything about the forty days before Jesus Christ ascended to heaven.

Notably, the decision to begin the concept of a trinity also began there. Athanasius, the Trinitarian from Alexandria answered the question put forth: Is Jesus absolutely equal to the Father: all powerful? "Yes Jesus is absolutely equal to the Father. He has always existed beside the Father. He is of the very same essence as the Father. He is absolute God and must be worshipped as God. Only a very small minority of Western Bishops agreed.

Arius expressed the view of the vast majority of bishops; "Jesus is not God, although he could be called divine. He was made by God so there was a time when he did not exist! He must not be worshipped as the one true God. Somehow, even though the Trinity was backed by only a few, it became canonical law.

And that very day dualism was achieved by the early Christian church!

The Council unified the Christians of the Roman Empire with one official story of Jesus' life, death, burial, resurrection and ascension. Unofficial versions were chased down and weeded out on penalty of death. Biblical Gospels don't include the mysterious and controversial, and apparently they no longer included the worship of God, alone.

None of the dealings of men, however, can detract from the precious revelation of Jesus, the Christ. Or the powerful effect His words have had on unifying people all over the earth.

"Consider and call thou to mind the days whereon the Spirit of God appeared, and Herod gave judgement against Him. God, however, aided Him with the hosts of the unseen, and protected Him with truth, and sent Him down unto another land, according to His promise. He, verily, ordaineth what He pleaseth. Thy Lord truly preserveth whom He willeth, be he in the midst of the seas, or in the maw of the serpent, or beneath the sword of the oppressor."
(Baha'u'llah, The Summons of the Lord of Hosts, p. 83)

Christianity and Islam

Today many blame Mohammad and Islam for the acts of terrorists and madmen. But is that how a faith should be judged? If so, how about the Crusades? How about this image of their arrival in Jerusalem. After they had slaughtered every living man, woman and child; they went to the Church of the Holy Sepulcher, covered in gore, to give thanks to God for delivering Jerusalem to them.

Should we blame Christ for this? Oh How Christ's, and Mohammad's hearts must break!

Mohammad was never the enemy of Christians or Jews. In fact, He was a very strong voice for their protection. His holy Book is filled with praises for Moses, Christ and Mary, and He strongly admonished any who would bring harm to their followers.

"Among the great religious systems of the world is Islam. About three hundred million people acknowledge it. For more than a thousand years there has been enmity and strife between Muslims and Christians, owing to misunderstanding and spiritual blindness. If prejudices and imitations were abandoned, there would be no enmity whatever between them, and these hundreds of millions of antagonistic religionists would adorn the world of humanity by their unity.

All Islam considers the Qur'án to be the Word of God. In this sacred Book there are explicit texts, stating that Christ was the Word of God that He was the Spirit of God, that Jesus Christ came into this world through the quickening breaths of the Holy Spirit and that Mary, His mother, was holy and sanctified. In the Qur'an a whole chapter is devoted to the story of Jesus. It records that in the time of His youth He worshipped God in the temple at Jerusalem, that manna descended from heaven for His sustenance and that He uttered words immediately after His birth. In brief, in the Qur'an there is eulogy and commendation of Christ such as you do not find in the Gospel.

The Gospel does not record that the child Jesus spoke at birth or that God caused sustenance to descend from heaven for Him, but in the Qur'an it is repeatedly stated that God sent down manna day by day as food for Him.

Furthermore, it is significant and convincing that when Muhammad proclaimed His work and mission, His first objection to His own followers was, 'Why have you not believed in Jesus Christ? Why have you not accepted the Gospel? Why have you not believed in Moses? Why have you not followed the precepts of the Old Testament? Why have you not understood the prophets of Israel? Why have you not believed in the Disciples of Christ? The first duty incumbent upon ye, O Arabians, is to accept and believe in these. You must consider Moses as a Prophet. You must accept Jesus Christ as the Word of God. You must know the Old and the New Testaments as the Word of God. You must believe in Jesus Christ as the product of the Holy Spirit.'

His people answered, 'O Muhammad! We will become believers, although our fathers and ancestors were not believers, and we are proud of them. Tell us what is going to become of them?' Muhammad replied, 'I declare unto you that they occupy the lowest stratum of hell because they did not believe in Moses and Christ and because they did not accept the Bible; and although they are my own ancestors, yet they are in despair in hell.' This is an explicit text of the Qur'an; it is not a story or tradition but from the Qur'an itself, which is in the hands of the people.

Therefore, it is evident that ignorance and misunderstanding have caused so much warfare and strife between Christians and Muslims. If both should investigate the underlying truth of their religious beliefs, the outcome would be unity and agreement; strife and bitterness would pass away forever and the world of humanity find peace and composure. Consider that there are two hundred and fifty million Christians and three hundred million Muslims. How much blood has flowed in their wars; how many nations have been destroyed; how many children have been made fatherless; how many fathers and mothers have mourned the loss of children and dear ones! All this has been due to prejudice, misunderstanding and imitations of ancestral beliefs without investigation of reality. If the Holy Books were rightly understood, none of this discord and distress would have existed, but love and fellowship would have prevailed instead. This is true with all the other religions as well. The conditions I have named will apply equally to all. The essential purpose of the religion of God is to establish unity among mankind. The divine Manifestations were Founders of the means of fellowship and love. They did not come to create discord, strife and hatred in the world. The religion of God is the cause of love, but if it is made to be the source of enmity and bloodshed, surely its absence is preferable to its existence; for then it becomes satanic, detrimental and an obstacle to the human world." (Abdu'l-Baha, The Promulgation of Universal Peace, Pp. 201-202)

MOHAMMED THE SEAL OF THE PROPHETS

The Adamic Cycle began with Adam and ended with Mohammad Who is the "Seal of the Prophets." For that age was completed on May 23, 1844. But, who was Mohammad? He is often maligned by ignorant masses. If only the world knew and embraced this gentle, yet potent Manifestation of God's Word—and gave Him fair hearing. The planet would advance immediately!

You may recognize some of the trials that assailed this One known as "The Apostle of God," are very similar to earlier Prophets, like Noah, Hud and Salih, as taught in His Book the Qu'ran. It would seem that the people of Arabia have turned a deaf ear more than once. Even in the face of such contentiousness, Mohammad brought humankind to the brink of nationalism, as a state of unity.

Note: This section, as well as the one to follow, with regard to the Baha'i Faith, will consist to a large degree of quotes, since they deal with historic and recent time, news of which circled the globe.

Early Life of the Apostle of God

"Mankind has always surrounded the birth of its Saviors with beautiful stories. We know of the shepherds and angels on the night of the Nativity. The Zoroastrians say that when Zoroaster was born even the trees and rivers rejoiced, and a divine light shone around the house. On the night Muhammad was born His mother (Aminih) saw light, streaming from Him, reaching up to the stars; the idols of the Ka'bih toppled over and lay face downward; across the world, in all the fire temples of the Magians, the fire died on the altars. The year was 570." (Tabari Vol. 2).

Muhammad was either born before his father died ('Abdu'llah, 'Servant of God'); or soon after. A shepherd's wife cared for Him in the mountains until He was five; this was the custom. He tended sheep. At six, He lost His mother, and then His grandfather took Him in (much like Krishna). He used to sit by the old chieftain on a rug spread out in the shade of the Ka'bih. At eight, He lost His grandfather; then He was lucky enough to have an uncle, who cared for Him.

Muhammad was a poor young man and he practiced several trades to make ends meet. He tended herds, kept a little shop, went on caravan expeditions and to the great fairs. He became known for the purity of His life and they called Him al-Amin – the 'Trusted One.'

There was a prominent and beautiful woman in Mecca, who had been twice widowed and was now about forty. She was a merchant, and Muhammad, as her agent, successfully conducted one of her caravans to Syria. (They caught each other's eyes.)

When it came to love and romance, she was the one for Mohammad, who was now in his twenties. Khadijih had refused the leaders of Mecca, but fell in love with her poor kinsman, who was sixteen years her junior.

Their marriage is one of the true love stories in history; until her death twenty-three years later, Muhammad married no other, although polygamy was almost universally (practiced). We read that there was a great wedding featuring some leather bottles of precious grape wine in the inner court under the torches, the bride's slave girls danced and sang to the tambourines; a camel was slaughtered on the door-step and its flesh divided among the poor... Muhammad and Khadijih had several children; the sons all died; then she became the mother of Fatimah, the holiest woman in Islam.

Published by Guillaume Rouillé (1518?-1589) ("Promptuarii Iconum Insigniorum") [Public domain], via Wikimedia Commons

Muhammad was now a man of considerable means, but He did not enter public life. The times were lawless, and except for serving the poor He kept to Himself. He retired often to a high, cone-shaped mountain north of Mecca, and stayed in a cave there. From Mt. Hira He could look out east and south on other mountains, and elsewhere on bare, blackened hills, grey hills, and white sandy valleys. It was on this mountain that He first saw the Archangel Gabriel veiled in light, on a throne of fire, and because this vision He was greatly troubled, in deep anguish, He went to Khadijih and she comforted Him. Ever since, Mt. Hira has been called Jabal-i-Nur, the Mountain of Light.

Later, Muhammad said of His wife Khadijih, 'When I was poor, she enriched me; when all the world abandoned me, she comforted me; when they treated me as a liar, she believed in me.' An account relates that in the early stage of the Revelation, when Muhammad was still in anguish, He asked Khadijih to wrap Him in His robe, as a kind of protection, whereupon Gabriel appeared before Him and said, 'O Thou, enwrapped in thy mantle! Arise and warn, and glorify Thy Lord!' " Noted in the Surih, The Enwrapped (Qur'án 74:1-3).

(Marzieh Gail, Six Lessons on Islam, Pp. 3 – 6)

Other sources: The Life of Mohammad from Original Sources Muir, Elibron Classic Series, 2005; Adamant Media Corporation p 38

A Dark Environment

The stage for the vast revelation of Mohammad is set by this quote of Gary L Matthews in his pamphlet "*Muhammad: Defender of Christians,*" Stonehaven Press, 2001.

"The Arabs of the early seventh century were nomadic tribesmen, tending meager flocks and herds in the semi-desert regions of the Arabian Peninsula. Steeped in idolatry, they were prone to violence, cruelty, feuding, drinking, gambling and prostitution. Women, typically living as virtual slaves in poorly treated harems of enormous size, were held in such contempt that unwanted infant girls sometimes were buried alive.

Mecca (like 'Ad and Thamud) was (an Arabian) crossroads between the Orient and the Mediterranean world. The Byzantines found indispensable the Arab caravans of jewels, spices from India, silk from China, skins, metals, perfumes, gums, and dates. In addition to commerce and herding, the Arabs' 'national industry' was the seizing of booty. Muhammad strictly regulated this, the bulk going to charity and army upkeep." (Dermenhagem, Emile "Muhammad and the Islamic Tradition" Pp. 4-25, 175; 1983)

After their journeys, the Arabs gambled and drank and speculated. There were constant tribal wars, brawls and blood-feuds. The poets enjoyed prominence as the journalists and historians of the time, and held annual poetry competitions; famed among the Arabs were the Seven Golden Odes, poems written in letters of gold on Egyptian silk. Skill at arms and horsemanship were also valued; and hospitality to the point of profligacy; an Arab poet comments, 'Wealth cometh in the morning, and ere the evening it hath departed.'

In Mecca, also called Becca, the leaders lived in the central, flat part of the city, around the Ka'bih the commoners lived surrounding this area, in the sloping streets; foreigners, slaves, and the rabble lived on the outskirts. Beyond, in the desert, were the Bedouin, tent-dwellers and nomads. The Bedouin were scornful of both tillers of the soil and merchants.

The most important thing in Mecca was the Ka'bih, or cube: the oblong stone House, which was a center of pilgrimage for all Arabia. The Arabs were members of innumerable isolated clans, worshipping different idols, but all would come and gather at the Ka'bih. It is a structure 55 feet long, 45 wide and something over 55 high. It has a covering of cloth, which was renewed annually, even in Muhammad's day.

Abraham traditionally built the Ka'bih, its site being granted to Him and Ishmael for a place of worship that would be monotheistic and universal (Qur'an 22:27). The Qur'an says of it: "The first temple that was founded for mankind was that in Becca, Blessed... In it are evident signs, even the standing-place of Abraham: and he who entereth it is safe. And the pilgrimage to the temple is a service due to God from those who are able to journey thither." (Qur'an 3:90-91). The Black Stone (Hajaru'l-Aswad) is set in the south-east corner of the Ka'bih wall; it is semi-circular, about six inches in height and eight wide, and reddish-black in color.

Four months of the year were months of general amnesty and truce, and it was then that pilgrims made their journeys to Mecca and to the merchandise fairs."

In and around the Ka'bih in the time before Muhammad – the Days of Ignorance (Jahiliyya) – were 360 idols, marked the days of the year. Their chief was Hobal, a bearded man made of red agate, with one hand of gold, and dressed in multi-colored clothing. People consulted him about marriage, where to dig a well, and other problems, using divining arrows. We read of a poet who wished to avenge the murder of his father, consulting one of the idols with three divining arrows symbolizing "Proceed," "Abandon," "Delay." Three times he drew "Abandon." He became furious, broke the arrows and threw them at the idol, crying 'Had it been thy father who was murdered, thou wouldst not have forbidden me to avenge him." (Matthews, 2001)

Statues of Hobal, also called Hubal, were sights of arrow pointing divination. The way the cast arrows fell in front of the statue dictated to answers to questions posed by the controlling Quraysh tribe, and others.

Even then Arabs had acknowledged a vague supreme Deity, called Allah; but they joined partners with Him. Muhammad taught "La ilaha illa'llah" – "There is no ilah (God) but Allah" as had Abraham.

Matthews continues, *"Islam revolutionized these conditions. Virtually overnight, idolatry was replaced by strict monotheism; drinking, gambling, infanticide and prostitution were abolished; polygamy was greatly curtailed and the status of women immensely elevated; tribal warfare gave way to spiritual brotherhood.*

As a result the Arabs, within a mere one hundred years became masters of an empire vaster than that of Rome at its peak. As Western Europe sank into the Dark Ages, Islam adorned its cities with paved and lighted streets, built flourishing universities and libraries, introduced algebra, Arabic numerals, table etiquette and soap, and many more useful innovations. During its centuries in Spain, Islam indirectly triggered Europe's Renaissance."

The Friend

"How shall we know him?' asked Ananda (Buddha's disciple). The Buddha replied, 'He will be known as Maitreya which means kindness or friendliness.' ..."

Christ also refers to the coming of the Friend (Then the Spirit of Truth). Mohammad is known as the "Friend of God."

Since the days when Moses sought to build a single Universal Faith for Mankind, the process had advanced during the turbulent time of Jesus the Christ, and now it most assuredly rushed forward in the revelation of Mohammad.

The Faith of God was once again purged of its corrosion and filth. And Mohammed changed the world on a massive scale.

This gentle Being was born to earth 1442 years ago. Even though he received no formal education, He penned one of the greatest Books of all time; the Qu'ran. For those who have not read the Qu'ran and expect that it might be full of frightful and violent references, everybody just take a big sigh of relief; it is not!

Mohammad retells the tales of God's unfolding Faith and His role of as the Seal of the Prophets, Who ends the Adamic Cycle. There are many adoring references to Christ, and to the station of His beloved mother Mary, and Mary Magdalene. He recounts the stories of the Prophets of old and how they were treated by the people to which they appeared. Many such references have been used in this paper.

There is no "kill the infidels" here! Instead we find The Oath of Muhammad to the Followers of the Nazarene. By Anton F. Haddad, 1902; Published by Bahá'í Board of Counsel, N.Y.

This call for the protection of Christians and Jews, was written by 'Ali, Mohammad's son-in-law, and signed by twenty-two leading companions of the Prophet. It was issued to the monks of St. Catherine at Mt. Sinai. (For an Arabic version, see Sunnajatu't-Tarab by Naufal Effendi Naufal.)

"This letter is directed to the embracers of Islam...as a Covenant to the followers of the Nazarene....who(ever) disobeys that which is therein will be regarded as one who has corrupted His Testament, rejected His Authority, despised His Religion, and made himself deserving of His Curse... Whenever monks, devotees and pilgrims gather together...Verily we are back of them and shall protect them, and their properties..." Exempted from all but a voluntary tax *"they must not be offended, or disturbed, or coerced or compelled."*

"Their judges and monks are to be free, no churches are to be plundered, no poll taxes are to be imposed on those whose occupation is worship (judges, monks) "Verily I shall keep their compact in the East or the West, in the North or the South, for they are under My protection and the testament of My safety, against all things which they ab-

hor." The wealthy and able Christians were to pay the about 12 dirhams a year in poll tax, but none were to be obliged to carry arms, "for the Muslims have to fight for them."

"Do not dispute or argue with them. No Christian woman is to marry a Muslim without her consent; she is not to be prevented from going to her church for prayer..." The Muslims must protect them and defend them against others. It is positively incumbent upon every one of the Muslim nations not to contradict or disobey this oath until the Day of Resurrection...."

From Ocean (Islamic Miscellaneous "The Oath of Mohammad to the Followers of the Nazarene," Gail Six Lessons on Islam, p. 25)

It is important to remember that the Revelation of Mohammad was meant for the whole world.

Anticipation of the Prophet

A pious Persian man named Salman had, as a boy tended the sacred Zoroastrian fire in his village, but left when he was gripped by a burning desire to seek a new Prophet. He became the student of four different teachers, all of whom had now passed, but the fourth said that the coming of the Prophet was indeed imminent. Below is that story of anticipation...

Bahá'u'lláh tells us in The Kitab-i-Íqán: **...when the hour draweth nigh on which the Day-star of the heaven of justice shall be made manifest, and the Ark of divine guidance shall sail upon the sea of glory, a star will appear in the heaven, heralding unto its people the advent of that most great light. In like manner, in the invisible heaven a star shall be made manifest who, unto the peoples of the earth, shall act as a harbinger of that true and exalted Morn."**

..."Likewise, ere the beauty of Muhammad was unveiled, the signs of the visible heaven were made manifest. As to the signs of the invisible heaven, there appeared four men who successively announced unto the people the joyful tidings of the rise of that divine Luminary. Ruz-bih, later named Salman, was honoured by being in their service. As the end (death) of one of these approached, he would send Ruz-bih unto the other, until the fourth who, feeling his death to be nigh, addressed Ruz-bih saying: 'O Ruz-bih! When thou hast taken up my body and buried it, go to Hijaz for there the Day-star of Muhammad will arise. Happy art thou, for thou shalt behold His face!' " (Baha'u'llah, The Kitab-i-Iqan, Pp. 62 – 65)

Mohammad's Mission

"The Faithful Spirit taught Him to pray, perform ablutions, stand and kneel in worship. One day as He and Khadijih were praying together young 'Ali (Muhammad's cousin, as well as His son-in-law) entered the room. He saw them bowing down before empty space. He said, "What are you doing? Before whom are you bowing down?" Muhammad said, "Before God, Whose Prophet I am." 'Ali accepted the Faith, and in the future he was called "Him whose face was never sullied," because he was so young.

"When three years had passed, Muhammad was commanded to preach in public, and withdraw from the idolaters. (Qur'an 15:94). He invited His kinsmen, who were Meccan leaders, and over a meal of a sheep cooked in milk, He freely told them of His station. "Never before has an Arab bestowed on his people what I now bring you . . . Who will act as my brother and helper? " There was icy silence. Then young 'Ali cried out, "I will help you, Prophet of God!" And they all laughed, and the meeting broke up."

Emile Dermenghem, *Muhammad and the Islamic Tradition*; Overlook Press 1983, Pp 44, 73-74).

Muhammad preached, and the Meccans scoffed. They didn't believe he could write the spiritual scriptures known as Surahs, since He was never educated and had not learned how to write. So they called Him a liar. They asked Him to perform miracles: turn the hills to gold, make a book fall from heaven, show them Gabriel, bring a well of pure water, or prophesy the approaching price of goods. They spoke much as the materialists of our own day.

They said, "There is only this present life: we die and we live, and naught but time destroyeth us." (Qur'an 45:23); (Marzieh Gail, Six Lessons on Islam, Pp. 3 – 6)

A Reckoning

Besides insisting that there was only one God, and telling people to follow righteousness as they would be called to account in the next world, Muhammad spoke to them repeatedly about the coming of "The Hour" and the "Meeting with God." Once He held up two fingers and said that He and The Hour were as close as the two fingers. The Qur'an states: *"Aye, they have treated the coming of 'the Hour' as a lie. But a flaming fire have we got ready for those who treat the coming of the Hour as a lie." (25:12). It was the Judgement day, a "Day that shall abase! Day that shall exalt!" Sometimes He called it "The Blow" or "The Striking": this chapter begins: In the surih of The Daybreak, He told them: "and thy Lord shall come, and the angels rank by rank . . ." (Surih 89).*

In later life, as Muhammad was entering the mosque, a disciple said, "Ah, Thou for Whom I would sacrifice father and mother, white hairs are hastening upon Thee!" And the Prophet raised up His beard with His hand and gazed at it; and the disciple's eyes filled with tears. "Yes," said Muhammad, "(the Surih of) Hud and its sisters have hastened my white hairs." They asked what He meant by its "sisters," and He replied" 'The Inevitable,' and 'The Blow.'" (Rodwell, Qur'án, 225-226).

Mohammad taught us about the "Great Disappointments" because The Holy Spirit with Him, had also been with those Blessed Prophets. The possibility of a recurrence of the "Blow" is always imminent, as the people of Moses found when He descend with the Pentateuch and found them reveling in debauchery and indecency; and a terrible storm came from the frightening vale of Horeb, which threatened all with destruction and destroyed many, for joining gods with God in the very site of the Tabernacle.

Like Moses, He bellowed to the disbelievers around Him, "Do ye indeed disbelieve in Him . . . do ye assign Him peers? The Lord of the worlds is He!"

"Then the unbelievers appealed to Muhammad's uncle and protector, Abu-Talib who was also, the head of His clan. Abu-Talib then, begged The Friend of God to desist from teaching, as He was bringing ruin on Himself and His family.

Muhammad answered, "Were the sun to come down on my right hand and the moon on my left, and the choice were offered me of abandoning my mission until God himself should reveal it, or perishing in the achievement of it, I would not abandon it."

(Marzieh Gail, *Six Lessons on Islam*, Pp. 3 – 6); (Ameer Ali Syed, *The Spirit of Islam*, Kessinger Press 1952 13-14).

The Quraysh, was a powerful Arab tribe to which Mohammad's family belonged. They held religious control over Mecca and were in charge of the Ka'bih. They distributed water and food to the pilgrims, took charge of the council hall, and raised the banner in war. "Muhammad's grandfather 'Abdu'l-Muttallib, was the foremost chief of Mecca. He and Abu-Talib, the uncle who was next in line to lead, told their Prophet-kinsman, that by tearing down the Ka'bih gods Muhammad was – -in their view – destroying His own family.

"For three years (617-619 A.D.) they blockaded Him and His kinsmen in a remote (mountainous) quarter of the town and forbade the other towns-people to have any dealings with them whatever. Then Khadijih died (December 619 A.D.) and five weeks later, Muhammad's uncle and protector (also died).

... His disciples had hungered and suffered, (until) the ban was lifted. Then the black days came, when the Prophet lost the two whom He loved dearest, His protector and chief defender, and His wife.

'When I was poor she enriched Me. When all the world abandoned Me, she comforted Me.' They had lived together over a score of years, and contrary to the way of His times He had married no other.

He spoke with the tribes, who came into Mecca for trade and to circle around the Ka'bih. He then went to another city – Ta'if, a beautiful place about seventy miles distant, where fruit trees grew – but the people stoned Him away. Shouting, 'If God had wanted to send a Prophet, could He not have chosen a better one than Thee?'"

Still the Noble Muhammad taught, and none listened, and He put His agony into the words of the Prophet Noah: 'My cry only maketh them flee me the more.'

"You would say this was the end of the story of Muhammad: He and a tiny group, shut away in the sand, alone on the planet, encircled by men so wild, they buried children alive as a point of honor, who killed casually, and who – because His teachings meant the destruction of the national religion and the loss of their own wealth and power – had for thirteen long years been waiting to shed His blood. An enemy of His has written: 'We search in vain through the pages of profane history for a parallel to the struggle in which for thirteen years the Prophet of Arabia, in face of discouragement and threats, rejection and persecution, retained thus his faith unwavering, preached repentance . . . he met insults, menace, and danger with a lofty and patient trust in the future.' " (Marzieh Gail, Six Lessons on Islam, Pp. 3 – 6)

Bahá'u'lláh says of Mohammad, **"I recognize, O Thou Who art my heart's desire, that were fire to be touched by water it would instantly be extinguished, whereas the Fire Thou didst kindle can never go out, though all the seas of the earth be poured upon it."** (Prayers and Meditations, 150).

Night Journey

When Mohammad returned to Mecca, He had the vision of the Night Journey (Mi'raj, "Ascent"), when He rose in spirit through the seven heavens to the throne of God. Surih 17 of the Qur'an is called the Night Journey; in the Íqán Bahá'u'lláh refers to Muhammad as the "Lord of the Mi'raj" and says that the mirror of the heart must be purified to understand its mystery. (H.M. Balyuzi, Baha'u'llah – The King of Glory, Pp. 187-280)

Elsewhere, Mr. Balyuzi goes into greater detail:

"But later in vision He journeyed by night to where the Lote-Tree flowers beside God's invisible throne; and He found thousands of choirs of angels, bowed down and motionless, in utter quiet, and then He felt Himself in the light of His Lord. He beheld God with His soul's eyes, and He saw what the tongue cannot express."

This verse is the basis for the account of the Prophet's 'Night Journey' from Mecca to Jerusalem, and the 'Ascent' from Jerusalem to Heaven. Sir William Muir relates the full story of the Mi'raj in his book, The Life of Mahomet, 1861. The world of Islam has accepted the literal fact of this Night Journey, just as Christendom has accepted the literal fact of the Resurrection and the Ascension of Christ. (H.M. Balyuzi, Muhammad and the Course of Islam, p. 41)

The Road to Ultimate Victory

Still, the ignorant and defiant Quraysh Tribe stopped Mohammad from praying in the Ka'bih. "They pursued Him, covered Him and His precious disciples with filth when they were praying, they incited children and the rabble to follow and mock them, a woman strewed thorns where He would walk."

Bahá'u'lláh says: "How abundant the thorns and briars which they have strewn over His path! ... Such sore accusations they brought against Him that in recounting them God forbiddeth the ink to flow ...or the page to bear them ... For this reason did Muhammad cry out: 'No Prophet of God hath suffered such harm as I have suffered.'" Baha'u'llah (Íqán, 108-109).

"To kill a man as influential as Muhammad would have meant a civil war, and so the Meccans tortured His poor disciples instead. Balal, the Ethiopian, they exposed, day after day, to the desert sun, stretched out with a rock on his breast. They told him he must renounce Muhammad or die, and he could only whisper, 'There is only one God, only one. He lived to become the first muezzin (one who calls the people to prayer).

The Christians of the period used the clapper to call to prayer, the Jews, trumpets, the Zoroastrians, bonfires," says Dermenghem, on page 267.

Bahá'u'lláh says of him, **"Consider how Balal, the Ethiopian, unlettered though he was, ascended into the heaven of faith and certitude . . ."** (Gleanings, 83).

And Muhammad sorrowed over the wrong that was done His disciples, and He cried out: 'I fly for refuge unto the Lord of the Daybreak, that He may deliver Me from the mischief of those things which He hath created... I fly for refuge unto the Lord of men, the King of men, the God of men...'"

By Bahá'u'lláh, *Gleanings from the Writings of Bahá'u'lláh*, translated by Shoghi Effendi, (Bahá'í Publishing Trust, Wilmette, rev. ed. 1952), no. xxxv]

From Marzieh Gail (referenced below): **"And they reviled Him, saying, 'Know this, O Muhammad, we shall never cease to stop Thee from preaching till either Thou or we shall perish.'**

So Mohammad "sent His followers into Ethiopia, to the pious Christian king. The Negus questioned them, and bade them speak, and they answered: 'O King, we adored idols, we lived in unchastity, we ate dead bodies, we spoke abominations ... when God raised up among us a Man ... and He called us to the unity of God, to fly vices and to shun evil.'

And the Negus traced a line on the ground with his stick, and he said: 'Truly, between your faith and ours, there is not more than this little stroke.'"

"Then the Meccans gathered to plot against Muhammad: 'Would you say He is a sorcerer?' 'No, He hath not the emphatic tone, the jerky language.' 'A madman then?' 'He hath not the bearing.' 'A poet inspired by a jinn?' 'He doth not speak in classic verse.' 'A magician?' 'He doth not perform wonders.' And since great converts had now been made, they bargained with the Prophet, offering gold and honours in exchange for silence, saying, 'We shall make Thee our chieftain and our king.' He answered them, 'I am only a man like you. It is revealed to Me that your God is one God: go straight, then to Him, and implore His pardon... Do ye indeed disbelieve in Him?... Do ye assign Him peers? The Lord of the worlds is He!'" (Marzieh Gail, Six Lessons on Islam, p. 7)

Momentum at Last

"A full decade had passed since the day Muhammad received His call in the wilderness of the hills overlooking the House of Ka'bah. Still the idols stood around the Ka'bah, and Muhammad was tolerated in His native town only by the fiat of an idolatrous chieftain, unrelated to His own clan. At the end of that decade, in the summer of A.D. 620, an event occurred, at first apparently insignificant, which was to open the way to the total triumph of Muhammad's ministry." That is... the first seven converts from Yathrib (Medina).
(H.M. Balyuzi, Muhammad and the Course of Islam, p. 41-42)

"Now at last the men of Yathrib asked of Him to come and rule among them, so that He sent His disciples ahead, out of Mecca. And the Meccans gathered around His house in the dark to kill Him, but when the dawn showed white, they saw that He had gone. The Meccans united to murder Muhammad. Members of all the clans came to attack Him together, so the blood-guilt would not rest on any one of them. They waited outside His house, watching as He lay in His cloak on the bed, but when the dawn came, they saw it was not Muhammad there but 'Ali.

And Yathrib became Medina, which means 'The City of the Prophet.' "Muhammad entered in triumph; a shaykh put his turban on the end of a lance for a banner, and a parasol of palm branches was held over the Prophet's head, while the Helpers (Ansar), the Medina believers, surrounded Him, brandishing swords and spears. He dismounted on the outskirts, and turned toward the Point of Adoration, Jerusalem (later Muhammad changed the Qiblih to Mecca. He prayed, with all the multitude; then, the accounts say, He let His camel go free into the town, and where it knelt, a mosque was later erected. As He entered, He greeted all the people, even the children...

So the Meccans were cheated of their prey. The despised outcast, the one they had called a crazed poet, a madman, a liar, was now the Head of a State. And now all Arabia rose against Medina; the Meccans rallied the tribes, including a "fifth column" within Medina itself. The battle was on, between idolatry and true worship, between Hobal (the chief idol) and the Omnipotent Lord, between freedom and death." (Marzieh Gail, Six Lessons on Islam, p. 9)

"Muhammad never first withdrew His hand out of another man's palm, nor turned away before the other had turned. He visited the sick, He followed any bier He met, He accepted the invitation of a slave to dinner. His food was dates and water, or barley bread; the people of His house 'did not eat their fill of barley bread, two days successively, as long as He lived.' He mended His own clothing and sandals, and milked the goats, and wiped sweat from His horse with His sleeve. He gave alms when He had anything to give. Once a woman brought Him a cloak, which He needed sorely, but they came and asked for it to make a shroud, and He gave it up, 'for He could refuse nothing.' He loved perfumes, and dyed His fingernails with henna, and was immaculate. Men said He was more modest than a virgin behind her curtain. Those who came near to Him loved Him. His countenance shone 'with a majestic radiance at the same time impressive and gentle.' A follower said of Him: 'I never saw anything more beautiful than Lord Muhammad; you might say the sun was moving in His face." (Marzieh Gail, Dawn Over Mount Hira, and Other Essays Oxford; George Ronald 1976 p. 5)

The Prophet of God now had ten more years to live. They were years of intense activity . . . At the Battle of Badr, the Meccans were put to flight. They rose again, 3,000 strong, and attacked Muhammad with His thousand men at the hill of Uhud, three miles from Medina. Muhammad did not love war, but He had no choice. He was so gentle and mild that His enemies called Him womanish. When He fell at Uhud, a disciple asked Him to curse the enemy; He answered, "I have not been sent as a curse to mankind, but as an inviter to good and as a mercy." – Maulana Muhammad, *Muhammad the Prophet*, Ahmadiyya Anjuman-i-Isha 'at-i-Islam, Lahore, India, 1924; 262.

"It was at Uhud that the idolatrous women marched to battle, beating their timbrels and singing: 'We are the daughters of the morning star; soft are the carpets we tread . . . our necks are adorned with pearls, and our tresses are perfumed with musk. The brave who confront the foe we will clasp to our bosoms, but the dastards who flee we will spurn – not for them our embraces!' It was here that these women mutilated the dead, and that Hind, notorious wife of Muhammad's chief enemy, Abu Sufyan, ripped out the liver of a Muslim hero and devoured it. It was this battle that the Muslims lost, because the archers who were holding the Meccan cavalry in check disobeyed Muhammad and left their positions to look for booty. Muhammad was wounded in the mouth and on the temple, and reported killed. 'Ali wept in despair when he saw Him, and brought water in his shield, saying, "Wash the blood from Thy face, O Apostle of God, that Thy men may know Thee . . ." (Chronique de Abou Djafar Mohammed-ben-Jarir Ben Yazid Tabari, tr. By M.H. Zotenberg, Paris, 1871; III, 33).

"Then 'Ali raised up the Prophet's banner and rallied the defeated Muslims. The idolaters' victory was costly; they dispersed for a time, but in 627 they came again, 10,000 strong, and besieged Medina. On the advice of Salman the Persian, a stratagem previously unknown in Arabia was now used: a trench was dug around the city. The Prophet Himself worked with the others at digging the trench. An account Says He seized a pickaxe . . . and with it, he struck a flint which had defied those who were digging; a spark came out of it, and he – -peace be with him – said 'In this spark I saw the cities of Chosrau (King of Persia.)' Then he struck another blow, and another spark came out; and he said 'In it I saw the cities of Caesar. Verily God will give them to my nation after me.'" -'Ali Tabari, *The Book of Religion and Empire*, tr. By A. Mingana, Manchester, University Press, 1922; pg. 44.

"There was a fifteen day siege, but the trench saved Medina and a storm put the enemy to flight. Islam had conquered.

After the battle, Muhammad went to His daughter, Fatimah, and she began to weep and to kiss his mouth; and he said to her: 'O Fatimah, why art thou weeping?' And she said 'O Apostle of God, I see thee shabby, weary, and clothed in worn out garments.' And he said 'O Fatimah, God has revealed to thy father that it is He who places dignity or lowliness in every house, be it of clay or of hair; and He has revealed to me that my lowliness will be (soon over)."

For partaking in war to defend this seed of renewed Faith and the precious followers in whose breasts this new fire burned, He has been derided by some, but Abdu'l-Baha, son of Baha'u'llah, the Glory of God has said:

"Look at it with justice. If Christ Himself had been placed in such circumstances... Culminating in the flight from His native land – if in spite of this, lawless tribes continued to pursue Him, to slaughter the men, to pillage their property, and to capture their women and children – what would have been Christ's conduct with regard to them?

If this oppression had fallen only upon Himself, He would have forgiven them... but if He had seen that these cruel and bloodthirsty murderers wished to kill, to pillage and to injure all these oppressed ones, and to take captive the women and children, it is certain that He would have protected them and would have resisted the tyrants...To free these tribes from their bloodthirstiness was the greatest kindness, and to coerce and restrain them was a true mercy." (Marzieh Gail, Six Lessons on Islam, p. 9)

"The old blood-tie was now replaced throughout Arabia by a new, much wider loyalty. For the first time, hundreds of hostile Arab tribes were now united under one banner – Islam. Muhammad took Mecca in 630 A.D. making an entry so peaceful as to be unparalleled in history, and telling the Meccans: – 'I say to you what my brother Joseph said to his brothers: 'No blame be on you this day. God will forgive you, for He is the most merciful of those who show mercy." (Qur'an 12:92).'

And He struck down the Ka'bih gods, saying: "Truth is come and falsehood is gone. Verily, falsehood is a thing that perisheth." (Qur'an 17:83). The Arabs now came into the religion of God by troops. As each tribe accepted, Muhammad sent them a teacher of Islam, telling him: "Deal gently with the people, and be not harsh; cheer them, and condemn them not . . . the key to heaven is to testify to the truth of God and to do good works." (Ameer-'Ali, op. cit., 208).

"Muhammad also sent out missives and embassies declaring Islam to rulers of the day, the King of Persia, the Negus of Abyssinia, Heraclius the Greek emperor, the ruler of Egypt, the governor of Yaman, the chief of the Bani Hanifa.

The King of Persia, enraged at seeing Muhammad's name before his own on the letter, tore it up. Muhammad said, 'God will tear up his kingdom in the same way.' "

(Marzieh Gail, Six Lessons on Islam, p. 10)

Muhammad fell ill with intense fever. A disciple laid his hand on Muhammad's forehead and said, "How fierce is the fever upon thee!" "Yea, verily," said Muhammad, "but I have been during the night season repeating in praise of the Lord seventy surihs, including the seven long ones." The disciple said, "Why not rest and take thine ease, for hath not the Lord forgiven thee?" "Nay," replied Muhammad, "wherefore should I not yet be a faithful servant unto Him?" (Cf. Muir, op. cit., 488).

"As He grew worse, He asked if there was any gold in the house; on being told there was, He insisted that His wife 'Ayesha give it away to the poor, and could not rest until she had done this. He said, "It would not have become me to meet my Lord, and this gold still in my hands." (Citation above)

Betrayal

While He lay dying, He called for pen and ink to write His will, but 'Umar said, "Pain is deluding God's Messenger; we have God's Book, which is enough." They disputed at the bedside, whether to bring the pen and ink, and He sent them away. He was praying in a whisper when He ascended, June 8, 632. (Gail, p. 12)

In retrospect, it is possible that the will, had it been drawn might well have stopped the immediate break of Mohammad's Faith into the Sunni and Shia sects, upon His death. (Marzieh Gail, Six Lessons on Islam, p. 10)

A Perfect Example

The Qur'an says: "An excellent pattern have ye in the Apostle of God." (33:21).

"He was stern in punishing criminals, but always forgave personal enemies; for example Habrar, who drove the end of his lance against the Prophet's daughter, as she was mounting her camel to flee from Mecca. She was far advanced in pregnancy; she fell to the ground, and later died from the injury. Habrar threw himself on Muhammad's mercy, and was pardoned." (Ameer-'Ali, 178).

If ever there was a reason for Mohammad to cry out "kill the infidels" as the negative propaganda would have us believe – this was it – instead, there was only mercy and forgiveness.

The God of the Qu'ran is a God of mercy; over and over, we hear of His mercy; we are told never to despair of it; God says, "I will answer the cry of him that crieth, when he crieth unto me: but let them hearken unto me, and believe in me." (2:182).

"This teaching seems to have freed the Muslims from the burden of conscious and unconscious guilt which weighs so heavily on many Christians."

"Repeatedly, we are directed in the Qur'an to be thankful: "forsooth is God rich without you: but He is not pleased with thanklessness in His servants: yet if ye be thankful He will be pleased with you." (39:9). (Marzieh Gail, Six Lessons on Islam, p. 10)

Submission to the Will of God: Islam

Muhammad had not founded a new religion, but renewed the one religion brought by successive holy Prophets before Him, and Who were on the same plane as Muhammad Himself (2:130).

"The soul is immortal and accountable for its actions. The Muslims do not believe in original sin, or vicarious atonement; salvation is not only for Muslims but for the followers of all 14 previous faiths: 'Verily, they who believe, and the Jews, and the Sabeites, and the Christians – whoever of them believeth in God and in the last day, and doth what is right, on them shall come no fear, neither shall they be put to grief.'" (Qur'án 5:73). (Marzieh Gail, Six Lessons on Islam, p. 13-14)

Islam has no priesthood. the 'ulama, meaning the learned ones – the qadis (judges), muftis (exponents of the religious law), mujtahids, and mullahs – are not a priesthood in the Christian sense, but expounders of the law.

"The Muslims do not worship Muhammad. "It is the one, universal God Who is worshipped in Islam; One closer to man than his neck-vein (50:15), and aware of all things:

'no leaf falleth but He knoweth it.' (6:59), and God is characterized by ninety-names given throughout the Qur'án, and another name, the Greatest Name, not made known at that time. Qur'án 7:179; 17:110; 59:24) He said, "The idols which ye invoke...can never create a single fly...and if the fly snatches anything from them, they cannot recover the same...." (Qur'án 22:72).

He was at everyone's disposal. He was a "witness, and a herald...and a warner; And one who, through His permission, summoneth to God, and a light-giving torch." (Qur'an 33: 44-45).

We read that in His lifetime "The meanest slaves would take hold of his hand and drag him to their masters to obtain redress for ill treatment or release from bondage." (Khwaja Kamal-ud-Din, *The Ideal Prophet*, Woking, 1925; 194).

"The oneness of religions is unequivocally stated: 'Verily We have revealed to Thee as We revealed to Noah and the Prophets after Him, and as We revealed to Abraham, and Ishmael, and Isaac, and Jacob, and the tribes, and Jesus, and Job, and Jonah, and Aaron, and Solomon; and to David, gave We Psalms.'" (4:161).

"Muhammad said, 'He who wrongs a Jew or Christian will have Me as his accuser.'" (Dermenghem 331).

"Before the Hejira, the Mussulmans had endured persecution without defence; later they put up a legitimate resistance and when they became victors they demonstrated tolerance... The idolater was not allowed to remain on Moslem soil; but the People of the Book both Jew and Christian, by paying tribute, had a right to protection, could practice their faith freely, and were considered a part of the community."

"In Spain as elsewhere, Ameer-'Ali points out, Muslim rule brought great progress, order, peace and plenty, promotion of freedom and equality, and regard of rulers for their subjects. Spain had greatly suffered from barbarian hordes, and the people had been weighted down with feudal burdens, while vast areas were deserted; under the Muslims, people and land were enfranchised, cities sprang up, order was established, Muslims and non-Muslims – Suevi, Goth, Vandal, Roman and Jew – were placed on equal footing, and intermarriage took place.

The Qur'an forbids drinking, gambling, usury, all forms of vice, and is the first of the sacred Books to put a restriction on polygamy. Muhammad forbids the vengeance of blood and all blood feuds. He prepared the way for the abolition of slavery, encouraging the manumission of slaves by His own example, and greatly ameliorating their lot; slavery as practiced in the West is unknown in Islam; slaves, such as the Mameluke sultans of Egypt, could become kings.

As for women, Muhammad has been called the greatest champion of women's rights the world has ever seen; Islam gives to women the same property rights as her husband; she can inherit and dispose of property, has various alimony and other rights, and must be treated with respect. There is no color or race prejudice in Islam – color is "a sign of God" (30:21; 35:25). Islam teaches love of country (nationalism is its great contribution, the Guardian, Shoghi Effendi; told Emeric Sala). The Muslims have no caste system, and the Hajj brings them all together, as equals.

Islam imposes only five obligations on the faithful: They must affirm that there is no God but God and that Muhammad is the Apostle of God; they must pray five times a day; fast one month out of the year; pay the poor-rate annually; and make one pilgrimage to Mecca in their lifetime, if they are able. The Muslims pray wherever they happen to be at the appointed hours, facing the Ka'bih; they must be in a state of cleanliness and have performed the ablutions.

"Muhammad tells of "the meadows of Paradise" (42:21); He says Paradise has "storied pavilions beneath which...the rivers flow." (39:21). He speaks of the gardens of delight, and the cup that shall not oppress the sense, of the houris with faces fair as ostrich eggs, of the ever-blooming youths going round about with goblets, of lote-trees and acacias, of soft green cushions and delicate carpets. He says of the believers in Paradise, "No vain discourse shall they hear therein, nor any falsehood, but only the cry, 'Peace! Peace!'" (56:24-25).

"The true Muslims are humble, known by the dust on their foreheads ...their tokens are on their faces" (48:29) – from bowing down in prayer. In prosperity, an individual forgets God, returning quickly to Him when in trouble: "When We are gracious to man, he withdraweth and turneth him(self) aside; but when evil toucheth him, he is a man of long prayers." (41:51). A believer whose custom it was to slip discreetly away from over-long meetings, was somewhat dismayed to come upon this: "God knoweth those of you who withdraw quietly from the assemblies, screening themselves behind others." (24:63).

"We shall hurl the truth at falsehood, and it shall smite it, and lo! It shall vanish." (21:18). The Imam 'Ali, who loved Muhammad, remembered Him as follows: "He was of the middle height, neither very tall nor very short. His skin was fair, but ruddy, His eyes black; His beard, that surrounded all His face, luxuriant. The hair of His head was long and fell to His shoulders; it was black. His neck was white...His gait was so energetic you would have said He was wrenching His foot from a stone, yet at the same time so light He seemed to float...But He did not walk with pride, as the princes do. (Elsewhere we read that He sometimes walked very rapidly, and that He never turned, even if His mantle caught in a thorny bush).

There was such sweetness in His face, that once you were in His presence you could not leave Him; if you were hungry, it fed you just to look at Him...When they entered His presence, the afflicted forgot their anguish. Whoever saw Him declared that he had never found, before or afterward, a man of such entrancing speech. His nose was aquiline, His teeth somewhat far apart. Sometimes He would let His hair fall free, sometimes He wore it knotted in two or four strands. At sixty-three...age had whitened but some fifteen of His hairs..." (Tabari, Chroniques, III, 202-203). (Marzieh Gail, Six Lessons on Islam, Pp. 13-15)

Laws and Duties

"He said, "The duties of Muslims to each other are six...When you meet a Muslim, greet him, and when he inviteth you to dinner, accept; and when he asketh you for advice, give it him; and when he sneezeth and saith, 'Praise be to God,' do you say, 'May God have mercy upon thee'; and when he is sick, visit him; and when he dieth, follow his bier."

"Modern societies for the prevention of cruelty to animals owe much to Him. He taught kindness to animals, and said that an adulteress was forgiven her sin because, seeing a dog suffering from thirst, she tied her shoe to her garment and lowered it into a well, to draw up water for the dog.

It was said that He loved cats and kept one Himself. In the Hadith it tells of a time when Muhammad cut off His own sleeve, rather than disturb the cat who was sleeping on it.

"He was endlessly patient. The Qur'an enjoins patience in over seventy passages. It states: 'How goodly the reward of those who labor, who patiently endure, and put their trust in their Lord!' (29:58-59); and 'Verily those who endure with patience shall be rewarded: their reward shall not be by measure.' (39:13).

"He taught people to love the next world; He said this world was only a vapor in a desert. Again He said, "Verily, the world is no otherwise than as a tree...when the traveler hath rested under its shade, he passeth on." (Cf. Muir, op. cit., 330 n.). As He was dying He told them, "God hath a servant to whom He hath said: Dost thou desire this world or the next? The servant hath chosen the next, and God hath approved his choice, and hath promised to call him into His presence." And one of the believers who was there understood, and wept. (Tabari, Chronique, III, 208-209).

He taught them to give alms, this being contrary to their wishes. Muhammad said, "Fear the Fire by giving alms, although it be but one half of a date." ('Ali Tabari, The Book of Religion and Empire, pp. 26-27). A Persian boasted that his father and grandfather died poor. Poverty is highly prized by the true Muslims, because Muhammad said "Poverty is My glory." He ate sitting on the ground; His pillow was His arm; He lived in a row of modest rooms, made of sun-dried brick, furnished with leather water-bags, and leather mats stuffed with palm-fibre, and cots of palm-fibre rope. He kindled the fire, swept the floor, patched His own garments and shoes, and milked the goats. He said, "I am a servant, I eat and sleep like a servant." (A. Tabari).

(Marzieh Gail, *Six Lessons on Islam*, p. 13-14)

Many of the things we take for granted as being a part of Western social graces, were brought to the world by Mohammad.

He was immaculate in His person, and loved fragrances; He would use musk and ambergris, and burn camphor or odoriferous wood. It is said that once His revelations ceased unexpectedly, and He remarked to some people who were present, "How can revelations not be interrupted when you do not trim your nails, nor clip your moustache...." -'Ali Tabari, The Book of Religion and Empire, Pg 27). The Qur'an says, "God loveth the clean." (9:109). " WOW!

It is true that Mohammad was the Seal of The Prophet's, the closer of the door at the end of an Age, yes. But it would be foolish to think that the visits of the Holy Spirit would end here for eternity.

A NEW DAWN: THE BAHA'I ERA

The appearance of these divine educators – Krishna, Buddha, Zoroaster, Abraham, Moses, Christ, Muhammad and, in our own age, the Báb and Bahá'u'lláh – has signified the founding of a new religion, and yet none of these religions is really new; they are stages in the unfoldment of the same religious truth proceeding from the same God. (Baha'i International Community, 1993 Feb 18, Eliminating Religious Intolerance)

"**Bestir yourselves, O people, in anticipation of the days of Divine justice, for the promised hour is now come. Beware lest ye fail to apprehend its import and be accounted among the erring.**"

In regard to people's inability to recognize a Manifestation of God, (Baha'ullah quoted in Advent of Divine Justice, p.28):

"*Consider the past. How many, both high and low, have, at all times, yearningly awaited the advent of the Manifestations of God in the sanctified persons of His chosen Ones. How often have they expected His coming, how frequently have they prayed that the breeze of Divine mercy might blow, and the promised Beauty step forth from behind the veil of concealment, and be made manifest to all the world. And whensoever the portals of grace did open, and the clouds of divine bounty did rain upon mankind, and the light of the Unseen did shine above the horizon of celestial might, they all denied Him, and turned away from His face the face of God Himself....*

Not for a moment hath His grace been withheld, nor have the showers of His loving-kindness ceased to rain upon mankind. Consequently, such behavior can be attributed to naught save the petty-mindedness of such souls as tread the valley of arrogance and pride, are lost in the wilds of remoteness, walk in the ways of their idle fancy, and follow the dictates of the leaders of their faith... having weighed the testimony of God by the standard of their own knowledge, gleaned from the teachings of the leaders of their faith, and found it at variance with their limited understanding, they arose to perpetrate such unseemly acts....

Consider Moses! Armed with the rod of celestial dominion, adorned with the white hand of Divine knowledge, and proceeding from the Paran of the love of God, and wielding the serpent of power and everlasting majesty, He shone forth from the Sinai of light upon the world. He summoned all the peoples and kindreds of the earth to the kingdom of eternity, and invited them to partake of the fruit of the tree of faithfulness. Surely you are aware of the fierce opposition of Pharaoh and his people, and of the stones of idle fancy which the hands of infidels cast upon that blessed Tree. So much so that Pharaoh and his people finally arose and exerted their utmost endeavor to extinguish with the waters of falsehood and denial the fire of that sacred Tree, oblivious of the truth that no earthly water can quench the flames of Divine wisdom, nor mortal blasts extinguish the lamp of everlasting dominion. Nay, rather, such water cannot but intensify the burning of the flame, and such blasts cannot but insure the preservation of the lamp, were ye to observe with the eye of discernment, and walk in the way of God's holy will and pleasure....

And when the days of Moses were ended, and the light of Jesus, shining forth from the Day Spring of the Spirit, encompassed the world, all the people of Israel arose in protest against Him. They clamored that He Whose advent the Bible had foretold must needs promulgate and fulfil the laws of Moses, whereas this youthful Nazarene, who laid claim to the station of the divine Messiah, had annulled the laws of divorce and of the Sabbath day – the most weighty of all the laws of Moses... These people of Israel are even unto the present day still expecting that Manifestation which the Bible hath foretold! How many Manifestations of Holiness, how many Revealers of the light everlasting, have appeared since the time of Moses, and yet Israel, wrapt in the densest veils of satanic fancy and false imaginings, is still expectant that the idol of her own handiwork will appear with such signs as she herself hath conceived!

To them that are endowed with understanding, it is clear and manifest that, when the fire of the love of Jesus consumed the veils of Jewish limitations, and His authority was made apparent and partially enforced, He, the Revealer of the unseen Beauty, addressing one day His disciples, referred unto His passing, and, kindling in their hearts the fire of bereavement, said unto them: "I go away and come again unto you." And in another place He said: "I go and another will come, Who will tell you all that I have not told you, and will fulfil all that I have said." Both these sayings have but one meaning, were ye to ponder upon the Manifestations of the Unity of God with Divine insight.

Every discerning observer will recognize in the Dispensation of the Qur'án both the Book and the Cause of Jesus were confirmed. As to the matter of names, Muhammad, Himself, declared: "I am Jesus." He recognized the truth of the signs, prophecies, and words of Jesus, and testified that they were all of God. In this sense, neither the person of Jesus nor His writings hath differed from that of Muhammad and of His holy Book, inasmuch as both have championed the Cause of God, uttered His praise, and revealed His commandments. Thus it is that Jesus, Himself, declared: "I go away and come again unto you." Consider the sun. Were it to say now, "I am the sun of yesterday," it would speak the truth. And should it, bearing the sequence of time in mind, claim to be other than that sun, it still would speak the truth.

When the Unseen, the Eternal, the Divine Essence, caused the Day Star of Muhammad to rise above the horizon of knowledge, among the cavils which the Jewish divines raised against Him was that after Moses no Prophet should be sent of God.

Behold how the sovereignty of Muhammad, the Messenger of God, is today apparent and manifest amongst the people. You are well aware of what befell His Faith in the early days of His Dispensation. Such sore accusations they brought against Him that in recounting them God forbiddeth the ink to flow, Our pen to move, or the page to bear them. These malicious imputations provoked the people to arise and torment Him... Consider, how great is the change today! Behold, how many are the Sovereigns who bow the knee before His name!

> *It is evident that the changes brought about in every Dispensation constitute the dark clouds that intervene between the eye of man's understanding and the Divine Luminary which shineth forth from the day spring of the Divine Essence. Consider how men for generations have been blindly imitating their fathers, and have been trained according to such ways and manners as have been laid down by the dictates of their Faith.*
>
> *It behoveth us, therefore, to make the utmost endeavor, that, by God's invisible assistance, these dark veils, these clouds of Heaven – sent trials, may not hinder us from beholding the beauty of His shining Countenance, and that we may recognize Him only by His own Self."* (Baha'u'llah, *The Kibab – I- Iqan*, p.3)

There is a great deal of information to be found on the Baha'i Faith www.bahai.org, so only a small discussion will be found here.

THE BAB

The dispensation of the Bab which means Gate, or Door sets the tone of the events surrounding the coming of Baha'u'llah. Here is a glimpse of the environment and times of the Declaration of the Bab and the dawn of a new Day of God.

Much of the goodness of Mohammad's Faith had faded, and become laden with the dust and degradation of human contamination. Yet there were great Muslim teachers who knew the world was close to a great upheaval. They told everyone to prepare for the coming of the Qaim (Promised one) by purifying their thoughts, actions and deeds; and through fasting and incessant prayer. After the passing of one such inspired teacher named Shaykh Ahmad, students like the great Mulla Husayn took refuge with another revered leader of the Messianic Shaykhi movement called Sayyid Kazim Rashti.

Later Mulla Husayn would not only be blessed by becoming the first to recognize the enigmatic Bab, but also later to suspect that Husayn-'Ali, later known as Baha'u'llah, was the Promised One of all Ages! Mullah Husayn's full tale is that of a shining spiritual hero, who became aware that he was indeed in the presence of the Promise of God, he had so diligently been seeking! (Source: *God Passes By*; Bahai Publishing Trust 1995, intro)

Mirza Ali Muhammad (The Bab's birth name) was born into a Merchant family. He was known for his innate intelligence and quiet, pious nature.

As he matured, He was well thought of and was described as a good looking, man with a thin beard. He wore a black turban, a green shawl and a quiet expression. The youth married happily at age 23. His 20 year old wife was Khadijih Bagum. They lost their only son in the first year of life, and Khadijih could bear no others.

In 1844 the gentle Bab released a shocking and powerful Message. Before He was put to death the Bab proclaimed at His trial:

"I am," He exclaimed, "I am, I am the Promised One! I am the One Whose name you have for a thousand years invoked, at Whose mention you have risen, Whose advent you have longed to witness, and the hour of Whose Revelation you have prayed God to hasten. Verily, I say, it is incumbent upon the peoples of both the East and the West to obey My word, and to pledge allegiance to My person." (Shoghi Effendi, God Passes By, p. 21)

The selections here depict both the gentleness, and tremendous power which emanated from the Bab. It is said that even before Creation, the other Manifestations of God were in awe of the one chosen to turn the whole, violent world on its ear, and prepare the way for the Glory of God, Himself, to arise on this planet.

Anticipation

Shrine of the Bab. By Deror avi (Own work) [Attribution], via Wikimedia Commons

From Nabil in the Dawn Breakers:

"My days were spent in the service of Siyyid Kazim (a revered Messianic teacher), to whom I was greatly attached. One day, at the hour of dawn, I was suddenly awakened by Mulla Naw-Ruz, one of his intimate attendants, who, in great excitement, bade me arise and follow him. We went to the house of Siyyid Kazim, where we found him fully dressed, wearing his aba, and ready to leave his home. He asked me to accompany him. 'A highly esteemed and distinguished Person,' he said, 'has arrived. I feel it incumbent upon us both to visit Him.' The morning light had just broken when I found myself walking with him through the streets of Karbila. We soon reached a house, at the door of which stood a Youth, as if expectant to receive us. He wore a green turban, and His countenance revealed an expression of humility and kindliness which I can never describe. He quietly approached us, extended His arms towards Siyyid Kazim, and lovingly embraced him. His affability and loving-kindness singularly contrasted with the sense of profound reverence that characterized the attitude of Siyyid Kazim towards Him. Speechless and with bowed head, he received the many expressions of affection and esteem with which that Youth greeted him.

We were soon led by Him to the upper floor of that house, and entered a chamber bedecked with flowers and redolent of the loveliest perfume. He bade us be seated. We knew not, however, what seats we actually occupied, so overpowering was the sense of delight which seized us. We observed a silver cup which had been placed in the centre of the room, which our youthful Host, soon after we were seated, filled to overflowing, and handed to Siyyid Kazim, saying: 'A drink of a pure beverage shall their Lord give them. Siyyid Kazim held the cup with both hands and quaffed it. A feeling of reverent joy filled his being, a feeling which he could not suppress. I too was presented with a cupful of that beverage, though no words were addressed to me. All that was spoken at that memorable gathering was the above-mentioned verse of the Qur'án. Soon after, the Host arose from His seat and, accompanying us to the threshold of the house, bade us farewell. I was mute with wonder, and knew not how to express the cordiality of His welcome, the dignity of His bearing, the charm of that face, and the delicious fragrance of that beverage.

How great was my amazement when I saw my teacher quaff without the least hesitation that holy draught from a silver cup, the use of which, according to the precepts of Islam, is forbidden to the faithful. I could not explain the motive which could have induced the Siyyid to manifest such profound reverence in the presence of that Youth – a reverence which even the sight of the shrine of the Siyyidu'sh-Shuhada' had failed to excite.

Three days later, I saw that same Youth arrive and take His seat in the midst of the company of the assembled disciples of Siyyid Kazim. He sat close to the threshold, and with the same modesty and dignity of bearing listened to the discourse of the Siyyid. As soon as his eyes fell upon that Youth, the Siyyid discontinued his address and held his peace. Whereupon, one of his disciples begged him to resume the argument which he had left unfinished. 'What more shall I say?' replied Siyyid Kazim, as he turned his face toward the Báb. 'Lo, the Truth is more manifest than the ray of light that has fallen upon that lap!'

I immediately observed that the ray to which the Siyyid referred had fallen upon the lap of that same Youth whom we had recently visited. 'Why is it,' that questioner enquired, 'that you neither reveal His name nor identify His person?' To this the Siyyid replied by pointing with his finger to his own throat, implying that were he to divulge His name, they both would be put to death instantly. This added still further to my perplexity. I had already heard my teacher observe that so great is the perversity of this generation, that were he to point with his finger to the promised One and say: 'He indeed is the Beloved, the Desire of your hearts and mine,' they would still fail to recognize and acknowledge Him. I saw the Siyyid actually point out with his finger the ray of light that had fallen on that lap, and yet none among those who were present seemed to apprehend its meaning. I, for my part, was convinced that the Siyyid, himself, could never be the promised One, but that a mystery inscrutable to us all, lay concealed in that strange and attractive Youth."
Ocean (Shoghi Effendi, The Dawn-Breakers, p. 25)

The Baha'i Faith was born on the night of 22 May 1844. Siyyid 'Ali-Muhammad, known as the Bab or "Gate," declared Himself to Mulla Husayn, in the upper chamber of His house in Shiraz. He was the promised Qa'im.

Shortly thereafter the Báb circumambulated the Ka'bih, performed all the rites of worship, then stood before the Black Stone and declared His mission. He also abrogated Muslin laws which were no longer necessary.

He called upon kings and rulers to govern with Justice. And He explained that idle words were not sufficient. God's servants must exhibit moral purity and righteous deeds. The Bab gathered a company of devoted, heroic believers, and He aroused the spirit of hope among the sorely oppressed masses. As one might expect, this caused the clergy and civil authorities to be fearful of losing their position, privileges and power.

Transfiguration

Here is a precious jewel. Throughout history, we have understood that God's Manifestation becomes transformed, even glows with radiant light when anointed by the Holy Spirit. But, here in the story of the Bab, we have an actual eye-witness account of the transfiguration.

The story of how the Bab's wife, Khadijih Bagum, became a believer (The Dawn-Breakers, p. 191)

"The wife of the Bab . . . perceived at the earliest dawn of His Revelation the glory and uniqueness of His Mission and felt from the very beginning the intensity of its force." Through her close association with the Bab and her observation of every aspect of His life, Khadijih Bagum, long before His declaration to Mulla Husayn, had discovered her husband's extraordinary spiritual endowments. However she was unaware of the claim He was to make and the nature of His mission until she experienced something unique which confirmed her belief in Him." (Baharieh Rouhani Ma'ani "Leaves of the Twin Divine Trees," George Ronald Press 2008 p. 33)

In His historical manuscript, her great nephew, Haji Mirza Habibu'llah Afnan has recorded the following account which was related to him by the wife of the Bab, Khadijih Bagum: "The sun was setting . . . when the Countenance of the Peerless Beloved illumined His home with the light of His effulgent Face. According to the usual custom, tea was served in the chamber of His mother and the dinner table was set. That night His blessed Person was not hungry, but accompanied others and had a little food; then He went to bed.

Around midnight His wife noticed His absence. She became worried and searched the courtyard of the House and the room of His mother, but did not find Him anywhere. As she was not yet aware of His inner heart's secret her anxiety heightened with the passing of every second. She involuntarily climbed up the staircase leading to the second floor and, lo and behold, she saw the upper chamber of the House immersed in light. What was the source of all this light and where had the lamps come from, she asked herself. But this was not tangible light; it was divine light, and she did not see it with her outward eyes but with her inner sight. She proceeded towards the guest room. There she saw that world-illuminating Sun and light-shedding Moon standing in the middle of the room with His hands raised heavenward. While her eyes were fixed upon the dazzling light emanating from His Being, a feeling of awe and fright came over her. She wanted to return downstairs, but was unable to move. Her awe grew to such intensity that she felt stupefied.

At this point His Blessed Person relieved her of her bewilderment. By uttering the words 'go back' He gave her new life and revived her faculties. She returned to bed, but could not sleep. She communed with the Almighty saying 'O my God, what power and grandeur! What greatness and glory! What is the wisdom in your revealing to me that effulgent Sun? Is He my Siyyid 'Ali-Muhammad? Will I henceforth be able to live with that luminous Sun? Nay, nay, the rays of this Resplendent Sun will consume me, and will reduce me to ashes. I possess not the power to withstand it.'

Her thoughts were all night revolving around this episode until she heard the voice of the mu'adhdhin [A Muslim crier who calls the hour of daily prayers.] from the adjacent mosque. At that time the Immaculate Being descended the steps. His esteemed wife, who had beheld the majesty and greatness of her glorious husband, was trembling as she thought of meeting Him face to face, and tried to conceal herself. When the breakfast table was spread and she went, according to the usual practice to the room of His mother, she was still trembling, and would not lift her head.

The Exalted Being poured tea and offered it to her. He enquired, 'What is the matter with you?' She replied, 'What was the condition I saw you in?' The Tongue of Grandeur uttered such words that caused her anxiety to vanish, and confirmed her in what she had seen. He spoke words such as these: 'Know thou that the Almighty God is manifested in Me. I am the One whose advent the people of Islam have expected for over a thousand years. God has created Me for a great Cause, and you witnessed the divine revelation. Although I had not wished that you see Me in that state, yet God had so willed that there may not be any place in your heart for doubt and hesitation.'

Just as Khadijih, the wife of the Prophet Muhammad witnessed the first emanations of the Spirit of Truth manifesting in her exalted husband and became the first to perceive the divinity of the mission with which He had been entrusted, so it was nearly 13 centuries later when a descendant of hers, also named Khadijih, became the first to recognize the Sun of Reality shining through the person of Siyyid 'Ali-Muhammad, a lineal descendant of Prophet Muhammad and His wife Khadijih.

Khadijih Bagum was the recipient of this tremendous bounty without preparation and expectation, for despite her awareness that her husband was above other men in stature and spiritual endowments, she never imagined that her intimate and loving companion would be the promised Qa'im. The discovery was no doubt an overwhelming and awe-inspiring experience. "(Leaves of the Twin Divine Trees, pp. 34-35)

"The Qa'im literally means 'He Who Arises': in Shia Islam, a reference to the Twelfth Imam, the Mihdi, who was to return in the fullness of time and bring a reign of righteousness to the world. The Bab declared Himself to be the Qa'im and the Gate to a greater Messenger, 'Him Whom God shall make manifest'"

From 1844 when The Bab took his name meaning "Gate," and began to proclaim His mission, until the time of His execution 6 years later, at the age of 25; this precious youth was persecuted and imprisoned; for His Revelation of God's Word, the laws He gave us and the call to arise and seek the imminent appearance of no less than The Promised One of all ages!

Independently 18 purified souls recognized the Bab and became His Disciples. They are known as The Letters of the Living.

The Bab and thousands of His followers were viciously tortured and killed in horrific ways, by Muslims who, like the Pharisees, could not tolerate the thought that the sacred promises had been fulfilled and that their dynasty was about to crash into evil descent. In the first year of His mission, fanatics and cruelly ignorant fools murdered 4000 of His followers.

It was for the love of Baha'u'llah, the Glory of God, that the Bab would sacrifice His life. His dramatic martyrdom took place in the windswept barracks square of Tabriz at noon on July 9, 1850." – Robert L. Gulick Jr February 1, 1975 (Preface to Seven Valleys and Four Valleys)

By order of church and state the Bab was denounced as a heretic and a rebel. He had been bastinadoed, isolated and imprisoned in castle dungeons, twice. In 1850 this heroic Prophet was publicly executed in the city of Tabriz.

His last words to the crowd, as the regiment prepared to fire its volley were:

"**O wayward generation! Had you believed in Me every one of you would have followed the example of this youth, who stood in rank above most of you, and would have willingly sacrificed himself in My path. The day will come when you will have recognized Me; that day I shall have ceased to be with you.**"

Nor was this all. The very moment the shots were fired a gale of exceptional violence arose and swept over the city. From noon till night a whirlwind of dust obscured the light of the sun, and blinded the eyes of the people. In Shiraz an "earthquake," foreshadowed in no less weighty a Book than the Revelation of St. John, occurred in 1268 A.H. which threw the whole city into turmoil and wrought havoc amongst its people, a havoc that was greatly aggravated by the outbreak of cholera, by famine and other afflictions.
Ocean (Shoghi Effendi, God Passes By, p. 52)

Within a year, the entire 752-man firing squad was wiped out, as were the officials in charge of the Bab's execution.

Many thousands of people accepted the Bab's Message and began to follow His teachings, and many were cruelly and horribly put to death. Irrefutably a new Day had dawned. The world was changed forever! The way had been paved for the Promised One of all ages!

"**Is there any remover of difficulties save God? Say: Praised be God! He is God! All are His servants, and all abide by His bidding**" – prayer Revealed by the Bab

BAHA'U'LLAH THE GLORY OF GOD

The Day of Judgement had arrived. The One promised by all Messengers had come to unite the world in peace and through justice! Baha'u'llah The One foretold by all of the previous Messengers was announced to mankind. Baha'u'llah the Gory of God had come to earth. In this Age the Kingdom of God will be Fullfilled. The world will be united in peace under One Almighty God through the power of Justice!

He was born in Tehran, Iran on November 12, 1817, as Husayn-'Ali. After transfiguration His title, Baha'u'llah meant the "Glory of God." Like Buddha He was a son of a noble, wealthy and respected family. As a boy he spent a great deal of time seeking out the quietude of nature. He especially loved mountain forests, according to His son 'Abdu'l-Baha.

Even as a youth, Husayn Ali was respected and admired for His virtuous qualities, and quiet dignity. He could have accepted an eminent position under the Shah. But that was not His path. His spiritual Mission was a continuation of the path of sacrifice laid down by 'Ali-Muhammad, known to history as the Bab; Who from May 22, 1844 to July 9, 1850, proclaimed the birth of a new Age. The degree of unity would be the peoples of a World Faith.

Crisis and Victory

"His life was a litany of exile, imprisonment and suffering. After the martyrdom of the Bab, Husayn – 'Ali became the beloved leader of the Babi's. For His beliefs He was imprisoned in a deep dark sewer in Teheran. He wore 200 pound chains around His neck, which, He fought, to keep His head from falling into the muck." Robert L. Gulick Jr February 1, 1975 (Preface to Seven Valleys and Four Valleys)

In the end His was a stunning tale of crisis after cruel subjugation and victory! The world of the 1840's, 50's and 60's was in upheaval, and people everywhere fought the tyranny and oppression of unjust overlords. Men and women would no longer stand for cruel subjugation.

Baha'u'llah exclaimed: "The Ancient Beauty hath consented to be bound with chains that mankind may be released from its bondage, and hath accepted to be made a prisoner within this most mighty Stronghold that the whole world may attain unto true liberty. He hath drained to its dregs the cup of sorrow, that all of the peoples of the earth may attain unto abiding joy, and be filled with gladness. This is of the mercy of your Lord, the Compassionate, the Most Merciful. We have accepted to be abased, O believers in the Unity of God, that ye may be exalted, and have suffered manifold afflictions, that ye might prosper and flourish. He Who hath come to build anew the whole world, behold, how they that have joined partners with God have forced Him to dwell within the most desolate of cities!"

"Baha'u'llah continued to reveal the Word of God for more than forty years and brought so much love and spiritual energy into this world that the final victory of His Cause is certain" (Baha'u'llah, Gleanings from the Writings of Baha'u'llah, p99)

"Forty years of exile and imprisonment had begun. From Tihr'an, Baha'u'llah, members of His family and a company of followers of the Bab were sent over the high cold mountains to Baghdad, in the middle of January with the expectation that His absence from Persia (Iran) would further weaken the remnant of believers. From Baghdad Baha'u'llah was exiled to Constantinople, which transferred jurisdiction of the civil and ecclesiastical charges from Persia to the Sultan, who was head of Sunni Islam. Under the Sultan, the policy of repression and of refusal to give Baha'u'llah a hearing continued. From Constantinople the party was dispatched to Adrianople. In 1868 the Turkish regime committed Baha'u'llah and His party to the pestilential prison-fortress of 'Akka, in Syria (then), now Israel."

"Before leaving Bagdad for Constantinople, Baha'u'llah declared His Mission (1863) in the Garden He referred to as Ridvan (pronounced Rizwan) to the company of Babi's, and from that time the believers have been Baha'is save for the few who rejected His claim and sought to perpetuate Babism beyond its destined time."

(Quoted selections by Horace Holley, in the introduction to Baha'i World Faith, Second edition 1956)

"'Upon Our arrival We were first conducted along a pitch-black corridor, from whence We descended three steep flights of stairs to the place of confinement assigned to Us. The dungeon was wrapped in thick darkness, and Our fellow-prisoners numbered nearly one hundred and fifty souls: thieves, assassins and highwaymen. Though crowded, it had no other outlet than the passage by which We entered. No pen can depict that place, nor any tongue describe its loathsome smell. Most of those men had neither clothes nor bedding to lie on. God alone knoweth what befell Us in that most foul-smelling and gloomy place!" Bahá'u'lláh's feet were placed in stocks, and around His neck were fastened the Qara-Guhar chains of such galling weight that their mark remained imprinted upon His body all the days of His life. (p. 72)

A heavy chain,' 'Abdu'l-Bahá Himself has testified, 'was placed about His neck by which He was chained to five other Bábís; these fetters were locked together by strong, very heavy, bolts and screws. His clothes were torn to pieces, also His headdress. In this terrible condition He was kept for four months.' For three days and three nights, He was denied all manner of food and drink. Sleep was impossible to Him. The place was chill and damp, filthy, fever-stricken, infested with vermin, and filled with a noisome stench.

Animated by a relentless hatred His enemies went even so far as to intercept and poison His food…an attempt which, though it impaired His health for years to come, failed to achieve its purpose.

Even in this dark gloom all hope was not lost, for in this pestilential hole, The Glory of God received His anointment, from The Maid of Heaven.

During the year 1853, while He was suffering this affliction (in Teheran) the Maid of Heaven descended and revealed to Husayn 'Ali His Mission as Baha'u'llah, the Promised One of all religions and nations. In a letter addressed in a later year to the Shah of Persia, Baha'u'llah wrote:

'O king! I was but a man like others, asleep upon My couch, when lo, the breezes of the All-Glorious were wafted over Me, and taught Me the knowledge of all that hath been. This thing is not from me, but from One Who is Almighty and All-Knowing, and He bade me lift up My voice between earth and heaven...'

The Maid of Heaven appeared, glowing, above Him and in the sweetest voice announce to heaven and earth the station of Bahá'u'lláh." – Citation from Dr. J.G. Esselmont, *Baha'u'llah and The New Era*.

Shoghi Effendi compared the Maid of Heaven with the Holy Spirit, which had also manifested as the Burning Bush of Moses, the Dove to Jesus, and the angel Gabriel to Muhammad.

Baha'u'llah speaks poignantly of the fates of His peers.

"O Jews! If ye be intent on crucifying once again, Jesus, the Spirit of God, put Me to death, for He hath once more, in My person, been made manifest unto you. Deal with Me as ye wish, for I have vowed to lay down My life in the path of God. I will fear no one, though the powers of earth and heaven be leagued against Me. Followers of the Gospel! If ye cherish the desire to slay Muhammad, the Apostle of God, seize Me and put an end to My life, as ye like, for the deepest longing of Mine heart is to attain the presence of My Best-Beloved in His Kingdom of Glory. Such is the Divine decree, if ye know it. Followers of Muhammad! If it be your will to riddle with your shafts the breast of Him Who hath caused His Book the Bayan to be sent down unto you, lay hands on Me and persecute Me, for I am His Well-Beloved, the revelation of His own Self, though My name be not His name. I have come in the shadows of the clouds of glory, and am invested by God with invincible sovereignty. He, verily, is the Truth, the Knower of things unseen. I, verily, anticipate from you the treatment ye have accorded unto Him that came before Me. To this all things, verily, witness if ye be of those who hearken. O people of the Bayan! If ye have resolved to shed the blood of Him Whose coming the Bab hath proclaimed, Whose advent Muhammad hath prophesied, and Whose Revelation Jesus Christ, Himself, hath announced behold Me standing, ready and defenseless, before you. Deal with Me after you own desires." –Gleanings of the Writings of Baha'u'llah Pp. 101-102

His works include The Seven Valleys and the Four Valleys, The Hidden Words, Prayers and Meditations, a Tablet to the Christians and many others. He proclaimed God's wish for rulers to be just. He sent appeals and warnings to corrupted heads of religion. He unlocked the meanings of the Sacred Scriptures, and formulated laws. He also appointed His son, 'Abdul-Baha as Center of His Covenant after His own Ascension.

No prior Revelation had so fully provided for the preservation and spread of its teaching in their essential purity. Baha'u'llah exhorted humanity to constantly hone virtues and to serve all mankind. In the Kitab-i-Iqan Baha'u'llah gives us the Tablet of the True Seeker:

"Be generous in prosperity, and thankful in adversity. Be worthy of the trust of thy neighbor, and look upon him with a bright and friendly face. Be a treasure to the poor, an admonisher to the rich, an answerer of the cry of the needy, a preserver of the sanctity of thy pledge. Be fair in thy judgement, and guarded in thy speech. Be unjust to no man, and show all meekness to all men. Be as a lamp unto them that walk in darkness, a joy to the sorrowful, a sea for the thirsty, a haven for the distressed, an upholder and defender of the victim of oppression. Let integrity and uprightness distinguish all thine acts. Be a home for the stranger, a balm to the suffering, a tower of strength for the fugitive. Be eyes to the blind, and a guiding light unto the feet of the erring. Be an ornament to the countenance of truth, a crown to the brow of fidelity, a pillar of the temple of righteousness, a breath of life to the body of mankind, an ensign of the hosts of justice, a luminary above the horizon of virtue, a dew to the soil of the human heart, an ark on the ocean of knowledge, a sun in the heaven of bounty, a gem on the diadem of wisdom, a shining light in the firmament of thy generation, a fruit on the tree of humility" (Baha'u'llah, *Kitab-i-Aqdas*. 233)

The kindness of Baha'u'llah can be found in many stories. This is but a sample.

May Bolles, an early pilgrim, heard `Abdu'l-Bahá tell the touching story about a hermit.

"On a freezing journey through the mountains to another prison, His small group met a hermit near a high cave. When Bahá`u'lláh arrived at that spot the hermit knelt down and kissed the dust before His feet, and said to Him: 'Oh, my Lord, I am a poor man living alone in a cave nearby; but henceforth I shall account myself the happiest of mortals if Thou wilt but come for a moment to my cave and bless it by Thy presence.' Then Bahá`u'lláh told the man that He would come, not for a moment, but for three days, and He bade His followers cast their tents, and await His return.

The poor man was so overcome with joy and gratitude that he was speechless, and led the way in humble silence to his lowly dwelling in a rock. There the Glorious One sat with him, talking to him and teaching him, and toward evening the man bethought himself that he had nothing to offer his great Guest but some dry meat and some dark bread, and water from a spring nearby. Not knowing what to do, he threw himself at the feet of his Lord and confessed his dilemma. Bahá`u'lláh comforted him and by a word bade him fetch the meat and bread and water; then the Lord of the Universe partook of this frugal repast with joy and fragrance as though it had been a banquet, and during the three days of His visit they ate only of this food which seemed to the poor hermit the most delicious he had ever eaten. Bahá`u'lláh declared that He had never been more nobly entertained nor received greater hospitality and love. 'This,' exclaimed the Master, when He had finished the story, 'shows us how little man requires when he is nourished by the sweetest of all foods – the love of God.'"

May Bolles Maxwell, http://bahai-library.com/may_ellis_maxwell_bw

The Coming of the Glory of the Lord

"Concerning the uniqueness of Bahá'u'lláh's station and the greatness of His Revelation, Shoghi Effendi affirms that the prophetic statements concerning the 'Day of God', found in the Sacred Scriptures of past Dispensations, are fulfilled by the advent of Bahá'u'lláh:

To Israel He was neither more nor less than the incarnation of the 'Everlasting Father', the 'Lord of Hosts' come down 'with ten thousands of saints'; to Christendom 'Christ returned in the glory of the Father'; to Shi'a Islam the return of the Imam Husayn; to Sunni Islam the descent of the Spirit of God (Jesus Christ); to the Zoroastrians the promised Shah-Bahram; to the Hindus the reincarnation of Krishna; to the Buddhists the fifth Buddha. (Baha'u'llah, *Kitab-i-Aqdas*. 234)

Bahá'u'lláh describes the station of 'Divinity' which He shares with all the Manifestations of God as ...the station in which one dieth to himself and liveth in God. Divinity, whenever I mention it, indicateth My complete and absolute self-effacement. This is the station in which I have no control over mine own weal or woe nor over my life nor over my resurrection. And, regarding His own relationship to God, He testifies: 'When I contemplate, O my God, the relationship that bindeth me to Thee, I am moved to proclaim to all created things 'verily I am God'; and when I consider my own self, lo, I find it coarser than clay!' (Adib Taherzadeh, *The Revelation of Baha'u'llah* Vol.1, p.59)

Baha'u'llah ascended in 'Akka in 1892, His Revelation completed, His Mission fulfilled. His Shrine is considered by Baha'is to be the Holiest Spot on earth. It is located near Akka Israel. Each Baha'i travels there once in his life, if able.

Baha'u'llah has drawn the circle of unity, He has made a design for the uniting of all the peoples' and for the gathering of them all under the shelter of the tent of universal unity. This is the work of the Divine Bounty, and we must strive with heart and soul until we have the reality of unity in our midst, as we work, so will strength be given unto us." 'Abdu'l-Baha cited in Adib Taherzadeh, The Revelation of Baha'u'llah v 3, p. xiii.

HONORING ALL FAITHS

We celebrate all paths that lead to the recognition of the Divine.

We honor Shamanism as a path of the inward journey and soul travel.

We honor Hinduism as a path of recognizing the Divine in each person.

We honor Judaism as a path of law.

We honor Taoism as a path of recognizing the perfect order and balance of the universe.

We honor Buddhism as a path of Compassion and Peace.

We honor Christianity as a path of Love and Forgiveness.

We honor Islam as a path of Constant Prayer.

We honor Baha'i as a path recognizing the oneness of all religion.

We honor New Thought as a path of healing and the power of the Mind.

WE HONOR ALL PATHS YET TO BE REVEALED.

Read at Sunday services at many Centers for Spiritual Livings – source unknown.

The sacred is never lost!
Religion is a Procession.